P9-DNA-341

THIS BOOK BELONGS TO:

_____

PRESENTED BY:

_____

DATE:

_____

Devotions
from the
world of
SPORTS

John & Kathy Hillman

CVP

Chariot Victor Publishing
A Division of Cook Communications

DEDICATION

"To our children, Marshall, Michael, and Holly,
their friends, and the boys and girls at church
and camp who served as our inspiration."

Chariot Victor Publishing,
A division of Cook Communications, Colorado Springs, Colorado 80918
Cook Communications, Paris, Ontario
Kingsway Communications, Eastbourne, England

DEVOTIONS FROM THE WORLD OF SPORTS
© 1998 by John and Kathy Hillman.

All rights reserved. Except for brief excerpts for review purposes,
no part of this book may be reproduced or used in any form
without written permission from the publisher.

All Scripture quotations in this publication are from the *Holy Bible*,
New International Version. Copyright © 1973, 1978, 1984, International Bible
Society. Used by permission of Zondervan Publishing House. All rights
reserved.

Designed by Andrea Boven
Edited by Jeannie Harmon and Elisabeth Brown
Interior text formatting by Cheryl Ogletree

First printing, 1998
Printed in the United States of America
02 01 00 / 15 14 13 12 11 10 9 8 7 6

Hillman, John.
    Devotions from the world of sports / John & Kathy Hillman.
       p.   cm.
    ISBN 0-78143-033-X
    1. Athletes–Prayer-books and devotions–English.   2. Sports
spectators–Prayer-books and devotions–English.   3. Sports–
Religious aspects–Christianity.   I. Hillman, Kathy.   II. Title.
BV4596.A8H55   1998
242'.68–dc21
                                      98-22230
                                          CIP

Sports permeate American society. Sports information surrounds us. Newspapers, radio, and television provide instant scores and up-to-date statistics.

All ages relate to sports and sports heroes. A recent survey indicated 90 percent of Americans watch an athletic event either on TV or in person at least once a month.

Sports have influenced my life since childhood. Playing baseball helped me attend college, travel around the country, play for the New York Yankees in the World Series, and earn a living doing what I love.

But success in sports means nothing without belief in God. My Christian faith provides me with a framework for living.

It takes more to be a Christian than just going to church. It's a 24-hour-a-day life. You can't separate God from everyday experiences whether you're on the mound, in the dugout, at school, at work, or with family or friends.

Some people view sports and religion as incompatible. They see athletes as selfish, pampered, spoiled, overgrown children. But sports and athletes, Christian or not, are still part of God's world. We can see His truth in sporting events just as we can in all things.

I can think of no better way to blend the nation's favorite pastimes with daily spiritual reflection than *Devotions From the World of Sports*. A quiet time with God drawn from the athletic world provides a great way for fans of all sports to start or end the day. Devotional books have often helped me focus on God especially since it's difficult for me to attend church at home during the long days of baseball season.

Devotions from the World of Sports will appeal to all ages. Youngsters emulate athletes almost as soon as they can walk. They revel in tales of their heroes. Older persons remember past glories and championships. The authors of this book bring together events from the spectrum of sports history that entertain, enlighten, and inspire.

But *Devotions from the World of Sports* is more than just an average devotional book full of enjoyable anecdotes. John and Kathy Hillman review intriguing sports events, couple them with strong spiritual insights, and devise an activity to reinforce each lesson. No parent, child, coach, or teacher could ask for more.

Andy Pettitte
Pitcher, New York Yankees

Look for these special features . . .

From the Playbook—A key Scripture from God's Word.

From the Pressbox—Glimpses from the pages of sports history and how we can see God's principles at work in the world around us.

From the Coach—An action point or activity that will demonstrate to us personally our need to follow God, and show us how we can be a winner if we "practice" being like Him.

Trust in the Lord with all your heart and lean not on your own understanding; in all your ways acknowledge him, and he will make your paths straight. —**PROVERBS 3:5-6**

Early in the 1929 Rose Bowl, with the score tied 0–0, Roy Riegels plucked a fumble from the air and rumbled untouched toward the end zone. Like all young men, the California linebacker dreamed of making the big play in a big game. In the confusion of the moment, however, he turned the wrong way and headed for his own goal line rather than his opponents'! Teammates chased after him, yelling for Riegels to stop. Benny Lom caught the runaway Golden Bear around the 3-yard line and wrestled him to the ground. Cal kept the ball, but it rested on the 1-yard line.

California chose to punt on first down, but a Georgia Tech lineman broke through to block it. The safety gave the Georgia Tech Yellow Jackets a 2-0 lead.

Both teams scored touchdowns later in the game, but the safety provided the winning margin in an 8-7 Georgia Tech victory. Because of his mistake, Riegels forever gained the nickname "Wrong Way."

So many things influence our lives, it's sometimes hard to know which ones are good and which ones are bad. In the excitement of the moment, it's easy to turn the wrong way.

God's Word is a road map we use to lead us on the right path. He guides us through Bible study and prayer. If we rely only on our own strength and intelligence, we will eventually become "Wrong Way" Christians.

Detours happen, and hazards appear on life's journey. Sometimes the path is clearly marked. Other times, it's blurred and fuzzy. But having faith in God and obeying His teachings keep us from going astray.

Make sure your family has an up-to-date road map in the car or somewhere easily accessible. Be certain you know how to use it as a guide. Make sure you also have a copy of God's road map, the Bible, on hand at all times. Pray for God's guidance on this New Year's Day so that, unlike Roy Riegels, you will head in the right direction.

We continually remember before our God and Father your work produced by faith, your labor prompted by love, and your endurance inspired by hope in our Lord Jesus Christ. —1 THESSALONIANS 1:3

Coach Don Shula could hardly believe the scoreboard. The opening quarter of the 1982 playoffs had not ended, but his Miami Dolphins already trailed the San Diego Chargers 24–0.

By the end of the third quarter, substitute signal caller Don Strock had tied the score. Miami's mood changed from despair to hope. After watching the lead evaporate, the sleeping Charger offense finally woke up.

It was anybody's game, with the tide turning back and forth toward San Diego or Miami. Finally, with only sixty-seven seconds to go, James Brooks made the tying touchdown at 38–38.

Strock moved the Dolphins into position for the winning score. At the Chargers' 25-yard line, Shula called for a field goal. As the ball arced toward the goal posts, Kellen Winslow's outstretched arm batted it away and forced the game into overtime.

San Diego's drive stalled on Miami's 9-yard line, and Rolf Benirschke attempted a field goal, but the ball mysteriously went wide. The Dolphins reached the San Diego 16, but, unbelievably, the Chargers blocked a second kick, and the game stayed tied. The tables turned when Dan Fouts reached the Miami 10. Coach Don Coryell called on Benirschke once again. This time the kick sailed true. One of pro football's longest playoff games finally ended.

Either the Dolphins or the Chargers could have given up during the game. But the desire to win inspired them.

Christians often consider giving up, too. Temptations and pressures make us wonder if our faith is worth the price. In difficult times, prayer brings us closer to God and sees us through. Prayer does not require fancy words or lots of time, just a brief moment with God. Like most things, prayer becomes easier with practice.

Practice kicking field goals in your backyard. While you're at it, practice some prayer. Thank God for always being there and seeing you through the hardest times.

for everyone born of God overcomes the world.

—1 John 5:4a

The Houston Oilers and Buffalo Bills tangled in an AFC wild card playoff game in 1993. Houston quarterback Warren Moon performed brilliantly in the first half, connecting on four touchdown passes. The Bills could muster only a field goal and trailed at halftime, 28-3.

Safety Bubba McDowell of the Oilers appeared to nail the victory early in the second half, returning an interception 58 yards for a touchdown. Never in NFL history had a team overcome a 35-3 deficit.

But Bills quarterback Frank Reich, subbing for an injured Jim Kelly, refused to quit. A 50-yard drive, capped by Kenneth Davis' 1-yard run, gave Buffalo its first touchdown.

Kicker Steve Christie recovered an onside kick, and Reich threw a 38-yard touchdown pass four plays later. Following a short Oiler punt, another four-play touchdown drive put Buffalo within striking distance.

Henry Jones intercepted a Moon pass to set up an 18-yard scoring strike to Andre Reed. Trailing 35-31, the Bills needed one touchdown to take the lead.

Reich engineered a 74-yard, seven-play drive late in the fourth quarter. The substitute signal caller connected on a 17-yard pass to Reed for his fourth touchdown pass of the second half, giving Buffalo the lead, 38-35.

Moon rallied the Oilers to a last-second field goal, sending the playoff game into overtime. But on the first possession in the extra frame, Henry Odomes intercepted the Oiler quarterback.

Steve Christie kicked a 32-yard field goal three plays later. The Bills had overcome the largest deficit in NFL history for a 41-38 victory.

Buffalo made an improbable comeback. Every Christian can do the same. Faith in God gives us the power to overcome impossible odds. We may feel inadequate. But God has promised that if we call on Him, He will help us do great and mighty things. The key is having the faith to call.

Look around your home for items that lock and need a key to open. How many can you find? Ask God to help you use the keys of faith and prayer to overcome the world.

Enter his gates with thanksgiving and his courts with praise; give thanks to him and praise his name. —PSALM 100:4

College basketball scouts drooled as they watched Cheryl Miller. The older sister of Indiana Pacer Reggie Miller could do it all—dribble, pass, shoot, and rebound. In 1982, the prep forward set an unbelievable mark.

Miller's high school, California's Riverside Poly, faced Norte Vista. The senior hit 46 of 50 from the floor, a sizzling 92 percent. At the charity stripe, she went 13 for 15. The high school All-American set a scoring record of 105 points. Riverside defeated Norte Vista by a stunning 179-15.

No one doubted that future stardom awaited Miller. She quickly established her reputation as one the nation's top college players.

Her school, the University of Southern California, won NCAA basketball championships in Miller's freshman and sophomore seasons. She received final-four tournament MVP honors both times.

The four-time collegiate All-American led the United States to a gold medal at the 1984 Olympics. In 1986, she anchored the U.S. team to the Women's World Basketball title in Moscow.

Following graduation, Southern Cal retired its superstar's jersey, the first basketball player so honored. Miller's university hired her as head coach, and she went on to television as a commentator.

If anyone ever entered the basketball courts with praise, it was Cheryl Miller. Imagine scoring 105 points in a single contest and hitting nearly 90 percent of your shots, both field goals and free throws. Picture yourself with 2 NCAA basketball championships, 2 final-four tournament MVP trophies, and an Olympic gold medal. See yourself accepting the thanks of your university by having your jersey retired. Awesome!

But God is even more amazing. He created the world. He made each person. He cares for us individually. He deserves all of our praise and our thanks.

Read Psalm 100 out loud as a prayer of praise and thanksgiving to God.

> They will lift you up in their hands, so that you will not strike your foot against a stone. —LUKE 4:11

Kickers lead roller coaster lives. They perform for only a few seconds, but every eye focuses on them. If they succeed, people praise them. If they fail, others ridicule them. In a 1986 playoff game, New York Giant punter Sean Landeta fell victim to the high-profile pressure.

The Chicago Bears hosted the Giants at Soldier Field. Midway through the first quarter, Chicago forced a New York punt from deep in its territory.

Landeta lined up near his own goal line for the snap. The Bears came with a massive rush.

The Giants punter caught the ball, dropped it, swung his leg, and missed. The pigskin barely grazed his instep and trickled off to the side.

Chicago defensive back Shaun Gayle grabbed the loose football at the 5-yard line. He scampered into the end zone to put the Bears in front, 7-0.

The play demoralized the Giants. Their offense never regained its poise. New York lost the game, 21-0.

Officially, Landeta's kick went into the records as a minus 7-yard punt. Unofficially, it should have been a swing and a miss.

The punter might as well have struck his foot against a stone. He was embarrassed and largely blamed for ending the Giants' season. Landeta must have felt awful. We feel awful when we make terrible mistakes like that, too. But God lifts us up after we fall. He gets us back on track and enables us to move forward. He helps us to regain our footing when we stumble.

Take a short hike with a friend or relative. Be aware of rocks in the path that cause problems. Pick up a small stone as a reminder of God's helping hand.

This is the one I meant when I said, "A man who comes after me has surpassed me because he was before me."

—JOHN 1:30

A coach experiences many victories and defeats during a career. In 1995, the Atlanta Hawks' Lenny Wilkens reached the pinnacle of his profession.

Wilkens began his NBA journey as the mentor of the Seattle Supersonics in 1969. After three seasons, he moved on to the Portland Trailblazers.

Seattle brought their former coach back in 1977. He remained there until 1985. Head positions in Cleveland and Atlanta followed.

In his twenty-second season, Wilkens tied Arnold "Red" Auerbach for the most NBA victories with 938. Another win would surpass the legendary Boston Celtics coach for the record.

The Hawks failed three times to push their headmaster to the summit. For attempt number four, the Washington Bullets traveled to the Omni. Wilkens' team jumped on the visitors for a quick double-digit lead. Washington never closed the gap, and the Hawks collected win number 939 for their coach, 112–90.

Coach Lenny Wilkens' name moved ahead of Red Auerbach's on the all-time coaching victories list. Wilkens came after Auerbach but surpassed him. Others will eventually surpass Wilkens, but no one surpasses God.

In the Bible, Jesus was born after His cousin, John the Baptist. But Jesus surpassed John because He was God from the beginning of time. Christ was the greatest man who ever lived. No one will ever surpass Him.

Look for information about Lenny Wilkens and Arnold "Red" Auerbach in a sports encyclopedia. Then read John 1:1 in your Bible. Note that the "Word" refers to Jesus. Thank God for sending Jesus to the earth to give His life for all people.

> All men are like grass, and all their glory is like the flowers of the field. —ISAIAH 40:6b

The Philadelphia Flyers blazed the ice to open the 1979–80 season. After splitting the first two games, the hockey team put together a streak unparalleled in professional sports.

From October 14, 1979, to January 6, 1980, coach Pat Quinn's charges never lost. During that period, the Flyers recorded 25 victories and 10 ties.

On January 7, Philadelphia traveled to Minnesota to engage the North Stars. A standing-room-only crowd of 15,962 filled the Metropolitan Sports Center to watch two of the NHL's best in action.

Bill Barber gave the Flyers an early 1-0 lead. But North Star goalie Gilles Meloche shut the door on Philadelphia the rest of the way.

Minnesota tied the score on a late first-period goal and quickly tallied 2 more for a 3-1 lead. The Flyers never recovered. The North Stars won easily 7-1, and the streak ended.

The Flyers learned the sad lesson that all things in life must end. Their glory faded. Other stars replaced them in new seasons. Their feat moved to memories.

The Bible tells us that people are like grass. Our accomplishments bloom for a while but eventually fade like flowers. Other flowers replace our blossoms.

The good news is that Isaiah spoke only of our earthly lives. If we trust Jesus and give ourselves to God, we live on with Him for eternity.

Go outside and look at the grass. Is it covered with snow? Picture it green and lush several months from now in the springtime. Plant a tulip or daffodil bulb. Depending on your climate, plant it outside or in a pot inside. Care for it, and watch it grow. Thank God for His gift of eternal life.

That night the Lord appeared to him and said, "I am the God of your father Abraham. Do not be afraid, for I am with you." —GENESIS 26:24a

In 1982, two small California colleges, UC Santa Cruz and West Coast Christian College, met on the basketball court. The Knights of West Coast suited up only eight players due to injury.

The Sea Lions of UC Santa Cruz trailed by 15 midway through the second half. Foul trouble, however, began to reduce the West Coast roster.

When the fourth player received violation number five, the Knights played one short. Players five, six, and seven soon fouled out. Even with the advantage, the Sea Lions narrowed the gap to only 70–57 at the 2:10 mark.

West Coast Christian had a single eligible player left on the floor, junior guard Mike Lockhart. Since NCAA rules allow a basketball team to play with one player if the team leads or has a chance to win, the game continued. But if Lockhart fouled out, the Knights would lose by default.

The solo player's greatest problem was inbounding. Rules forbid the inbounder to touch the ball until another player makes contact. The Knights' guard solved the dilemma by bouncing the ball off an opponent or rolling it on the floor and going for the steal.

The Sea Lions lost their composure and made stupid mistakes and turnovers. Amazingly, UC Santa Cruz fouled Lockhart and gave him six tries at the free-throw line. Five went through the hoop.

The full strength squad scored only 10 points against a lone defender. At contest's end, the Knights, led by a lonesome guard, won 75–67.

Surely Lockhart felt fear when he realized he would be playing one-on-five. He knew he had to do it all—shoot, rebound, dribble, inbound, and play defense.

But the guard put his fears aside. God was with him, win or lose. God promises us His presence. We do not need to be afraid.

Sometime during the week, practice free throws. As you finish, try six. Can you make five like Lockhart did?

The tempest comes out from its chamber, the cold from the driving winds. The breath of God produces ice, and the broad waters become frozen. —JOB 37:9-10

Terrible weather conditions plagued the 1982 AFC championship between the Cincinnati Bengals and San Diego Chargers. The thermometer registered minus 9 degrees. The wind gusted to 35 miles per hour, making the wind chill factor 59 degrees below zero. NFL commissioner Pete Rozelle considered postponement.

The Bengals led by an early field goal. On the following kickoff, San Diego fumbled, and Cincinnati recovered. A short pass to M. L. Harris made the score 10–0.

Charger quarterback Dan Fouts battled the high winds and completed a 33-yard second-quarter touchdown pass to Kellen Winslow. Twice San Diego's signal caller directed drives deep into Bengal territory. Interceptions off cold, stiff hands killed both.

Cincinnati's Ken Anderson marched his team downfield late in the first half. Pete Johnson smashed into the end zone, giving the Bengals a 17–7 lead.

San Diego's offensive woes continued as the gloved defense held the Chargers scoreless. The conservative Cincinnati offense padded its lead with a 38-yard field goal and a 3-yard touchdown pass to Don Bass. The Bengals advanced to their first Super Bowl with a 27-7 rout.

On a warm day, the outcome might have been different. But the Chargers were not used to playing in such cold. Players huddled around heaters as they left the field. Every player who could, wore gloves. Noses, fingers, and toes became numb. Everyone was miserable.

God is God on freezing days and blazing hot ones. He produces the weather. Even the wind obeys Him. He sends cold and ice. He warms the earth with the radiant sun and cools it with a gentle breeze. He is in control.

If there's snow today, make a snowball. If not, get an ice cube. Let the frozen water melt in your hands as long as you can. Think of how cold the Bengals and the Chargers must have been. When you feel cold and sad, remember God's love can warm your heart. Just ask Him.

We were therefore buried with him through baptism into death in order that, just as Christ was raised from the dead through the glory of the Father, we too may live a new life. —ROMANS 6:4

The San Francisco '49ers faced the Dallas Cowboys in the 1981 NFC title game. Experts gave the Bay Area team little chance.

The Cowboys owned an edge in experience. The Niners entered the playoffs for the first time in over a decade. In 1978 and 1979, they had finished dead last. Dallas had won two Super Bowls and missed postseason play only once over the same time.

The championship game far exceeded expectations. The lead seesawed back and forth until the Cowboys went ahead 27–21 in the fourth quarter.

The '49ers took over the ball on their own 11-yard line with under five minutes to play. San Francisco needed an immediate touchdown.

Third-year quarterback Joe Montana triggered the offense. Mixing runs and passes with expertise, San Francisco moved downfield to the Cowboys' 13-yard line.

A first-down pass fell incomplete. A run on second down moved the ball to the 6. Only fifty-eight seconds remained. Montana called a pass to Freddie Solomon in the left corner of the end zone. The route was covered. The quarterback rolled, looking for Dwight Clark.

Massive defensive end Ed Jones closed quickly. Falling backwards, the youthful Montana lobbed a pass off the wrong foot deep into the end zone. Many thought he threw the ball away. Miraculously, Clark broke free and made a fingertip reception. With the extra point, the Niners led 28-27 and held on for one of pro football's greatest comebacks.

Joe Montana breathed new life into his team when everyone thought the championship was lost. To save a lost world, Jesus Christ gave mankind new life with His own death on the cross. His salvation is available to all. It costs commitment, but lasts forever.

List some great sports comebacks. A sports encyclopedia can help. Think about the great biblical comeback of Paul recorded in Acts 21:37–22:21. Thank God for the gift of salvation.

Who is it that overcomes the world? Only he who believes that Jesus is the Son of God. —I JOHN 5:5

A cold, biting wind blew off Lake Erie as the Denver Broncos faced the Cleveland Browns in the 1987 American Football Conference championship. Cleveland's ferocious defense, the Dawgs, made them the favorite to advance to the Super Bowl.

With just under six minutes remaining, the 79,915 Brown fans visualized their heroes in football's ultimate game. Bernie Kosar put Cleveland ahead 20–13 with a 48-yard touchdown pass to Brian Brennan.

The crowd cheered as Denver botched the kickoff and recovered the ball on the 2-yard line. The Dog Pound crowd smelled victory.

A grim and determined John Elway took command. His scrambling and passing moved Denver to midfield inside the three-minute mark. The Browns' defense stiffened, however, and sacked the Denver quarterback for an 8-yard loss.

Facing third and 18, coach Dan Reeves signaled time-out. He called for a 10-yard pass over the middle, but Elway noticed safety Ray Ellis playing deep. Number 7 hit Mark Jackson at the Cleveland 28 with seventy-nine seconds to play.

A couple of passes and an Elway run put the ball on the Browns' 5. Facing third and 1, the Denver quarterback rifled a pass to Jackson. With seconds to go, the Broncos tied.

The Browns failed to score in overtime. Denver forced a punt, and Elway marched his offense to the Cleveland 15. Rich Karlis kicked a 33-yard field goal to give the Broncos a victory. Professional football fans refer to Denver's tying touchdown march as, "The Drive."

Christians often feel backed against their own goal lines facing unbelievable odds. We're afraid to move forward. In troubled times, there is no alternative but Jesus. We must rely on His strength and make choices with Christ's teachings and example as our guide.

Look at the front page of a daily newspaper. Find a story about someone facing a difficult situation. Pray for God to direct his or her actions.

His heart is secure, he will have no fear; in the end he will look in triumph on his foes. —PSALM 112:8

John Elway reigns as king of the fourth-quarter comeback. The Denver quarterback directed one of his best in the 1992 AFC divisional playoffs.

The visiting Houston Oilers romped to a 21–6 first-half lead. With six minutes remaining, however, Bronco Steve Atwater intercepted a Warren Moon pass.

Elway connected on 6 of 6 passes on an 88-yard drive. Greg Lewis dove over from the one to narrow the gap to 21–13.

David Treadwell added three with a 49-yard third-quarter field goal. But the Oilers matched it on their next possession to lead 24–16 at the end of three.

The Broncos gained possession on their own 20. Twelve plays later, Greg Lewis plunged over for his second 1-yard touchdown. The Oilers' lead fell to a single point.

Houston's next drive stalled, and Elway took over on his own 2-yard line. With no time-outs and 2:07 to play, the Denver signal caller converted two fourth-down plays, moving the ball to the Oiler 19.

Twenty ticks remained as David Treadwell lined up for the game-winning field goal. The ball sailed true, and Elway and the Broncos had recorded another patented comeback, 26–24.

As the game wound down, Denver players and partisans showed no fear. They felt confidence in Elway's prowess. And they were right. In the end, the Broncos triumphed.

As Christians, we have that same security in God through Christ. So if we trust Jesus, we should not be afraid.

Make a list of your fears. Talk to God about them. Ask Him to help you put each one aside or deal with it if necessary. Cross each off the list as you pray specifically about that concern.

I will search for the lost and bring back the strays. I will bind up the injured and strengthen the weak.

—EZEKIEL 34:16

Bo Jackson had incredible talent. The Heisman Trophy winner is the only player ever named to both baseball's and football's All-Star squads. But in 1991, the running back and outfielder suffered a career-ending injury.

The Los Angeles Raiders faced the Cincinnati Bengals in the AFC playoffs. Jackson played sparingly. The Raiders limited the dual sport star to take advantage of his great breakaway speed.

The Raiders received the second-half kickoff. On the second play, quarterback Jay Schroeder ran a sweep and handed off to Jackson. The play gained 34 yards before Kevin Walker made the tackle from behind. Jackson bounced awkwardly to the turf. Something felt wrong, and the speedster left the game.

Jackson never returned. Los Angeles pulled ahead on a third-quarter touchdown pass to Ethan Horton. The Silver and Black defense shut out the Bengals after halftime, and LA won 20–10. Doctors diagnosed Jackson's injury as a serious fracture dislocation of the left hip. Its severity eliminated football as an option.

Baseball remained a possibility, but the Kansas City Royals released their power hitter rather than take a chance. Jackson signed with the Chicago White Sox. The weakened hip prevented him from patrolling the outfield and forced him into the designated hitter's role.

Jackson never regained his preinjury form. The 1989 All-Star MVP struggled for four seasons and called it quits in 1994.

Life sometimes hands us injuries and illnesses. Like Bo Jackson, the ailments may keep us from doing something we want or reaching a goal we've set. While God might not heal our bodies completely, He will make us strong enough to handle the disappointment.

Think of a friend, relative, or someone you know who is injured or sick. Ask God to make her strong. Call her or write her a note of encouragement.

Aim for perfection . . . be of one mind, live in peace. And the God of love and peace will be with you. —2 CORINTHIANS 13:11

The Miami Dolphins approached Super Bowl VII in 1973 with high emotions. No other professional football team had equaled their perfect 14-0 regular season record. The Aqua and Coral stood on the brink of history.

The contest matched Miami with the Washington Redskins. Analysts predicted a defensive struggle pairing Miami's "No Name Defense" with Washington's "Over the Hill Gang."

The game lived up to its billing. Neither team scored early. Quarterback Bob Griese finally cranked the Miami offense into gear. Using runs by Jim Kiick, Larry Csonka, and Eugene "Mercury" Morris and passes to Paul Warfield, the Dolphins moved into Redskin territory. The Miami signal caller hit Howard Twilley to put the Dolphins up 7–0.

Miami's middle linebacker Nick Buoniconti intercepted a pass in the waning minutes of the first half. The patient Griese worked the clock. Jim Kiick carried the ball in for the touchdown.

The second half stayed scoreless until the final minutes. The Dolphins attempted a 42-yard field goal to ice the game. But Bill Brundage blocked Garo Yepremian's kick. The kicker grabbed the loose ball and vainly tried to pass. Mike Bass snatched the pigskin and raced 49 yards to Redskin pay dirt.

Miami's No-Namers snuffed a final Washington threat to win 14–7. The Dolphins aimed for perfection and finished the season undefeated. They played with one mind.

Paul wrote asking the church to do the same. He told the Corinthian Christians to aim for the best, to be a team, and to live in peace. And he promised that if they did, God would be with them.

As you read back through the description of Super Bowl VII, write down the names of all the Dolphins mentioned. Each one was important to the team. Think about teams you are on—sports, church, or otherwise. Do you all aim for perfection? Do you have the same goals? Do you get along? Seek God's help to change any no answers.

So that you are proved right when you speak and justified when you judge. —PSALM 51:4b

The AFL Kansas City Chiefs challenged the NFL Minnesota Vikings in Super Bowl IV. Most believed the Purple People Eaters would handle the second-place Chiefs easily.

Coach Hank Stram devised a strong game plan for the Chiefs. He utilized short, quick passes and a moving pocket to neutralize Minnesota's fierce pass rush.

On their first possession, Kansas City played ball control and moved into Viking territory. Jan Stenerud kicked a 48-yard field goal for the early lead.

The soccer-style kicker from Norway booted two more in the second quarter to boost the margin to 9–0. Moments later, Viking return man Charlie West muffed the kickoff. Remi Prudhomme recovered for Kansas City on the Minnesota 19.

Alan Page sacked Len Dawson on first down. But a trap up the middle caught the defensive front off guard, and a pass to Otis Taylor set up first and goal at the 5. Mike Garrett's countersweep put the Chiefs up 16–zip at halftime.

Kansas City kept the ball on the ground in the second half. The Vikings drove for a touchdown, narrowing the gap to 16–7. But the Chiefs countered with a 46-yard scoring strike to Otis Taylor.

Hank Stram and his team prevailed 23–7. After four Super Bowls, the final tally showed NFL 2–AFL 2. The new league had proven itself. The evidence was on the field. Television viewers and fans in the stands saw the results. The scoreboard showed the world.

We don't usually think of sacks, counters, traps, muffs, and kicks as positive words in life. But they make a difference in football, especially when they're well planned and practiced. God also asks us to plan and practice doing right to make a difference for Him.

Diagram a trap up the middle and a countersweep. Get assistance if you have difficulty. Ask God to help you plan to do right.

No, in all these things we are more than conquerors through him who loved us. —**ROMANS 8:37**

Sports fans dream about matchups between two undefeated teams ranked number one and two in the nation. In 1995, when the University of Tennessee Lady Volunteers and the University of Connecticut Lady Huskies basketball teams tangled, their wishes came true.

The number-one-ranked Lady Vols traveled to the home court of the Lady Huskies. Number two Connecticut longed to conquer Tennessee.

The home team took the floor using a mixture of man-to-man and 2–3 zone defenses. The scheme confused the Lady Vols, and they hit only 12 of 34 shots in the first half. Connecticut rolled to a 41–33 halftime lead.

But UConn's star center Rebecca Lobo collected her fifth personal foul with 5 minutes to play. Tennessee narrowed the gap to 52–47 but could get no closer.

The Lady Huskies kept their poise and forced Tennessee into turnovers. Kara Wolters scored 12 of her 18 points in the second half, and Jen Rizzotti added 17 to pace a balanced attack. UConn upset the number one Lady Vols, 77–66.

The Connecticut women became conquerors through strategy, skill, and selflessness. In life, we become conquerors of selfishness and sin through Jesus Christ. Bible study, prayer, and other Christians help guide us.

Put together a pickup basketball game. Make sure everyone has a chance to play. Practice both man-to-man and zone defenses. Ask God to help you conquer selfishness.

Do not gloat when your enemy falls; when he stumbles, do not let your heart rejoice. —PROVERBS 24:17

Football fans expect to see professional football's best teams in the Super Bowl. But in 1971's Super Bowl V, they witnessed a matchup many called the Blooper Bowl.

The Dallas Cowboys, making their first appearance in the big game, met the Baltimore Colts. Both teams possessed strong running games and tough defenses. But neither quarterback, Johnny Unitas nor Craig Morton, played at full strength.

Dallas opened the scoring with 2 quick field goals. Unitas tied the contest with a 75-yard scoring pass to John Mackey. Baltimore missed the extra point for a 6–6 tie.

The Cowboys regained the lead before halftime on Morton's 7-yard scoring toss to Duane Thomas. Dallas and Baltimore botched several opportunities with fumbles and interceptions. The Colts knotted the score 13–13 early in the fourth quarter as Tom Nowatzke carried in the ball from 2 yards out.

Just after the two-minute warning, Dallas took possession. Morton attempted a pass to Dan Reeves, but Jerry Logan blasted the running back as the ball arrived. Mike Curtis intercepted and returned the pigskin to the Dallas 28-yard line with fifty-nine seconds to go.

The Colts ran the clock down to nine seconds and called time-out. Rookie kicker Jim O'Brien entered the game to try a 32-yard field goal. Despite the Doomsday Defense taunts, the kick sailed true. Baltimore won 16–13 in a game featuring 5 fumbles, 6 interceptions, dropped passes, tipped passes, and a missed extra point.

Sometimes, as in Super Bowl V, we gain when someone else messes up. We win, not because we should, but because others fall. It's easy to gloat when an enemy suffers. We're tempted to rejoice when an opponent fails.

But God urges us to show good sportsmanship. He warns us not to be pleased when others do poorly or grin over their losses.

Define good sportsmanship. Then ask some friends or relatives for their definitions. Write down your favorite one. Pray that God will help you be a good sport in athletics and in life.

And the God of all grace, who called you to his eternal glory in Christ, after you have suffered a little while, will himself restore you and make you strong, firm and steadfast. —1 PETER 5:10

The Associated Press selected Jim Thorpe as the greatest athlete of the twentieth century. The Sac and Fox Indian won gold medals in the pentathlon and decathlon in the 1912 Olympic games.

A month later, however, the Amateur Athletic Union stripped Thorpe of his honors when it learned he had received money for playing baseball during summer vacations. The AAU believed that accepting any money in any sport made an athlete a professional in every sport. Thus they felt Thorpe had been ineligible for the all-amateur Olympics. This action pained the Native American the remainder of his life.

Sports fans protested for years against the AAU's injustice but to no avail. In 1983, the International Olympic Committee finally admitted its error and returned the medals to Thorpe's family. It also deservedly added his name to the list of 1912 champions.

Jim Thorpe died in 1953. His family waited over seventy years to have his name and honor restored.

The world idolized Jim Thorpe for his athletic ability. People quickly turned their backs on him, however, when he could no longer perform. God, on the other hand, never leaves. When a Christian calls, He answers. He restores.

Recall a tough time. Think about people who turned their backs on you. Remember the ones who stuck with you. Thank God for supportive friends. Praise Him for always sticking by you.

> But as for me, my feet had almost slipped; I had nearly lost my foothold. —PSALM 73:2

The Pittsburgh Steelers entered Super Bowl X as heavy favorites. But the wild card Dallas Cowboys provided plenty of fireworks.

Roger Staubach put Dallas on the scoreboard first with a 29-yard scoring pass to Drew Pearson. But Terry Bradshaw quickly evened the points with a 7-yard touchdown toss to Randy Grossman.

The Cowboys kicked a 36-yard field goal to take a 10–7 halftime lead. After a scoreless third quarter, the Steel Curtain turned the tide with a big special teams play.

Reggie Harrison broke through the line to block Mitch Hoopes' punt for a safety. Although Dallas still led 10–9, momentum shifted. Two Roy Gerela field goals put the Gold and Black in front 15–10.

Bradshaw appeared to clinch the Steelers' victory with a 64-yard strike to Lynn Swann. But Staubach found rookie Percy Howard alone in the end zone for a 34-yard touchdown. Howard had never caught a single pass in an NFL game nor would he ever catch another.

Dallas had one final shot at a come-from-behind upset win, but Glen Edwards intercepted Staubach's desperation pass. Pittsburgh won its second straight championship, 21–17.

As time ran out, the Cowboys almost pulled out the victory. The Steelers almost let the championship slip away. But almost isn't close enough. Almost doesn't get the job done.

The same holds true in life. Sometimes an almost can let us know we'll make it next time. But for the moment, almost doesn't count. In the Book of Acts, King Agrippa was almost persuaded to become a Christian. The rich young ruler almost followed Jesus. The pharaoh of Egypt almost let the Israelites go before his son died.

Almost is a sad word. God doesn't want us to almost trust Him. He doesn't want us to almost do good or almost spend time with Him in prayer. He wants us to be completely committed to Him.

Think of a skill you almost have. Practice until you have acquired it. Pray that God will keep you from almost serving Him.

I will give them an undivided heart and put a new spirit in them. —EZEKIEL 11:19a

Michelle Kwan took to the ice as naturally as a bird takes to flight. In 1993, at age 13, the Californian gained instant acclaim as the youngest U.S. Olympic Festival champion. And at the United States Figure Skating Championships in 1996, Kwan proved her maturity and excellence.

The former World Junior Champion changed her hairstyle from a youthful ponytail to a braided bun. Her coach, Frank Carroll, developed a new long program that captured the judges' attention.

Her performance exhibited a complete figure skating package: elegance, athleticism, grace, and discipline. Kwan received 32 points and totally dominated all challengers.

With wins in the short program and free skate, the youthful skater led throughout the competition. Kwan left little doubt of a first-place finish. All indecision vanished when defending champion Nicole Bobek withdrew the final night due to an ankle injury.

At age 17, Kwan became the youngest U.S. champion since Peggy Fleming, and the third youngest ever.

Michelle gracefully made the move from junior to senior competition. She showed spirit and left the judges undivided in their admiration and in their scoring. By putting herself in the hands of her coach, Kwan was able to put it all together.

God promises us a new spirit and a new hope. But we must first give Him our whole hearts. We must put ourselves in His hands. We must become His package. He will make us someone very special.

Prepare a package for a friend or relative. Make it your package, but something special the other person will enjoy. Ask God to help you put yourself in His hands.

And I pray that you, being rooted and established in love, may have power, together with all the saints, to grasp how wide and long and high and deep is the love of Christ.

—EPHESIANS 3:17-18

A bucket from beyond half court either stuns or electrifies the crowd. In 1980, Les Henson of Virginia Tech used nearly all of the court to make an unbelievable shot.

The Florida State Seminoles hosted the Gobblers of Virginia Tech. The two Metro Conference schools battled the entire contest. Nine ties and nine lead changes marked the hard-fought affair.

With the score knotted at 77, FSU rebounded a Tech miss. Twenty-two seconds remained. The Seminoles ran off 12 ticks and called time-out to work for the final basket.

The clock showed 5 seconds when Pernell Tookes fired a 14-foot jumper. The shot bounced off the rim and over the heads of all defenders.

Henson, a 6-foot-6 forward, grabbed the errant attempt in the corner. At the 2-tick mark, he whirled and flung the sphere the length of the court.

The buzzer sounded with the ball in midair. The ball hit the back of the iron and slammed through the net. Virginia Tech won on an incredible basket, 79-77. Using television replays, officials determined the shot length to be 89 feet, 3 inches.

Les Henson quickly mentally figured the width, length, depth, and height needed for his shot. He figured accurately and canned the ball.

Sometimes we try to calculate people's love. Is my parent's love greater than my sister's or brother's? Which friend loves me the most? Whom do I love more? Does he or she like me enough?

But God's love cannot be measured. The Bible says it's impossible to understand how wide and long and high and deep it is.

What are the dimensions of a basketball court? If you don't know, ask a coach, official, or player, or look them up in an encyclopedia. Subtract Henson's shot from the length to determine how much space he had to spare. Thank God there are no limits to the dimensions of Christ's love.

Now it is God who has made us for this very purpose and has given us the Spirit as a deposit, guaranteeing what is to come. —2 CORINTHIANS 5:5

Joe Namath guaranteed the New York Jets would defeat the Baltimore Colts in Super Bowl III. New York went three plays and out on the game's first possession. Baltimore sustained a long drive but came up empty.

The Colts pounced on a George Sauer fumble to set up on the Jets' 12-yard line. But Al Atkinson tipped Earl Morrall's end zone pass, and Randy Beverly intercepted the ball.

The turnover energized New York. Alternating runs and passes, Namath led an 80-yard touchdown march. Matt Snell scored to give the Jets a 7-0 lead.

The Colts rallied, but Johnny Sample picked off Morrall once more, killing the scoring opportunity. Baltimore missed another chance in the first half when Morrall failed to see Jimmy Orr alone in the end zone.

The contest's turning point came on the first play of the second stanza. Tom Matte fumbled, and the Jets recovered on the Baltimore 12. Five plays later, Jim Turner kicked a field goal, upping the lead to 10-0.

New York played ball control. Two more field goals increased the lead to 16-0. Baltimore scored a meaningless late touchdown, and the Jets upset the highly favored Colts, 16-7.

Namath walked off the field with his index finger showing number one. It was almost as if Joe Namath had been made for that one season and that one Super Bowl. Virtually the entire world scoffed when the quarterback guaranteed victory. But they could not see what Namath's spirit felt.

God has made each of us for a special purpose. He gave us the Holy Spirit to live in us and to guide us. Our Heavenly Father guarantees our victory if we follow Him.

Look through your home for an appliance or a food or clothing item with a guarantee. Read the wording. Are there conditions that would keep the manufacturer from making good on the promise? Thank God that there are no conditions on His guarantees.

I am the vine; you are the branches. If a man remains in me and I in him, he will bear much fruit; apart from me you can do nothing. —JOHN 15:5

The 1982–83 Houston Rockets struggled on the court. Most nights victory eluded them. Tight games gave some measure of respect, but one overtime contest left the NBA team wondering if it really belonged in the league.

The Rockets hosted the Portland Trailblazers. With a 6-win and 34-loss record, Houston could have played without spark or enthusiasm. But the game stayed nip and tuck for four full quarters.

Allen Leavell hit a 3-pointer with 7 seconds left to tie at 96. Time expired, and the contest went to overtime.

Coach Del Harris ran into bad luck immediately. Joe Bryant and James Bailey fouled out less than a minute into OT.

Calvin Natt and Kenny Carr hit 2 buckets apiece and put the Trailblazers up by 8. The lead limited Houston's strategy to shooting wild jumpers and gambling on defense. Nothing worked.

In the 5-minute extra period, Portland tallied 17 points, and Houston got none. The game became a rout with the Trailblazers winning 113–96. No other NBA team had ever been shut out in overtime.

No points—imagine scoring nothing. The Bible tells us that apart from God, we are nothing.

A branch cut off from a tree will die. A branch attached to a healthy fruit tree will bear fruit. That's the way it is with God. As long as our lives are attached to Him, we will do good things. We will bear fruit.

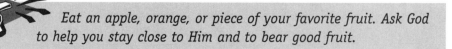

Eat an apple, orange, or piece of your favorite fruit. Ask God to help you stay close to Him and to bear good fruit.

Much dreaming and many words are meaningless. Therefore stand in awe of God. —ECCLESIASTES 5:7

Averaging 1 goal per game in the National Hockey League seems almost impossible. In the league's first 65 years only one player, Maurice Richard, achieved the awesome feat.

Richard played a 50-game schedule in 1944–45 and scored 50 goals. His achievement set the benchmark for all NHL players.

In 1981, Mike Bossy entered his 50th contest against the Quebec Nordiques with 48 goals. More than 15,000 fans packed the Nassau Coliseum. Most gave up hope of seeing the record when the New York Islander didn't take a single shot on goal in the first two periods.

With the score tied 4–4 midway through the final frame, the team worked a power play. Bossy found the puck on his backhand side. He waited a split second and shot it through an opening for goal number 49.

Two-and-a-half minutes later, a Nordique pass struck John Tonelli's skate. The puck bounced to Bryan Trottier inside the Quebec blue line.

Bossy, left unguarded, screamed for the puck. Trottier flicked a perfect pass, and the Islander sent a bullet flying through Nordique goalie Ron Grahame's legs for his 50th score. His teammates swarmed the ice to offer congratulations.

Bossy's New York Islander teammates dreamed the dream just as he had. Their assists and passes made his record possible. They helped make his dream come true.

Dreams don't mean much unless they're backed by action. God is always a God of action. He helps us define our dreams. He guides us to act on our dreams. He is awesome.

Do you have a dream in your life? Talk to God about it. Share it with a special friend or favorite relative. Discuss what actions you need to take to make it come true. Begin.

The name of the Lord is a strong tower; the righteous run to it and are safe. —**PROVERBS 18:10**

The Green Bay Packers and New England Patriots met in 1996's Super Bowl XXXI. The Pack had not played for the title since 1968, and the Patriots had been absent for over a decade.

Experts considered Green Bay a 2-touchdown favorite. They confirmed their reputation quickly. Quarterback Brett Favre threw a 54-yard touchdown to Andre Rison on his first pass of the game. Chris Jacke added a field goal to give the Packers a 10–0 first-quarter lead.

But New England answered with two Drew Bledsoe touchdown passes to pull in front, 14–10. The lead evaporated quickly, however, as Favre hit Antonio Freeman with an 81-yard scoring strike, the longest in Super Bowl history.

The Green Bay signal caller scored the Pack's third touchdown on a 2-yard run, upping the margin to 27–14. New England refused to buckle, and Curtis Martin's 18-yard touchdown run closed the gap to 27–21.

But the Green and Gold iced their third world championship on the very next play. Adam Vinatieri kicked off for the Patriots. Desmond Howard fielded the ball on his own 1-yard line. Reading blockers perfectly, Howard wove through the coverage for a 99-yard touchdown return.

Favre passed to Mark Chmura for a 2-point conversion, and the Packers held on for a 35–21 triumph. Howard's 99-yard kickoff return, combined with 6 punt returns for 90 yards, brought him MVP honors.

Howard fielded the ball, carefully tucked it away, and glanced at the towering goal post. He darted. He slipped into holes. He eluded tackler after tackler, obstacle after obstacle. The kick returner reached safety and 6 points.

Obstacles fill our lives, too. God provides the tower of strength. He offers safety if we run to Him.

Take your Bible and read about the Tower of Babel in Genesis 11:1-9. Thank God that He is the only tower that cannot be destroyed.

And we pray this in order that you may live a life worthy of the Lord and may please him in every way . . . being strengthened with all power . . . so that you may have great endurance and patience. —COLOSSIANS 1:10-11

Peter Snell broke the mold of most distance runners. The 1960 Olympic gold medalist relied on stamina rather than speed.

In 1962, running on a grass track in his native New Zealand, Snell lagged to the back of the pack as the mile run began. He finished the first lap in a slow 60.7 seconds.

As the runners entered lap two, the distance runner slowly passed each competitor. Snell lowered his time to 59.9.

Heading into the third leg, the 24 year old took the lead. Running at a strong clip, Snell reduced his lap time to 59.0.

On the bell lap, the stout-hearted runner positioned himself perfectly. He ran unchallenged, far in front of the field. Snell's reserved strength pushed him far out in front. He crossed the finish line 40 yards ahead. The man from down under ran his fastest time on the final lap, 54.8 seconds. His total time of 3:54.4 broke a world record by a tenth of a second. Stamina had triumphed over speed.

Snell ran the fastest mile ever run. The New Zealander used his patience and endurance to achieve new heights. He proved once again that strength and power must be coupled with stamina and discipline.

The Apostle Paul appreciated the runners of his day. He prayed that the Colossian Christians would be strong like great athletes. He wanted them to endure and be patient in how they lived. He desired that they please God.

Have you ever started something and moved so quickly that you burned out? You ran out of gas. Try to run as fast as you can. Then pace yourself and run or walk a mile. The point is not how fast you did it but that you finished. Ask God to help you please Him by finishing what you start.

Folly delights a man who lacks judgment, but a man of understanding keeps a straight course. —**PROVERBS 15:21**

Super Bowl XXV in 1991 pitted two teams from the Empire State, the New York Giants and the Buffalo Bills. The odds favored the Bills when the Giants lost starting quarterback Phil Simms to injury. But backup signal caller Jeff Hostetler responded in one of the most exciting championships in NFL history.

The Giants struck on a 28-yard Matt Bahr field goal. Buffalo matched the 3-pointer with a 23-yarder by Scott Norwood.

Jim Kelly marched the Bills downfield late in the first quarter. Don Smith's 1-yard touchdown plunge put Buffalo in the lead.

The Bills added a safety when Hostetler tripped in the end zone. But the reserve quarterback engineered an 87-yard drive before halftime to narrow the margin to 12–10.

New York's defense tightened, shutting out Buffalo in quarter number three. The Giants punched in a second touchdown and took the lead.

But Thurman Thomas reeled off a 31-yard fourth-quarter touchdown run to put the Bills back on top. Hostetler showed his poise. He directed a drive that ended with Bahr's 21-yard field goal, giving New York a 20–19 edge.

Kelly took Buffalo from its own 10 to the Giants' 29 in the final two minutes. With four seconds remaining, Norwood attempted a 47-yard field goal. The kick had the distance, but it drifted wide to the right. The Giants captured their second Super Bowl victory.

Even though he was the backup, Hostetler used good judgment and steered the Giants on a straight course. His efforts paid off. And the Giants went down in history as the winners of Super Bowl XXV.

The Bible says when we use poor judgment, we do foolish things. But if we think before we act, we'll stay on the right course.

Remember something really dumb or silly you've done. If you can, share the story with someone else. Why did you do it? Was it because you didn't think first? Ask God to help you use good judgment.

He tends his flock like a shepherd: He gathers the lambs in his arms and carries them close to his heart; he gently leads those that have young. —ISAIAH 40:11

Winning a Grand Slam tennis tournament takes incredible resolve. Becoming a champion as a teenager staggers the imagination. But in 1991, Monica Seles made tennis fans take notice.

Seles defeated opponent after opponent in the Australian Open and met Jana Novotna in the finals. Novotna won the first set 7–5 over the 17-year-2-month-old Yugoslavian. But a pulled hamstring muscle suffered at the end of set one weakened the 22-year-old Czech player.

The teenaged Seles shook off her lethargy and began making her trademark deep grunts with each shot. She angled ground strokes closer and closer to the lines, forcing Novotna to stretch and lunge. The strategy prevented Novotna from dropping shots just over the net and kept her running the baseline.

Seles held serve in the fourth game of the second set to even the match with a 6–3 win. In the deciding set three, the teenager won 6 straight games to defeat Novotna 6–1 for the crown.

The Yugoslav native became the youngest player ever to win the Australian Open. She edged out the legendary Margaret Court by two months.

Novotna tried her best to beat the teenager. However, Seles showed her ability and her determination. She used outstanding strategy and excellent shot selection. She deserved to win.

Seles received no special treatment because of her age. But Jesus does have a special place in His heart for the young. Isaiah compares them to lambs he holds close like a shepherd. And God tenderly guides their parents as well.

If you have a pet or pets, spend extra time playing with them today. Be especially gentle if you have kittens, puppies, or other baby animals. Thank God for His tender loving care.

Whatever you do, work at it with all your heart, as working for the Lord, not for men. —COLOSSIANS 3:23

Most basketball fans prefer a run-and-gun attack rather than a controlled, deliberate offense. Spectators who witnessed Loyola Marymount host U.S. International in 1989 saw the scoreboard light up like the Fourth of July.

When the Lions and Gulls met at the Gersten Pavilion, they averaged a point every 7.3 seconds. The teams shot almost continuously. The longest time between any 2 buckets was 59 seconds, the shortest a mere 2.

Hank Gaithers canned 41, and Jeff Fryer added 34 to pace the Loyola attack. Eleven players hit for double figures.

Coach Paul Westhead used his total roster of sixteen players, but no tactic could put a lid on the scoring. Loyola Marymount won the track-meet-like contest, 181–150. The game set an NCAA record for most combined points scored.

Gaithers led the nation in both scoring and rebounding in 1989. Thirteen months later in the West Coast Conference Tournament, the 23 year old collapsed in a game against Portland. In less than two hours, the Loyola Marymount star died due to a heart arrhythmia.

Players on both teams worked hard every second of the Loyola Marymount–U.S. International contest. The scoreboard showed it. Hank Gaithers played each game with his whole heart, a heart that proved to be defective. But rather than give up his great love for basketball, he continued to play as for the Lord and not for men.

God asks that in everything we do, we do it to the best of our ability. He wants us to expend all of our energy in His service. Death comes to every person at a time no one but He knows. So we should accomplish the most we can and give our all every day we live.

Think of a time you were tempted to give less than your best. Did you give in to the urge or did you work hard anyway? What happened? Write yourself a reminder of the occasion. Ask God to help you live life with your whole heart. Refer to the note whenever you're tempted.

> Therefore, if anyone is in Christ, he is a new creation; the old has gone, the new has come! —2 CORINTHIANS 5:17

Steffi Graf possesses an intimidating forehand, an explosive serve, and a devastating backhand. In 1988, she put together a string of victories unequaled by any player in recent history.

In the Australian Open finals, the 18 year old faced veteran Chris Evert. Graf dominated the first set, winning 6-1. The West German edged Evert for the title with a 7-6 tiebreaker victory in set number two.

The Grand Slam triumph vaulted Graf to the pinnacle of women's tennis. June brought a repeat victory in the French Open. July saw the teenager win at Wimbledon, and September witnessed a U.S. Open triumph. Graf became only the fifth player in tennis history to win all four Grand Slam tournaments in the same year. An Olympic gold medal capped her incredible twelve months.

The German player claimed her Grand Slam on four different surfaces. The Australian Open used rubberized hardcourt, and France featured slow red clay. Wimbledon played on fast grass, and the U.S. Open utilized hard DecoTurf II.

Steffi Graf put away the older, more experienced stars. She burst on the scene as the new player to beat.

When we become Christians, Christ makes us new. God enters our lives with new thoughts, new attitudes, and new actions. He gets rid of the old self-centered person we were.

Clean out a drawer or closet. Get rid of the old and prepare for the new. Thank God for the new life He brings.

But you are a chosen people, a royal priesthood, a holy nation, a people belonging to God, that you may declare the praises of him who called you out of darkness into his wonderful light. —1 PETER 2:9

Joe Gibbs chose some interesting players for the starting line-up against the Denver Broncos in Super Bowl XXII. The Redskins coach picked Doug Williams to quarterback over Jay Schroeder. Gibbs selected speedy Timmy Smith at running back. Neither Williams nor Smith had played much.

Williams performed poorly in the game's early stages, suffering from an abscessed tooth. He had undergone a five-hour operation the day before.

But with Denver leading 10–0 in the second quarter, the pieces fell in place. The Super Bowl's first black quarterback hit Ricky Sanders with an 80-yard scoring strike. Minutes later, Williams connected with Gary Clark to put Washington in the lead.

The scoring didn't stop. Smith broke to the outside and went 56 yards for a TD. Williams hooked up for another touchdown pass to Sanders and finished the half with a 4-yard toss to Clint Didier.

The Redskins scored 5 unanswered second-quarter touchdowns. Smith, the unheralded rookie, added a final scoring run in the second half as Washington won 42–10.

Sports writers selected Williams as MVP for his 4 touchdown passes and 340 passing yards. The seldom-used Smith rushed for a Super Bowl record 204 yards.

Gibbs chose two unlikely stars. The two chose to give their all. Of course, when the Redskins won, Williams, Smith, fans, and sports writers praised the coach for bringing the backups into the spotlight.

God chooses us. But we must choose to give Him our all. If we do, He brings us into His spotlight.

On a piece of paper, draw three columns. Label the first, "Super Bowl"; the second, "Participants"; and the third, "Winner." Try to list the participants and winners of each Super Bowl. Use an almanac or a sports encyclopedia if you get stuck. Don't be afraid to ask a librarian for help. Thank God for choosing you.

Serve wholeheartedly, as if you were serving the Lord, not men. —EPHESIANS 6:7

Basketball statisticians credit an assist to a player whose pass sets up a score. In 1995, John Stockton took over as the NBA's all-time assistant.

The Utah Jazz hosted the Denver Nuggets. Stockton had 9,911 career assists—10 short of Magic Johnson's NBA record.

The point guard had been creeping toward the mark for weeks. This night's game provided an excellent opportunity to achieve top honors.

The Jazz dominated the Nuggets from beginning to end. Stockton played his usual steady game, running the offense to perfection. He quickly earned assist number 1, a pass to Jeff Hornacek, who hit a 19-footer. Number 2 came on a fast break resulting in a Karl Malone layup. Stockton collected the tying number 10 passing to Tom Chambers, who canned an 18-footer.

Longtime teammate Malone put the playmaker at the top. The Mailman gathered Stockton's pinpoint pass and posted up for a 15-foot fadeaway. The long-awaited record went into the books.

The Jazz point guard made 12 assists before halftime. He finished the night with 16 as Utah blew away Denver 122–90.

Stockton earned a record and a reputation. Assists not only show passing skill but also the ability to spot an open man. The stat further measures unselfishness. The player must be willing to pass up the glory of making points to help the team. He allows others to score more than himself.

Such service is the kind of unselfishness God wants in His followers. As Christians, He asks us to serve Him with our whole hearts and work for His glory, not the praise of people. His teachings encourage us to put our own desires last.

Look for ways this week to assist others and to do so without calling attention to yourself. Ask God to help you be unselfish. Volunteer to take out the trash or bring in the groceries. Give someone else the last cookie or larger piece of meat. Watch the video or television program your friends or family choose.

You must have accurate and honest weights and measures, so that you may live long in the land the Lord your God is giving you. —**DEUTERONOMY 25:15**

Marine Corporal John Uelses pole-vaulted higher than anyone before him. But at the 1962 Millrose Games in Madison Square Garden, an overzealous photographer almost cost him an opportunity for world recognition.

The slender, 170-pound marine barely attracted notice at the meet. Few believed the 16-foot mark could be conquered with a 15-foot pole.

But Uelses switched poles from bamboo to fiberglass. The revolutionary new pole bent almost double, then abruptly straightened, pushing the vaulter over the bar.

As the German native ran down the wooden runway, the crowd sensed something special. The Garden grew silent. Everyone held his breath until Uelses sailed over the bar without even brushing it.

Spectators erupted with cheers. The Miami High grad cleared 16 feet, 1/4 inch—a world record.

A photographer, rushing to capture the event, brushed against the upright. The bar fell into the sawdust pit.

Track and field regulations require measurement before and after a record vault for certification. Controversy reigned regarding whether the new mark would count.

Uelses made the arguments moot the following day. The corporal vaulted higher, clearing 16 feet, 3/4 inch. The crowd carefully avoided the pit area so that a officials could measure. The new mark stood.

Track and field rules were clear. The measure had to be accurate. The first apparent record couldn't count because the tape couldn't verify it.

In one of the Books of the Law, the Bible cautions about using accurate weights and measures. Honesty is important to God. He demands it.

Cut a piece of paper about an inch wide. Measure and cut an inch-wide piece using the first or last inch of a ruler. Make the one-inch cut using a different part of the ruler. Try using a meter stick or tape measure. Were there differences in the one-inch pieces of paper? Ask God to help you be honest and accurate in all of your dealings.

We were under great pressure, far beyond our ability to endure. . . . But this happened that we might not rely on ourselves but on God. —2 CORINTHIANS 1:8-9

The entire United States Olympic team performed poorly at the 1964 Innsbruck games. Through the halfway point, the Americans had won only a silver and a bronze, by skier Jean Saubert. But Terry McDermott burst onto the speed skating scene to give the Red, White, and Blue reason to cheer.

Soviet skater Yevgeny Grishin held the world record in the 500-meter and arrived as the prohibitive favorite. Another Russian, Vladimir Orlov, appeared to be his successor.

No one had ever accused Terry McDermott of hogging the media spotlight. He preferred to let his skates do the talking.

McDermott's coach, Leo Freisinger, decided the young man from Michigan needed pressure. The 1936 bronze medalist purposely scheduled McDermott for a dangerous late run. The ice might soften and increase the time, but the American headmaster took the risk.

Grishin, Orlov, and Norway's Alv Gjestvang tied for the fastest time in the early heats at 40.6 seconds. Fortunately for McDermott, the ice improved as the day wore on. The temperature warmed just enough to create a thin layer of lubricant on the surface.

The American, wearing a pair of borrowed skates, took off at the gun. Flying furiously around the rink, he sped to a gold medal in an Olympic record time of 40.1. Terry McDermott salvaged America's pride and prevented the United States' first gold medal shutout in Olympic history.

Pressure brought out the best in the quiet speed skater. Coaches wonder why pressure destroys some athletes but improves others.

Pressure in life either destroys us or strengthens us. It strengthens when we respond by relying on God. Pressure destroys when we look only to ourselves.

Think of some things that have measured pressure. Perhaps you listed balls, balloons, tires, or a steam engine. What happens when the pressure drops too low? What happens when there's too much pressure? Ask God to help you rely on Him when you're under great stress.

Therefore we do not lose heart. Though outwardly we are wasting away, yet inwardly we are being renewed day by day. —2 CORINTHIANS 4:16

The long NBA season often wears down its teams and players. Many never win a championship.

The Sacramento Kings have experienced their share of bad games. One of the worst occurred in 1987 when they visited the Forum to play the Los Angeles Lakers.

The powerful Purple and Gold jumped to a 10–0 lead. Sacramento coach Phil Johnson called a quick time-out. Two minutes later Johnson stopped play a second time.

Nothing seemed to help. Laker guard Byron Scott stole the ball and scored on a breakaway jam. The hometown crowd roared. Trailing 22–0, the Kings burned a third time-out trying to regroup.

With just under 3 minutes remaining in period number one, the Kings' Derek Smith drew a foul. Behind 29–zip, Smith went to the line. He took a deep breath. The ball swished the net. The Laker partisans gave a standing ovation as the Kings finally put points on the board.

At the first-period buzzer, Los Angeles led by the score of 40–4. The Kings had missed every shot from the field. It was the lowest single total for one quarter since the NBA had installed the 24-second clock in 1954.

Both coaches emptied their benches. The Lakers coasted to another win, and the final tally read Los Angeles 128, Sacramento 92.

Many of us face days like that of the Sacramento Kings. Nothing seems to go right. We lack faith in our abilities and label ourselves losers. But we're never losers in God's eyes. He sticks with us, win or lose, and renews us for a new day.

The path to a winning lifestyle starts with faith in God. The closer we grow in our relationship with Him, the easier it becomes to handle life's setbacks.

Recall a day when everything went wrong. Share your story with a friend. Imagine how difficult it would have been without God. Thank Him for His constant support.

Do everything without complaining or arguing, so that you may become blameless and pure, children of God without fault in a crooked and depraved generation, in which you shine like stars in the universe. —PHILIPPIANS 2:14-15

The National Football League Pro Bowl game provides an opportunity for the stars to showcase their talents. The postseason contest played in Hawaii allows a chance to relax.

Strong rivalry exists between the AFC and NFC. With the National Conference dominating the Super Bowl, the American Conference often exacts revenge in the Pro Bowl. In 1995, that's exactly what happened.

Behind a strong All-Pro line, the AFC rushed for a record 400 yards. Colts rookie Marshall Faulk led the way, setting a new individual mark of 180 yards in 13 attempts. He bolted 49 yards for a touchdown on a fourth-quarter fake punt to set the new high.

Seattle's Chris Warren contributed 127 yards, and Pittsburgh's Eric Green hauled in 2 TD passes. Charger linebacker Junior Seau anchored the defense, logging 7 tackles.

The AFC allowed its National Conference counterparts only 41 yards rushing and 209 total yards. Despite spotting its rivals a 10-point first-quarter lead, the American Conference routed the NFC All-Pros, 41-13, for its third win in five tries.

AFC and NFC players continually argue about who's the best. The Super Bowl normally proves the NFC argument. The Pro Bowl usually supports the AFC claim. But true stars don't need cheap talk. They don't have to show off. They shine purely by their actions on the field.

God's children who star in life don't need to argue, complain, or show off either. Dedication, hard work, kindness, loyalty, hope, commitment, truth, honesty, faith, and love all shine through their lives.

Consider some qualities you like and don't like in All-Pros. Then list some qualities you like and don't like in yourself. Think of those you really want in your life. Do arguing and complaining develop any of them? Ask God to help you work on one quality. Concentrate on letting His love shine through you.

The hour has come for you to wake up from your slumber, because our salvation is nearer now than when we first believed. —ROMANS 13:11

Darryl Sittler, captain of the Toronto Maple Leafs, had been playing as if he were asleep. Team owner Harold Ballard publicly criticized him for scoring only 5 goals in 17 games. But in 1976, the center awoke from his slumber with a vengeance.

The 25 year old opened the first period against the Boston Bruins with a pair of assists. Sittler lit up the scoreboard in stanza number two. He scored 3 goals and helped with 2 more.

Number 27 continued the torrid pace in the final frame. He added another 3 goals, giving him 6 for the game. The Maple Leafs routed the Bruins, 11-4.

Sittler made some unbelievable shots. He slapped the puck on one goal from just inside the blue line. The shot dribbled between goalie Dave Reece's legs and into the net.

The 6th and final goal defied logic. The Maple Leaf captain passed the puck from behind the net. It caromed off two pairs of skates before setting off the red light.

Sittler's half dozen scores plus 4 assists totaled 10 points. The offensive barrage broke the single game record of 8 shared by Maurice "Rocket" Richard and Bert Olmstead.

Sometimes, like Sittler, we move through life as if we're asleep. We halfheartedly do what we're supposed to do. Perhaps we're daydreaming. We might be angry at someone. Or maybe we're just plain tired.

Whatever the cause, we need to wake up like the Maple Leaf captain, take charge, and move forward. God demands it because life is shorter than we think.

Evaluate your sleep, exercise, and eating habits for the past three days. Are you going to bed early enough? Are you eating too much junk food or too many fats? Are you including enough fruits, vegetables, and milk in your diet? What about exercise? Are you playing a sport, riding a bike, or walking? Ask God to help you move enthusiastically through life.

[The Lord] blesses the home of the righteous.

—PROVERBS 3:33b

In 1972, Japan hosted the Winter Olympics for the first time. The Land of the Rising Sun, however, had produced only a single silver medal, by skier Chiharu Igaya, in all previous competitions. But this year the Japanese ski jumpers gave their countrymen reason to cheer.

Twenty-eight-year-old Yukio Kasaya won three straight meets in Europe the month prior to the Olympics. Hopes for a gold medal rested on the shoulders of the young man from Hokkaido.

Kasaya's former schoolmates from Yoischimachi High School awaited him at the bottom of the slope, waving the flag of their alma mater. The Japanese jumper flew off the lift as he never had before. He soared 84 meters in his first attempt.

More surprising, two other natives of Hokkaido jumped well. Seiji Aochi and Akitsugu Konno placed second and third in the first round.

The hometown favorites felt enormous pressure, but they refused to yield. Kasaya, Konno, and Aochi responded with shorter second leaps but still sailed farther than all challengers.

At the conclusion of competition, Kasaya took gold, Konno claimed silver, and Aochi won bronze. The entire nation of Japan celebrated the 70-meter jump sweep.

Why did the Japanese win? Were they better than their competitors? That day they were, but not normally.

Most believed the jumpers excelled because they skied at home. Their friends and family cheered. The threesome felt comfortable, and they were blessed with all the medals.

God also promises to bless our homes if we do right and honor Him. He makes our houses, apartments, or condos places of comfort and support.

Walk through your home. As you walk, pray for the people who live there. Ask God to bless the actions in each room. Thank Him for the homes of the righteous.

The sun has one kind of splendor, the moon another and the stars another; and star differs from star in splendor.

—1 CORINTHIANS 15:41

No other golfer on the Ladies Professional Golf Association tour has the recognition and charisma of Nancy Lopez. The four-time LPGA Player of the Year achieved her fame faster than any female golfer. She collected her first professional title at Bent Tree Country Club's Sarasota Classic in 1978.

In 1987, Lopez survived a late round charge by Kathy Baker and repeated as champion in the Sarasota. Her 7-under-par 281 carried her to a 2-stroke victory.

The championship marked win number 35 for the California golfer. That magic total earned the well-liked and intense competitor automatic enshrinement in the LPGA Hall of Fame. Though she had qualified earlier, LPGA rules requiring ten years of membership forced Lopez to wait until July 1987 for induction.

Each star in every sport differs from the others. Nancy Lopez's unorthodox swing, fierce concentration, and relaxed attitude set her apart from the ten golfers who preceded her into the Hall of Fame.

God has made each of us a star. Some of us shine brightly in knowledge. Others excel in sports, music, or art. Many display winning personalities. But the splendor He gives is different for every person.

Gaze into the night sky. Marvel at the soft reflected glow of the moon. Notice the difference in brightness of stars. Praise God for the unique person that you are.

May the Lord now show you kindness and faithfulness, and I too will show you the same favor because you have done this. —2 SAMUEL 2:6

The Winter Olympics have included bobsledding since its inception in 1924. In 1956, one of Italy's most popular athletes, Eugenio Monti, won silvers in both the two-man and four-man competitions. Lack of facilities at Squaw Valley forced cancellation of the event in 1960.

At the 1964 games, the British team of Anthony Nash and Robin Dixon prepared for their second run when they noticed a broken axle bolt. Monti learned of their problem and pulled one off his own sled so they could compete. Nash and Dixon took the gold while the red-haired Italian managed only a bronze.

At age 40 in 1968, Monti had the odds for the gold stacked against him. After three runs, the Italians trailed the Germans by one-tenth of a second.

Monti drove the bobsled to a course record 1:10.05 and watched the Germans race their final leg in 1:10.15. Incredibly, both teams tied in total time.

The judges first announced dual gold medals. Later, they reversed their decision, citing the international rule giving the victory to the team with the fastest run. After twelve years, Monti had won the gold.

Sometimes being kind and doing the right thing carries a personal price. Kindness cost Eugenio Monti a medal in 1964. But he was faithful to his sport and to his training. The judges returned the favor in 1968 by awarding his team the victory.

In the Bible, David asked God to show kindness and faithfulness to those who had been kind and faithful. And David promised to reward favor with favor. Today, those rewards may come on earth as in Monti's case, or they may come in heaven. But kindness never goes out of God's style.

Put yourself in Monti's place in 1964. What would you have done? Discuss your answer with a friend or relative. Ask God to help you be kind even when it may cost you.

"I will shake all nations, and the desired of all nations will come, and I will fill this house with glory," says the Lord Almighty. "The silver is mine and the gold is mine," declares the Lord Almighty. —**HAGGAI 2:7-8**

Bonnie Blair reigns supreme in the world of women's speed skating. But in the 1992 Olympics, she held her breath and watched others skate before learning if she had earned silver or gold.

The female speedster entered the Albertville games as the favorite. Since her 1988 triumphs occurred indoors, skeptics questioned her ability to race on the outdoor rink.

Blair and China's Ye Qiaobo raced head-to-head in the 500. Blair edged ahead by 18 hundredths of a second for back-to-back Olympic victories.

In the 1,000, the two-time 500 champion posted a brilliant time of 1:21.90. Blair watched and waited as Qiaobo and Germany's Monique Garbrecht prepared to compete.

Qiaobo found stamina, strength, and speed at the 600-meter mark. The crowd waited breathlessly for her time to be posted. Finally, it appeared.

The Chinese skater doubled over in anguish. Blair's time bested her by only 2 hundredths of a second. The 27 year old became the first American woman speed skater to capture three golds.

Bonnie Blair filled the USA's house with glory during those 1992 Olympics. She watched, waited, and shook the nations. The skater filled her own home with gold medals.

Earthly sports stars like Blair bring glory to their homelands through winning. However, God's glory shines brighter. He fills the whole world with it. He created gold, silver, and all things. He is all-powerful, all-knowing, and forever present. But He loves each of us individually.

Do you know a superstar like Bonnie Blair? How do you feel when you're around her or him? Are you so in awe that you can't say an intelligent word? If you don't know a well-known person, how do you think you would feel? Remember, you know God, the greatest superstar ever. But you can still talk to Him any time you want about anything you like. Talk to Him now.

See, I am doing a new thing! Now it springs up; do you not perceive it? —ISAIAH 43:19a

Most people recognize Dick Button as a figure skating commentator. Few remember his electrifying Olympic performances.

Two days prior to the free-skating portion of the 1948 games, the Harvard freshman successfully completed his first double axel, a move never before done in competition. Dick knew he could win by playing it safe. But he wanted to advance his sport.

Button glided forward on one foot, leaped from the outside edge, whirled two-and-a-half times, and landed backward on the opposite foot. Eight of nine judges awarded first place. The former chubby 12 year old whose teacher remarked he would never learn to skate totaled the most points ever in earning gold.

The Harvard student continued polishing. In 1952, he could have played it safe and easily repeated. Instead, he chose to add another never-attempted move—the triple loop.

Button, in a momentary panic, forgot which shoulder went forward. But the hours of practice took over as he leaped and spun three times. He landed cleanly and pulled away breathlessly. The applause thundered.

All nine judges gave Button first place. Dick Button achieved the impossible. He performed new, never-been-done-before, very difficult jumps. And he did it in international competition. The Olympic winner served as a springboard. He moved figure skating to a new level of athleticism and grace.

God does new things in us everyday. He helps us grow. He shows us ways to help others.

Sometimes we'd rather play it safe. We find it easier to stick with what we already know. We resist God's nudge. We refuse to attempt the double axels and triple loops of life. But God knows we can achieve things we never dreamed possible.

If it's possible where you live, go ice skating. Think about Dick Button and his story as you glide. If you can't skate, plan to watch figure skating on television. Pay close attention to the jumps. Ask God to help you make a leap of faith doing new things for Him.

And we rejoice in the hope of the glory of God. Not only so, but we also rejoice in our sufferings, because we know that suffering produces perseverance; perseverance, character; and character, hope. —ROMANS 5:2-4

Hall of Fame baseball manager Leo Durocher once remarked, "Nice guys finish last." That label seemed to apply to Dan Jansen. Bad luck plagued the polite, soft-spoken American speed skater early in his Olympic career. In 1988, Jansen fell in both the 500 and 1,000-meter races. Analysts blamed his lack of concentration on his sister's death from leukemia during the games. At the 1992 Albertville contest, the Wisconsin native placed fourth in the 500. He slipped to 26th in the 1,000.

Sportswriters quickly classify athletes. They tabbed Jansen a skater who couldn't win under pressure. The tag lingered when the speedster slipped in the 1994 Olympic 500.

The 28-year-old skater had one remaining chance, the 1,000. Jansen stumbled on the next-to-last curve. But the American remembered his coach's advice. "Don't panic, and don't compensate too soon."

Jansen relaxed. His time of 1:12.43 not only won, it set a new record. The nice guy finished first.

Dan Jansen suffered—from the untimely death of his sister, from sportswriters' barbs, from glassy ice, from unrealized dreams. As he warmed up for the 1,000 meters, the strain showed on his face and in the faces of his watching family.

But the man's suffering produced great perseverance; perseverance, character; and character, hope. The strain turned to exuberant smiles as Jansen skated his victory lap, carrying his young child and waving the American flag.

Life doesn't always fulfill our dreams. And when that happens, the world can be cruel. God promises that if we stick with it, He'll stand by us.

In your Bible, read Romans 5:1-8. If you have not yet trusted Jesus, talk with a pastor or friend about becoming a Christian. Thank God for His great love. If you already know Jesus, think of a time He helped you through suffering. How did you change because of your experience?

Do not conform any longer to the pattern of this world, but be transformed by the renewing of your mind. Then you will be able to test and approve what God's will is—his good, pleasing and perfect will. —ROMANS 12:2

Leroy Burrell couldn't believe the strange turn of events at the 1991 Madrid indoor meet. First he set a world record of 6.40 seconds in the 60-meter dash. Then officials nullified it, ruling the sprinter had left the blocks too soon.

The judges finally decided to rerun the race. Burrell took his mark on the starting line. He carefully watched the starter, waiting to explode the moment the smoke appeared from his gun.

The former University of Houston runner bolted cleanly. Arms pumping and feet flying, Burrell barreled down the straightaway. Timers clocked the sprinter in 6.48 seconds, 2 hundredths of a second less than Lee McRae's world record. In two consecutive races only ten minutes apart, the American established two new marks in the 60-meter.

Burrell had ten minutes to renew his mind and body before running the second race. He was tested and came through with a world record that held.

God offers to renew us if we will become His and follow His pattern. He wants us to put aside what the world wants and look at Him. Only then can we discover what He will do in our lives.

With a friend or relative, time yourself running the 60-meter dash. How far were you off of Burrell's 6.48 seconds? Ask God to help you follow His pattern rather than the world's.

> My people will live in peaceful dwelling places, in secure homes, in undisturbed places of rest. —ISAIAH 32:18

A home court can be a great advantage to a basketball team. For over four years, the University of Nevada at Las Vegas defeated every opponent who set foot on its home turf.

UNLV hosted the University of Louisville in 1993. The Nevada Runnin' Rebels had not lost to a visiting team since the University of Oklahoma came calling on January 28, 1989.

Although the Louisville Cardinals ranked lower in the polls, they refused to be intimidated. Using superior height, they led 49–37 at the half.

UNLV's tallest player, 6-foot-7-inch Evric Gray, fouled out with 6:27 to play. The Runnin' Rebs remaining big man, 6-foot-5-inch J. R. Rider, couldn't control the boards.

Louisville led by as many as 16 points. A furious UNLV rally closed the margin to 4, but at game's end, the scoreboard favored the Cardinals, 90-86. The Runnin' Rebels' four-year home winning streak had ended.

Most teams play their best at home. Familiar surroundings may be a factor. Vocal fan support plays a role. Avoiding the hassles of travel helps, too.

But the biggest advantage may be undisturbed rest before the game in the player's own home. He feels peaceful and secure.

Life can be stressful. But in our home, God gives us security, peace, and rest. Of course, He expects us to do our part. We must treat others with respect and do more than our share of work. Fighting and whining don't help the team. But God can make our home a place of safety.

List some ways you can help make your home peaceful. Make an effort to do one or more of them. Ask God to help you make your home more restful and secure.

Let them praise his name with dancing and make music to him with tambourine and harp. —**PSALM 149:3**

The International Olympic Committee introduced ice dancing as a sport in 1976. Its beauty, grace, and skill quickly made it a spectator favorite.

Ice dancers skate extremely close to each other and must remain in unison and contact throughout the program. They cannot separate for more than a few seconds. Rules prohibit the strong, athletic moves such as lifts and jumps seen in pairs skating.

At the 1984 Sarajevo games, Great Britain's Jayne Torvill and Christopher Dean performed their free dance program to Ravel's "Bolero." Their interpretation and execution awed not only the crowd but also the judges.

The entire panel of nine judges awarded perfect 6.0s for artistic impression. Three gave perfect scores for technical merit.

Torvill and Dean achieved more than a gold medal. They set a new standard for ice dancing and musical performance.

Music and dance appear in the Bible, too. In the Book of Psalms, King David encourages us to praise God with music and dance. The psalmist says to rejoice with tambourines and harps.

Listen to your favorite piece of Christian music. Note the intensity and change of tempo and volume. Sing a praise to God.

It is God who arms me with strength and makes my way perfect. He makes my feet like the feet of a deer; he enables me to stand on the heights. He trains my hands for battle.

—2 SAMUEL 22:33-35a

Most Americans don't understand biathlon. The sport combines cross country skiing and shooting. Athletes cover a set route, carrying an 11-pound, .22-caliber rifle. At various intervals, the competitor stops and shoots at five targets. Each time is adjusted by adding 1 minute for each missed target. The fastest time wins the event.

In 1968, a 31-year-old Norwegian policeman, Magnar Solberg, attracted little attention. Even in the world of biathlon, few knew much about him.

Solberg completed the 20-kilometer course in 1 hour, 13 minutes, and 45.9 seconds. The Soviet Union's Aleksandr Tikhonov finished slightly over a minute sooner.

But the policeman accomplished a feat for the very first time. He sighted and hit every target. Tikhonov missed twice, adding 2 minutes to his total time. His misses made Solberg the winner.

As photographers crowded around the surprised gold medal winner, he exclaimed, "I am very happy, but too tired to smile." Solberg repeated his top performance at the 1972 games.

Imagine trying to ski for several miles. Picture yourself attempting to slow your heartbeat, take a deep breath, aim, and shoot at a distant target. Think about throwing the weapon back over your shoulder and doing it all over again. It's not easy. But Solberg did it and did it with strength and perfection.

God provides our strength, our endurance, our swiftness, and our training to live life for Him. He assists us through hard times and lifts us when we're too tired to smile. He guides us to aim for perfection.

Pick up a 10-pound bag of flour or another item that weighs about the 11 pounds of a biathlon rifle. Carry it with you for a few minutes or equal to the time needed for the event. Thank God for the help He gives.

for the Lord is our judge; the Lord is our lawgiver; the Lord is our king, it is he who will save us. —ISAIAH 33:22

Everyone expected Jean-Claude Killy to become a champion. The Frenchman grew up in the Alps at his father's ski lodge. At 3, he donned his first pair of skis. But attitude, illness, and adversity delayed his development.

In 1968, however, the pieces began to fall in place at the Grenoble Olympics. The skier set a goal to win all three alpine events. Only Austria's Toni Sailer had performed the feat.

Two rivals stood in Killy's way—Guy Perillat in the downhill and Karl Schranz in the slalom. Perillat opened the competition and clocked a strong 1:59.93.

Killy, nicknamed Casse-cou (breakneck), knew what he had to do. Skiing full throttle, he finished at 1:59.85, winning gold by .08 seconds.

Three days later, France's favorite son easily won the giant slalom.

A thick fog shrouded the mountain on the day of the slalom. The athletes asked for the event to be postponed, but officials refused.

The sun broke through briefly. Killy turned in the event's early best time.

Norway's Hakon Mjoen later bettered Killy's time, but judges disqualified him for missing two gates. Schranz ran the course but stopped when a mysterious figure crossed in front of him. Officials granted a rerun.

The Austrian beat Killy's time and won the gold. But hours later, he received a stunning announcement. Judges ruled Schranz had missed two gates before stopping on the first run. The rerun was disallowed. Killy had equaled Sailer's sweep.

The judges decided. They made the laws. They ruled. And they ultimately saved Killy's gold and goal.

God created us. He made our laws. He serves as judge. He rules as king. But He also saves us from our sins and death.

If you're not familiar with skiing, learn about the three alpine events—slalom, downhill, and giant slalom. Consider the differences and skills needed. Thank God for the unique skills He has given you.

And we, who with unveiled faces all reflect the Lord's glory, are being transformed into his likeness with ever-increasing glory, which comes from the Lord, who is the Spirit.

—2 CORINTHIANS 3:18

Kristi Yamaguchi's performance in the 1992 Olympics could not be classified as perfect. But steady and controlled skating enabled her to equal her girlhood inspiration, Dorothy Hamill.

As a child, the two-time World Figure Skating champion took the ice clutching a Dorothy Hamill doll. In 1992, moments before the final portion of the Albertville games, Hamill—winner of the 1976 gold medal—paid a surprise backstage visit to Yamaguchi.

The artistic skater held a large advantage after the first round. Every competitor had fallen on the ice except Yamaguchi.

The California native opened the free skating program. Midway through, she suffered a near fall on a triple loop. She compensated by reducing her next move, a triple salchow, into a double. Yamaguchi finished without another flaw.

The judges awarded 5.7s and 5.8s for technical merit, and eight of nine gave the graceful American 5.9s for artistic impression. No other skater came close to catching her. Yamaguchi became the first American to capture the women's figure skating gold medal since her idol Dorothy Hamill had in 1976.

From her childhood, Kristi Yamaguchi dreamed of being like Dorothy Hamill. Kristi emulated her moves and control. She wanted to be a reflection of her. And Dorothy encouraged and inspired her.

We choose many different earthly stars to idolize. But none of them is perfect. None is really worthy of our worship. As Christians, we should try to be like our Lord, reflecting Him in all that we think, say, and do.

Question several friends about who they want to be like. Answer for yourself. Ask God to help make you more like Him.

A friend loves at all times, and a brother is born for adversity. —**PROVERBS 17:17**

World-class athletes often fare poorly in the Olympic games. Identical twins Phil and Steve Mahre shared the strange jinx. Both won numerous World Cup skiing races, but Phil's silver medal in the 1980 slalom represented their sole Olympic glory.

In 1984, the American brothers announced they would retire following the World Cup season. Neither was considered a medal hopeful at the Sarajevo games.

One hundred one skiers lined up for the final event, the slalom. Heavy snowfalls turned the course into a treacherous maze.

Athlete after athlete failed to finish. But the twins from Washington felt at home.

Steve led the pack after his first run with a time of 50.85. Phil fell into third at 51.55 with Sweden's Jonas Nilsson in between.

Phil, skiing third from last in the second leg, glided through the course and moved into number one. He grabbed a walkie-talkie and described the intricacies of the downhill run to brother, Steve, the only skier left who could best him.

Steve went for broke, hoping to surpass his four-minutes-older brother, but taking chances caused several minor slips. His total time of 1:39.62 held up for the silver, but the unselfish Phil kept gold.

The Mahre twins completed their Olympic competition on top. The one–two finish swept away years of frustration.

Phil didn't have to think before radioing tips to his brother in the start house. He didn't worry about losing the gold to his twin. Love took over as he chose to help his brother.

We love our friends and enjoy being together. But in difficult times, we usually count on a brother or sister. And as a brother or sister, we come through. The Bible says that's how it should be.

If you have brothers or sisters, thank God for them. Write them notes telling them what they mean to you. If you don't have a sibling, ask God to give you a friend who can be as close as a brother or sister to you.

Our people must learn to devote themselves to doing what is good, in order that they may provide for daily necessities and not live unproductive lives. **—TITUS 3:14**

Some nights NBA teams play at incredible levels. Other times, one franchise completely dominates another. On rare occasions, both appear as if neither wants to win.

The Philadelphia 76ers hosted the Miami Heat in 1996. At the end of quarter one, the home team had banked only 13 points. The visitors fared little better, hitting for just 18.

The Sixers improved slightly, scoring 20 points in the second period. The Heat cooled almost to the freezing point, ringing up a mere 10. The intermission score of 33–28 seemed more appropriate for a high school game than the NBA.

Philadelphia never got untracked in the second half. The 76ers put a paltry 24 points on the scoreboard after intermission. Miami almost matched its opponent's incompetence but managed to add 38 and won 66–57.

The 76ers tied the NBA record for fewest points in a single game.

The Philadelphia and Miami players simply weren't in the game. They were unproductive at best. And the results showed. Who wants to be remembered for being the worst? Not the Apostle Paul.

Paul writes to Titus that as Christians, we should devote ourselves to doing what is good. He says we should work hard to be productive and provide the necessities of life. God does not want His people to be lazy.

Make a list of the things that you need to live. How do you meet those needs? Next make a list of the things that you want. Are you willing to work hard to get them? Ask God to help you be productive.

"Where were you when I laid the earth's foundation . . . while the morning stars sang together and all the angels shouted for joy?" —JOB 38:4,7

The NBA All-Star game brings together basketball's best. Fans flock to the arena to watch the elite East and West teams in action. Millions tune in their television sets to see the galaxy of stars.

The 1993 midseason classic took place in Utah's Delta Center. The press focused on Shaquille O'Neal and Michael Jordan and virtually ignored hometown participants Karl Malone and John Stockton. But in the Sunday afternoon contest, the duo exhibited the grace and style they had practiced for years.

West's coach Paul Westphal called the pick-and-roll play numerous times. Malone and Stockton ran it to perfection. The Mailman delivered 28 points and 10 rebounds while the Utah point guard contributed 9 points and 15 assists.

Patrick Ewing nailed a 15-footer from the baseline with 8.1 seconds left to knot the score at 119. But Stockton blew past Isaiah Thomas with 2:36 remaining in overtime to put the West ahead 126-123. Charles Barkley's 3-pointer at the 1:32 mark pushed the lead to 6. The West prevailed over the East 135–132.

The media couldn't pick a single outstanding player. They voted to split the award between the Jazz combo. Stockton and Malone shared MVP for only the second time in NBA All-Star history.

On that day the NBA stars sang together, and the crowd shouted for joy. Two stars shone brighter than the rest. Malone delivered points and rebounds. Stockton scored his share but provided great assistance.

God created each of those All-Stars and every person in the crowd. He created the earth and all living things.

After dark, go outside and look at the Milky Way. Pick out the brightest stars. Thank God for His creation.

"What are we going to do with these men?" they asked. "Everybody living in Jerusalem knows they have done an outstanding miracle, and we cannot deny it." —ACTS 4:16

The 1980 United States Olympic hockey team faced a challenge. It survived to the medal round but was pitted against the talented Soviet team.

Prior to the Lake Placid games, the Americans had played an exhibition against the Russians. The older, more experienced Soviets had totally dominated, winning easily 10–3.

But Herb Brooks' team had trained well. The players had practiced six months prior to the Olympics and had played a grueling 62-game exhibition schedule.

The Soviets scored first, but Buzz Schneider tied on a first-period goal. Shortly afterward, the U.S.S.R. team pulled ahead, but Mark Johnson tied again with a single second remaining in the first half.

Early in the second frame, the Soviets led once more 3–2, and the Americans failed to counter before the period ended. But the fact they trailed by a single goal inspired the USA squad to press onward.

Tension built. Mark Johnson's tying goal at 8:39 in the final period brought the partisan crowd to the edge. Eighty-one seconds later, captain Mike Eruzione swiped the puck and fired it past the Soviet goalie to gain the lead, 4–3. The rink erupted with shouts of, "U-S-A, U-S-A."

Ten minutes remained. The Soviets mounted numerous scoring threats, but the Red, White, and Blue defense turned each away. With less than a minute to play, the crowd roared.

The fans began the countdown. At last, the Americans triumphed. The press and media dubbed the game the "Miracle on Ice."

The Bible tells of many miracles. But we tend to discount miracles today. We don't usually think of advances in science or doctors treating patients as miracles, but they are. God provides the knowledge.

Ask some older people to list the inventions they've seen in their lifetimes. Question them about what life was like without them. Praise God for those who seek knowledge. Pray they will use it to honor Him.

I press on toward the goal to win the prize for which God has called me heavenward in Christ Jesus. —**PHILIPPIANS 3:14**

The 1980 Winter Olympics in Lake Placid, New York, provided the world with many champions. Eric Heiden, a 21-year-old Wisconsin native, put on an exhibition in speed skating unlike anyone had ever seen.

Heiden won the 500-meter sprint in a time of 38.03, setting an Olympic record. The skater followed with gold medals in the 1,000, 1,500, and 5,000-meter events. In every one, the young American set world or Olympic records.

The final speed skating competition was the longest. The 10,000-meter race, covering a grueling 6.2 miles, required not only great speed but also endurance.

Heiden pushed, pounded, and drove himself around the rink. Skating in the second pair, he crossed the finish line not only in first place, but more than six seconds under the world record. The Olympian speed skater had captured the gold medal in every event, the only skater in Olympic history to accomplish the amazing feat.

Eric Heiden set a goal like no other skater before him. Throughout his long and difficult training and the excitement and pressure of the Olympic games, he never lost sight of it.

The Apostle Paul understood how goal-setting drives individuals to achieve. Before accepting the Christian faith, he sought to destroy the early church. After meeting Christ, Paul became one of Christianity's greatest missionaries.

Paul set a goal to spread Christ's message throughout the known world. Through his journeys and travels, he did. Ultimately, he gave his life in service to Christ.

Make a list of personal goals. Keep it where you see it often. Pray for God's help in achieving your goals.

Never be lacking in zeal, but keep your spiritual fervor, serving the Lord. —**ROMANS 12:11**

The 1980 United States Olympic hockey team met Finland with the gold medal on the line. However, the USA squad had played one of the most emotional contests in Olympic history by defeating the Russians two days earlier. It would be difficult to maintain focus and skate with the same intensity of the previous game.

But what the team lacked in talent, it compensated for in heart. The Americans had an entire nation rooting for them and were determined to win the gold.

The mental and physical fatigue showed early against the Finns. Finland led 2-1 at the end of period number two.

Aggressive checking finally wore the Finnish team down. Phil Verchota tied the score a little over 2 minutes into the final frame. Three minutes and forty seconds later, Rob McClanahan's goal put the USA in the lead.

Penalties forced the Americans to play most of the closing minutes a man short. Goalie Jim Craig held off three desperate Finn power plays.

Mark Johnson broke free and slapped the puck into the net, giving the American squad a 4-2 advantage. The clock ticked down to 0:00, and shouts of "U-S-A, U-S-A, U-S-A" filled the Olympic field house.

The United States hockey team could have wilted under the pressure and intense media exposure, but resolve carried it to victory. A Christian's faith should be just as strong.

The grind of daily living wears on all of us. There are days we want to quit. But no matter how tired or weary we become, God stays with us. We only forget His presence when we focus on our pain rather than serving Him.

Service to God is an obligation for every Christian. Through service, not only do we do our duty, but we also receive the peace and comfort that comes from listening to our Creator.

Recall the last time you participated in a contest. Did you compete with zeal and excitement? Resolve to serve God with the same energy.

I will tell of the kindnesses of the Lord, the deeds for which he is to be praised. —ISAIAH 63:7a

Anton "Toni" Sailer had already won the giant slalom and the slalom in the 1956 Cortina Olympics. The Austrian skier felt confident about winning the downhill since he held the course record of 2:46.2. But a simple piece of equipment almost prevented him from competing.

As Sailer tightened the straps holding the skis to his boots, one snapped. The problem happens so infrequently, the skier had not brought any spares. None of his teammates had extra straps either.

The time approached for Sailer to run the course. If he had to withdraw, his hopes of an alpine sweep (winning every downhill skiing event) would be dashed.

Hans Senger, trainer for the Italian team, walked by and noticed the Austrians in a panic. Senger removed the straps from his own skis and offered them to Sailer.

The course record holder met his starting time. Strong winds and a glassy surface had downed twenty-eight competitors and sent eight to the hospital.

But Sailer survived a near spill and finished the course 3.5 seconds faster than any challenger. The Austrian became the first Olympian to win an alpine sweep. Senger offered kindness. The world praised Sailer for his unmatched feat. Sailer praised Senger for making it possible. God deserves all our praise for His kindness to us every day.

The Bible is filled with examples of God's kindness. Read 1 Kings 17:7-24. The widow praised God for Elijah's kindness to her and her son. Praise God for His kindness.

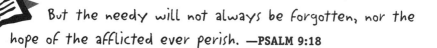

But the needy will not always be forgotten, nor the hope of the afflicted ever perish. —PSALM 9:18

As a youngster, Tenley Albright had polio, a disease that stiffens a person's muscles. Like many children stricken with polio, Albright took to the ice to strengthen her legs. Eventually her figure skating went far beyond exercise.

The young woman from Massachusetts claimed the silver medal in the 1952 Olympics. Two weeks before the 1956 games, the surgeon's daughter hit a rut in the ice while training. Her left skate blade cut through three layers of boot, slashed a vein, and severely scraped a bone.

Her father arrived two days later and stitched the laceration. Albright competed on her injured foot.

Ten of eleven judges awarded the skater first place. The American easily scored more points than her fellow countryman, Carol Heiss, for the gold.

Following her gold medal performance, Albright lost the World Figure Skating Championship to Heiss. The doctor's daughter enrolled in Harvard Medical School and became a surgeon.

Lying in a bed battling polio could have left Tenley Albright ready to die. Instead she found hope. She worked to walk and skated for strength. The hope didn't perish but turned to gold and a surgeon's scalpel.

Whatever our circumstance, God offers hope.

Doctors today rarely see cases of polio because of Jonas Salk's vaccine. Read an encyclopedia article about the disease. Can you name the president of the United States who also overcame polio? Thank God for the hope He gives.

Again Jesus said, "Peace be with you! As the Father has sent me, I am sending you." And with that he breathed on them and said, "Receive the Holy Spirit." **—JOHN 20:21-22**

Millions recall the excitement of the 1980 U.S. hockey team. But few remember the United States' 1960 gold medal upset.

The Americans entered the Squaw Valley games with an unimpressive record. The collegians had lost to Michigan Tech, Denver University, and the Warroad Minnesota Lakers. But when the games counted for real, the squad stepped up.

The opening match paired the United States with a strong Czech team. Trailing 4–3 after two periods, the U.S. scored 4 straight goals and won 7–5.

Impressive victories over Australia, Sweden, Germany, and Canada followed.

The wins vaulted the U.S. into a contest against the defending champion Soviet Union. The Soviets led 2–1 until brothers Billy and Roger Christian scored the tying and winning goals. The Americans defeated the U.S.S.R. for the first time in Olympic competition.

To win the gold, the U.S. team had to beat Czechoslovakia at 8:00 A.M. the following morning. The exhausted players couldn't sleep or relax.

The Czechs jumped to a 4-3 lead after two periods. Then, Soviet captain Nikolai Solobugov paid a surprise visit to the Red, White, and Blue locker room.

Unable to speak English, he pantomimed for the team to inhale oxygen. Officials brought in a tank, and the revitalized amateurs took the ice.

Scoring 6 goals in the final 20 minutes, the Americans blitzed the Slavic team, 9–4. The United States captured its first-ever Olympic hockey gold medal.

The Soviets sent their captain! He brought the gift of air. When the Americans breathed oxygen, they received the gift with renewed spirit.

God sent Jesus to earth to tell people about Him. In turn, Jesus sends us to tell others. But first He breathes the Holy Spirit into us.

Hold your breath for as long as you can. How do you start to feel? Take several deep breaths. Of course, you feel better. Thank God for His wonderful gifts. Share them with a friend.

For there are three that testify: the Spirit, the water and the blood; and the three are in agreement. —1 JOHN 5:7

When the NCAA introduced the 3-point basket to college hoops in 1986, it created new excitement. Teams could bring up their score in a hurry by hitting a few quick threes.

In 1993's final regular season game, the Lamar University Cardinals took on the Louisiana Tech Bulldogs. The Cardinals played a four-guard offense, shooting 3-pointers with abandon.

In the Sunday afternoon contest, Lamar's outside shooting was unstoppable. Quincy Dockins hit 9 of 15 3-point shots, and Shawn Clifton canned 6 of 7.

The Cardinals set a Sun Belt Conference record 49 attempts outside the 3-point arc. Twenty-three went through the rim to establish a new NCAA high, breaking the old mark of 21 shared by Kentucky, Loyola Marymount, and UNLV.

Louisiana Tech never caught up with the furious pace. Quickly down 10–0, the team trailed 59–26 at intermission. The Bulldogs eventually fell 113–76.

Three points in a single shot changed the face of basketball. Coaches rethought strategy. Tempo increased. New shooters emerged. Teams came back to win from seemingly impossible low scores.

Three-in-one changed the face of the world—God the Father, God the Son, and God the Holy Spirit. All are God. And all have the power to change our hearts.

Eat an apple or other piece of fruit. Notice that the peel, the pulp, and the seeds are all three different, but all three part of the same fruit. Thank God for His presence.

"But after me will come one who is more powerful than I, whose sandals I am not fit to carry." —**MATTHEW 3:11b**

Wayne Gretzky worshiped Gordie Howe as a boy. In 1988, when the Great One became the National Hockey League's all-time assist leader, he surpassed his boyhood hero.

The 16,615 spectators watching the Los Angeles Kings tangle with the Edmonton Oilers didn't wait long to see number 99 in action. In the first period, Gretzky circled behind the net to pick up a loose puck. He passed to Jari Kurri on the left side of the crease. Kurri banged the puck past goaltender Rollie Melanson to give Los Angeles a 2-1 lead.

Gretzky's assist, number 1050 in a 681-game career, broke Howe's record established over 26 seasons and 1,767 games. The Great One expressed pleasure that Kurri, his longtime teammate, had a hand in shattering the mark. Number 99 assisted on 298 of Kurri's 387 career goals.

The Kings broadcast a taped message from Gordie Howe after the superstar set the new standard. The former Red Wing thanked Gretzky for being the one who exceeded his mark.

Gretzky and Howe stand as two of hockey's all-time greats. Surely Howe couldn't help being a bit sad when his record fell. And yet Howe knew Gretzky admired him. He knew Gretzky's success came in part from the quest to be like the retired star. So Howe was grateful that one who had admired him had exceeded him.

John the Baptist found himself in a similar position in the Bible. One who had come after him exceeded him. That one was Jesus Christ, the Savior.

Almost everyone has someone who wants to be like him. Odds are someone admires you even if you don't know it. So do your best to be worthy. Always treat everyone with kindness and respect. Ask God to help you set a good example.

The Lord will watch over your coming and going both now and forevermore. —**PSALM 121:8**

The Philadelphia Warriors engaged the New York Knickerbockers in a meaningless late season game in March 1962. The small town of Hershey, Pennsylvania, hosted the contest. A city better known for chocolate than sports witnessed professional basketball's greatest offensive spectacle.

The 7-foot-1-inch Wilt Chamberlain scored at will. He hit 36 of 63 shots from the field and canned 28 of 32 free throws, tallying an even 100 points. No professional basketball player has ever come close to matching his brilliant display.

Only 4,124 spectators saw the center's awesome performance. No film or video exists. If not for newspaper coverage, Chamberlain's electrifying feat would have gone unnoticed.

Few capture the spotlight like professional athletes. Most of our actions occur out of sight. We perform good deeds but receive no thanks and commit wrongs but go unpunished. But God knows every act.

He watches daily over our lives. Our goodness pleases Him, and our failings make Him sad.

Name some people who do good but receive little notice. Make an effort to show appreciation to one or more of them. Pray for courage to do what is right even when no one is watching.

The Lord upholds all those who fall and lifts up all who are bowed down. —PSALM 145:14

No one enjoys falling with thousands watching. At the 1977 World Figure Skating Championships, Linda Fratianne attempted a triple salchow jump in the free skate. Weakened from a sore throat, the 16 year old fell. Quickly, she regained her balance and flew into a successful triple toe loop, dazzling the crowd.

Coach Frank Carroll worried dizziness might force the young skater to withdraw from competition. But the delicate Fratianne possessed nerves and fortitude of steel. She completed the program with grace and technical control.

A Soviet, Yelena Vodorezova, finished first in free skating. However, Fratianne's high scores in compulsory figures and the short program brought her the championship. Eight of nine judges awarded the Californian first place with East Germany's Anett Poetzsch taking second.

Linda Fratianne fell in front of thousands in the arena and millions at home by television. How embarrassing! At that moment she had to make a choice. She could quit. She could finish halfheartedly. Or she could finish to the best of her ability and try to make the judges forget the slip. She chose the latter. And she took gold.

It's not easy to get up when we fall or suffer embarrassment. Maybe we strike out in baseball or softball, miss the backboard completely in basketball, don't touch the ball on a tennis serve, or drop a pass in football. The key is not what we do, but how we handle our mistakes.

God promises that He will hold us and lift us up when we fall. He is there on good days and in tough times. Through prayer, Bible study, and the words of other Christians, we feel Him near.

Jump up in the air and try to spin around three times. Can you do it? If you can't, try twice. What about once? Remember, the champion, Linda Fratianne, fell on a triple jump but got up and completed a different triple. Thank God for His presence when you fall.

He spreads out the northern skies over empty space; he suspends the earth over nothing. —JOB 26:7

A hockey goalie's job is to block shots, not score goals. On the very rare occasion when a goaltender tallies a point, people notice.

In 1996, the Detroit Red Wings took on the Hartford Whalers. Late in the third period, Hartford pulled its goalie out of the crease, attempting to tie the score at 3.

The Red Wings' goaltender, Chris Osgood, blocked the power-play shot. Normally after such a play, the Detroit goalie simply kicked the puck over to a defenseman.

But with time expiring, the Red Wings shot blocker spied the empty Hartford net at the opposite end of the ice. He slapped the puck across the rink with all his might.

Somehow, the hard rubber disk avoided eleven pairs of skates and sticks. It skidded into the net, capping a 4–2 Detroit victory.

The win gave the Red Wings a franchise record 48 victories. Osgood became only the third goalie in National Hockey League history to score in a regular season contest.

When Chris Osgood looked up, he saw eleven players spread over empty space. His shot hit nothing but net. He achieved the seldom-achieved, and his name made the record books.

God suspended the earth in nothingness and stretched the sky over empty space. He created what no one else could.

Watch the news for information about the space shuttles and space stations. If you have a chance, watch one streak across the night sky. Think about what it would be like to be suspended in the nothingness of space like the astronauts. Praise God for His creation.

Know [the love of Christ] that surpasses knowledge—that you may be filled to the measure of all the fullness of God. —EPHESIANS 3:19

In boyhood, Scott Hamilton suffered from Schwachman's syndrome, an inability to absorb food. Doctors recommended skating to develop his brittle legs. The more he practiced, the stronger his body became. In 1981, the once-sickly child made the world take notice.

The 22 year old entered the final phase of the World Figure Skating Championships in third place behind David Santee and Jean-Christophe Simond. Performing next-to-last, the 5-foot-3 1/2-inch skater electrified the crowd with his whirling and leaping. His scores of one 5.7, nine 5.8s, and eight 5.9s catapulted the Pennsylvania native into first place.

Santee, skating last, could not match Hamilton's fervor and energy. The Illinois native stumbled slightly on his first triple jump and never regained the form needed to win gold.

The man in the boy's body earned the second World Championship for an American since 1970. The one–two finish by Hamilton and Santee represented the first sweep by American men in the championship since its beginning in 1892.

Scott Hamilton stands small in height but tall in heart. That is the true measure of a man or woman. People look at the outside, but God looks at the inside.

Recall the story of David and Goliath in the Bible. You can find the details in 1 Samuel 17. Pick up a small, smooth stone. Keep it in your room or on your desk as a reminder that God values the heart.

> There is a time for everything, and a season for every activity under heaven. —ECCLESIASTES 3:1

Most professional sports leagues have existed for many years. Over time, others have been formed and faded away. In 1983, the United States Football League opened with high hopes for success.

The League fielded twelve teams. Los Angeles, New Jersey, Boston, Tampa Bay, Chicago, Washington, Philadelphia, Denver, Oakland, Arizona, Michigan, and Birmingham jumped on the bandwagon for springtime professional football.

Few took the new franchises seriously until the signing of one marquee player. Heisman trophy winner Herschel Walker skipped his senior year at the University of Georgia and signed a contract with the New Jersey Generals. The USFL obtained instant credibility.

An average of 40,000 fans attended the weekend openers. The teams played reasonably high caliber football, but fans had difficulty identifying and bonding with the players.

Over time interest waned. Financial problems developed. The league that opened with high expectations fell victim to low television ratings.

Despite the presence of big name players like Walker, Steve Young, and Jim Kelly, the USFL lasted just three seasons. A lawsuit against the National Football League yielded only three dollars in damages. The League turned into nothing more than bad memories and unpaid bills.

The time seemed right for a new football league. The spring season appeared to be perfect. But the time wasn't right. The season wasn't perfect. The experiment failed.

We force things in life. We want to move forward. We charge ahead. God often answers our prayers yes. Sometimes He says no. But often He asks us to wait because the time isn't right.

Think of a time you wanted something very badly, but you had to wait. How did you feel? Did God later give you what you wanted or maybe something even better? Ask God to help you be patient and wait for the right times in life.

Remember your Creator in the days of your youth.

—ECCLESIASTES 12:1a

It's unimaginable for a teenager to compete with veterans twice her age. But in 1990, that's exactly what Jennifer Capriati did.

Tennis fans watched the young girl as a junior player for several years, anticipating her move from the amateur ranks. At age 13, Capriati debuted professionally in the Virginia Slims of Florida tournament.

The New York native drew 28-year-old Mary Lou Daniels in the first round. Playing an opponent more than a decade older never fazed the youngster.

Capriati moved quickly and efficiently. She won the first game on a backhand smash. A service ace clinched game two, and a sizzling forehand brought victory in the third.

The young pro won her first match in straight sets, 7-6 and 6-1. A crowd of 5,000 spectators and a horde of media witnessed Capriati's first professional triumph. The teenager quickly broke into the World Tennis Association's top ten. She won a gold medal in the 1992 Barcelona Olympics and remained ranked until 1993.

Capriati accomplished much during her teen years. Older opponents soon quit taking her lightly.

Sometimes people discount the importance of a child or teenager's relationship with God. But the Heavenly Father doesn't take it lightly. He wants to be remembered by each person, no matter how young or how old.

Make a list of ways that a young person can serve God—at home, at church, and in the community. Thank God that He uses everyone of every age.

"'Rise in the presence of the aged, show respect for the elderly and revere your God. I am the Lord.'" —**LEVITICUS 19:32**

The 1972–73 Philadelphia 76ers may have been pro basketball's worst team, winning just 9 games and losing 73. But at season's end, the Philly fans honored a longtime star. Hal Greer, a fifteen-year veteran, moved to the Sixers when the franchise relocated from Syracuse in 1963. He ran the offense with precision on Philadelphia's 1967 championship squad.

Kevin Loughery took over the 76er coaching reins in midseason 1973. The new headmaster benched the aging veteran in favor of younger players.

Greer watched from the sideline for 20 straight games. In game 21, the New York Knickerbockers visited the Spectrum. Midway through the third quarter, with New York leading 73–57, Loughery put the 36 year old on the court.

The crowd quickly responded. It rose and cheered. The applause started low and rose to a vibrating crescendo. Fans paid their respects to a legend, saying farewell.

Greer stayed on the court 17 minutes, scoring a basket, grabbing a rebound, and making 4 assists. The point guard had played in 1,117 career games, the most for any NBA player at that time.

The Philadelphia fans cheered the aging star. They rose in Hal Greer's honor. They respected him for all he had done for so many years. And they showed it.

Society often emphasizes the young and their accomplishments. We race past older people or put them aside. We view them as less valuable because their steps have slowed and their hair grayed. But God's law says we ought to honor those who are old by standing in their presence. We should respect senior citizens and show reverence to God.

Think of an older person in your church or in your neighborhood. Call and go by for a visit. Listen to what she has to say, and share what's going on in your life. Ask God to help you show respect for seniors.

"'The Lord bless you and keep you; the Lord make his face shine upon you and be gracious to you; the Lord turn his face toward you and give you peace.'" —**NUMBERS 6:24-26**

The Fighting Irish of Notre Dame have been linked with college football for decades. But in 1970, Austin Carr proved the Notre Dame offense could shine on the hardwood as well as on the gridiron.

Notre Dame met the Ohio University Bobcats in the first round of the NCAA basketball playoffs. Carr sizzled in the field and at the free-throw line.

The 6-foot-3-inch forward connected on 25 of 44 buckets and 11 of 14 free throws. His 61 total points broke Bill Bradley's NCAA scoring record of 58. Notre Dame blew away the Bobcats, 112–82.

The Fighting Irish advanced to the Mideast Regionals and drew the top-ranked Kentucky Wildcats. Carr and Kentucky's Dan Issel put on a shooting clinic for the fans. Carr racked up 52 points, and Issel tallied 44 to lead Kentucky over Notre Dame, 109-99.

In a meaningless third-place game, Notre Dame faced the Iowa Hawkeyes. The Fighting Irish lost 121-106, but Carr lit up the scoreboard for 45. His 52.7 scoring average remains the highest in NCAA tournament history.

God blessed Austin Carr throughout the playoffs. God has richly turned His face toward Notre Dame. The University ranks as one of the top Christian schools in the world, athletically and academically. The school has a wonderful reputation for its commitment to scholarship and its commitment to Christ.

When early Christians said good-bye, they often parted with a blessing. Surprise your pastor or a special Christian teacher or friend by blessing them as you say good-bye with Numbers 6:24-26.

I lift up my eyes to the hills—where does my help come from? My help comes from the Lord, the Maker of heaven and earth. **—PSALM 121:1-2**

Skiing enthusiasts first considered downhill skier Picabo Street a "flash in the pan." But in 1995 and 1996, the Lillehammer Olympic silver medalist accomplished more than any American female skier.

The Colorado native, whose name is pronounced "Peek-a-boo" and means "shining water," had never won a World Cup event until 1995. But the 24 year old rose to new heights on the European circuit.

The daredevil skier won 6 of 9 races including her final 5 in a row. Street became the first American downhill champion in World Cup history.

History repeated in 1996. Although the free-spirited racer's victory total dropped to 3, she accumulated enough points to capture the downhill crown for the second straight year.

The exuberant and outspoken skier topped off 1996 by winning the World Alpine Ski Championship downhill at Sierra Nevada, Spain. Her time of 1:54.06 bested runner-up Katja Seizinger by .57 of a second. The United States Olympic Committee named her Sportswoman of the Year.

Watching a downhill event means looking up from the spectator area to the hills above. The skier first appears as a small dot swirling alone down the mountain but grows larger with each passing meter. Near the finish, the person finally becomes life-size. Some even become larger than life as a reputation grows.

But only the Lord who made those hills is larger than life. We look up to Him. The One who made all of heaven and earth offers us help. We are never alone when we trust in Him.

Walk up a hill or even up some stairs. Look at how small everything appears below. As you move back down, notice the size changing. Remember that size depends on your perspective and no matter how big something seems, God is always greater. Praise Him for His presence.

How beautiful on the mountains are the feet of those who bring good news, who proclaim peace, who bring good tidings, who proclaim salvation, who say to Zion, "Your God reigns!"

—ISAIAH 52:7

Professional golfers try to avoid controversy. Drawing the wrath of officials leads to sanctions or disqualification.

In 1990 at the Honda Classic in Coral Springs, Florida, John Huston lined up on the first tee. Tournament marshals noticed the pro's Weight-Rite shoes.

The footwear inserts a wedge on the outer edge of the sole, forcing weight toward the inside. The player gets better posture for striking a golf ball.

Officials ruled the shoes illegal. The quick-thinking Huston shucked the outlawed spikes and bought a new pair of shoes in the pro shop.

The change in footwear didn't affect Huston's play. He shot a 4-under-par 68 and led by 2 strokes after the first day. Still wearing the off-the-rack shoes, the 28-year-old golfer fired a second round 73 and clung to the lead.

A legal pair of Weight-Rites arrived on Saturday. Huston finished with rounds of 70 and 71. The third-year pro captured the Honda Classic by 2 strokes over Mark Calcavecchia for his first PGA Tour victory.

Professional Golf Association officials obviously check everything, including the golfers' feet. Now John Huston knows the rules and makes sure his footwear complies.

God also checks our feet. But He looks for something different. He considers how we use them. The Lord wants us to go and tell others the good news that Jesus died for our sins. No matter what our feet look like, they appear beautiful to God when we use them for Him.

List all the special shoes available for exercising or playing sports. A trip to a sporting goods or athletic shoe store will help. How many of the different kinds do you own? Remember, God doesn't care about our shoes, just where we go in them. Ask Him to help you share Christ with those who don't know Him.

for he does not willingly bring affliction or grief to the children of men. —**LAMENTATIONS 3:33**

Gail Devers has established a reputation as one of the world's top women sprinters. But a debilitating disease almost ended her track career.

After setting an American record in the 100-meters in May 1988, Devers failed to make the finals in the Seoul Summer Olympics. For the next two years, a mysterious ailment sapped her strength, weakened her muscles, attacked her skin, and caused weight and hair loss. The runner feared her feet might have to be amputated.

Doctors diagnosed her illness as Graves' disease. Appropriate treatment cured the affliction. Devers returned to her world-class form, winning the 100-meter gold medal in the 1992 Barcelona Olympics.

In March 1993, the speedster faced 60-meter world record holder Irina Privolova in an indoor meet in Toronto. The American broke quickly from the blocks.

In less time than most people cross a room, Devers bolted across the finish line. She set a new American record of 6.95 seconds, only .03 off Privolova's world mark.

Diseases and illnesses are a part of life. God does not willingly bring us grief but stays by our side when bad things happen. He guides doctors and provides knowledge to researchers. He gives the strength to live no matter what the circumstance.

Talk to a Christian doctor or nurse about how God helps her or him in everyday practice. Thank the Heavenly Father for the knowledge and guidance He gives to medical personnel.

for he has delivered me from all my troubles, and my eyes have looked in triumph on my foes. —**PSALM 54:7**

No team has dominated collegiate indoor track and field like the University of Arkansas. From 1984 to 1992, the Razorbacks captured 9 straight indoor championships. One more title would pass Iowa's string in wrestling and Southern Cal's in outdoor track.

Erick Walker's long jump victory gave the Fayetteville school a giant boost on the first day of the 1993 competition. The Hogs earned 30 points on opening day and led second-place Ohio State by 18. With four qualifiers in the mile run, Arkansas seemed a cinch to repeat.

Every piece fell into place for the Razorbacks on day two. Walker repeated his double wins of 1992 in the long and triple jumps. Niall Bruton and Michael Morin placed first and third in the mile. Arkansas collected 66 points and easily captured its 10th consecutive indoor track and field title. The Hogs outscored runner-up Clemson by a whopping 36 points and stood alone atop the NCAA record book.

The Razorbacks had no trouble winning the championship and setting the record. Each team member trained and did his part. Everything went perfectly, and the University of Arkansas track team triumphed—10 times in a row!

In Psalm 54, King David praised God for delivering him from King Saul. Assuming our motives are pure, God will help us triumph over our foes. Maybe even 10 times in a row!

At the local track or on soft ground, practice the long jump. Remember, putting your hand down behind you or falling backward shortens the jump. Thank God that even though you may not always win, He helps you triumph in life.

"Suppose a woman has ten silver coins and loses one. Does she not light a lamp, sweep the house and search carefully until she finds it?" —**LUKE 15:8**

A fall sometimes eliminates any chance of success. But in 1982, Elaine Zayak proved recovery is possible.

Two months prior to the World Figure Skating Championship, Zayak fell three times in the United States Nationals. The slipups resulted in a second-place finish.

In the World Championship, the 16 year old slipped on the ice in the short program. Her first-round stumble on a combination double flip and triple toe loop left the New Jersey native in seventh place. Few gave the skater any serious hope of top honors.

In the free skate program, however, Zayak dazzled the judges by completing seven triple jumps without faltering. At the end of her four-minute segment, the teenager leaped into the arms of her coach, Peter Burrows. He tossed her playfully into the air as she cried, "I didn't fall, I didn't fall."

Six of seven judges awarded Zayak first place. Katarina Witt of East Germany received one first-place vote, finishing second.

In the competition, Elaine Zayak and her coach weren't too concerned about losing one judge. It didn't affect the gold medal. In fact, the skater could have lost another without changing the results.

But when God loses one person, He's like the woman who sweeps her house to find one valuable coin. The Heavenly Father seeks us individually because each of us is important to Him.

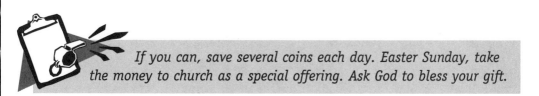

If you can, save several coins each day. Easter Sunday, take the money to church as a special offering. Ask God to bless your gift.

The prayer of a righteous man is powerful and effective.

—JAMES 5:16b

The opening rounds of the NCAA basketball tournament often produce odd results. In 1981, the University of Louisville Cardinals entered the playoffs as defending champions. Their talent had been depleted, but the team fought to keep its title.

A gifted University of Arkansas Razorback squad battled the Cardinals. The Razorbacks gained a 71–67 advantage with 1:33 to play.

Poncho Wright's free throws narrowed the gap to 71–69 at the 47-second mark. Eleven ticks later, U.S. Reed hit 1 of 2 from the free throw stripe to put Arkansas up by 3.

Wright came back and hit a 25-foot corner jumper with 20 seconds left. The Razorbacks foolishly overthrew the in-bounds pass, and Louisville regained possession.

Derek Smith grabbed Wright's offensive rebound and laid it in the hoop, giving the Cardinals a 73–72 lead. With 5 seconds remaining, Arkansas called time-out.

Without time for a set play, the Razorbacks inbounded to Reed. Despite the double team, the guard fired a shot at the buzzer from just inside the midcourt stripe.

The ball hung high in the air before arcing downward. The sphere swooshed through the net as the Razorback fans erupted and wildly called the hogs. Arkansas triumphed 74–73.

Coach Eddie Sutton described Reed's shot as "throwing up a prayer and having it answered."

Sutton spoke figuratively when he described the shot. God loves the players on both sides of any game. But we all can and should pray.

Praying isn't hard. We simply talk to God as we would to someone in the same room who loves and cares about us. When we pray to the Lord earnestly with a right and unselfish attitude, our prayers become powerful. He answers them.

Read the Lord's Prayer in Matthew 6:9-13. Learn it if you haven't already. Think of it as a model you can use in your own prayer life.

Then I looked up—and there before me was a man with a measuring line in his hand! —ZECHARIAH 2:1

Sergei Bubka has broken the world pole vault record 35 times. In 1991, at a meet in San Sebastian, Spain, the Ukrainian vaulter set a new mark especially for the American people.

The previous week at the Indoor World Championships in Seville, the 27 year old attempted to top the 20-foot standard three times and failed. Bubka cleared the height cleanly on his first try in San Sebastian.

Bubka soared above his competitors through a combination of speed and strength. His speed converted to height, and his strength allowed the use of a stiffer pole. The stiffer pole creates a greater slingshot effect to thrust the vaulter over the bar.

The Eastern European dedicated his record to America's track and field fans. Since all countries except the United States use the metric system, a 20-foot pole vault is considered special only in the U.S.

Measurements are important in sports. Tracks, fields, courts, nets, hurdles, and various pieces of equipment must adhere to specific size requirements. Measurements determine placement and records in all field events.

While most of the world uses the metric system and America uses the traditional English system, God sets His own standard. And the only way we can measure up is by depending on Him for direction.

Label each of the following as either part of the metric or U.S. system: liter, quart, yard, meter, centimeter, inch, mile, kilometer, gram, and ounce. If you get stuck, a dictionary or encyclopedia normally includes a table of weights and measures. Ask God to help you measure up to His standard.

"Is not my word like fire," declares the Lord, "and like a hammer that breaks a rock in pieces?" —JEREMIAH 23:29

In 1996, the Texas Tech Red Raiders faced the two-time NCAA champion University of North Carolina Tar Heels in the Eastern Sub-Regionals in Richmond, Virginia. Despite a 28–1 record, the team from Lubbock, Texas, had struggled in its first-round game, defeating Northern Illinois by a single point. Most expected the Tar Heels to give Texas Tech all it could handle.

UNC fell behind in the early minutes, but outscored Tech 14-9 to take a 16-14 lead 8 minutes into the contest. Suddenly, Red Raider Darvin Ham delivered a slam to knot the game at 16.

The dunk accomplished more than just tying the score. The powerful jam shattered the backboard and stopped play for over 30 minutes. *Sports Illustrated* recorded the scene and ran the picture on its cover the following week.

After the delay, the Tar Heels blew ice cold, and the Raiders got red hot. Texas Tech went on a 10-0 run and led at intermission, 44–32.

North Carolina never got untracked in the second half. The third-ranked Red Raiders captured the East Sub-Regional with a 92–73 victory.

Imagine seeing the backboard broken into little pieces. How scary! What a display of power!

God's Word contains that kind of power. The Bible guides, comforts, encourages, gives examples, and points the way to salvation and right living. It is the greatest story ever written and the best selling book of all time.

Read your favorite Bible verse and psalm. If you haven't yet chosen one, begin to note meaningful Scriptures. Memorize some special ones.

"Do not be fainthearted or afraid; do not be terrified or give way to panic before them." —**DEUTERONOMY 20:3b**

The NCAA basketball tournament sometimes becomes unpredictable. Every team plays to win, but low-ranked schools have the toughest job.

In 1993, the Santa Clara University Broncos advanced to the playoffs with an upset victory in the West Coast Conference Tournament. The NCAA selection committee ranked SCU fifteenth due to a mediocre 18–11 record. The Broncos drew the second-ranked University of Arizona Wildcats.

Arizona led 35–33 at the halftime, but the Broncos remained confident. They refused to surrender.

Santa Clara out-rebounded the taller Wildcat team, 50–36. Although the Broncos shot an unimpressive 37.7 percent from the field, Arizona hit only 30.9.

In the final minute, the Wildcats made crucial mistakes. They missed rebounds. They allowed tip-ins. They dropped the ball.

Damon Stoudamire missed a desperation 3-point shot at the buzzer. Arizona fell to Santa Clara, 64–61.

The Broncos could have been content just to make the tournament. Instead, Santa Clara played its best. The Broncos refused to be afraid or panic.

Sometimes we face difficulties. We play a higher-ranked opponent. We make a hard choice. We move away or a friend does. We lose someone we love.

In those times, God helps us stay calm and control our fears. Praying and reading the Bible in a quiet place allows Him to guide us.

Review the following situations. How could you calmly handle each one?
- *The weather service issues a tornado warning.*
- *Two cars crash on the street outside your home.*
- *A friend begins to choke during lunch.*

Ask God to help you remain calm in tough times and handle each crisis with confidence.

Live in harmony with one another. Do not be proud, but be willing to associate with people of low position. Do not be conceited. —ROMANS 12:16

Fans pair college basketball and the University of Kentucky Wildcats like peanut butter and jelly. But in 1966, number one Kentucky met its equal in the NCAA finals.

Few considered Texas Western a contender. But Don Haskins' gritty team of Miners advanced round after round.

The Wildcats' starting team had no one over 6 feet, 5 inches. The media called them "Rupp's Runts."

Texas Western surprised Kentucky with quickness. Coach Haskins controlled the tempo using a three-guard offense. His big men dominated inside.

The Texas collegians led at intermission, 34–31. The Miners stretched the margin to 68–57 and forced Kentucky to foul. Texas Western won one of the greatest upsets in NCAA tournament history, 72–65.

Why did Kentucky lose? Were the Wildcats proud and overconfident? Did they consider Texas Western beneath them? Or was the El Paso team for real? Did its quickness, tempo, and coaching simply make it better, at least on that day?

Whatever the reason, Texas Western took the crown.

In life we sometimes look down on other people. We think we're better. Maybe we believe we're smarter or have more money or are more outstanding athletes. We don't want to associate with them.

But God wants us to live in harmony. He wants us to put away false pride and associate with different kinds of people. And most of all, He wants us not to be conceited or stuck up, but to welcome everyone just as He does.

Experiment with peanut butter. Instead of the traditional jelly, try mixing it with bananas, applesauce, raisins, honey, or even chocolate. How does your sandwich taste? Different but good. Remember, people are different, too. Keep your old friends, but branch out to make new ones. God will approve. Ask Him.

Those who sow in tears will reap with songs of joy.

—PSALM 126:5

Michael Jordan's personal burdens drove him away from basketball. After a seventeen-month layoff, however, the love of roundball brought the superstar back to the court.

Jordan left the hardwood for the baseball diamond. Bulls' owner Jerry Reinsdorf allowed the forward to play in the White Sox minor league system. But the experiment failed. Jordan knew where he belonged. And it wasn't with the Birmingham Barons.

The three-time MVP rejoined his teammates in Indianapolis. He wore number 45 rather than the familiar 23, but everyone knew Michael was back.

The effects of the long absence couldn't be disguised. Jordan missed his first six shots. The once fluid and graceful moves appeared jerky and unnatural. The superstar hit just 7 of 28 from the field and finished the game with 19 points.

The Chicago Bulls took the contest into overtime but fell to the Indiana Pacers, 103–96. Despite the loss, all welcomed Jordan back. His talent and ability had not been lost. The world's most recognizable athlete needed only time to resharpen his skills.

Michael Jordan left basketball in tears, his own and those of his fans. But after time he was renewed. Air Jordan returned to his love, bringing great joy.

When tragedy strikes, sometimes we need change and time by ourselves to shed our tears. In those quiet, alone times with God, He begins to give us songs of joy.

Think about a friend you haven't seen in a long time because of something sad in his life. Call or go by to renew your friendship. Thank God that He can turn tears into laughter.

He is before all things, and in him all things hold together. —COLOSSIANS 1:17

An athlete doesn't always have to place first to finish on top. In 1986, Debi Thomas proved runners-up can sometimes be just as good.

The premed student from Stanford competed in the World Figure Skating Championships in Geneva. The two-time defending champion, Katarina Witt, received the nod as the favorite.

But Thomas upstaged Witt in the short program to take an early lead. The question remained, however—could the black skater hold her own against the German veteran in the five-minute long program?

Thomas knew a first- or second-place showing would give her the title. She came out skating hard to a combination of Duke Ellington and ballet music.

The 18 year old landed four triple jumps, including a tricky triple-double-toe-loop combination. Thomas followed the maneuver with a double axel in which she seemed to float on air.

The performance brought the crowd to its feet. But Witt enthralled them. Her finesse and style edged Thomas and made the double defending champion the star of the four-minute segment.

Two judges awarded Witt perfect scores. The German skater took first in the long program. But Thomas placed second, and her early strong showing gave the American the title.

Debi Thomas held together throughout the competition. She built a lead and stayed close enough to win. Sometimes the winner isn't the showiest or the flashiest. Often steady beats inconsistent.

God holds things together in the world and for each of us. He's steady, consistent, and always there. He existed before He formed the earth and will last forever.

Name some objects that hold other objects together. Examples might include tape or Velcro. Usually you don't even notice them. Then think about some teams you've played on or watched and who held them together. Is it the star everyone sees, or the steady player few notice? Ask God to help you be a person who holds things together.

> Though one may be overpowered, two can defend them-
> selves. A cord of three strands is not quickly broken.

—ECCLESIASTES 4:12

Hockey players describe scoring 3 goals in a game as a "hat trick." In 1952, Bill Mosienko pulled off a very special trick.

The Chicago Black Hawks traveled to Madison Square Garden for the season finale. Since neither team would participate in the Stanley Cup play-offs, the New York Rangers started rookie goaltender Lorne Anderson.

Mosienko, a 28-goal-scorer heading into the final game, hoped to reach the 30 plateau. But with New York leading 6–2 early in the 3rd period, his chances appeared bleak.

Gus Bodnar passed the puck to the wingman following a face-off. Mosienko darted around defenseman Hy Buller and fired a low-wrist shot into the goal. The clock showed 6:09.

Bodnar took the next face-off. He sent the puck to his right winger at the blue line. Mosienko slipped past Buller and sent another screamer past Anderson. Eleven seconds had elapsed between goals.

When play resumed, left wing George Gee passed to Mosienko streaking into the Ranger zone. He faked left and flipped the puck into the net. The time read 6:30. His unbelievable scoring feat rallied Chicago past the Rangers, 7–6.

Mosienko did the fastest hat trick on record—3 goals in less than 30 seconds. But he had help, first from Bodnar, and then from Gee. One couldn't have done it. Neither could two. It took three to make the three.

Life becomes easier when we rely on God and have help from family, friends, and church. Of course, we also return the favor by helping them.

Cut a piece of thread. Try to break it. Cut two pieces of thread and wind them together. Try to break the strand. Finally, cut three pieces of thread and wrap them together. Can you break the triple strand without using scissors? Thank God for His help and the help of others.

> Great is the Lord and most worthy of praise; his great-ness no one can fathom. —**PSALM 145:3**

Wayne Gretzky has earned his nickname, the Great Gretzky. Over a seventeen-year career, he has rewritten the National Hockey League record book.

The Edmonton Oiler, Los Angeles King, St. Louis Blue, and New York Ranger superstar has won the League's Hart Trophy as Most Valuable Player nine times. He set the record for most goals with 92 in 1982. The Great One also holds the highest number of NHL scoring titles with nine.

In 1994, the center nailed goal number 802 to surpass former Detroit Red Wing Gordie Howe. It came on a power play in the second period against the Vancouver Canucks and tied the game at 2–2.

Teammate Luc Robitaille brought the puck into the Vancouver zone. He passed to Gretzky, who fed Marty McSorley streaking down the right side. McSorley drove for the net, but the Vancouver goalie came out to cut down the angle.

McSorley managed a cross pass to the Great One, and Gretzky fired the puck into a wide-open net. The record-breaking goal sent the Kings celebration onto the ice, and the crowd roared. Play stopped to show a highlight film from the careers of Howe and Gretzky.

Wayne Gretzky proved that day and on many others that he was worthy of praise. But even a great hockey player like Wayne Gretzky cannot compare with God. No one matches the Lord's strength and power.

God's greatness surrounds us. We see it in the majestic beauty of the earth. We find it in the love of our families and friends. We experience it in prayer.

List at least five things that show the power of God. For help, read Genesis 1. Praise God for His greatness.

Perseverance must finish its work so that you may be mature and complete, not lacking anything. —JAMES 1:4

The Detroit Red Wings and Montreal Maroons faced off in the first game of hockey's 1936 Stanley Cup semifinals. Both teams skated up and down the ice. Both teams fired the puck at the net. But at the end of regulation play, neither team had scored.

The contest moved to overtime. The fourth period matched the other three. Periods five, six, seven, and eight produced similar results. The Red Wings and Maroons played eight 20-minute rounds, but their goalies refused to yield. The scoreless contest went into the ninth frame.

Nearly 6 minutes into the period, Montreal started a power play. Detroit goalie Norman Smith blocked the shot and cleared the puck.

Red Wing Her Kilrea picked up the loose puck. He and rookie forward Mud Bruneteau broke for the Montreal net. Kilrea passed to Bruneteau, who skated around the Maroon defense. Goalie Lorne Chabot moved out to intercept the skater, but the rookie dodged him. The forward who had scored only 2 goals the entire season slapped the puck between the goal posts. Detroit won on Montreal's ice, 1–0, in the NHL's longest game. The contest took over six hours to complete, and the players skated 2 hours, 56 minutes, and 30 seconds.

How easy it would have been for the players to let up. Their skates began to feel heavier. The players needed more effort to move their sticks.

But each man persevered. Each played his best. Each finished his work. Each completed his task.

Sticking to a task, especially one that takes a long time, isn't easy. We may be tempted to quit or give weak effort. It's difficult to finish a job, giving our best all the way. But that's what God demands.

Is there something you need to finish? It could be reading a book, learning a sports skill, doing chores, or completing a project. It could be almost anything. Finish it now or set a specific time and stick to it, no matter how long it takes.

"Dominion and awe belong to God; he establishes order in the heights of heaven." —JOB 25:2

Dynasties sometimes dominate sports. During the late 1960s and early 1970s, the UCLA Bruins ruled college basketball as no team has before or since.

From 1967 to 1972, the Bruins won 6 straight NCAA championships. In 1973, UCLA faced the Memphis State Tigers for title number 7.

A crowd of 19,301 filled the St. Louis arena. UCLA focused its offense around 6-foot-11-inch center Bill Walton. The Tigers relied on guard Larry Finch and center Larry Kenon.

The underdogs from Memphis battled even in the first half. The two Larrys combined for 30 points, and the teams went into intermission tied at 39.

But Walton and his UCLA gang erupted in the second half. The red-haired center played almost perfect basketball. He hit 21 of 22 from the field and 2 of 3 at the free-throw line. His 44 points set an NCAA championship game record. The Bruins' big man held Finch and Kenon to 19 second-half points.

UCLA demolished the Tigers, 87–66. John Wooden's team captured its 75th consecutive victory and 7th straight title.

UCLA ruled. With their consecutive wins and championships, the Bruins had indeed become a dynasty. The dictionary defines dominion as supreme authority or power and dynasty as a succession of kings or rulers in one line or the length of time one family holds power. UCLA held power for seven years, a long time in sports, but not so long in life. Unlike teams or earthly kings, God's dominion and dynasty last forever.

Make a list of what you think are the greatest sports teams of all time. Include both colleges and professional franchises. Discuss your list with another sports enthusiast. How many championships has each won? How many were in a row? How many were won without losing a contest? Praise God for His dominion over the world.

We will shout for joy when you are victorious and will lift up our banners in the name of our God. —PSALM 20:5

Sheryl Swoopes may have been the best female collegiate basketball player of all time. In her final game, she showed a national television audience why.

The Texas Tech Red Raiders met the Ohio State Buckeyes for the 1993 NCAA crown. The Buckeyes took great pride in their defense, but the Ohio State women couldn't stop Swoopes.

Marsha Sharp's Tech team led by as many as 11 points in the second half, but a determined Ohio State squad narrowed the margin to 75–73 with 2 minutes to play. Then Swoopes shifted into higher gear and turned on the afterburners.

The All-American hit 2 clutch free throws. On Tech's next possession, Buckeye freshman Katie Smith left Swoopes alone at the top of the key. The rest of the Red Raiders cleared out. The Player of the Year glided past Smith through the lane for an easy layup. Ohio State fouled, and Swoopes completed the 3-point play.

The 5-point run gave the Texans an 80–73 lead with 58 seconds to play. Texas Tech held on for an 84–82 victory and its first title.

Swoopes scored 47 points against the Buckeyes, breaking the NCAA championship game mark of 44 held by Bill Walton. She hit a perfect 11 of 11 free throws. The media selected her the tournament's Most Valuable Player.

The Red Raiders lifted the 1993 NCAA Women's Basketball Championship banner over the Lubbock Municipal Coliseum. Shouts echoed over the plains for months. Swoopes, Coach Sharp's other players, and Tech fans everywhere celebrated.

God gives us great cause for celebration. He endows us with the talent and support needed for joy and peace in what He chooses for us in life. And He presents us with eternal life through the death and resurrection of Jesus Christ, His Son.

Make a banner, flag, or door decoration you can display during the Easter season. Celebrate God.

Do not swerve to the right or the left; keep your foot from evil. —**PROVERBS 4:27**

Millions have watched Vinko Bogataj on television every week. But few recognize his name or sport.

In 1970, Bogataj competed in the World Ski Flying Championship in Oberstdorf, Germany. As the ski jumper neared the bottom of the hill, he veered right. Instead of soaring through the air, the Yugoslav hurtled over the solid barrier and crashed.

Incredibly, Bogataj escaped serious injury and sustained only a slight concussion. But an ABC television crew captured the breathtaking spill on videotape.

For over two decades, the network used the footage to introduce its weekly program "ABC's Wide World of Sports." Every Saturday afternoon, countless sports fans heard Jim McKay's famous words, "the thrill of victory—the agony of defeat," voiced over Bogataj's death-defying plunge.

Bogataj's spill became famous because he veered off course. He swerved to the right and couldn't correct the mistake. The skier paid the price.

God warns us to remain on His straight path. When we disobey Him, we veer off course. We do wrong. And we pay the price in disappointment, lack of respect, loss of friends, and separation from God. We may also face fines or imprisonment if we break man's laws as well as God's.

Walk along a not-very-high ledge or on a line of masking tape placed on the floor. Try to stay exactly on the path. Ask God to keep you on His straight path.

He mounted the cherubim and flew; he soared on the wings of the wind. —2 SAMUEL 22:11

Skeptics wondered if Michael Jordan could return to his pre-retirement form. Just nine days after rejoining the Chicago Bulls, Michael showed everyone he was back.

Chicago took on the New York Knicks in Madison Square Garden. Jordan carried his team as if he had never left.

Number 23 wearing number 45 hit 21 of 37 from the floor. From the free-throw stripe, Jordan barely missed perfection, canning 10 of 11. The 55 points were the NBA's high for the season and an arena record for the new Madison Square Garden.

The prodigal looked like the superstar of old in the game's final seconds. A jumper at the 25.8-second mark put Chicago up 111-109. John Starks tied the score with 2 free throws at 14.6.

Scottie Pippen inbounded to the Air Man. He drove the ball straight upcourt before Starks and Patrick Ewing double-teamed him.

Rather than dribble through or around, Jordan spotted a wide-open Bill Wennington. The forward threaded the ball to the center, who slam-dunked it for the winning basket with 3.1 seconds remaining.

Michael Jordan came back home, and it was as though he had never gone. He flew across the court and soared on the wings of air. The lost player had returned. And the crowd rejoiced.

Jesus told about another man, the Prodigal Son, who returned home to a great celebration. Read the story in Luke 15:11-24. Remember, the father represents God. He celebrates when we come to Him.

It is not good to have zeal without knowledge, nor to be hasty and miss the way. —**PROVERBS 19:2**

No NCAA basketball final in recent history featured as many future pro stars as the 1982 championship. Patrick Ewing, Eric "Sleepy" Floyd, and Fred Brown led the Georgetown Hoyas. James Worthy, Sam Perkins, and freshman Michael Jordan anchored the North Carolina Tar Heels.

The championship matchup exceeded its hype. Strong inside play from Ewing allowed Georgetown to claim a 32–21 halftime lead.

In the second half, neither team could dominate. The scoreboard never registered a margin greater than 4.

The Hoyas inched ahead 62–61 on Floyd's short jumper with under a minute to play. North Carolina worked the ball.

Worthy found Jordan uncovered with 15 seconds remaining. The forward canned a 17-foot jump shot to put the Tar Heels up by one.

Without calling time-out, the sure-handed Fred Brown brought the ball up court. Crossing the midcourt stripe at the 8-second mark, the point guard searched for an open man.

Brown thought he glimpsed an open Eric Smith. He fired a quick chest-high pass. But the player turned out to be UNC's James Worthy.

Worthy snared the errant throw and dribbled toward his basket. Georgetown intentionally fouled him with 2 seconds left. The Tar Heel missed both free throws, but they didn't matter. Time expired, and the University of North Carolina reigned.

Because of an ill-advised pass, the Hoyas missed a chance for victory. Just like Fred Brown, our desire to achieve is so great we lose sight of the main goal—to lead a Christ-centered life.

Busyness often shoves aside quiet time and God. We rush from place to place, from event to event.

Jobs, school, sports, and recreation are important, but they shouldn't dictate our lives. We do not serve them. They should serve us.

Create a time line of your last two days. Calculate how much time you spent in every activity. How many minutes did you spend alone with God? How can you change your schedule to make God number one?

Put your hope in the Lord, for with the Lord is unfailing love and with him is full redemption. —PSALM 130:7

Defending champions face enormous pressure. The University of Tennessee Lady Volunteers captured their 4th NCAA basketball championship in 1996. Hopes ran high for an encore in 1997. Injuries and a tough schedule, however, combined to leave UT at 23-10.

The team's record earned an NCAA tournament invitation and a chance for redemption. The Lady Vols ripped through Grambling and Oregon to win the Midwest Sub-Regional.

In the Regional opener, Tennessee defeated Colorado, 75–67. It faced the University of Connecticut Lady Huskies in the finals.

The Lady Huskies had defeated UT, 72–57, during the regular season. But in the showdown, Tennessee upset top-ranked UConn, 91–81.

In the Final Four semifinal, Notre Dame fell to the Lady Vols, 80–66. The Volunteer victory set up a title match with the Old Dominion University Lady Monarchs.

Despite an earlier loss to the Lady Monarchs, 83–72, the Lady Vols jumped to a 16-point lead. Old Dominion regrouped and tied the contest at 49 with 6:42 to play.

But Chamique Holdsclaw handed out 2 quick assists, a couple of layups, and a blocked shot. The Lady Monarchs abdicated, and Tennessee captured its 2nd consecutive and 5th overall basketball crown, 68–59.

The Lady Vols hoped for a second chance in 1997, and they got it. The UT team redeemed itself in postseason play. It even revenged earlier losses against Connecticut and Old Dominion. The Lady Vols captured the crown.

Life doesn't offer many chances for redemption. Usually what's done is done, but not so with God. He loves us and rescues us from our sins and its penalties if we ask.

On a United States map, locate the sites of Tennessee (Knoxville) and the teams they played: Grambling (Grambling, Louisiana), Oregon (Eugene), Colorado (Boulder), Connecticut (Storrs), Notre Dame (South Bend, Indiana), and Old Dominion (Norfolk, Virginia). Imagine the geographic impact of UT's victory. Thank God for the impact of His redemption.

> "The kingdom of heaven is like a mustard seed, which a man took and planted in his field. Though it is the smallest of all your seeds, yet when it grows, it is the largest of garden plants." —MATTHEW 13:31-32a

The path to the NCAA basketball championship is never easy. The University of Arizona Wildcats received a fourth ranking in the 1997 regional tournament. Analysts scoffed due to three previous first-round upsets.

After beating two average teams, South Alabama and College of Charleston, the Wildcats faced a strong field. Arizona shocked March Madness followers with an 85–82 upset of number-one-ranked Kansas. A 96–92 victory over Providence in the Regional finals reinforced confidence in Arizona.

The Wildcats entered the Final Four as the only non-number-one team. First came North Carolina in the semifinal. Arizona prevailed 66-58, and the Cinderella story continued.

The victory set up a title game with defending champion Kentucky. Basketball experts considered Arizona a heavy underdog.

The Hoosier Dome crowd witnessed a classic. The lead jockeyed back and forth.

Kentucky rallied from a 4-point deficit to send the game into overtime, 74–74. But Arizona hit 10 free throws in the extra period to garner its first national championship, 84–79. No team had ever defeated three number-one-ranked teams en route to a title.

Coach Lute Olson always believed in his young players. He cited their hard work as the reason they refused to falter under the intense pressure.

Christians should never back away from a challenge. Christ recognized individuals could accomplish great deeds despite heavy odds. He used the mustard seed as His example. The tiny seed, no bigger than a pinhead, grows into a flowering plant of tremendous height.

Go to the grocery store and look at a jar of mustard seed. Compare the tiny seed to a six-foot mustard plant. Imagine the effort God uses to make that seed grow. Consider what He uses to develop you. Thank Him.

O Lord, you are my God; I will exalt you and praise your name, for in perfect faithfulness you have done marvelous things, things planned long ago. —ISAIAH 25:1

The NCAA basketball championship is an exciting single-game, winner-take-all match. The 1985 title game featured two Big East teams—the Georgetown Hoyas and the Villanova Wildcats.

Georgetown had defeated Villanova twice in the regular season. Few gave Rollie Massimino's squad any chance against John Thompson's charges led by center Patrick Ewing.

The press asked Massimino what it would take to win. He replied, "We're going to have to play a perfect game. . . . And that may not be enough."

The Hoyas relied on pressure defense to create turnovers and generate easy baskets. Villanova used a controlled offense and deadeye shooting.

The contest opened as expected. Georgetown jumped to a 20–14 lead despite the Wildcats hitting 7 of their first 8 shots. But the Hoyas turned cold, and Villanova led at intermission, 29–28.

The second half mirrored the first. Villanova shot only 10 buckets but connected on 9. Georgetown's high-pressure tactics resulted in turnovers and fouls. The Wildcats tallied 19 second-period free-throw points, including their last 11. When the whistle sounded, the Wildcats stunned the nation with a 66–64 victory.

Massimino's prediction of a perfect game came close. His Wildcats made 22 of 28 field goals for 78.6 percent and 22 of 27 free throws.

Athletic teams, however, like the men and women on them, are seldom perfect. True perfection is found only with God. The prophet Isaiah praised God for His perfect faithfulness. He recognized God had a plan for his life and realized the plans were laid even before his birth.

The God of Isaiah is our God. Through eternity, He has not changed. He remains perfectly faithful and asks that we remain faithful to Him.

Make a list of equipment you rely on everyday at home, at school, or at your job. What happens when one breaks down? God relies on us in the same way. Ask Him to keep you faithful, and thank Him for His perfect faithfulness.

Be very careful, then, how you live—not as unwise but as wise, making the most of every opportunity.

—EPHESIANS 5:15-16a

The North Carolina State Wolfpack had only an outside chance of receiving a 1983 NCAA basketball tournament bid. Its 17-and-10 record hardly rated a second glance. But the Wolfpack swept 3 straight in the Atlantic Coast Conference tournament to receive an automatic invitation.

Jim Valvano's team had senior leadership but limited talent. In their March Madness opener, NC State forced Pepperdine into double overtime and escaped with a 69–67 triumph.

The second game of the sub-regional pitted the North Carolina squad against the University of Nevada–Las Vegas Rebels. The Rebels led by 12 with 11 minutes remaining, but the Wolfpack scratched and clawed to a 71–70 victory.

Advancing to the Sweet Sixteen gave North Carolina State great confidence. The nation embraced the Wolfpack as a Cinderella.

NC State blew out the University of Utah in the Western Regional opener. The final matched the team with ACC rival the University of Virginia Cavaliers. The Cavaliers sought revenge but misfired twice in the closing seconds and fell 63–62.

North Carolina State drew the University of Georgia in the Final Four semifinal. Valvano's team played tight defense and prevailed 67–60. The victory gave the Wolfpack a chance to play for the national title.

It took luck for North Carolina State to march into the NCAA basketball final. But when the opportunity came, the Wolfpack leaped toward it. The Christian faith is no different.

The Apostle Paul warned early church members to be on guard. He knew how easily Christians could slip. But if we stay alert, we have countless opportunities for service. Wisely taking advantage of them brings unmeasured joy.

Walk around your neighborhood. Count the warning signs you see. Thank God for friends who warn you of danger so that you have the opportunity to lead a safe and productive life.

I have seen something else under the sun: The race is not to the swift or the battle to the strong, nor does food come to the wise or wealth to the brilliant or favor to the learned; but time and chance happen to them all. —ECCLESIASTES 9:11

Eight consecutive wins propelled the North Carolina State Wolfpack to the 1983 NCAA basketball title game. It faced the University of Houston Cougars, whose twin towers, Clyde Drexler and Hakeem Olajuwon, had earned the nickname "Phi Slamma Jamma."

Experts considered the championship match an afterthought. Houston needed only to go through the motions. But the Wolfpack had other ideas. Another contest as an underdog didn't faze Jim Valvano's team.

NC State employed the same strategy that had carried it on its winning streak. The team stuck to controlled offense, tight defense, and planned to foul late to force pressure free throws.

The tactics worked well. The Wolfpack led 33–25 at intermission.

Houston regrouped and went on a 17–2 run. With 3 minutes remaining, the Cougars forged ahead 52–46.

NC State began to foul. The ploy worked. Houston missed free throws, and the Wolfpack hit buckets.

With the game knotted at 52, Valvano ordered his team to work for the final shot. But the Pack offense couldn't click. Time ticked away.

Dereck Wittenberg fired a desperation shot that touched nothing but air. Suddenly, two monstrous hands reached up, grabbed the ball, and stuffed it through the hoop as the buzzer sounded. The hands belonged to NC State's Lorenzo Charles. The Wolfpack reigned as the NCAA basketball champ.

NC State proved things don't always go as planned. The strongest and the swiftest don't always win. The writer of Ecclesiastes observed the same thing. Time and chance happen to all. And God controls both.

Remember when you received an unexpected letter, telephone call, or present at just the right time. How did you feel? Pray for readiness to receive the unexpected from God.

"When you pass through the waters, I will be with you; and when you pass through the rivers, they will not sweep over you." —ISAIAH 43:2a

Janet Evans moves through the water with amazing speed. The California native holds world records in the 400, 800, and 1500-meter freestyle. She earned five medals—four gold and one silver —in Olympic competition. In 1993, the woman with the neon smile moved one step closer to becoming the top American swimmer of all time.

At the United States Indoor Championships, Evans swept the long-distance freestyle events. She won the 400 in 4:11.01, the 800 in 8:34.99, and the 1,500 in 16:16.38.

Although the times were slower than her world records, the 1989 Sullivan Award winner continued her dominance. The three first places gave Evans 33 national titles and moved her into third place behind Johnny Weismuller and Tracy Caulkins. Before retiring in 1996, the Californian captured 45 American championships and fell just short of Caulkins' record of 48.

Janet Evans loves to swim. She passes through the pool with speed and grace. But sometimes water becomes dangerous.

A rising river covers everything it contacts with a destructive wall. The flood sweeps away any person or animal in its path. Unless they can find something to grab, they drown in the swift current.

Sometimes life seems that way. Pressures sweep over us, and we feel we're drowning in troubles. When that happens, we can claim God's promise in Isaiah 43:2. He will be with us and will use His power to protect us.

Recall pictures of a flood you've seen on television or in a newspaper. If you've been in a flood, think about the experience. Learn water safety rules. Remember never to swim, walk, or drive through water unless you know its depth and current. Thank God for the promise of His presence.

For there is a proper time and procedure for every matter. —ECCLESIASTES 8:6a

College basketball fans had high expectations for the University of Michigan Wolverines' Fab Five. Michigan's prize freshman recruits—Chris Webber, Juwan Howard, Ray Jackson, Jalen Rose, and Jimmy King—advanced to the 1992 title game but lost. Although the road to the 1993 Big Dance proved rocky, Michigan squared off against the University of North Carolina Tar Heels in the final. UNC fielded a well-balanced team. Four starters—Eric Montross, George Lynch, Donald Williams, and Brian Reese—carried double-digit scoring averages.

The matchup seesawed. The Tar Heels gained the early lead, but Michigan jumped in front by 10. UNC surged back. The Wolverines countered, going up by 4 with 4 1/2 minutes to play.

North Carolina made another run. Michigan trailed 73–71 with time running out. With under 20 seconds, Chris Webber grabbed a rebound and dribbled downcourt.

Two Tar Heels trapped him. Suddenly, Webber called time-out with 11 seconds to go. But Michigan had already used its allotment.

The Wolverines received a technical foul. UNC got 2 free throws and the ball. The contest was all but over. The final score read 77–71, but Webber's illegal time-out really ended the game.

The player lost track of one of the most important tools in basketball, the time-out. When used properly, a well-timed break can fuel a win. If time-outs are burned too early, a team faces no chance to regroup.

God gives us the gift of time, but it's up to us to use it wisely. Sometimes we watch television or play video games when we ought to mow the lawn or clean. We shoot hoops when we ought to study or work.

Like Chris Webber, we pay the price. We miss a movie because the lawn isn't mowed. We do poorly because we didn't prepare.

Make a list of responsibilities you have this week. Write next to each the time you plan to do it. Ask God to help you use time wisely.

He who has been stealing must steal no longer, but must work, doing something useful with his own hands, that he may have something to share with those in need.

—EPHESIANS 4:28

In 1996, the Minnesota Twins never considered holding Detroit Tiger Cecil Fielder at first base after he walked to lead off the top of the ninth. After all, in 1,097 major league baseball contests, Fielder had yet to steal a base. In five previous attempts, he had zero swipes.

But with one out and a full count on Melvin Nieves, Tiger manager Buddy Bell put on a play. He signaled for a hit-and-run, not a straight steal.

Fielder took off with the pitch, lumbering toward second. Nieves swung and missed to strike out, and Twins catcher Greg Myers fired the ball to second.

The massive first baseman appeared out by a couple of steps, but the ball glanced off Fielder's batting helmet as he slid into the bag. Umpire Tim Tschida waved his arms safe, and the official scorer credited the Tiger slugger with a stolen base. The record-setting streak of most games played without a stolen base had ended.

Base stealing is an important part of baseball strategy, although a big man such as Cecil Fielder rarely uses it.

However, stealing cannot be a part of our personal lives. We learn at an early age that taking things that belong to other people is wrong.

But we can be thieves and not realize it. Borrowing but never returning items, damaging or using up another person's property, or taking little things like pens and pencils she won't miss is stealing.

Instead, God expects us to do something useful to meet our needs. He also wants us to work so that we can share with others.

Look at needs in your community. How could your family or your church work to meet some of those needs? Ask God for guidance as you make plans.

> Awake, and rise to my defense! Contend for me, my God and Lord. —PSALM 35:23

New York Ranger coach Lester Patrick faced a quandary. In game two of the 1928 Stanley Cup playoffs, goalie Lorne Chabot took a shot from Nels Stewart just above the eye.

Chabot required immediate medical attention. Since National Hockey League teams of that era carried only one goalie, Patrick had very few alternatives.

Rather than insert a player with no experience in the crease, the 44-year-old headmaster donned the gear himself. The determined New Yorkers stepped up their checking to reduce the Montreal Maroons' shots.

The contest remained scoreless until the third period. New York took a 1–0 lead, but the Maroons knotted the game and sent it into overtime.

Montreal kept up the pressure, but the Silver Fox blocked shot after shot. Frank Boucher stole the puck and threaded his way through the Maroon defense.

His goal at 7:05 brought the Rangers victory. The New Yorkers carried their coach-turned-goalie off the ice on their shoulders. Inspired by Patrick's courage and his 18 stops, New York swept the next three games to claim its first Stanley Cup.

Coach Patrick chose to enter the rink to defend his players. He chose to put himself on the line for them. He could have been hurt. After all, he had already retired as a player. He could have allowed some perfectly understandable goals. But he didn't. He brought home victory.

God is our defender. He's always on our side. But He won't get into the game of our lives unless we ask Him.

Ask a friend, relative, or coach to help you perfect a skill in your favorite sport. Thank him or her for being on your side. Ask God for His help and then remember to thank Him.

"My heart is changed within me; all my compassion is aroused." —HOSEA 11:8b

Switch-hitting gives a batter a slight edge over a pitcher. But with a baseball heading to the plate at over 80 mph, a hitter looks for every advantage.

A switch-hitter in the lineup makes an interesting situation when the opposition changes pitchers. The batter switches sides if the manager puts in a left-hander instead of a right-hander. Cleveland Indians second baseman Carlos Baerga faced the situation in 1993 against the New York Yankees.

The Tribe led 6–5 in the bottom of the seventh. Batting right, Baerga worked the count full against southpaw Steve Howe. The second baseman drove the next pitch over the fence for a 2-run homer.

Six runs later in the same inning, Baerga batted for the second time. Righty Steve Farr manned the hill for New York.

Hitting left, Baerga launched a shot into the stands for Cleveland's final run in a 15–5 rout. In baseball's entire history, no one had ever hit 2 homers in the same inning from opposite sides of the plate.

Switching from batting right to batting left didn't change the outcome for Carlos Baerga. But accepting Christ causes a powerful change in His followers.

Becoming a Christian doesn't affect our outward appearance. The change occurs on the inside. But the difference is noticeable.

We leave our selfish and self-centered ways. We give service priority. We shift our focus from material gain to spiritual growth.

Look at some of your baby photographs. Then look at some current pictures. What outward changes do you see? How have you changed inside? Ask God to help others see Christ in you.

"For nothing is impossible with God." —**LUKE 1:37**

Sportswriters debate whether some baseball records will stand forever. Many believe Joe DiMaggio's 56-game hitting streak or Nolan Ryan's 5,714 strikeouts are impossible to surpass. But in 1974, a long-standing mark once thought unbreakable finally fell.

Yankee slugger Babe Ruth retired in 1935 with 714 career home runs. Simple math indicates a player must average 35 homers for 20 years to come close to Ruth's standard.

In 1968, 35-year-old Henry "Hank" Aaron belted homer number 500. Statisticians began to reexamine Ruth's totals. They pondered. Perhaps Aaron could continue his record-setting pace.

Over the next 5 seasons, the Braves outfielder hit 44, 38, 47, 34, and 40 home runs. At the end of the 1973 campaign, Aaron had amassed 713, 1 short of the Sultan of Swat.

Scribes discussed the impact of shattering Ruth's record endlessly during the off-season. Aaron quickly brought the matter to a head by homering in his first at bat of 1974.

The Braves outfielder sat out the season's second game and went hitless in the third. Aaron returned to Atlanta, and a national TV audience watched breathlessly as the Alabama native attempted to surpass the Bambino.

Los Angeles Dodger pitcher Al Downing walked the outfielder in his first plate appearance. In his second at bat, Aaron took ball one. On the next pitch, the power hitter swung, and the ball skyrocketed over the left field wall. Ruth's record had fallen.

The seemingly impossible had happened. A nearly 40-year-old record fell. Aaron moved ahead of Ruth.

In life, many things seem impossible. And, of course, some are unrealistic and won't happen. But nothing is impossible if we follow God's will and give our best effort.

Make a list of sports records you think won't ever be broken. Use a sports encyclopedia if necessary. Begin to note new records. Praise God for the possibilities He provides.

By day the Lord directs his love, at night his song is with me—a prayer to the God of my life. —PSALM 42:8

When winning or losing doesn't affect the final standings, teams can afford to concentrate on individual performance. On the final day of the 1978 basketball season, the Denver Nuggets and San Antonio Spurs pulled out all the stops to give their superstars the scoring title.

Denver hosted the Detroit Pistons in an afternoon contest. The Nuggets constantly fed guard David Thompson.

The former North Carolina State star pumped in 73 points. His scoring binge represented the third highest single game total in National Basketball Association history. Only Wilt Chamberlain's 100- and 78-point games exceeded Thompson's mark.

But Thompson's 1978 scoring title wasn't secure. San Antonio Spurs forward George "The Iceman" Gervin viewed the Denver–Detroit contest from his hotel room, waiting for a night game with the New Orleans Jazz.

Knowing he needed 58 points to pass Thompson's season record, Gervin erupted for 53 in the first half. The Iceman finished the game with 63 to edge his Denver rival for the scoring crown.

By day, Gervin directed his thoughts toward the title. By night, he focused his desire into action and won his dream.

The psalmist understands that by day, God directs His love toward man. By night, God's mighty song surrounds him. He focuses his praise into prayer and hope for eternity.

During a busy day, it's hard to think constantly about God. But God thinks about us and loves us. At night, when the world echoes in quiet stillness, we should focus our praise into prayer.

Before you go to bed, listen to or sing your favorite Christian song or hymn. Offer it as a prayer of praise to God.

"A son honors his father, and a servant his master. If I am a father, where is the honor due me? If I am a master, where is the respect due me?" says the Lord Almighty. —MALACHI 1:6

No golfer has dominated the sport like Jack Nicklaus. His 20 Grand Slam victories still rank number one. But no tournament exceeded the drama of the 1986 Masters.

Nicklaus trailed coleaders Seve Ballesteros and Tom Kite by 4 strokes heading into the final four holes. On the par-4 15th, the former Ohio State Buckeye cleared the water fronting the green on his drive.

The ball landed pin high, 12 feet from the hole. Nicklaus sank the putt for an eagle.

The Golden Bear nailed a 40-footer for a birdie on 16. He took the lead with a second straight birdie on 17. Nicklaus finished his final round with a 7-under-par 65 and a 279 total.

The five-time champion waited in the clubhouse, watching his challengers. Kite missed a birdie putt on 18 to fall one stroke back.

Australian Greg Norman made a last-minute charge with four birdies. The Shark, however, made an errant approach shot on the final hole for a bogey.

Nicklaus claimed the green jacket for the sixth time. At age 46, he became the oldest Masters champion ever.

Jack Nicklaus mastered both the game of golf and the Masters. From his young years to the height of his game, the Golden Bear earned the respect of players and spectators of all ages. He has been honored with every golfing award imaginable.

God has mastered both heaven and earth. He deserves the respect of everyone on earth. He has earned that honor by His love, His faithfulness, and His very being.

Write down definitions of the words honor and respect. How are they different? Think of ways we show honor and respect toward people. Your list might include things like standing in their presence or naming buildings for them. How can you demonstrate honor and respect toward God?

Are you so foolish? After beginning with the Spirit, are you now trying to attain your goal by human effort?

—GALATIANS 3:3

As a young boy, Cornelius "Dutch" Warmerdam began pole-vaulting in a cabbage patch, using a bamboo pole. He soon soared to heights others dared not even try.

The California collegian raised the world record from 14 feet, 11 inches to 15 feet, 7 3/4 inches. He had cleared the 15-foot barrier 43 times before any other vaulter accomplished the feat.

Dutch appeared to have the 1940 Olympic gold medal cinched. However, circumstances destroyed Warmerdam's chances. World War II canceled both the scheduled 1940 Tokyo and 1944 London events. The 29-year-old track star retired from competition in 1944 and began coaching at Fresno State.

During each stage of life, we set goals and objectives. Sometimes, however, doors close, and like Cornelius Warmerdam, our dreams cannot come true.

In frustration, we blame God for missed opportunities and wonder why He failed. But God never fails. We fail when we try to accomplish our goals on our own, without God's help. Or maybe, our goals are not the goals God has for us.

By submitting ourselves to His master plan, our objectives match His. For every closed door, He opens another. We reach our goals with God's help.

Ask God to help you set a goal in each of the following areas: spiritual, physical, social, and intellectual. Write them down. Ask God to guide you as you strive to reach them.

The glory of young men is their strength.

—PROVERBS 20:29a

The Masters receives more attention than other golf tournaments. The stately trees, shimmering water, luscious grass, and blooming azaleas make it America's favorite.

The beauty of the course hides its difficulty. The added stress of tradition and large crowds creates unbelievable obstacles.

In 1997, Eldrick "Tiger" Woods challenged Augusta National for the first time as a professional. Twice before he had joined the field as the U. S. Amateur Champion.

Nervousness affected the 21-year-old's game. His scorecard tallied a 4-over-par 40 on the front nine.

Then confidence forged by years of practice took over. Tiger shot a 30 on the back nine for a first-round total of 70, 2 under par.

On Friday, despite the ultrafast greens, Wood's 66 gave him the lead. He bettered his score by one on Saturday.

The young golfer went into Sunday's round up by nine. The odds favored him, but the Masters had a long history of miracle finishes.

Under intense scrutiny, Tiger survived the final round. Even when his drives went awry, incredible approach shots salvaged pars. He finished the day at 69 for a total of 270.

The Stanford grad rewrote the Augusta National record book. Not only did he become the youngest Masters winner, he also set new marks for lowest score and greatest margin of victory.

It's not unusual to be frustrated as a young person. The world worships youth but often denies it a chance to achieve. But young people's strength and enthusiasm can overcome difficulties.

God uses everyone. No one is too young or too old. Mission trips, church athletic teams, and Bible study groups provide opportunities to grow both spiritually and physically.

Make an appointment with your pastor or another church staff member. Pray for and discuss the various youth activities at your church. Try to think of some new ones that offer chances for youth to grow, serve, and excel. If appropriate, offer to help begin one of them.

The unfolding of your words gives light; it gives understanding to the simple. —PSALM 119:130

Shooting basketball free throws appears to be a simple skill. The goal rests only 15 feet from the foul line. The shooter lines up directly in front of the basket. No one blocks his way. Yet crowd noise, pressure, and mental blocks often make them difficult. Without a doubt in 1990, New Jersey Net Chris Dudley proved the point.

Dudley, a notoriously poor career free-throw shooter, missed virtually every attempt. His inept performance at the free-throw line aided the visiting Indiana Pacers in their 124 to 113 victory.

The Meadowlands crowd sensed the comic aspect and joined in the action. Every time the struggling pivot man touched the ball in the fourth quarter, they shouted, "Foul him! Foul him!" Each time he stepped to the line, they loudly cheered, "Dudley! Dudley! Dudley!"

Their chanting ignited a brief rally, but the Pacers snuffed it by deliberately fouling the New Jersey center in the game's final minutes. Without points from the free-throw line, the hometown team never could catch up. The Nets lost a winable game, and Dudley's 17 of 18 misses set an inglorious National Basketball Association record.

Faith in God is simple. But like Chris Dudley, we let the world and its influences distract us. We seek acceptance from the crowd and shove God and His teachings aside. We believe we can somehow survive without Him.

But when times get desperate and our lives unravel, we quickly return. A compassionate God welcomes us back. He knows our weaknesses and simply loves us in spite of them.

Make a list of ways you can show your faith in God. Share your ideas with a Christian relative or friend. Ask God to keep you focused on Him.

It is unthinkable that God would do wrong, that the Almighty would pervert justice. —JOB 34:12

Every golfer dreams of winning the Masters. The tournament takes place on one of the country's most beautiful courses and comprises the first step in golf's Grand Slam. But in 1968, a partner's blunder cost Roberto de Vicenzo.

Under the rules of golf, a player has responsibility for his own score. His partner, however, records the strokes on the scorecard.

On the 17th hole of the final round, de Vicenzo scored a birdie 3. Tommy Aaron recorded it as a par 4. At the conclusion of the 18 holes, the Argentine golfer looked casually at the card and signed it. He rushed over to watch Bob Goalby, his closest challenger, finish the round.

Goalby came into the clubhouse with a 277, the same as the Argentine. Officials prepared for a playoff.

Moments before it was to begin, they realized the error. Aaron's mistake gave de Vicenzo a 278 rather than a tying 277. Because he had already signed the card, the playoff was canceled. De Vicenzo had to settle for second.

Tommy Aaron accidentally did wrong. Roberto de Vicenzo had a chance to catch the mistake and correct it. In his haste to watch his rival, he wasn't careful. Still, the results seem unfair and unjust.

But de Vicenzo knew the rules and agreed to them when he joined the pro tour. His signature on the card became his bond. By writing his name, he showed he agreed with the score.

People make mistakes. Sometimes they're intentional. Sometimes they're not. But God never makes a mistake. He will never let us down on purpose or accidentally. He is always just. He is perfect.

If you play golf, spend some time practicing your swing and thinking about the game. If you don't play, talk with someone who does. Ask him or her to review some of the basic rules. Praise the perfect God.

No one whose hope is in you will ever be put to shame.

—PSALM 25:3a

Hope abounds on opening day. Every baseball player visualizes a berth in the World Series. In 1940, Bob Feller treated followers of the national pastime to the sport's most memorable first day.

The Cleveland Indians visited Chicago's Comiskey Park. Feller, a 21-year-old right-hander, drew the starting assignment against the White Sox. Nearly 14,000 attended the game.

Chicago threatened in the second. The White Sox loaded the bases without a hit. But Feller struck out third baseman Bob Kennedy to end the inning.

The Indians scored in the fourth to lead 1–0. Then the Cleveland ace found his rhythm, retiring fifteen Chicagoans in a row. Feller entered the ninth with 8 strikeouts, 4 walks, but no hits.

Rapid Robert easily put out the first two White Sox batters. All-star shortstop Luke Appling refused to go down easily. He fouled off four pitches before drawing Feller's fifth base on balls.

Taft Wright batted next and hit a hard shot. Ray Mack dove to his left, knocked the ball down, barehanded it, and fired to first to nip Wright. Cleveland won 1–0 as Feller pitched baseball's only opening day no-hitter.

Every pitcher hopes for a no-hitter. Every player hopes for a win. Every batter hopes for a hit. Every fielder hopes for a clean play.

Few pitchers pitch no-hitters. Half the players win and half lose every game. A batter is considered great if he connects for a hit every third time up. Fielders make errors. Teams lose hope, and so do fans.

But when we hope in God, we never lose. He makes no errors. He never puts us to shame.

Who do you hope will win the pennants this year? Who do you think will win the World Series? If you didn't make predictions on opening day, write your choices down now. In October, see how close you came. Thank God there is never any doubt with Him.

"The Lord's right hand is lifted high; the Lord's right hand has done mighty things!" —**PSALM 118:16**

Spectators stand in awe when a batter clouts a home run. Scoreboards flash the distance allowing followers to marvel at the star's power. In 1953, baseball fans witnessed quite a homer.

The New York Yankees visited the Washington Senators. Yankee center fielder Mickey Mantle stepped to the plate in the fifth inning with Yogi Berra on first. Batting right-handed, the Oklahoma native connected off Chuck Stobbs for a 2-run homer.

The blast cleared Griffith Stadium's 60-foot left center field fence located 391 feet from home plate. The ball continued to rise and ricocheted off the football scoreboard sitting atop a 50-foot wall.

The horsehide landed in the backyard of a home a block away. Yankee publicist Arthur "Red" Patterson retrieved the ball from a young boy who found it. He measured the massive shot and calculated the distance to be 565 feet.

No other ball had ever been hit out of Griffith Stadium. Mantle unofficially holds baseball's record for the longest home run.

Mantle's right arm lifted the ball high into the air. His power did a mighty thing. That ball traveled higher and farther than any ever had.

But as powerful as Mickey Mantle's swing was, nothing matches the power of God. Nature demonstrates His strength, and man His might.

Estimate and walk 565 feet. Remember that's nearly the length of two football fields. Then look up at a tower or tall building. Guess how high 110 feet would be. That's how far and how high Mantle powered the ball. Praise God for His power unmatched by any person.

"Rejoice in that day and leap for joy, because great is your reward in heaven." —**LUKE 6:23a**

Preschoolers Shannon Miller and her older sister, Tessa, got a trampoline for Christmas. Within two weeks, the Oklahoma youngster could perform a front flip.

Her parents enrolled their daughter in gymnastics class to reduce the risk of injury. After several years of lessons, Shannon turned into a world-class gymnast.

In the 1993 World Gymnastics Championships, the teenager faced stiff competition from Romanian Gina Gogean. An unsteady dismount from the beam, Miller's favorite event, dropped the 16 year old from second place to fifth.

But the winner of two silver and three bronze medals at the 1992 Olympics hit two solid vaults to regain the lead. Her first leap scored an impressive 9.775. The second improved to 9.800.

Gogean had a chance to pass Miller in the floor exercises. She needed a 9.808. But the Romanian came up short with a 9.800 and claimed the silver.

Miller became the second American to win the world title. In 1994, the physics professor's daughter repeated as world champion.

Shannon Miller leaped with joy all right, right into two world championships. The world rewarded her with medals, money, and fame.

Though most of us won't leap with the joy of a world gymnastics championship, we can leap for joy because of God. He loves us so much He sent His Son to earth to live and die for us. If we believe, He has promised us great rewards in heaven.

If you can, try jumping on a trampoline. If you can't, leap as high as you can. How does it feel? Thank God for the rewards He gives.

Oh, my anguish, my anguish! I writhe in pain. Oh, the agony of my heart! My heart pounds within me, I cannot keep silent. For I have heard the sound of the trumpet; I have heard the battle cry. —JEREMIAH 4:19

No other race requires the stamina of the marathon. The 26-mile, 385-yard course saps the strongest runners. In 1996, Germany's Uta Pippig needed every ounce of strength to complete the Boston Marathon.

The two-time defending champion trailed most of the way. The long-distance runner developed cramps at the 4-mile mark and considered dropping out. But Pippig continued, struggling all the way.

With less than a mile to go, pack leader Teglo Loroupe's thighs tightened. The Kenyan runner faltered.

The German marathoner heard the cries of the crowd. The Bostonians chanted in unison, "You can catch her! You can catch her!"

Pippig kicked into overdrive. Loroupe could barely move.

The crowd favorite passed the Kenyan as a deafening roar rumbled along the course. Pippig won her third straight Boston Marathon in a time of 2:17:12.

Uta Pippig agonized in pain throughout the race. Her heart surely pounded as the sound of the crowd urged her to battle Loroupe. She heard its cry, and she responded. She claimed victory.

The crowd kept Uta going. Sometimes God keeps us going. When life becomes painful, we agonize. We feel sorry for ourselves. We may even want to quit.

But God is there. He's our biggest fan and our greatest support. If we listen through prayer and Scripture, we can hear His voice urging us on.

Who are your biggest fans? Your parents? A special friend? A coach? Your pastor? A favorite teacher from years ago? Let them know you appreciate them. Thank God for their support and for His.

The Lord is my strength and my shield; my heart trusts in him, and I am helped. My heart leaps for joy and I will give thanks to him in song. —**PSALM 28:7**

Star forward Michael Jordan electrifies the crowd every time he steps on the basketball court. No one matches his majestic jumping and shooting.

A 1986 scoring display earned the Chicago superstar a place in playoff history. Although Chicago lost in double overtime to the Boston Celtics 135 to 131, Michael set a playoff scoring record with 63 points. In one of the greatest shows ever at the Boston Garden, on national TV, and in the playoffs, Jordan hit 22 of 41 from the field and 19 of 21 free throws. He scored almost half of Chicago's points.

Boston appeared to have the game won in regulation, leading 116 to 114. The quick-handed Jordan, however, stole the ball from Robert Parish. Chicago called time-out.

John Paxton inbounded the ball to Michael, who shot a 3-pointer at the buzzer. It bounced off the iron, but the referee called Kevin McHale for pushing on the rebound. Jordan calmly hit both free throws to send the game into overtime. His awesome performance kept the Bulls in contention and almost led them to victory.

The Bulls fell short when Boston backup guard Jerry Sichting put the Celtics ahead in the second overtime, 133–131. The Boston victory, however, could not outshine number 23's offensive display.

No other player in professional basketball can leap and control his body like Michael Jordan. Few have the heart of the superstar.

Many dream of flying high above the rim and slamming the ball in for two points. However, through God's love, our spirits can fly, and our hearts can soar much higher than any basketball hoop.

Name the people you actually know who can slam-dunk a basketball. It's probably a short list. Pray for God's love to fill your soaring heart with joy.

"You also must be ready, because the Son of Man will come at an hour when you do not expect him." —**LUKE 12:40**

The Dallas Stars anticipated the 1997 Stanley Cup playoffs. They finished the regular season with the second best record in the National Hockey League and played great down the stretch.

In the first round, the Stars drew the Edmonton Oilers. Few gave the Oilers any chance. Dallas had defeated them four times without a loss during the regular season.

The form chart held true in the initial meeting. The Stars bested Edmonton 5–3. Their confidence continued to grow.

The tables turned in game two, however. The Oilers offense erupted, and their defense rose to the occasion. The seemingly invincible Stars fell victim to a 4–0 shutout.

The turning point of the series came in game three. Dallas held a 3-goal lead late in the third period. Suddenly, the Edmonton offense sprang to life.

The Oilers scored 3 goals in the last 4 minutes to send the contest to overtime. Kelly Buchberger fired the puck past goalie Andy Moog at the 9:15 mark in sudden death to lead Edmonton to victory.

The comeback win fueled the underdog Oilers. Twice more they forced the favorites to overtime and emerged victorious. Edmonton took the series in game seven with another 4–3 extra-period win.

Edmonton's fierce defense took Dallas unaware. The Stars' lack of focus led to an early exit from Stanley Cup competition.

As the Stars found out, inattention can be costly. If we don't focus on Christ, we drift into a lifestyle without meaning. Wealth, athletics, health, and friends can't substitute for a personal relationship with God.

Life is complicated. Countless activities and responsibilities demand our time and energy. However, no matter what we do, God must be involved. If He's not, our neglect will leave us unprepared for eternity.

Prepare a list of your commitments. Number them in order of importance. Where does God rank?

The Spirit of the Lord will come upon you in power, and you will prophesy with them; and you will be changed into a different person. —1 SAMUEL 10:6

David Robinson changed the San Antonio Spurs. In 1989–90, the 7-foot-1-inch center made the franchise one of the National Basketball Association's best.

San Antonio acquired the Naval Academy graduate in 1987. But Robinson's military service obligation required two years to fulfill.

The year before "the Admiral" joined the Spurs, San Antonio won 21 games and lost 61. Coach Larry Brown replaced almost the entire roster. Only guard Willie Anderson and backup center Frank Brickowski remained.

With the pivotman anchoring the defense, grabbing 12 rebounds, and scoring 24 points per game, the team improved to 56 and 26. The margin of 35 represented the greatest turnaround in NBA history.

The Spurs defeated Phoenix in the season finale, 108–93, to edge Utah for the Midwest Division crown. San Antonio and Portland battled for seven games in the Western Conference playoffs. The Trailblazers squeaked by the final contest in overtime.

The change created by David Robinson and an almost new roster brought great things to San Antonio. The team won a division title. But the change proved painful for those players cut and the fans who loved them. Change isn't always easy, but it's often necessary.

When we become Christians, the Spirit of the Lord enters our lives. He changes each of us into a new person, a person who wants to follow Him. Sometimes the difference means leaving some actions and some people behind. But we begin new activities and become friends with other believers. Our hearts seek right and good rather than wrong and evil.

Think of some major changes you've experienced in your life. Discuss with a Christian friend or family member how you felt about those changes. What did you learn from those experiences? Thank God for the changes He brings through the Holy Spirit.

You have become great and strong; your greatness has grown until it reaches the sky, and your dominion extends to distant parts of the earth. —DANIEL 4:22b

Few hockey fans would deny Wayne Gretzky deserves the title the "Great One." But when he reached age 36, most expected his skills to wane. In game four of the first round of the 1997 Stanley Cup playoffs, the New York Rangers drew the defending champion Florida Panthers. Florida took game one, 3–0. The New York press criticized Gretzky for his almost invisible play. The Ranger superstar silenced the critics in game two. He scored the winning goal.

The series moved to Madison Square Garden, where schedule conflicts forced back-to-back games. The Rangers took the contest into overtime when Luc Robitaille tied the score. They won on Esa Tikkanen's slap shot 3 1/2 minutes into the extra period.

Experts next predicted a Panther victory. They believed the veteran Rangers couldn't win without rest.

Gretzky proved them wrong. The aging superstar tied the game with a second-period goal.

Less than 4 minutes later, Gretzky fired a rocket into the net to put New York ahead. Teammate Mark Messier whispered, "Keep sniffing," an encouragement to try for 3 goals or in hockey slang, the hat trick.

Gretzky faked goalie John Vanbiesbrouck and bounced a shot off the left post. The Great One turned his 58th career hat trick, and the Rangers held on for series win number three.

Every professional athlete dreads the day his skills fade and he must leave the playing field. The great ones fight hard to remain on top.

Unlike men, the greatness of God never fades. He never grows old or gets tired. He is the same yesterday, today, and forever.

The Heavenly Father watches over us our entire lives. When we grow into adulthood, He gives us direction and strength. In our later years, the Lord comforts us.

Talk to a retired person. Ask about his church activities when he was a child, and how God has blessed him through the years.

So then, let us not be like others, who are asleep, but let us be alert and self-controlled. —1 **THESSALONIANS 5:6**

Losing track of the number of outs in an inning is not smart baseball. Neither is giving away a ball still in play to a fan in the stands. In a 1994 spring game, Montreal Expo outfielder Larry Walker pulled both dumb stunts.

With one out and a man on first, Los Angeles Dodger catcher Mike Piazza lifted a fly ball down the right field line. It drifted foul. Walker caught the ball and thought the inning was over.

After snagging the ball, the Expo outfielder walked over to the seats and handed the souvenir to a young boy in the first row. Walker trotted toward his dugout.

Much to his chagrin, he noticed Los Angeles shortstop Jose Offerman rounding second on his way to third. Walker then realized his mistake.

The outfielder quickly returned to the stands and retrieved the ball from the youngster. He threw home just in time to prevent Offerman from scoring. Had the Dodger shortstop tagged and scored on the foul out to right field, Walker would have suffered one of baseball's ultimate embarrassments.

Larry Walker let his mind fall asleep. It made him look foolish and almost cost his team a run.

We can fall asleep as Christians as well. Our lives become predictable, and we approach each day without thinking.

It's not easy to get ourselves off cruise control. When things are comfortable, we want them to remain that way. But Christians need to be challenged.

Be alert for new opportunities. Take a close look at your local school, church, and community. What are some things you can do to make them better? With God's help, choose at least one thing and do it. Ask Him to keep you alert.

Let your eyes look straight ahead, fix your gaze directly before you. —**PROVERBS 4:25**

It takes tremendous concentration to shoot a free throw. The action stops on the court, but the crowd screams and waves to distract the shooter. Usually, Michael Williams shut out everything when he stepped to the free-throw line.

In 1993, the Minnesota Timberwolves played the Utah Jazz in the season finale. Williams entered the contest with a string of 74 consecutive free throws without a miss. Four more would tie Calvin Murphy for the NBA record.

The point guard had canned 3 straight when John Stockton fouled him with 11:17 left in the third quarter. The Timberwolf stepped to the foul line for two shots.

Williams took the ball, bounced it, and eyed the basket. With a motion honed by hours of practice, he let the ball fly. The net cords ripped as the ball swooshed through, tying Murphy's mark.

After a moment of frantic cheering, the guard took his second shot. The result was the same. Williams broke the record.

The playmaker extended his string to 84 before the contest's end. His 29 points led the Timberwolf scoring and propelled Minnesota to a 113–111 win.

Three ingredients led Williams to break the record: practice, confidence, and concentration. Of course, they were coupled with God-given ability.

We can't all break records or play professional sports. But we can do our best with the talents God gives us. It may be athletics, music, art, speaking, writing, being a friend, or just about anything. If we fix our eyes on what we do best, God will make us successful.

Identify one or more talents you possess. If you have trouble deciding, ask an objective friend. Spend some time during the next few days practicing. Thank God for the talents He has given you.

Blessed is the nation whose God is the Lord. —**PSALM 33:12a**

In 1976, Rick Monday saw two spectators leap from the stands of Dodger Stadium in the fourth inning. The visiting Chicago Cub center fielder watched as they unfurled an American flag and soaked it in lighter fluid.

Suddenly, the Arizona State product realized their intention. The protestors were preparing to burn Old Glory.

The first match blew out before the flag could be ignited. The wind delayed their action. Before the two men could light another, Monday rushed over, grabbed his nation's symbol, and sprinted away.

Security guards arrested the two men. The Dodger scoreboard flashed, "Rick Monday—You made a great play." The crowd spontaneously burst into singing *God Bless America*.

Monday kept the flag as a remembrance of that day. It hangs in his den on a staff presented by Richard Daley, the former mayor of Chicago.

Rick Monday risked being burned to stop the two men. He showed great patriotism in protecting the flag of the United States of America. He demonstrated his pride in his country. And the crowd and the mayor agreed with his actions.

The Pledge of Allegiance to that flag says in part, "one nation under God, indivisible, with liberty and justice for all." The psalmist wrote that the nation is blessed whose God is the Lord. We are indeed blessed we live in a country where we can worship our Heavenly Father.

Think about the flag. How many stripes are there? Why was that number chosen? How many stars appear? Why? If you don't know the answers, ask someone who has recently become a U.S. citizen. She had to know to pass the citizenship test. Of course, you can look up the information in an encyclopedia. Thank God for the United States of America.

So do not throw away your confidence; it will be richly rewarded. —HEBREWS 10:35

Few baseball pitchers threw harder than Nolan Ryan. Thousands of batters faced his heat and went down.

In 1983, the Houston Astros faced the Montreal Expos on the road. The team was struggling to climb from the National League West cellar. But on this Wednesday afternoon, baseball fans focused on the Astro pitcher.

Ryan entered the contest with 3,504 career strikeouts. Five more would move the Astro ace past Walter Johnson for the all-time lead.

The Express sat Tim Wallach and Tim Blackwell down on strikes in the second. Two innings later, the Texan hit one by Bryan Little for number 3.

In the eighth, Ryan struck out Blackwell again and tied Johnson's record. Montreal inserted Brad Mills as a pinch hitter. Ryan had faced the left-handed hitter only once. But the fireballer threw two quick fastballs for strikes.

On a 1–2 count, Big Tex switched to a curveball. The breaking pitch completely fooled Mills as he took a called strike three. The all-time strike-out record belonged to Ryan.

Nolan Ryan was a great pitcher. But part of his success was throwing with confidence. He believed he could strike out anyone, and he often did. Just facing the Express made batters nervous, and they had a right to be.

The writer of the Book of Hebrews in the Bible cautions us about confidence. With belief in God and in ourselves and our abilities, we can achieve great things. Without it, our efforts often fall short. We fail, not because we can't, but because we don't think we can.

Think of something giving you trouble. It might be a sports skill. It could be learning something new. It might be getting up in front of a group to speak. Whatever it is, practice. Then, tell yourself over and over that you can do it. Ask God to give you confidence.

I consider everything a loss compared to the surpassing greatness of knowing Christ Jesus my Lord, for whose sake I have lost all things. —**PHILIPPIANS 3:8a**

The 1988 Baltimore Orioles lost on Opening Day. The team went down in defeat the following game and the next, and the next, and the next. Loss after loss accumulated for the O's.

Management attempted to halt the streak by firing manager Cal Ripken Sr. His replacement, Hall-of-Famer Frank Robinson, fared no better.

April's end approached, and Baltimore's record stood at 0 wins and 21 losses. The despairing Orioles traveled to Chicago's Comiskey Park.

The game began well for the cellar dwellers. Eddie Murray hit a 2-run homer in the top of the first. Cal Ripken Jr. broke out of a hitting slump with 2 singles, a double, and a home run.

Baltimore tallied 9 runs. Mark Williamson and Dave Schmidt combined to shut out Chicago. The Orioles defeated the White Sox 9–0, breaking the longest American League losing streak ever.

Imagine how awful it would be to lose that many games. No loss goes down easily. In fact, losing anything is hard.

The Apostle Paul suffered many losses in his life. He lost freedom through imprisonment. He lost friends through his choice to follow Christ. He lost comfort and safety as he traveled the world on missionary journeys.

But Paul considered all his losses victories because he knew Jesus Christ as Lord. He chose loss on earth to taste God's greatness and win eternity.

Read about two of Paul's losses in Acts 9:20-30. Remember, he was called Saul before he met Christ. Thank God for turning losses into victories.

The heavens declare the glory of God; the skies proclaim the work of his hands. . . . In the heavens he has
pitched a tent for the sun. . . . It rises at one end of the heavens
and makes its circuit to the other; nothing is hidden from its heat.

—PSALM 19:1,4b,6

On a cool spring 1986 evening, Roger Clemens took the mound for the Boston Red Sox. Just two years removed from the minors, the tall Texas right-hander faced an uncertain future following shoulder surgery. The Seattle Mariners, however, saw nothing but hard heat as the Rocket Man's fastball clocked 95 mph.

Clemens got off to a rapid start, striking out the side. At the end of three, the fireballer had recorded six K's (strikeouts).

The game's middle third showcased Roger's humming fastball. He tied an American League record by whiffing 8 in a row. The crowd of 13,414 sensed another record.

The Rocket Man punched out two Mariners in both the seventh and eighth. Leading off the ninth, Roger faced his former University of Texas teammate Spike Owen. The Red Sox hurler blew a 1–2 pitch past Owen for strikeout number 19.

Phil Bradley came up next. A 2–2 fastball struck out Bradley for the fourth time, and Clemens had a new major league record of 20 strikeouts.

Nothing compares with watching someone perform at the top of his game. The Fenway faithful saw Roger Clemens' heat baffle baseball's best.

The psalmist felt the sun's heat and recognized that the giant star served as the greatest example of God's creation. The shining light warms our hearts.

A day without sunshine leaves us depressed. Plants convert the bright rays into food. Without the sun, the earth would die.

Just as our lives depend on the sun, they also depend on God. Without His presence, we feel empty.

Set your alarm clock and get up before daybreak. Watch the sunrise. Mentally calculate the number of sunrises since the beginning of time. Praise the sun's Creator and His Son.

This is what the Lord Almighty says: "Give careful thought to your ways." —HAGGAI 1:7

Come-from-behind victories always fuel a team's emotion. But nothing deflates an organization as quickly as a careless mistake.

In 1986, the Edmonton Oilers faced the Calgary Flames in the seventh game of the National Hockey League division finals. After spotting Calgary a 2–0 lead, Edmonton rallied with 2 third-period goals.

With less than 6 minutes to go in regulation, the Oilers worked to score the go-ahead goal or at least hold to move into overtime. Steve Smith, a rookie defenseman, made an unforgettable pass.

Smith, playing in place of the injured Lee Fogolin, shot a routine clearing pass from behind his own net. The puck nipped the ankle of Oiler goalie Grant Fuhr and skidded into the net.

Left wing Perry Berezan, the Flame nearest the goal, received credit for the score. Calgary held on for a 3–2 victory and eliminated Edmonton from competition. The Oilers lost a chance for a third straight Stanley Cup.

Smith's carelessness cost his team the opportunity for victory. He surely wished he could take back that one tiny moment and replay it. But he couldn't.

Life doesn't allow for such corrections. We can't change the past, but we can carefully live the present. We need to get things right the first time. That's why God commands us to give careful thought to our words and to our actions. We can't take them back.

Watch a sporting event on television and pay attention to the replays. Do outcomes change? Of course not. Only our perspectives change. Ask God to help you carefully think through the words you say and your actions.

Surely the Lord has done great things. —JOEL 2:21b

Although his body ached, Nolan Ryan took the mound for the Texas Rangers against the Toronto Blue Jays. The 44-year-old pitcher started with four days' rest instead of five to accommodate Arlington Appreciation Night.

Ryan experienced some touchy moments in the top of the first. He ran the count full on two hitters and walked Kelly Gruber. The right-hander escaped damage by popping up Joe Carter to end the frame.

Big Tex dominated the remainder of the 1991 game. He struck out the side in the second, all on called third strikes. The flamethrower retired eighteen batters in a row before walking Carter in the seventh.

Only one Blue Jay seriously threatened to spoil the gem. In the top of the sixth, Manny Lee hit a fastball to shallow right-center. But center fielder Gary Pettis got a great jump and made a streaking, knee-high catch.

Ruben Sierra's home run in the third gave the Ranger pitcher all the support he needed as the Rangers won 3–0. The Express completed his seventh no-hitter by striking out Roberto Alomar on a 93-mph fastball.

Ryan surely did the amazing when he threw his final no-hitter. He became the only pitcher to accomplish the feat in two decades—the 1970s and the 1980s. The right-hander became the only hurler to throw a no-hitter in his 40s, not once but twice. He earned the record for total no-hitters by three games. Ryan's closest competitor, Sandy Koufax, hurled only four no-hit masterpieces.

Nolan Ryan was one of the most outstanding baseball players of all time. But as great as his accomplishments, God does even greater things.

He created the world. He made every living thing. He formed each of us. He knows our every thought and hears our every prayer. God gave His Son to save us.

Praise God for His greatness. Decide on one great deed you can do for someone. Then do it.

Three times a day he got down on his knees and prayed, giving thanks to his God, just as he had done before.

—DANIEL 6:10b

Mac Wilkins often criticized United States Olympic officials and athletes. But his discipline in the discus brought the University of Oregon student great success.

In 1976, the bearded hurler reached the peak of his sport. In late April, he broke John Powell's world record with a throw of 69.18 meters at the Mount San Antonio Relays.

The following week, Wilkins competed in a meet in San Jose, California. He beat his own record on the first throw with a heave of 69.80 meters.

The controversial athlete could have stopped but chose to take his final throws. Amazingly, attempt number two traveled farther than the first. Wilkins' toss carried 70.24 meters, making him the first to go beyond 70 meters.

The record holder had one more try. Throw number three flew the farthest of all—70.86 meters.

Wilkins' three throws yielded three world records. In the Bible, Daniel saw the importance of discipline and doing something three times. He prayed morning, noon, and night. His disciplined prayers caused difficulty in the eyes of men. But they brought understanding and favor in the eyes of God.

Anything we practice consistently will improve. If we make prayer a habit, it will become a natural extension of our daily lives.

Read Daniel 6:1-23. Take note of Daniel's disciplined life. Ask God to give you spiritual discipline that you may gain His understanding.

Then the end will come, when he hands over the kingdom to God the Father after he has destroyed all dominion, authority and power. —1 CORINTHIANS 15:24

Kevin Johnson left the Key Arena feeling frustrated.

Although his game statistics appeared satisfactory, no athlete ever enjoys a loss, especially on the road. The Seattle Supersonics defeated the Phoenix Suns 116–92, ending the Suns' 1997 basketball playoff hopes and Johnson's season.

Instead of packing his bags and preparing for next year, however, Johnson made a surprise announcement. The Phoenix guard told everyone he had played his last professional basketball game. No fanfare, no farewell tour, no highlight film would precede his exit.

The three-time all-star enjoyed his playing days. In the record books, he belongs to an elite group. The guard is one of six National Basketball Association players to score over 11,500 points, snag over 2,000 rebounds, make over 6,000 assists, and gather over 1,000 steals. But Kevin Johnson knew his best days were behind him.

Few athletes, however, quit when they are at the top of their game. Most leave the playing field only when they are forced. They cannot accept the loss of their skills and ability.

Unlike athletic ability, however, our faith should improve with each passing year. Every day we spend seeking God strengthens us. Bible study, prayer, and service build lasting links with Him.

Too often we view the decision to accept Christ as a one-time event. But it is an everlasting experience. The greater effort we make to become more Christlike, the stronger our relationship grows.

How much have you grown in the past few years? Does your physical growth compare with your spiritual development? Ask God to help you continue to grow in Him.

"No servant can serve two masters. Either he will hate the one and love the other, or he will be devoted to the one and despise the other. You cannot serve both God and Money."

—LUKE 16:13

Statisticians calculate the odds of a baseball no-hitter at 13,000 to 1. But in 1917, the Chicago Cubs and Cincinnati Reds locked horns in a rare pitchers' duel.

"Big" Fred Toney and James "Hippo" Vaughn matched mound skills in Chicago's Weeghman Park. Both would win over twenty games in 1917 and conclude their careers with over one hundred victories.

Inning after inning passed without a hit. Nine complete stanzas went by without hits or runs. Never had two teams played a double no-hitter.

The Reds broke the spell in the tenth. With one out, Larry Kopf drilled a single for the first hit. The shortstop advanced to third when right fielder Cy Williams misplayed Hal Chase's flyball.

All-American halfback and Olympic-gold-medal-winner Jim Thorpe stepped to the plate. He barely topped the ball to the right of the mound. Vaughn fielded the ball but had no play. Kopf crossed the plate with the go-ahead run.

The Cubs hurler retired the side, but his teammates failed to rally. Toney put down the Chicagoans one, two, three, completing his masterpiece.

What a shame that one pitcher had to win and one had to lose his no-hitter. But such often happens in life. Only one can win. Only one path can be followed. Only one choice can be made. And those victories, paths, and choices eliminate all others.

The same is true with God. We either put Him first or we don't. We can't split our loyalties. We can't serve both God and money. God doesn't allow ties when He's involved.

What are your three most prized possessions? How much money would it take to buy them? Ask God to help you put money and material things in their proper places in your life.

for he himself is our peace, who has made the two one and has destroyed the barrier, the dividing wall of hostility.

—EPHESIANS 2:14

Milers tried for years to break the barrier of the sub-4-minute mile. In 1954, Roger Bannister, an Oxford medical student, took on the lofty goal.

The Englishman displayed remarkable maturity as a runner. He refused a berth on the 1948 Olympic team, believing he needed additional development.

At the 1952 Summer Games in Helsinki, he ran for the U.K. in the 1,500 meters, placing fourth. By 1954, the 25-year-old runner had reached his maximum potential.

Oxford classmates prearranged a race to encourage Bannister during his record-breaking attempt. Chris Brasher paced the first two laps at 1:58. Chris Chataway took over to finish lap number three at 3:00.7.

With the record within striking distance, the medical student stormed to the finish line, clocking in the final lap at 58.7. A new world's record of 3:59.4 for the mile went into the books.

Bannister had at last broken the barrier, the wall that had divided the possible from the impossible. Christ's birth, death, and resurrection also broke a barrier. His sacrifice made salvation possible for all mankind, not just a chosen few.

Ask a senior adult to share things he or she believed impossible as a child that have occurred. Talk about what you both still believe will never happen. Praise God for being the God of the possible.

Praise the Lord, O my soul, and forget not all his benefits. —PSALM 103:2

In the fast-paced world of basketball, players sometimes lose track of the score. On occasion, the lapse determines victory or defeat.

The Dallas Mavericks faced the Los Angeles Lakers at Reunion Arena in the 1984 playoffs. Trailing two games to one, the expansion franchise hoped to even the series.

The lead seesawed back and forth. With 31 seconds remaining, Maverick center Pat Cummings sank a left-handed hook to tie at 108. Magic Johnson fouled on the shot, and Cummings had an opportunity to give Dallas the lead.

With no time-outs remaining, Derek Harper moved to the sideline to discuss strategy with coach Dick Motta. Meanwhile, Cummings missed the free throw, but Harper mistakenly believed the shot was good.

The Lakers grabbed the rebound and worked the ball to Kareem Abdul-Jabbar. With time ticking down to 12 seconds, Jabbar arched his classic sky hook, but the ball bounced off the rim. Rolando Blackman snatched the rebound and looked for the winning shot.

Blackman quickly passed to Dale Ellis in the forecourt. He flipped it back to rookie point guard Harper to trigger the go-ahead basket. Thinking the game was won, he only dribbled the ball and watched time tick down to zero. In agony and disbelief, Harper realized the score had been tied.

The Lakers took command in overtime and won easily 122–115. What could have been a deadlocked series turned into a three-to-one advantage for the Lakers.

It's easy to forget. We rush in many different directions. Sometimes we can't remember where we've been or where we're going. Like Derek Harper, we focus on details and overlook the big picture.

We may lose sight of God in the frenzy of our daily lives. But God wants us to remember all He has done for us. If we do, our everyday problems won't seem so large.

Think about yesterday. How often did God enter the action? Did He come into focus at all? Try to spend at least ten minutes of quiet time with Him today and every day.

> "Act with courage, and may the Lord be with those who do well." —2 CHRONICLES 19:11b

The New York Knickerbockers faced the Los Angeles Lakers in the final game of the 1970 National Basketball Association finals. The Knicks had led the series 3-2, but a leg injury sidelined captain and defensive stalwart Willis Reed in game four.

While Reed received therapy, New York lost game six. Without the Knicks' center in the lineup, the outcome of game seven favored Los Angeles.

The capacity Madison Square Garden crowd watched glumly as the Knicks warmed up. Shortly before tip-off, Reed gingerly walked from the locker room.

The PA announced the starting lineup. A roar swelled through the throng as Reed's name was called.

The center limped downcourt but canned a jumper when his teammates kicked the ball out to him. The crowd erupted.

Reed hit a second shot. His courageous presence lifted the Knicks. The New Yorkers jumped to a 17–8 lead.

The pivotman soon reached his limit. Coach Red Holzman pulled Reed from the lineup, but his spirit remained on the floor. Buoyed by their captain's bravery, the Knicks waltzed to a 69–42 halftime margin and coasted to a 113–99 victory. The Knickerbockers captured their first championship.

Reed fought through pain to lead the Knicks. He certainly didn't have to. He could have stayed off the floor, and no one would have thought less of him. But Willis showed courage. He chose the difficult.

Courage means the ability to face danger, difficulty, or despair without giving in to fear. The writer of 2 Chronicles urges us to act with courage. He prays for God to be with those who do well. Often, like Willis Reed, we do well because we display courage.

Read a newspaper or newsmagazine or watch the news. Look for a story in which someone showed courage. How did he or she overcome difficulty? Ask God to give you the courage to do right even when it would be easier not to.

He was delivered over to death for our sins and was raised to life for our justification. —ROMANS 4:25

A sportswriter nicknamed Louisiana Tech's Karl Malone the "Mailman." He coined the term because Malone always delivered. The unique label carried over into the National Basketball Association.

The Utah Jazz faced the Los Angeles Lakers in game three of the 1997 NBA Western Conference semifinals. The Jazz had won five straight playoff games but took on the Lakers on their home court.

From the start, nothing clicked. Malone's team canned just 6 of 44 shots in the first half. Amazingly, the Jazz trailed only 49–36 because of the Lakers' foul trouble.

Unfortunately, Utah couldn't turn things around in the second half. Shooting barely improved, and the Jazz fell 104–84.

The Mailman experienced his worst professional game. He hit 2 of 20 shots from the floor. Malone scored 15 points, but it took an 11-of-12 performance from the free-throw line. Although the power forward has been one of the NBA's most consistent players, he occasionally plays a subpar game. Sometimes even the "Mail" gets sidetracked.

No one can be on top all the time except God. There is only one constant in this world, God's love. The Lord is always there.

Write a note to your mail carrier thanking him or her for faithfully delivering your mail. Put it in your mailbox. Give thanks to God for His constant love.

And we know that in all things God works for the good of those who love him, who have been called according to his purpose. —ROMANS 8:28

The Phoenix Suns dug themselves into a deep playoff hole in 1993 by losing the first 2 games at home. Another loss and the season would end.

The series moved to Los Angeles. The Suns defeated the Lakers in game three, 107–102, and four, 101–86. Game five returned to Phoenix.

The America West Arena filled with 19,023 frenzied fans. The Suns held a 10-point lead with 10 minutes to go. But the Lakers clawed back, led by James Worthy and Sedale Threatt. With 1:08 remaining, Los Angeles jumped in front 95–91.

Phoenix answered. Charles Barkley hit a baseline jumper. Dan Majerle canned an off-balance shot to send the contest into overtime.

Sun coach Paul Westphal called on backup center Oliver Miller. In the 5-minute extra period, the Arkansas rookie collected 9 points, 5 rebounds, and 1 blocked shot. The Suns put the Lakers away easily, 112–104.

Phoenix became the first team in NBA history to win a playoff series after losing the first 2 games at home. Miller led the way, averaging 14.7 points, 10 rebounds, and 3.7 blocks.

Miller answered Coach Westphal's call. Miller performed for the good of the team. He accomplished his purpose. The team won.

God calls each of us into His service. He doesn't promise we will always win as Phoenix did. He doesn't promise all of life will be good. But He does promise He will work whatever happens for our good if we love Him and hear His call.

Remember a time when you didn't win or something didn't go the way you wanted. Think of the good resulting from that experience. Perhaps you learned a lesson, practiced harder, developed a new skill, or grew closer to a teammate. Thank God for the good He brings from tough times.

When Jesus saw him lying there and learned that he had been in this condition for a long time, he asked him, "Do you want to get well?" —**JOHN 5:6**

A home run sometimes brings a baseball game to a quick and exciting conclusion. In 1984, Harold Baines' power hitting ended a contest, not quickly, but certainly with excitement.

The Milwaukee Brewers visited the Chicago White Sox. Milwaukee led 3–1 in the bottom of the ninth. Ace closer Rollie Fingers took the mound. But Chicago rallied to tie.

Neither could push across another run. After 17 frames, umpires halted play due to the 1:05 A.M. curfew.

The marathon resumed the next day. Brewer Ben Oglivie belted a 3-run homer in the twenty-first inning. But the White Sox battled back with run-scoring singles by Carlton Fisk and Tom Paciorek.

The scoreboard revealed nothing but goose eggs until the twenty-fifth. Baines' 1-out homer gave Chicago a 7–6 victory after eight hours and six minutes. The game set an American League record for innings played and a major league mark for time.

The two teams played for a long time. Fans could have asked, "Do you want to win?" Eventually Harold Baines hit the homer to show the answer, "Yes, I want to win!"

Jesus asked a similar question to a man who had been crippled for thirty-eight years. His question was "Do you want to get well?"

Instead of saying yes, the man replied that he had no one to help him into the healing pool. But Jesus asked the man to get up, pick up his bed, and walk. When the disabled man got up, he demonstrated the answer, "Yes, I want to be healed!"

We can think about God's teachings for a long time. We can talk about doing good things. We can plan to share Jesus with the lost. But until we act, we do not answer the Lord's call.

Read John 5:1-15. Ask God to help you answer His call to act.

Better a patient man than a warrior, a man who controls his temper than one who takes a city. —**PROVERBS 16:32**

A tennis player needs tremendous patience to remain on top. In 1996, Steffi Graf demonstrated the cost of impatience.

The world's number-one-ranked player met Martina Hingis in the quarterfinals of the Italian Open. Making her first appearance in Rome in nine years, Graf appeared worn and distraught. But she displayed her familiar dominance, acing the first set 6–2 in only 29 minutes.

Hingis, a 15-year-old Swiss prodigy, refused to buckle. She went ahead 2–1 in the second set, and Graf began to make uncharacteristic errors. Even as the world's twentieth-ranked player, Hingis went up 5–2 and put the set away with a backhand smash and a forehand off the baseline.

Graf panicked. She became impatient and lost control. Hingis placed shots in unexpected places and forced her opponent to run ragged across the baseline.

The young Hingis, who had turned professional only nineteen months before, won the deciding set 6–3 to advance to the semifinals. Graf took only her fourth loss in seventeen months.

Steffi Graf lost patience. She lost the match.

The writer of the Book of Proverbs puts the power of patience in perspective. He values it above the spoils of war because patience brings victory in life.

If you play tennis, arrange a friendly match with someone. Focus on being patient. Ask God to help you incorporate this quality into your daily life.

[He] satisfies your desires with good things so that your youth is renewed like the eagle's. —**PSALM 103:5**

When the Atlanta Braves released Gaylord Perry, the aging baseball veteran faced an uncertain future. The former Giant, Indian, Ranger, Padre, Yankee, and Brave needed only 3 wins to reach the magic 300 plateau. In 1982, the two-time Cy Young award winner got a final chance from the Seattle Mariners.

Perry's odds of staying in the majors appeared slim. But the five-time, 20-game winner made the opening day roster.

The 43-year-old right-hander lost his first two decisions. But two wins and a no-decision put Perry in position for the 300th win.

The New York Yankees visited the Kingdome. Seattle staked the Ancient Mariner to 7 runs.

Perry, who was often suspected of applying a foreign substance to the ball, allowed a single run in seven innings. In the eighth, the Yankees loaded the bases. But Perry fanned John Mayberry on three pitches. Two infield singles plated 2 runs, but Roy Smalley flied out to end the threat.

The Mariner pitcher breezed through the ninth. Rick Cerone lined out. Larry Milbourne popped up, and Willie Randolph grounded out. Seattle won 7–3, and Perry became baseball's first 300-game winner since Early Wynn in 1963.

Gaylord Perry appeared to be finished as a baseball player. His prime was past. The elusive 300-game plateau seemed out of reach because of age. But on that spring day, Perry's youth was renewed. He pitched with the strength of an eagle, and his desire for the milestone was satisfied.

Sometimes we feel finished. We just can't quite make it. We're not good enough. But God will satisfy us, maybe not with our desire, but with a good thing. The Lord will provide the strength to carry on.

Read about eagles in an encyclopedia. Think about why our early leaders chose it as the symbol for the United States of America. Thank God for the satisfaction and strength He gives.

The mind of sinful man is death, but the mind controlled by the Spirit is life and peace. —**ROMANS 8:6**

Strikeouts require great control. In 1952, Ron Necciai had the greatest control ever witnessed. The Pittsburgh Pirate farm-hand took the mound for the Appalachian League Bristol Twins against the Welsh Miners. Necciai struck out the side in the first. He repeated the feat in the second, and the third, and the fourth.

The Miners went down on strikes in the fifth. Necciai fanned three Welshmen in the sixth, seventh, and eighth. A hit batsman, a walk, and an error prevented the Class D minor leaguer from hurling a perfect game. But Necciai had 24 strikeouts and a no-hitter going into the ninth.

The fireballer notched strikeout number 25 for the first out. Center fielder Bobby Hammond stepped into the box. The 19-year-old Necciai whiffed Hammond, but the low pitch eluded catcher Harry Dunlop, allowing the outfielder to reach first.

Right fielder Bob Ganung grounded out. The pitcher faced Bob Kendrick. The Welsh left fielder went down on strikes for the game's final out. Necciai rang up 27 strikeouts en route to the no-hitter.

What a game! What control! Necciai deserved the no-hitter with an average of three strikeouts per inning. Control was the key.

Control is also an important key to living a peaceful and Holy Spirit-filled life. If we put our minds completely in God's hands, we give Him control.

Search your home for keys. Do you know what they all unlock? If you don't, try to find out by trial and error. Ask God to take control of your life and open the door to peace.

Remember this: Whoever turns a sinner from the error of his way will save him from death and cover over a multitude of sins. —JAMES 5:20

In spring training, pitchers and first basemen practice one routine play endlessly—ground balls hit to first. In 1990, Greg Maddux and Mark Grace worked the combination over and over again.

When the first baseman fields a ball far to his right, he can't reach the base in time for a force out. The pitcher has the responsibility of running to first, covering the bag, and taking the throw.

The pitcher must be alert and angle toward first to avoid colliding with the runner. The first baseman tosses a soft underhand throw, leading the pitcher as a football quarterback would a wide receiver.

In 1990, the Chicago Cubs visited the Los Angeles Dodgers. Maddux dominated, allowing Tommy Lasorda's team only 4 hits. Three times Los Angeles hitters grounded into double plays following a hit. No Dodger advanced past first base.

The Chicago pitcher's pinpoint control forced Los Angeles to hit weak ground ball after weak ground ball. Maddux set a new record for putouts by a pitcher with 7.

Andre Dawson gave Maddux all the offense he required with a sixth inning 3-run homer. Maddux, Grace, and the Cubs claimed a 4–0 victory.

The combination of Grace to Maddux worked seven times without error. The team turned three double plays. Greg's base coverage covered the hits he allowed.

God calls on us to work in combination with Him. He asks us to tell sinners about salvation through His Son. When we lead others to Christ, we help save them from eternal death and cover many sins.

Practice fielding grounders. If you like to pitch, also work on covering first. Ask God to help you lead someone to Christ, the One who covered our sins with His death.

"As for God, his way is perfect; the word of the Lord is flawless. He is a shield for all who take refuge in him."

—2 SAMUEL 22:31

Len Barker had great stuff on a cold May evening in 1981. His fastball clocked 96 mph, and his curveball broke precisely. But only 7,290 fans watched the Cleveland hurler write baseball history.

The Indians battled the Toronto Blue Jays. The Tribe scored 2 runs in the bottom of the first. Although Toronto shut them out until Jorge Orta's eighth-inning solo homer, Barker needed no additional support.

The Cleveland pitcher struck out no Blue Jays until the fourth. But from that point on, he sent eleven Toronto batters down swinging.

Barker's teammates played great defense. Center fielder Rick Manning ran down Damaso Garcia's line drive in the alley. Duane Kuiper backhanded Rick Bosetti's grounder behind second and nipped him with a throw to first baseman Mike Hargrove.

Kuiper made another outstanding play in the seventh. He fielded Alfredo Griffin's slow roller cleanly and gunned the ball to first, just beating the speedster to the bag.

With the pressure on in the ninth, Barker performed flawlessly. Bosetti popped out to third. Pinch hitter Al Woods struck out on three pitches. The final batter, Ernie Witt, ran the count to 1–2 before flying out to center.

Len Barker pitched baseball's 10th perfect game. Although his name was written in the record book, he didn't earn the honor alone. Manning, Kuiper, Hargrove, Orta, and the whole Cleveland lineup made the feat possible.

God alone is always perfect. We can count on His flawless Word, the Bible, to guide us. He needs no help from teammates, but allows us to be on His team.

Think about outstanding baseball players. Who would make your all-time greatest team? Would they win every game? Thank God that He is perfect.

When you walk, your steps will not be hampered; when you run, you will not stumble. —**PROVERBS 4:12**

Writers nicknamed the 1927 New York Yankees "Murderer's Row," because of their power hitting. But outfielder Bob Meusel proved they could run as well as hit.

The Yankees engaged the Detroit Tigers in a chilly afternoon contest. The Tigers took an early 2–0 lead.

But in the top of the third, Lou Gehrig hit a two-out solo homer. Meusel singled and stole second. Shortstop Tony Lazzeri walked.

Lazzeri wandered too far from first and got caught in a rundown. The alert Meusel broke from second and dashed for third.

The shortstop eluded the fielders and danced to and fro on the basepaths. The New York outfielder rounded third and headed for the plate.

Lazzeri returned to first safely. Detroit first baseman Lu Blue threw home to nail the base thief. But Meusel made a perfect hook slide around catcher Merv Shea's tag, tying the score, 2–2.

The Yankees broke open the contest with 2 runs in the seventh and 2 more in the ninth. Walter "Dutch" Ruether and Wilcy "Deacon" Moore combined to defeat Detroit, 6–2. Meusel's run led the way.

The Yankee shortstop ran but didn't stumble. The Tigers couldn't stop his steps. Even Meusel's slide worked to perfection.

If we follow God's teaching and His wisdom, God promises we will walk in His way without stumbling.

Work on base running and sliding. Thank the Heavenly Father for the promise of a secure path.

"I am sending you to Jesse of Bethlehem. I have chosen one of his sons to be king.". . . . But the Lord said to Samuel . . . "The Lord does not look at the things man looks at. Man looks at the outward appearance, but the Lord looks at the heart."

—1 SAMUEL 16:1b,7

A difficult course gives golfers fits. In 1992, Betsy King mastered one of the Ladies Professional Golf Association's toughest.

The LPGA championship took place at the Bethesda Country Club in Bethesda, Maryland. King found the zone from the opening round.

The 36 year old shot a 68 on the first day to take the lead. King improved to 66 on Friday and totaled a 67 on Saturday. She entered Sunday's final round with a 5-stroke lead.

The two-time LPGA Player of the Year never faltered. She fired a closing round 66 to win by 11 strokes. The margin broke Patty Sheehan's record of 10 set in 1984.

Only 13 of the 144 players broke par. The LPGA's all-time money leader became the only golfer to shoot four rounds in the 60s at a major tournament.

King reigned supreme that week on the golf course. Her heart stayed true to her game, and she set a new standard.

In athletics, heart often determines victory. A person may outwardly look like the better athlete but may not win.

A person's heart is most important to God. He doesn't judge by outward appearance or worldly success. He looks at the inside, at the spirit.

Read about an earthly king or queen. You might choose one from the Bible, one from modern history, or one currently on the throne. Contrast the outward appearance and the heart as shown by actions. Ask God to help you have a beautiful heart.

"For many are invited, but few are chosen."

—MATTHEW 22:14

With the baseball players' union on strike in 1995, owners considered using replacements. But the work stoppage ended before the substitutes took the field. In 1912, however, a strike forced a baseball team to choose its players from the crowd.

On May 15, Ty Cobb attacked a fan heckling him from the stands. American League President Ban Johnson slapped the Tiger outfielder with a fine and a 10-day suspension.

His teammates walked out in protest. The entire Detroit team boycotted the May 18 contest in Philadelphia.

If Detroit didn't play, Tiger ownership faced a $5,000 fine and possible franchise revocation. To field a team, manager Hughie Jennings called for volunteers from the Shibe Field stands.

Jennings selected nine participants, including several from St. Joseph's College. The skipper also pressed former players and Tiger scouts Jim McGuire and Joe Sugden into service.

The game turned into a complete fiasco. After five innings, the Athletics led 14–2. Several thousand fans demanded refunds. The final tally read Philadelphia 24, Detroit 2.

The replacement game brought the walkout to a rapid conclusion. The Tigers returned to the fold, and Cobb rejoined the team a week later.

Jennings carefully looked through the invited crowd to pick a team. He chose some willing men who seemed promising. Those the manager chose also chose to accept the invitation. They put on the uniforms and took the field.

God invites every man, woman, girl, and boy to follow Him. But He chooses for His team only those of us who also choose Him.

Think of an invitation you received but didn't accept. Why didn't you? Was the cost too high? Did the time conflict? Was the distance too far? Did the other guests seem uninteresting? Have you chosen God's invitation to follow Him? If you haven't, what's stopping you?

"Return to me," declares the Lord Almighty, "and I will return to you." —ZECHARIAH 1:3

Mario Lemieux broke his left hand in game two of the 1992 National Hockey League division finals against the New York Rangers. Without Number 66 in the lineup, the Pittsburgh Penguins struggled to win the series 4 games to 2.

The Penguin superstar played hurt much of the time. A sore back and bad shoulder limited him to 64 regular season games. When Adam Graves slashed Lemieux's hand in the playoffs, no one knew when the center would return.

Super Mario surprised everyone by missing only 5 games in two weeks. In his return, the center scored 2 goals and set up another to lead the Penguins to a 5–2 victory over the Boston Bruins. The win put Pittsburgh up 2 games to none in the semifinal series.

Inspired by their captain's return, the Penguins swept the Bruins and repeated the feat in the finals over the Chicago Blackhawks. Pittsburgh claimed NHL supremacy for the second consecutive year. Lemieux won his second straight Conn Smythe Trophy as the Stanley Cup's MVP.

The superstar's teammates surely got excited on his return to the line-up. And when Lemieux came back to his special brand of hockey, the Penguins returned to play their best, too.

Sometimes, we feel God is far away. We don't think about Him, read the Bible, worship, or pray. When we return to God, we feel Him return to us. Of course, He was right there all the time.

Compete with a friend or relative to see who can name the most things that can be returned. Examples might include a tennis serve or a library book. Thank God that He's always waiting when we return to Him.

[I] present to you the word of God in its fullness—the mystery that has been kept hidden for ages and generations, but is now disclosed to the saints. —COLOSSIANS 1:25-26

The Philadelphia Flyers visited the Buffalo Sabres for the third game of the 1975 National Hockey League Stanley Cup finals. The late May date forced the game to be played under unusual circumstances.

Buffalo's Memorial Stadium lacked air conditioning. The heat turned the rink into patches of puddles. A thick, waist-deep fog wafted over the ice.

Eleven times officials stopped play to circulate the air and improve visibility. The skaters circled en masse around the arena stirring the still, humid atmosphere.

Fans could not see the action. The players dripped with humidity and sweat.

The contest ended at 4–4 after regulation play. Eighteen minutes into the overtime period, Gilbert Perreault and Rene Robert broke into the Flyers' zone during a line change. Perreault fired the puck toward the corner. It ricocheted to Robert.

The Sabre wingman blasted a 24-foot shot. Flyers goalie Bernie Parent barely saw the players and never sighted the puck. The slap shot crashed into the net, and Buffalo won in the fog, 5–4.

The Buffalo Sabres didn't really win. The fog did. The mystery puck found the net hidden in haze.

Many people see God's Word as a mystery. They find it hidden in a fog of difficult Old Testament names and long-ago language. But Paul explains that, through Christ, God discloses the mystery to His followers.

If you have difficulty understanding the Bible, buy a modern language translation, perhaps one in everyday language written in paragraphs with verses noted but not separated. Start by reading the Book of Luke. Ask God to reveal Himself to you through His Word, but don't be afraid to ask your pastor or another church leader for help if you have problems.

My cup overflows. —**PSALM 23:5b**

Winning a Stanley Cup is not unusual for the Montreal Canadiens. But in 1986, the hockey team captured the crown with a surprising cast.

Eight rookies, including goaltender Patrick Roy, made the roster. The veterans and youngsters combined to form a team that scored sparingly but usually found a way to win.

When the Calgary Flames upset the defending champion Edmonton Oilers, the Cup became anyone's to claim. Montreal marched through Hartford, Boston, and New York to face Calgary in the finals.

The Flames claimed the opener on their home ice. But tough checking and young legs wore Calgary down, and Montreal won three straight.

In game five, the Canadiens led 4–1 late in the third period. The Flames pulled within 1 with 2 quick goals. Roy made a spectacular save on Jamie Macoun's shot to preserve the win. Montreal garnered a 23rd championship, the most of any professional team, and the goalie earned the Conn Symthe Trophy as Stanley Cup MVP.

The rookies and veterans together made an unbeatable combination. They won, and Montreal's cup overflowed with Stanley Cup victories.

As Christians, our lives overflow with God's blessings. He promises His guidance, His restoration, His comfort, His support, His goodness, His love, and His presence forever.

Read Psalm 23. Mark it in your Bible and refer to it often.

When the righteous triumph, there is great elation; but when the wicked rise to power, men go into hiding.

—PROVERBS 28:12

No one ran like Jesse Owens. In the 1935 Big Ten Conference Track Championship, he quickly showed his athletic prowess.

The Cleveland native anchored the Ohio State Buckeye track team, competing in Ann Arbor, Michigan. Fighting off the flu, Owens took his mark for the 100-yard dash at 3:15 P.M. The Ebony Express tied the world record 9.4 seconds later.

Ten minutes passed, and the Ohioan competed in the long jump. In his first attempt, Owens leaped 26 feet, 8 1/4 inches—a new world standard. The mark stood for twenty-five years.

Nine more minutes elapsed, and the graduate of East Technical High School broke from the blocks in the 220-yard dash. His 20.3-second run shattered another world record.

At 4:00 P.M., Owens competed in his final event, the 220-yard hurdles. The speedster won in 22.6 seconds, a fourth record-setting time.

But the star is better remembered, not for the four Big Ten record day, but for the four gold medals he won at the 1936 Summer Olympics in Berlin, Germany. Most of the world, including the German people, were elated over Jesse's triumph. But the performances of Owens and other outstanding black Americans embarrassed German Nazi leader Adolf Hitler.

Hitler believed blacks to be an inferior race and snubbed the athletes. The ruler later led in the persecution of another group he considered inferior—the Jews. Many hid to escape his wrath.

God understands the joy of living under a righteous leader and the pressures of living under a wicked one. His desire is that we choose good and faithful government officials.

If you are eligible to vote, make sure that you're registered and knowledgeable of the issues and platforms. Pray for righteous candidates and wisdom in voting. If you're too young to vote, begin learning now so that you'll be ready. Thank the Lord for godly leaders.

The end of a matter is better than its beginning, and patience is better than pride. —ECCLESIASTES 7:8

A reporter asked former Yankee catcher and baseball manager Yogi Berra if the pennant race was over. Berra profoundly answered, "It's not over until it's over." The Cleveland Indians proved the truth of Berra's adage in the American League's first season in 1901.

The Washington Senators led Cleveland, then called the Blues, 13–5 with two out in the bottom of the ninth. Spectators headed for the exits.

But Jack McCarthy singled. Bill Bradley followed with another. Candy LaChance punched one to center, scoring McCarthy.

Senator pitcher Casey Patten hit Bob Wood with a pitch to load the bases. Frank Scheibeck delivered a double. Frank Genins singled before manager Jimmy Manning pulled Patten and inserted Watty Lee.

Lee immediately walked Truck Eagan. Erve Beck pinch hit for the pitcher, Bill Hoffer, and belted a double off the left field wall.

Ollie Pickering, thrown out at first for the inning's second out, singled in his second chance and tied the game. The *Cleveland Plain Dealer* reported the crowd behaved wildly.

Jack McCarthy batted for a second time. A passed ball sent Pickering to second. McCarthy singled again, plating Pickering with the winning run. The Blues scored 9 runs with two out in the bottom of the ninth to win 14–13.

For the Cleveland Blues, the game wasn't over with two outs in the ninth. The third out never came. Like some of the Blues fans, we anticipate the end before it comes.

The Christian life is much the same. We assume growth ends by accepting Christ. But acceptance is only the beginning. If we develop our relationship with God, life gets richer every day. The end becomes better than the beginning.

Remember when you watched an event on television but turned the TV off before the end. Were the results different from what you expected? Pray for patience to see things to their conclusion.

He causes his sun to rise on the evil and the good, and sends rain on the righteous and the unrighteous. —**MATTHEW 5:45**

In the 1984 Italian Open, Manuela Maleeva battled her tennis opponents and the elements. Rain postponed play for several days and halted Maleeva's quarterfinal against Virginia Ruzici.

Matches could be delayed no longer due to the French Open. The 17 year old opened the day by disposing of Ruzici. The semifinals and final remained.

The Bulgarian defeated Canada's Carling Bassett, 6–2, 6–2, advancing to the finals against Chris Evert. Maleeva dominated the top-seeded American, winning 6–3, 6–3. No other tennis player in history has won three escalating matches in a single day.

Manuela won in the sunshine and the rain. Her opponents experienced the same weather. The sun shone on both. The rain pelted both.

God sends the sun and the rain to His followers and His enemies. He loves both, and He allows both hard times and good times. Jesus uses the illustration to explain that we should love our opponents. It's easy to love those who love us. The test of Christianity comes in loving enemies.

Of all the people you see frequently, whom do you like the least? Make a pact with yourself and God to go out of your way to be kind to that person. Plan one specific thing you can do. Ask for God's help to carry through.

They would put their trust in God and would not forget his deeds. —PSALM 78:7

In fifteen seasons, Eddie Johnson has scored 18,550 points, won the Sixth Man award, and gained a reputation as a deadly shooter. But only diehard basketball fans recognize his name. In the 1997 playoffs, however, the Houston Rockets swingman received recognition.

The Utah Jazz led the Western Conference finals, two games to none. Another Jazz victory would make a Rocket comeback difficult.

Utah jumped to a 13-point second-quarter lead. But Johnson came off the bench and lit up the scoreboard. The 38-year-old veteran hit 12 of 17 from the field, including 5 of 8 3-pointers. He finished the night with 31 points in 28 minutes as the Rockets cruised 118–100.

Game four was pivotal. A Jazz win would send the series back to Utah needing only one win. The Rockets, however, could even the series.

Karl Malone's fadeaway jumper tied the score at 98 with 1:08 to play. For a while it seemed as if neither team would score.

Hakeem Olajuwon turned the ball over. John Stockton missed a jumper. Greg Foster failed on two tip-ins, and Bryon Russell misfired.

Houston rebounded with 6.7 seconds left and called time-out. The Rockets set a play, but the Jazz double-teamed Clyde Drexler after he caught the inbound pass.

The home team improvised. Matt Maloney found Johnson open 5 feet beyond the 3-point line.

The sixth man shot his 27-footer with less than a second remaining. It swished the net. The 16,285 sellout crowd erupted in a frenzy as the Rockets won 95–92.

Houston Rocket fans won't soon forget Eddie Johnson's performance. Many sports fans even remember trivia from years past. So it's amazing we easily forget to talk to God.

We shouldn't. God hears and answers our prayers.

Share the story of an unforgettable experience with a friend. What made the time memorable? Ask God to keep you from being forgetful.

> The ransomed of the Lord will return. They will enter Zion with singing; everlasting joy will crown their heads.
>
> **—ISAIAH 51:11**

José Canseco combines power and speed. In 1988, he rewrote the record book, becoming baseball's first player to join the 40-40 club. The Cuban native clubbed 42 homers and swiped 40 bases. But in 1993, the power hitter really used his head.

The Texas Rangers engaged the Cleveland Indians in old Memorial Stadium. Canseco, a weak defensive player, manned right field.

In the fourth inning with Texas leading 3–1, Carlos Martinez lofted a high fly. The arcing ball backed Canseco to the wall.

At the last moment, the Ranger outfielder either misjudged the ball's flight or lost the sphere in the sun. The ball ticked off the top of Canseco's glove, bounced off the top of his head, and bounded over the wall for a cheap home run. The Indians tallied 2 more runs in the fourth and took the lead, 4–3.

Cleveland padded its margin to 7–3. Texas scored single runs in the seventh, eighth, and ninth but fell to the Tribe, 7–6. Canseco's heady play made the difference.

A baseball crowned José Canseco's head and embarrassed him and his teammates. According to the prophet, God's believers will someday wear crowns of joy, and all will rejoice. None will be embarrassed.

Heaven is a mysterious place. But one thing is certain for all Christians. Someday we will meet God. What a glorious day it will be.

Look up the word crown in an encyclopedia. Examine the photographs of the jeweled headpieces worn by kings, queens, and emperors. Think how insignificant they are compared to a Christian's crown of joy. Praise God.

But when perfection comes, the imperfect disappears.

—1 CORINTHIANS 13:10

On a cold and threatening evening in 1959, journeyman baseball pitcher Harvey Haddix sought his fourth win against the Milwaukee Braves. The two-time defending National League champions presented a powerful lineup, including future Hall of Famers Henry Aaron and Eddie Mathews.

Haddix retired the Braves one, two, three, in the bottom of the first. He repeated the feat in the second, third, fourth, and fifth. The three-up, three-down scenario continued through the sixth, seventh, eighth, and ninth.

A dilemma faced the Pirate pitcher, however. Pittsburgh failed to score. The game continued.

Haddix took the mound and pitched perfectly. The tenth, eleventh, and twelfth innings went into the scorebook without a single Brave reaching base. But the Pirates could not push a run across.

Disaster struck in the bottom of the thirteenth. Don Hoak's error allowed Felix Mantilla to reach first base. Perfection evaporated.

Mathews sacrificed Mantilla to second. Haddix intentionally walked Aaron to set up a double play.

Joe Adcock belted a 1–0 pitch over the right center field wall for an apparent 3-run homer. But the game ended on a strange note.

Aaron, not realizing the ball had left the park, touched second and headed for the dugout. The umpires ruled Adcock out for passing Aaron on his way to third.

The official scorer credited the Brave first baseman with a double. Haddix lost his twelve-inning perfect game in the 13th by a score of 1–0, and Adcock lost his 3-run homer.

Aaron's imperfection cost Adcock batting stats. Hoak's imperfection cost Haddix perfection. On earth, man is imperfect. In heaven, God makes everything perfect. There, we will see all things clearly and not as a reflection in a poor mirror.

Look in a mirror under dim light. Then look under bright light. Note that the image improved but was still just a reflection. Thank God for the promise of heaven when all will be perfect.

At this my heart pounds and leaps from its place.

—JOB 37:1

When a basketball lead rocks back and forth, suspense grips the heart of every player, coach, and fan. In 1995, the Orlando Magic held a 2–1 margin over the Indiana Pacers in the Eastern Conference finals. Indiana desperately wanted to win on its home court.

Orlando opened with a 15–3 run. But the Pacers rallied and led 53–47 at the half.

The contest continued nip and tuck. Indiana gained height advantage when Shaquille O'Neal and Horace Grant fouled out.

The Magic took the lead 90–89 with 13.3 seconds to play on Brian Shaw's 3-pointer. But the Pacers matched the feat when Reggie Miller canned a trey with 5.2 ticks remaining.

Orlando refused to concede. Anfernee Hardaway hit 3 to put the Magic up 93–92 with only 1.3 seconds left.

Indiana called time-out and set up a play for 7-foot-4-inch post Rik Smits. Derrick McKey inbounded the ball. Smits faked defender Tree Rollins into the air. The Dutchman stepped forward and swished the ball through the net. The Pacers won the heartstopper, 94–93.

Hearts pounded with each lead change. No one exited the arena until the final buzzer sounded. One of the most exciting contests of all time left both sides weak-kneed and totally exhausted.

The Bible tells us that the awesomeness of God left Job feeling the same way. His heart seemed to leap as he thought of lightning, thunder, ice, wind, rain, sun, and God's total power over nature.

Then Job was asked the question, "Do you know how God controls the clouds and makes His lightning flash?" While we may understand about high and low pressure, temperature readings, weather fronts, and wind speed, we cannot change the weather. Only God can.

For several days, check the weather forecast on television, in the newspaper, or on the internet. Was the meteorologist correct? Is he or she always right? Praise God for His power over the weather.

On arriving, he was a great help to those who by grace had believed. —ACTS 18:27b

The Utah Jazz acquired the reputation of a team that couldn't reach the National Basketball Association finals. Losses in the semifinals to Portland, Houston, and Seattle haunted the franchise.

In 1997, Utah led the series against the Houston Rockets, three games to two, but neither team had won off its home court. The Houston fans cheered loudly in game six.

Charles Barkley's foul shots put the home team up by 7, 98–91, with 2 minutes to play. Bryon Russell cut the Houston lead to 4 with a 3-pointer.

John Stockton drove the lane for an uncontested layup with 1:22 remaining. Fifteen seconds later, the point guard recovered a loose ball and laid it up to tie at 98.

Barkley's second free throw with 32 seconds on the clock put Houston ahead. But the Jazz worked an isolation play for Stockton. The guard dribbled past Sedale Threatt and scored to tie the game at the 22.4-second mark.

The Rockets set up for the final shot. Clyde Drexler worked the time under 5 seconds, spun, and missed a 12-footer.

Karl Malone grabbed the rebound. The Jazz called time. Russell inbounded to Stockton.

The NBA's all-time assist leader cocked and fired. His 3-pointer touched nothing but net. The Jazz won 103–100 and claimed its first Western Conference crown.

John Stockton is best known for assisting his teammates. But when a crucial basket is needed, he shoots as well as anyone.

As Christians, we should copy Stockton's style. Our role is primarily service. We not only serve God but also our church, our school, our family, and our community.

When we volunteer, we sharpen our leadership skills. We learn to organize and direct. We are ready to deliver when needed.

Look for a volunteer opportunity. Spend time assisting. Think about what you have gained from helping others. Thank God for the experience.

Remember your leaders, who spoke the word of God to you. Consider the outcome of their way of life and imitate their faith. —HEBREWS 13:7

Many professional athletes wear a single championship ring. No amount of personal or financial success can substitute for the winning feeling. In 1989, Calgary Flames cocaptain Lanny McDonald finally realized his hockey title dream.

The 36 year old announced that the 1988–89 season would be his last. McDonald played a backup role, but his younger teammates looked to him for leadership and inspiration.

The wingman achieved personal goals, scoring his 1,000th point on March 7 and netting his 500th goal two weeks later. But for the season, the veteran scored only 11 goals and often watched from the sidelines.

Calgary skated past Vancouver, Los Angeles, and Chicago to reach the Stanley Cup finals against the Montreal Canadiens. The Flames took a 3–2 lead in the series, but the red-bearded wing mostly warmed the bench.

Thirty minutes prior to game six at Montreal's Forum, coach Terry Crisp informed McDonald he would start. The news filled the sixteen-year player with rookie excitement.

Crisp's decision soon yielded dividends. McDonald took a pass from Joe Nieuwendyk and flicked a wrist shot past Montreal goalie Patrick Roy. His second-period goal gave Calgary a 2–1 lead. The Flames held on for a 4–2 victory and their first Stanley Cup title.

The celebrating Calgary fans imitated their leader by wearing large red moustaches. They considered the outcome of his career and chose to honor him.

The writer of Hebrews also urges us to remember Christian leaders from times past. We should think about their accomplishments for God and imitate their faith.

Remember a pastor, musician, Sunday School teacher, or other Christian leader who helped you learn about Jesus. Think of qualities he or she had that you would like to imitate. Praise God for the person's life.

The tongue is a small part of the body, but it makes great boasts. Consider what a great forest is set on fire by a small spark. —JAMES 3:5

The UCLA Lady Bruins faced the University of Arizona Lady Wildcats in the 1996 NCAA Softball World Series title game. UCLA pitcher Lisa Fernandez took the mound.

In the first inning, Lady Wildcat Amy Chellevold reached on shortstop Kristy Howard's error and advanced to second on a groundout. Leah O'Brien singled to center, plating Chellevold.

The contest turned into a pitchers' duel. Fernandez threw beautifully. Arizona's Susie Parra hurled with precision. The junior All-American threw 75 pitches, allowing just 2 hits and striking out 6.

The Lady Bruins never mounted a threat. Arizona won a 1–0 victory and the NCAA softball title. Fernandez finished her career with a 93–7 collegiate record and two no-hitters in World Series play.

One little mistake by Howard and a tiny one by Fernandez determined the outcome. Fernandez and UCLA couldn't repeat as champs.

Small things in life make a big difference. A tiny spark begins the destruction of thousands of trees. Looking away from the road for just a second causes a car crash. An unbuckled seat belt results in injury or death. A thoughtless word damages a reputation or relationship.

God knows the importance of the little things and urges us to consider them. A spark can light a fire that provides warmth and cooks food. Spotting another driver off course can keep an accident from happening. The moment taken to buckle a seat belt can save a life. An encouraging word spoken at just the right moment can change a life for good.

In a park or other appropriate place with your family, build a campfire. Roast hot dogs or marshmallows. Enjoy the tasty food. Talk about the importance of little things in life. Before you leave make certain the fire is completely out. Ask God to help you pay attention to details.

If only I may finish the race and complete the task the Lord Jesus has given me—the task of testifying to the gospel of God's grace. —ACTS 20:24b

Promoters billed the race as the match to determine the world's fastest man. In 1997, Olympic champions Donovan Bailey of Canada and Michael Johnson of the United States competed in a special 150-meter race with the winner claiming the title and a million-dollar prize.

Officials constructed a special track in Toronto's Skydome. Bailey, the 100-meter world record holder, and Johnson, the 200-meter pace setter, traded verbal jabs for a month prior to the race.

Television viewers in fifty-six countries tuned in to the event. The starter's gun sounded, and Bailey led out of the blocks. He gained a two-stride lead coming off the curve at the 75-meter mark. Johnson needed to make his move, or the race would be lost.

Suddenly, the double Olympic gold winner in the 200 and 400 grimaced in pain. He grabbed his left thigh.

Bailey continued to sprint and recorded a time of 14.93 seconds. Johnson limped to the finish line far behind. The 100-meter champion won the race and the million dollars, but the question of who was the fastest man remained unanswered.

While Donovan Bailey raced to the end, Michael Johnson struggled to cross the finish line. The task required effort, but he did it. He faced disappointment, but he finished and earned the runner-up prize.

God gives us all a race to run as Christians. Our contest is to tell others about Jesus and show we believe in Him by how we act. Sometimes we stumble. Sometimes we pull up lame.

But like Saint Paul, on those days we ask God to help us keep going. Only in His strength can we finish.

Challenge a friend or relative to a short race. Choose someone close to your speed. Thank God for the strength to run. Ask Him to help you run His race as a Christian.

> Draw water for the siege, strengthen your defenses! Work the clay. —NAHUM 3:14a

No American female tennis player has starred like Chris Evert. The young woman from Florida captured 18 Grand Slam titles, a dozen more than any of her fellow countrymen. In 1983, she demonstrated her methodical and effortless style at the French Open.

The 28 year old faced Mima Jausovec in the finals. The 16,500 fans roasted in the sun at Roland Garros Stadium. Evert limited their exposure to 65 minutes. The red clay surface suited the young woman well. Growing up in Florida, she played the majority of her matches on clay.

But Jausovec had vast clay experience as well. Both contestants mixed their shots, varied the tempo, and drew the opponent toward the net with drop shots.

Yet Evert prevailed. She missed only three shots, defeating her Slavic challenger with ease, 6–1, 6–2. The queen of the court won her 5th French Open title and her 15th Grand Slam championship overall.

On that hot June day, Chris knew what it would take to win. She had to stay hydrated by drinking plenty of water and other healthful liquids. She needed to play outstanding defense. And she had to work the clay surface to benefit her talents and abilities. The champion managed all three.

God asks the same of us. We must pay attention to our physical needs. We should guard against participating in activities opposed to Christian values. And we ought to use the intelligence, abilities, and talents God has given us for His good.

Use an encyclopedia, nutrition book, or the internet to determine how much liquid you should drink during a normal day and during exercise. How do the numbers differ? Drink a glass of water now, and make it a point to drink enough liquid each day, especially as you play a sport or exercise. Ask God to help you maintain a healthy body.

Jesus has been found worthy of greater honor than Moses, just as the builder of a house has greater honor than the house itself. —HEBREWS 3:3

For years, Edwin Moses dominated the 400-meter hurdles unlike any other runner. The 31 year old competed at a 1987 meet in Madrid. The two-time Olympic gold medalist started quickly and led the first half of the race.

But three-time NCAA intermediate champion Danny Harris caught Moses by the fifth hurdle. The world's best reached back for something extra to regain the lead.

Moses, however, tripped on the tenth and final hurdle and lost to the challenger. The Iowa State collegian posted a time of 47.56 seconds, clipping the long-time champion by .13.

The king of the hurdles had not lost since August 26, 1977. Nine years, nine months, and nine days had elapsed between defeats.

The winner of 107 consecutive races walked around the track, letting his fans honor his achievements. The crowd of 16,000 applauded 20 minutes in tribute.

Edwin Moses achieved an amazing track and field record. He deserved all the praise he received. But like any athlete, Moses eventually lost.

The biblical Moses achieved great things for God. He showed the Pharaoh God's tremendous power. He led the Israelite people out of slavery in Egypt. He received the Ten Commandments. He governed with wisdom. He remained faithful until his death. He deserves the honor we give him.

But Jesus, our Lord, is greater than the Moses of the Old Testament. The Creator surpasses the created. And we owe Him our greatest honor.

Find out who designed and built your house or a favorite building in your town or city. Remember that without the builder, the structure wouldn't exist. Thank God for the life He is building in you.

The Lord reigns, let the earth be glad; let the distant shores rejoice. —PSALM 97:1

A champion faces pressure to live up to the past. Annika Sorenstam won the 1995 U.S. Women's Open. The golfer led the field by three strokes going into the final round of the 1996 championship. The 25-year-old Swede felt nervous as she prepared for her last 18 holes. But when the 1992 World Amateur Champion stepped into the number one tee box, she played with calm self-assurance.

Sorenstam intended to play conservatively, hitting her shots in the middle of the greens and going for pars. But as she continued, the University of Arizona alum made birdies and 1 eagle. She tallied a final round 66 and a four-day total of 272, 8-under-par.

The defending champion finished 6 strokes ahead of runner-up Kris Tschetter. Sorenstam became only the sixth golfer to capture back-to-back U.S. Women's Opens.

When Annika won, Sweden rejoiced. Her countrymen were justly proud of her play and her victory.

Through His followers, God does great things every day. Christians in other parts of the world win people to Christ in spite of religious persecution. Missionaries make a difference as they offer water wells, food, medical care, education, and God's message. Some even teach sports skills or coach as a way to tell people about Jesus. We rejoice as we learn what God is doing on distant shores.

If you don't know any missionaries, ask your pastor or another church leader for the name and address of a missionary family. Ask God to bless their ministry, and rejoice in their work. If appropriate, write them a note of encouragement.

for prophesy never had its origin in the will of man, but men spoke from God as they were carried along by the Holy Spirit. —2 PETER 1:21

A broken right hand sidelined Louisiana State University's Warren Morris for 40 games in 1996. But the preseason baseball All-American returned to the lineup late in the season.

The LSU Tigers challenged the University of Miami Hurricanes in the College World Series final. The Hurricanes took a first inning 2–0 lead, but the Tigers surged ahead with 3 runs in the third.

Miami scored 3 in the fifth and 2 in the sixth and led 7–3. But LSU chipped away, tying the contest with 2 runs in the seventh and eighth.

The Hurricanes went up 8–7 in the top of the ninth. Freshman pitcher Robbie Morrison retired two LSU batters. The Hurricanes needed one more out to claim a third national baseball title.

Warren Morris stepped to the plate with a man on base. The second baseman hit a deep line drive to right. At first glance, it appeared the ball would be caught on the warning track.

But the horsehide carried farther and farther until it cleared the fence, plating the winning run. The entire LSU team erupted in wild celebration, mobbing Morris as he touched home plate. The Tigers won their third NCAA baseball championship, all in the 1990s.

The home run ball carried out of the park on the wind and on Morris' power. God carries us along by His power and the wind of the Holy Spirit.

Follow the College World Series this summer. Count how many balls are carried over the fence. How does the Holy Spirit carry you along in your Christian life? Thank God for the gift of His Holy Spirit.

"O house of Israel, can I not do with you as this potter does?" declares the Lord. "Like clay in the hand of the potter, so are you in my hand." —JEREMIAH 18:6

Jim Courier had won the 1991 and 1992 French Open titles. He wanted a third and promised to deliver his acceptance speech in French.

The world's number-two-ranked tennis player met eleventh-ranked Sergi Bruguera in the finals. The heat and humidity turned the red clay into an inferno.

Bruguera's ferocious forehand kept Courier off balance. The two-time champion fell 6–4.

Courier fought back. He took the second set. But the Spaniard battled, capturing the third.

The match seesawed. The reigning champ tied it at two sets.

Both players fought exhaustion and dehydration. After 3 1/4 hours, they began the final set.

Courier broke Bruguera's serve. But the challenger broke back. Suddenly, the American's legendary forehand failed. Bruguera's clutch serves and Courier's unforced errors led the Spaniard to victory.

The winner ran into the stands and fell into the arms of his coach, his father. He returned to the training room and collapsed.

Bruguera had been like clay in the elder Bruguera's hands. The father-coach molded him into an outstanding player. And that day on clay, he spent every ounce of energy.

God holds us in His hands like the potter holds clay. Sometimes clay becomes too wet, dries out, or includes straw. Then the potter can't mold it as he wants.

He adds water or lets the clay dry. He picks out the undesirable. Our Heavenly Father does the same for us if we let Him. Only then can He mold us into what He wants.

Watch a potter or mold some clay. Try to make a bowl or other small object. As you work the clay into what you plan, think of yourself as clay in the hands of God. Thank God for His plan for your life. Let Him be your potter.

No one knows what is coming—who can tell him what will happen after him? —ECCLESIASTES 10:14

The Houston Rockets traveled to the Orlando Magic for the opener of the 1995 National Basketball Association finals. The Magic blitzed to an early second quarter lead. But ignited by 8 3-pointers, the Rockets cut the margin to 61-50 at the half.

Houston continued its hot shooting and gained the upper hand. But Orlando recovered from its sleepwalking and moved in front 98-96 with 6:42 remaining.

The Magic led 110–107 with 10.7 ticks left on the clock. Nick Anderson stood at the free-throw line to shoot two. Unbelievably, he missed both.

Another foul gave the guard another chance. He blew it again.

Houston's Kenny Smith knocked down a trey to force overtime. Orlando's Dennis Scott hit a 3 with 5.5 seconds left to tie at 118.

The Rockets called time-out to set up a final play. Clyde Drexler drove the right side of the lane and missed over Shaquille O'Neal. But Hakeem Olajuwon's tip-in gave Houston the comeback win. The overtime victory set the stage for the Rockets' sweep and repeat championship.

The magic ran out for Orlando. Perhaps Nick Anderson knew what would happen when he missed the free throws. But he couldn't have been sure. Nor could the Rockets have known Olajuwon would score the winning bucket. The plan was for Drexler to take the shot.

No person on earth knows the future. Only God does. He knows everything that will happen to us. Our job is to trust Him.

Add three tablespoons of baking soda to an empty two-liter pop bottle. Have a small balloon ready to cover the top of the bottle. Pour in 1/4 cup of vinegar. Quickly snap the balloon over the top. Watch the balloon as it inflates. Did magic make it blow up? Of course not. It was something God created and knew would react that way—carbon dioxide. Thank God for creating such a magnificent world and for watching over your life.

Let us throw off everything that hinders and the sin that so easily entangles, and let us run with perseverance the race marked out for us. —HEBREWS 12:1b

None equaled Suzy Favor as a collegiate middle distance runner. In 1990, the NCAA outdoor track and field meet took place at Duke University. On the first day of competition, the University of Wisconsin star competed in the 800-meter race for the first time.

Favor not only captured the 800 crown, she also set an NCAA record. The senior's time of 1 minute 59.11 seconds broke Karen Bakewell's mark of 2:00.85.

But the collegian didn't stop. The following day, Favor ran the 1,500-meter. On the last lap, she pulled away on the final straightaway to best Tennessee's Jasmin Jones by 7 meters.

The defending champion captured her 4th consecutive NCAA 1500-meter title. She clocked the course in 4:08.26, setting another NCAA mark.

Favor's 2 titles in her final collegiate meet gave her a total of 9 over her four-year career. In 56 NCAA races, the Wisconsin runner won 54. Favor never lost in her final 40 competitions.

The 800 and 1,500-meter races demand perseverance. Suzy threw off everything that would hold her back and ran. She focused on the finish and broke the tape.

Runners look for every advantage. They choose lightweight shoes and wear minimal clothing. Some even cut their hair to lessen wind resistance.

The writer of Hebrews compared life to a race that God has marked out for us. Our Heavenly Father wants us to get rid of everything that would keep us from running His race and focus on the Christian life.

Wear heavy clothes and shoes and walk 400 meters. Then change to lightweight clothing and shoes. Walk the last 400 meters. Could you feel the difference? Thank God for the race He has marked for you. Ask Him to help you get rid of everything that would hold you back.

"Go into all the world and preach the good news to all creation." —**MARK 16:15**

In 1991, National Football League owners decided to experiment with football in Europe. They created the World League of American Football and placed teams in London, England; Barcelona, Spain; and Frankfurt, Germany.

The London Monarchs and Barcelona Dragons met in the first WLAF championship in England's Wembley Stadium. Over 61,100 European fans attended, just 838 less than the crowd at Super Bowl I.

Monarchs quarterback Stan Gelbaugh threw two first-half touchdown passes. Dan Crossman intercepted three Dragon passes, returning one 20 yards for a touchdown.

London defeated Barcelona 21–0, avenging its only loss of the season. Coach Larry Kennan proclaimed the Monarchs "Champions of the World."

Although football has not yet expanded past Europe, people on every continent watch or listen to NFL Football, especially the playoffs and the Super Bowl. Announcers broadcast the games in a multitude of languages.

Many people around the world already know about Jesus. But most people do not. Christ's command to tell everyone the Good News of His salvation is for us today just as it was for His disciples in His day.

A few of us may be called as missionaries to serve in the far corners of the world. But the world has come to us. Millions travel in the United States for business or pleasure every year. Thousands attend our colleges and universities. Others move to our country to work temporarily or to live permanently. Nearly 100 languages are spoken in large metropolitan school districts such as Houston, Texas.

If you know an international who lives in your community, be especially friendly. Invite him or her to join your family for a baseball or softball game or to attend a church or community program. Look for ways to tell the person about Jesus. Ask God to help you be sensitive to cultural differences as you make friends.

The Lord will sustain him on his sickbed and restore him from his bed of illness. —**PSALM 41:3**

The Utah Jazz had backed the Chicago Bulls into a corner. After Chicago opened the 1997 National Basketball Association finals with two wins, Utah rebounded to even the series. Game five would give either the Jazz or the Bulls the lead.

Chicago's Michael Jordan missed the morning practice with food poisoning. He spent the entire day in bed with an upset stomach but dragged himself to the arena and donned his familiar number 23.

Utah played as if it were the final game. The Jazz soared to a 21–8 lead and increased the margin to 16 before Jordan roared to life.

His Airness netted 17 points in the second quarter, and the Bulls briefly took the lead. The Jazz countered and led at the half, 53–49.

Michael scored only 2 points in the third as the Jazz upped its margin by one, 72–67. He seemed almost dehydrated.

Jordan canned 7 points in the first 3 minutes of the fourth quarter. He totaled 15 in the final period and hit 3 with 25 seconds remaining to put the Bulls in front for good. The ill man played 44 minutes and collected 38 points in Chicago's 90–88 victory.

Neither his teammates nor his opponents could explain how he did it. He was obviously sick and could barely get out bed. Some of the Bulls didn't expect the future Hall of Famer at the arena. They surely didn't expect his performance.

God promises that He will take care of us when we are sick. The illness may be physical. Or we may feel bad because of something we've done or haven't done. Either way, God can sustain us.

Take inventory of your family's first aid kit. Get rid of expired items. Make a list of things necessary to restore it. Then, make a list of things God does to restore you each day.

Is not wisdom found among the aged? Does not long life bring understanding? —JOB 12:12

Nolan Ryan's back still ached. The hard-throwing right-hander had come off the disabled list only five days earlier. But on a cool summer evening in 1990, the Texas Rangers called on their ace to challenge the world champion Oakland Athletics.

The rest seemed to improve Ryan's pitching. His fastball exploded to the plate, and his curveball broke sharply. The 33,436 A's fans watching the future Hall of Famer sensed history in the making.

Through six innings, Big Tex allowed no hits and walked two. Julio Franco and John Russell homered to give Texas a 5-run cushion. In the seventh, the fireballer retired the side in order, striking out Ron Hassey and Felix Jose.

Ryan's back stiffened, but he refused to quit. His son and Ranger batboy, Reese, massaged and offered encouragement.

The Ryan Express chugged through the eighth. In the ninth, pinch hitter Ken Phelps led off and struck out. Next came speedster Rickey Henderson. The hard-throwing righty worked the count to 2–2. Henderson tapped the next pitch, a curveball, slowly to short. Jeff Huson charged and threw out the swift runner.

One out remained. Veteran Willie Randolph stepped in. The second baseman lofted a shallow foul ball. Rightfielder Ruben Sierra gloved it. Nolan Ryan had made baseball history with no-hitter number six.

At age 43 years, 4 months, and 12 days, Ryan became the oldest man to pitch a no-hit major league game and the only pitcher to achieve the feat in three separate decades.

Just like Nolan Ryan, older people have accumulated vast knowledge. Past experiences give them insight and wisdom.

God has been around for eternity. When we need answers, He has the answers.

Spend some time chatting with an older person. Ask about his childhood, schooling, work, and church. Compare his experiences with yours. Ask God to help you gain wisdom from his experiences and your own.

Yet their Redeemer is strong; the Lord Almighty is his name. He will vigorously defend their cause so that he may bring rest to their land. —JEREMIAH 50:34a

A defensive struggle keeps every hockey fan on the edge of his seat. The excitement builds with each passing moment. The Colorado Avalanche held a 3-0 lead over the Florida Panthers going into game four of the 1996 National Hockey League finals. The Panthers were determined to avoid the sweep, especially with the game on their home ice.

The first period closed with no scoring. Colorado goalie Patrick Roy stopped 10 shots. His Florida counterpart John Vanbiesbrouck blocked 9.

The offenses fared no better in period two. Roy's blocked shot total increased to 27, and Vanbiesbrouck tallied 19.

The crowd grew anxious as the minutes ticked off. A single goal could win the game especially with the determined defenses. When the clock finally flashed 0:00, the scoreboard still read Avalanche 0, Panthers 0.

In overtime, both teams fought hard. But the offenses failed to score.

The contest went into a second overtime. The goalies continued their brilliant play. Roy blocked an incredible 18 shots on goal.

A third overtime began. The deadlock had to end. Uwe Krupp's wrist shot snaked its way through traffic and found the net at 4:31. Patrick Roy had stopped the puck 63 times, and the Stanley Cup belonged to the Avalanche.

Roy turned in one of the greatest defensive efforts in NHL history, but no defender is greater than the Lord. He protects us every day.

It's not easy to think of God as a defender. We tend to picture Him far removed from our daily lives. But He is really quite near.

There are many ways to grow closer to the Lord. Family or personal devotionals, Bible study, church attendance, worship, and prayer develop our relationships with Him.

List as many names of God as you can. Thank God for His role as defender.

"To whom will you compare me? Or who is my equal?"
says the Holy One.— ISAIAH 40:25

Since the founding of the American League in 1901, the two major baseball leagues have met only in the World Series. But in 1997, baseball owners decided to experiment with interleague games during the regular season.

The Texas Rangers hosted the San Francisco Giants in the first American–National League matchup. The media and fans flocked to the Ballpark in Arlington for the historic occasion. Giant great Willie Mays and Ranger legend Nolan Ryan together threw out the ceremonial first pitch.

Umpires applied the rules of the home team. Since the Rangers play in the American League, both teams could use a designated hitter. Giant manager Dusty Baker moved his regular right fielder Glenallen Hill to DH and slotted backup Stan Javier in right field. The switch proved to be shrewd.

Javier tied the game with a second-inning solo home run and drove in the go-ahead run with a seventh-inning double. San Francisco won baseball's first-ever interleague regular season game over Texas, 3–1.

Baseball fans usually prefer one league over the other. They think the National Leaguers or American Leaguers play better ball. AL fans believe using a DH makes for added excitement. Those who are pro-NL feel the DH isn't pure baseball and lessens strategy.

Comparing the two leagues is easy, especially when they play head-to-head. Each side has good reasons why theirs is the best.

But one thing is certain. There is no argument about God. No one can touch Him. None even compare.

Chat with another sports fan. Compare your ideas about the best all-time baseball teams and players. Do you agree? Praise God for His matchless greatness.

You were wearied by all your ways, but you would not say, "It is hopeless." You found renewal of your strength, and so you did not faint. —ISAIAH 57:10

The Chicago Bulls entered the 1992 playoffs with hopes of a repeat. The previous year, they had waltzed to their first National Basketball Association title with a 15–2 playoff record.

After posting 67 regular season wins, Chicago encountered surprising difficulties. The New York Knicks pushed the Bulls to seven games in the Eastern Conference semifinals. It took the Bulls six games to eliminate Cleveland in the conference finals.

The Portland Trailblazers emerged from the West. In game two, they shocked Chicago with a 115–104 overtime win on the Bulls' home court. But the Bulls took two of three in Oregon to return home with an edge.

The Trailblazers attacked and led 79–64 at the end of three quarters. Bulls coach Phil Jackson stunned the crowd by benching four starters. But the reserves and Scottie Pippen outscored the Blazers 14–2, shifting the momentum.

Michael Jordan reentered with 8:38 remaining. Number 23 electrified the 18,676 fans. He hit 12 of his 33 points in the final 5 minutes to lift the Bulls to a 97–93 victory. Chicago joined the Lakers, Celtics, and Pistons as the NBA's only repeat champions.

The coach made a risky move. Why would anyone bench Michael Jordan? Perhaps the coach believed his starters were tired and needed rest. Maybe he wanted to give them a wake-up call or to put a better matchup on the court. It's possible he saw the substitution as his last hope.

Whatever the reason, the move worked. The action renewed the Bulls. The stronger team won.

Sometimes situations in life seem hopeless. When that happens, God helps us find creative solutions. All we have to do is ask.

Put yourself in Coach Jackson's place. Think of three possible actions he could have taken. What would you have done? Thank God for creative solutions to problems.

I write to you, young men, because you are strong, and the word of God lives in you. —1 JOHN 2:14b

Experience often bests youth in tennis. In 1989, 17-year-old Michael Chang faced Stefan Edberg in the French Open finals. Odds favored Edberg. No one so young had won a Grand Slam. No American had triumphed at Roland Garros since Tony Trabert in 1955.

Chang reached the finals through determination. He suffered from leg cramps and fell behind Ivan Lendl in the fourth round.

In the semifinals, the teenager had met Andrei Chesnokov. Chang eventually won in 4 hours, 5 minutes. The young American suffered heat exhaustion and had to be carried to the locker room.

Now, in the finals, Edberg pushed his opponent to the brink of elimination. Behind two sets to one, Chang survived 10 break points. He rallied to win 6–4.

In the final set, the youthful pro took command. He defeated the Swede 6–2 to claim the title. At age 17 years, 3 months, Chang became the youngest Grand Slam winner in tennis history.

Michael Chang won the French Open through strength and dedication. In the Bible, John wrote his first letter to both young and old. He wrote to the young because they were strong and dedicated to God.

But even the young must be on guard. Michael Chang suffered heat exhaustion. Young Christians may suffer exhaustion and burnout from overinvolvement. Michael Chang had to be assisted off the court. Young Christians may need help to stay on God's path.

Review the following symptoms of heat exhaustion (two or more are usually present): pale, cool, and clammy skin; dry mouth; dizziness; weakness and fatigue; headache; nausea, sometimes with vomiting; weak, rapid pulse; muscle cramps.

First aid for heat exhaustion includes lying down in a cool place indoors or in the shade; drinking fluids like cool or cold water or a sports drink with salt; and eating saltine crackers or other salty foods.

How many of the above treatments could apply to your Christian life when you are exhausted? Ask God to keep you strong in your dedication to Him.

Above all, love each other deeply, because love covers over a multitude of sins. —1 PETER 4:8

Over the years, baseball fans and batters saw a multitude of strange pitches from knuckleballer Charlie Hough. But the tables turned on the soft-tossing pitcher in 1986.

The Texas Rangers pitcher baffled the California Angels for eight innings. Hough held the Angels hitless and entered the bottom of the ninth leading, 1–0.

With one out, California pinch hitter Jack Howell lofted a pitch down the left field line. George Wright, a defensive replacement, raced from left-center for the catch. But Wright overran the ball, and it bounced off his glove for a three-base error.

Wally Joyner singled to right-center, breaking up the no-hitter and tying the score. Joyner moved to second on a passed ball, but Doug DeCines struck out.

The contest should have gone into extra innings. George Hendricks struck out, but catcher Orlando Mercado allowed the ball to skip away. It rolled too far from the plate for Mercado to throw Hendricks out at first.

Joyner rounded third and saw Hough standing like a statue on the mound. With no one covering the plate, the Angel first baseman motored home with the winning run.

It's a sin in baseball to let the ball get past the catcher. But covering the plate prevents the opposition from scoring an easy run.

Love also covers many wrongs. They still hurt, but loving those who commit wrong can put them on the right track.

God loves us deeply. And with God's love and assistance, we can overcome sin.

Recall a time you wronged someone you loved. Think about the hurt you caused. Apologize if you have not already done so. Pray for forgiveness of past wrongs and for strength to prevent future ones.

Whatever happens, conduct yourselves in a manner worthy of the gospel of Christ. Then, whether I come and see you or only hear about you in my absence, I will know that you stand firm in one spirit, contending as one man for the faith of the gospel without being frightened in any way by those who oppose you. —PHILIPPIANS 1:27-28a

The Oakmont Country Club in Oakmont, Pennsylvania, favored low scores in the 1973 U.S. Open. Johnny Miller's third-round 76 removed nearly all hope of a title. His three-day total of 216 left the Californian 6 strokes back, trailing twelve competitors.

Low clouds and high humidity kept the greens soft for the final round. The former Brigham Young collegian opened his Sunday round brilliantly, with four birdies. Miller continued his red-hot play with birdies at 9, 11, 12, 13, and 15.

The blond golfer fired a record 63 in the final round. Due to his early tee time, Miller finished an hour ahead of the leaders.

As Miller waited in the clubhouse, the others fell. His final challenger, John Schlee, missed a birdie on 18 and finished one stroke behind. The California golfer captured the U.S. Open title with one of the sport's greatest closing rounds.

Though far behind, Johnny Miller conducted himself like a champion. He seemed unafraid of his opposition and contended. He proved himself worthy of the victory.

In Paul's letter to the Philippians, he urged them to conduct themselves in a manner worthy of Christ. He asked that they contend for their faith without fear. And he wanted what he heard about them to be good.

We should live our lives the same way. Our words and actions should be such that whatever others hear about us is worthy of Christ.

Think about two people you know, one with a good reputation and one whose is questionable. Make a mental note or written list of what led to each. Ask God to help you always think and act in a manner worthy of being a Christian.

Follow my example, as I follow the example of Christ.

— 1 CORINTHIANS 11:1

Joe Cronin quit playing baseball regularly following the 1941 season. He focused on managing the Boston Red Sox but occasionally pinch hit. In 1943, the Hall of Fame shortstop set an example for his team to follow.

Boston hosted the Philadelphia Athletics in the final 2 games of a 5-game series. Two days earlier in the first contest, Cronin had belted a 3-run pinch-hit home run.

Philadelphia led 4–1 in the first game of the Bunker Hill Day doubleheader. The Red Sox skipper batted for pitcher Lou Lucier with two on in the bottom of the seventh. The veteran drove the ball over the left field screen, tying the score. Boston rallied with a run in the ninth to take the opener, 5–4.

The Athletics cruised into the eighth inning of the twin bill's second half with an 8–4 margin. With Bobby Doerr and Lamar "Skeeter" Newsome on base, Cronin put himself in the lineup. The 36-year-old manager smacked his third pinch-hit 3-run homer in two days, cutting the A's margin to 8–7.

The Boston manager was willing to work hard and put his skills on the line for the team. He played a major role in the Red Sox success. Cronin set a worthy example for the players and the fans to follow. He practiced what he taught.

The Apostle Paul followed Christ's perfect example. In so doing, he became an example worth following. We should follow the examples of Paul and of Christ, always remembering that others will watch us and do what we do.

Whom do you admire and want to be like? Who admires you and wants to be like you? There probably is someone even if you don't know who it is. Ask God to help you be the kind of example others should follow.

I face daily the pressure of my concern for all the churches. —2 CORINTHIANS 11:28

Making a putt in a close golf match creates great pressure. In 1980, Detroit native Donna Caponi entered the final day of the Ladies Professional Golf Association championship with a 2-stroke lead. At the end of 17 holes, Caponi, Jerilyn Britz, and Pat Meyers moved into a three-way tie.

To make for a more exciting finish, officials shortened the last hole, a par 5, to 470 yards. In theory, a player could reach the green in 2 and card an eagle.

Britz hit a solid drive, forcing Caponi and Meyers to follow her lead. But her second shot clipped a tree and landed in the wet rough.

Caponi and Meyers played it safe. The coleaders hit short second shots and reached the green in 3.

Caponi, who had turned professional after high school graduation in 1965, made the best approach shot. Her ball landed 18 feet from the pin, lying slightly downhill.

The 5-foot-5-inch star sank the birdie putt. Britz and Meyers took pars as Caponi captured her second straight LPGA championship. Coupled with her two U.S. Women's Open titles, she became the first female golfer with four major championships.

The putting pressure must have been terrific, but Donna handled the stress with poise and calm. Her ball covered the 18 feet easily and dropped into the cup. Caponi had beaten two others on the final hole.

Pressure is a part of life. Sometimes it is applied by others. Often we create the stress ourselves. The Apostle Paul felt pressure. But the urgency came from God. The early Christian leader was concerned for the churches. His was healthy stress.

Find two envelopes. Lightly lick the first and gently put the flap down. Moisten the second thoroughly, and press firmly to make sure the flap closes well. Which one could lose its contents in the mail? Remember, some stress is necessary to make us strong. Thank God for the pressure He applies in our lives.

"For where two or three come together in my name, there am I with them." —MATTHEW 18:20

The Chicago Bulls met the Phoenix Suns in game six of the 1993 National Basketball Association finals. Chicago fans hoped for a third straight championship. The Bulls needed a final victory to bring the trophy home.

Both teams showed the effects of traveling 1,500 miles and playing two games in 48 hours. Phoenix, fueled by 19,023 fans, surged ahead 98–94. With under a minute remaining, however, Michael Jordan grabbed Frank Johnson's rebound. The superstar forward dribbled the length of the floor and effortlessly laid the ball in the basket to take the Bulls within 2.

The Suns brought the ball upcourt without calling time-out. Johnson dished the basketball to Dan Majerle. His 12-foot baseliner touched only air. The Bulls snared the ball and quickly stopped the clock.

With 13.1 seconds left, Jordan inbounded to B. J. Armstrong in the backcourt. Armstrong immediately passed it back, setting up the Bulls final shot. MJ dribbled toward midcourt and spotted Scottie Pippen.

Pippen drove the lane, then bounced a pass to Horace Grant. Grant looked, but instead of shooting, fired the ball to an open John Paxton just beyond the 3-point line.

Paxton's jumper popped the net and put Chicago ahead 99–98. Grant blocked a last-second Phoenix shot, and the Bulls brought a third straight NBA championship to Chicago.

The Bulls needed a full team effort for the three-peat. They entered the playoffs without the league's best record. The Suns held a home court advantage.

Sometimes as Christians we operate at a disadvantage. Nonbelievers poke fun at us. We get swept away by the popular crowd.

God recognized the pressures. The early church grew because believers found strength in fellowship. Today, we may shy away from involvement. Yet Christ reminded His followers He would be with us, especially when two or more gather in His name.

Review your church schedule. Examine the activities. How can you use your unique, God-given gifts to help out? You may be missing some wonderful opportunities.

Let your light shine before men, that they may see your good deeds and praise your Father in heaven.

—MATTHEW 5:16

The New York Mets hosted the Philadelphia Phillies in a 1964 Father's Day baseball doubleheader. Jim Bunning, the father of nine children, took the mound for the Phillies in the opener.

The Kentucky native breezed through the first two innings, retiring all six batters. With one out in the top of the third, Amado Samuel lined a smash toward short. Cookie Rojas leaped nearly 3 feet, snaring the drive for out number two.

In the following frame, Ron Hunt lofted a fly ball down the right field line. Outfielder Johnny Callison raced toward the chalk but had no chance for a catch. Fortunately, the ball landed just foul. Hunt worked the count full before striking out.

Bunning mowed down Met after Met. Staked to an early 2–0 lead, the right-hander experienced a final anxious moment in the eighth.

Hawk Taylor took a called third strike for the final out. But catcher Gus Triandos dropped the ball. He recovered and threw to first to end the inning.

The Shea Stadium crowd of 32,904 switched allegiance and cheered for Bunning in the bottom of the ninth. A foul out and two strikeouts completed baseball's eighth perfect game. The Phillie hurler received the perfect Father's Day gift.

Fathers like Jim Bunning play important roles in their children's lives. Our Father in heaven plays an important role in the lives of His children too. Just as earthly children strive to earn the praise of their fathers, we should also try to earn the praise of our Heavenly Father.

Write a special love note to your own father or to a father you admire. Thank him for the role he has played. Pray a prayer of praise to your Father in heaven.

Therefore, strengthen your feeble arms and weak knees.

—HEBREWS 12:12

No job in baseball demands more physically than catcher. The backstop must squat endlessly and endure the aches and pains of foul tips and collisions at the plate. In 1993, longtime American League catcher Carlton Fisk climbed to the top of games played behind the plate.

Fisk donned the catcher's gear in the major leagues with the Boston Red Sox in 1969. He exchanged Red Sox for White in 1981.

Throughout his career, the New England native accumulated records. Fisk heads the list for home runs by a catcher and home runs by players over age 40.

In 1993, the position's rigors caught up with the 45 year old. In Chicago's first 65 games, the veteran caught only 22. But when regular catcher Ron Karkovice injured his shoulder, the White Sox started Fisk in 3 straight games.

Game three put the future Hall of Famer first in games caught with 2,226. He edged runner-up Bob Boone by a single contest.

Six days later, Chicago quietly released its longtime star. He had the record, but he no longer had baseball.

For years Fisk strengthened his body and mind to catch. He developed an accurate arm, flexible knees, and steady concentration. He learned pitchers and batters. Fisk worked hard at hitting, too. Discipline made him successful longer than any other player at his position.

Success demands discipline. Whether it's sports or leading a Christian life, hard work pays off. In athletics, we must practice skills and follow instructions.

As Christians, we must read the Bible and practice its teachings. We must pray, worship, and listen to God.

Watch a baseball game on television or in person. Pay special attention to the catchers. Note their importance to their teams. Ask God to help you be as disciplined as a catcher.

Don't have anything to do with foolish and stupid arguments, because you know they produce quarrels.

—2 TIMOTHY 2:23

The Boston Red Sox hosted the Washington Senators in a 1917 baseball doubleheader. Babe Ruth drew the starting assignment for Boston in the first game.

Left-hander Ruth walked Ray Morgan to open the bottom of the first. Ruth argued the call violently with umpire Brick Owens and bumped him. The man in blue ejected the uncontrollable pitcher.

Manager Bill Carrigan brought in Ernie Shore to pitch for Ruth. He also substituted catcher Sam Agnew for Chester "Pinch" Thomas.

With number two hitter Eddie Foster at bat, Morgan broke for second. Agnew nailed the second baseman attempting to steal for the game's first out.

Of the 26 batters Shore faced, none reached base. He allowed no hits, no walks, and his fielders committed no errors. The substitute pitched 8 2/3 perfect innings and claimed a 4–0 win.

Ernie Shore didn't expect to enter the game so early. But Babe Ruth's argument put him in the spotlight.

Arguments rarely accomplish anything. Foolish quarrels accomplish even less. All Ruth's quarrel with the ump produced was ejection from the game. Ultimately Shore and the team benefited, but Ruth did not.

God's Word tells us that we should avoid silly arguments. Sometimes that may mean giving in. At other times, it simply means keeping our mouths shut.

Think back to the last time you argued with your best friend. Do you remember what it was about? What did the bickering accomplish? Have you asked your friend for forgiveness? Ask God to help you avoid quarreling.

"With his own hands he defends his cause. Oh, be his help against his foes!" **—DEUTERONOMY 33:7b**

A sparkling defensive play can ignite a baseball team. In 1997, Jim Edmonds lit up highlight films across the nation.

The Anaheim Angels visited the Kansas City Royals. In the bottom of the fifth of a 1–1 game, David Howard batted with two aboard for the Royals. The second baseman drove the ball over Edmonds' head to deep center field.

The Angel outfielder sprinted toward the wall. At the last second, Edmonds peeked over the brim of his cap. He glimpsed the ball falling from the sky.

The center fielder extended his body and lunged. He bellyflopped on the warning track. The ball landed in the webbing of his glove and bounced up. Edmonds, amazingly, grabbed the loose ball with his bare hand for the out.

In the top of the sixth, the defensive star came to bat. He doubled to score Darin Erstad and put the Angels in front. Anaheim added 4 more runs to defeat the Royals, 6–2.

Jim Edmonds used his own hands and his whole body to play defense. He defended his team. He was largely responsible for an important win.

God wants us to use our hands in service to Him and to aid those suffering from hunger, poverty, poor health, loneliness, and other problems. God will help us as we seek to defend His cause.

With a friend, practice catching fly balls. As you become comfortable with the skill, try some difficult catches. Ask God to help you use your hands to help others in difficult situations.

When Jesus spoke again to the people, he said, "I am the light of the world. Whoever follows me will never walk in darkness, but will have the light of life." —JOHN 8:12

No award has a more appropriate name than the World Cup. Every four years, millions watch their countries vie for soccer supremacy. In 1986, Germany and Argentina faced off for soccer's ultimate trophy.

The favored South American team scored the first half's only goal. Jorge Luis Burruchaga lofted a high floating pass from a corner kick. The flight of the ball completely fooled German goalie Harald Schumacher. Jose Luis Brown timed his leap perfectly to head the ball into the net.

Early in the second half, Argentina added another goal. A pass from Hector Enrique to Jorge Valdano put the forward one-on-one against Schumacher. Valdano's kick sailed straight and true.

But the Germans rallied to tie 2–2. The European squad focused on containing Argentina's star midfielder, Diego Armando Maradona. With 6 minutes to play, Maradona broke free of his defender, Lothar Matthaeus.

The midfielder spied Burruchaga in the clear. Maradona made a perfect pass. The forward dribbled downfield, beat Schumacher to the corner, and delicately tapped the ball into the net. Argentina held on for a 3–2 victory and captured the country's second World Cup.

In 1986, Argentina became the light of the soccer world. The win brought the Argentine stars fame in their native country for a short time.

But Jesus is the Light of the world, always and forever. He takes our lives out of the darkness of sin and death and brings them to the brightness of hope and eternal life.

Experiment with several light bulbs in a reading lamp. Use 25-, 60-, 75-, and 100-watt bulbs. How well can you read with each? Remember, Christ is the brightest light of all time.

> Train yourself to be godly. For physical training is of some value, but godliness has value for all things.

—1 TIMOTHY 4:7-8

The College World Series showcases the finest collegiate baseball talent. The best and the brightest have played in the event since its inception in 1948.

The first championship series pitted the winners of East and West regional tournaments in Kalamazoo, Michigan. The Yale University Bulldogs emerged from a field of New York University, Illinois, and Clemson. The University of California Golden Bears won over Texas, Oklahoma, and the University of Denver.

Future American Leaguer Jackie Jensen paced the California team. None of the Yale squad made it to the majors, but in 1988, first baseman George Bush won the U.S. presidency.

The Golden Bears routed the Bulldogs 17–4 in game one of the best of three series. Cal led 7–2 after four innings in game two. But Yale tied the contest in the sixth.

California scratched a seventh inning run to provide the margin in an 8–7 victory. The Golden Bears captured the first NCAA baseball crown, two games to none over Yale University.

Future president George Bush and all the players trained themselves physically. Their efforts took them to the 1948 Collegiate World Series. But the baseball glory lasted a short time. Their godliness and character lasted a lifetime.

How many athletes can you name who later became outstanding outside their sports? Use a sports encyclopedia or the Internet if you wish, or discuss the question with a group of friends. Ask God to help you train both physically and spiritually.

The lowly will be exalted and the exalted will be brought low. —EZEKIEL 21:26b

Jim Courier had his sights set on winning the tennis Grand Slam in 1992. Victories in the Australian and French Opens put him halfway to the goal.

Courier faced tennis' 193rd-ranked player, Andrei Olhovskiy of Russia, in the third round at Wimbledon. Fans who had waited all night for tickets expected a quick match. But the underdog played with ease and grace. The former Russian junior champion took the first set 6–4.

The top seed rebounded in set two, winning by an identical 6–4 score. Olhovskiy's zipping serves and volleys, however, kept Courier at bay. The Russian who trained on the synthetic courts of the Central Red Army captured sets three and four by the same 6–4 margin. Courier became the first number one player to lose to a qualifier at the British tournament. The monumental upset dashed Courier's Grand Slam aspirations. What happened? Was Courier overconfident? Did he take the young Andrei lightly? Was he so busy basking in glory he forgot the moment? Or did he just have a bad day?

What about Olhovskiy? Did he simply play the match of his life? Did he carefully study Courier's weaknesses? Or did he win because he had nothing to lose?

Whatever the reason, the champion fell, and the lowly player won. Some people are naturally exalted. They're great athletes. They're smart. They're popular and win all the awards.

But in God's kingdom, earth's exaltation fades. Honesty, obedience, kindness, mercy, friendship, truth, and love bring glory. God's standards measure differently from man's.

List the qualities that make someone popular. Then list the qualities you want in a friend. Which would God exalt? Ask Him to help you live up to His standards rather than man's.

Do not be surprised at the painful trial you are suffering, as though something strange were happening to you.

—I PETER 4:12

For the 1992 Olympics, a major shoe company planned to showcase American decathletes Dan O'Brien and Dave Johnson. They ran "Dan or Dave?" promos before the Olympic team was set.

Through the first seven events at the trials, O'Brien captured four first places. He led the field on pace to break the world record.

In the pole vault, O'Brien passed on the first four heights. He opened at 15 feet, 9 inches but bailed out.

He knocked the bar off on his way down on the second try. On the final attempt, the decathlon champion sailed under the bar. The zero score put him in eleventh place overall. On the other hand, Dave Johnson earned points in all events and a spot on the United States team.

If the American record holder had cleared 15 feet, 9 inches, he would have scored 849 more points and won the event by 56. Had he vaulted 14 feet, 5 1/4 inches, the 424 additional points would have been sufficient for third. As it was, decathlete Dan O'Brien missed an opportunity to compete for the gold.

The strange turn of events surprised Dan, Dave, and the entire sports world. The shoe company lost millions in commercials already filmed and fees already paid.

The trials proved painful for O'Brien. He suffered through an event he had mastered. He sat home when the team competed in Barcelona.

Some days strange and painful things happen. We make a wrong choice. We try, but we miss. Our normally successful efforts fall just short. We're the last one cut from the squad.

God warned us about those times. But He also promised to see us through. Four years later in Atlanta, Dan O'Brien captured Olympic gold.

Picture yourself four years from now. Imagine where you'll be and what you'll be doing. Ask God to guide you every step of the way.

For the eyes of the Lord are on the righteous and his ears are attentive to their prayer. —1 PETER 3:12

Interleague baseball play in 1997 forced American League pitchers to hit in National League ballparks. Analysts believed they wouldn't have a prayer.

The Texas Rangers visited Dodger Stadium. Los Angeles pitcher Ismael Valdes and Ranger Bobby Witt hooked up in a classic pitcher's duel. Texas scratched out the game's first run in the fifth.

With the 1–0 lead, Witt stepped to the plate in the sixth. Mickey Tettleton had just advised the pitcher to "swing hard in case you hit it." The right-hander felt confident having swung the bat with the Florida Marlins.

The Texas hurler never bothered to look over Valdes' pitches. He lined the very first one over the left centerfield wall to up the Ranger margin to 2–0.

The Ranger starter went eight innings before giving way to stopper John Wetteland. Texas won 3–2.

Witt became the first American League pitcher to hit a home run in 25 years. Baltimore's Roric Harrison had collected one on the final day of the 1972 season. The designated hitter rule had taken effect the following year.

Bobby Witt's swing was both powerful and effective. Witt approached the plate with the right attitude. Critics had to eat their words at the sight of the 398-foot shot.

For Christians, prayer is both powerful and effective if we ask sincerely with the right attitude. God sometimes answers yes. At other times He says no. Occasionally He lets us wait or gives us something we could not have imagined.

Go to a quiet place outside if possible. Talk to God or write a letter to Him. Use the following acrostic to guide your prayer:
Praise God for His creation, His love, and His power.
Ask for forgiveness for what you've done wrong or haven't done right.
Request God's help for yourself and others. Be specific.
Thank God for past and future answers to your prayers.

Everyone who wants to live a godly life in Christ Jesus will be persecuted, while evil men and impostors will go from bad to worse, deceiving and being deceived. —2 TIMOTHY 3:12-13

Stan Musial, Hall of Fame outfielder for the St. Louis Cardinals, had a long and illustrious career. He collected 3,630 hits, 475 home runs, and 1,951 RBIs in 22 seasons. But in 1959, he was deceived.

The Chicago Cubs and Cardinals faced off in Wrigley Field. Musial batted against Bob Anderson. With the count at 3–1, Anderson's pitch bounced past catcher Sammy Taylor. Vic Delmore, the home plate umpire, called "Ball Four."

Rather than retrieve the baseball, Taylor argued the call. "The pitch hit Musial's bat," he tiraded, "and should be strike two not ball four."

Stan the Man noticed the ball lying loose. Since time had not been called, he alertly rounded first and headed for second.

Meanwhile, Delmore, Taylor, and Anderson settled their differences. The umpire absentmindedly handed the pitcher a new ball, forgetting the old one was still in play.

Anderson noticed Musial approaching second base. He heaved the ball toward the bag, but the throw sailed into center field.

The Cardinal Hall of Famer took off for third. But Alvin Dark, an observant third baseman, had retrieved the original horsehide. He fired it to shortstop Ernie Banks. Musial ran straight into Bank's tag.

Confusion reigned. After a lengthy conference, the umpiring crew ruled Musial out. He was tagged with the ball officially in play. The second ball was nothing more than a deception.

Like Stan Musial, we sometimes find ourselves deceived, especially when life becomes confused. Yet God is not a God of confusion but of order. He is not a God of deception but of honesty.

Call a good-natured friend or relative on the phone. Try to disguise your voice. Give clues to who you are. How did she react to your deception? How do you react when someone tricks you? Ask God to keep you from being deceived by evil.

He who doubts is like a wave of the sea, blown and tossed by the wind. —JAMES 1:6

Many call Chicago the "Windy City." In 1990, the Comiskey Park breezes affected New York Yankee pitcher Andy Hawkins.

The right-hander pitched 7 2/3 innings without allowing the Chicago White Sox a hit. But neither Chicago nor New York could put a run on the scoreboard.

Sammy Sosa of the White Sox reached first on Mike Blowers' two-out error in the bottom of the eighth. Yankee Hawkins walked Ozzie Guillen and Lance Johnson to load the bases.

Robin Ventura hit a lazy fly ball to left. Rookie Jim Leyritz battled the sun and the swirling breeze. The Yankee outfielder dropped the ball for a three-base error as the runners raced home.

The next batter, Ivan Calderon, lofted a high fly to right. Outfielder Jesse Barfield misplayed it too, and Ventura scored the inning's fourth run.

New York went down in order in the ninth. Hawkins entered the record book as the second pitcher to lose a complete game no-hitter.

The baseball blew in the wind, and Leyritz couldn't make the catch. The wind continued to swirl, and Barfield missed the ball. Andy Hawkins lost the match.

Natural elements affect our lives. Hurricanes, tornadoes, high winds, hail, heavy waves, and floods can all harm us. In the Bible, James tells us doubts can damage us in the same way.

What should we do when we doubt? We must ask God for wisdom and have the faith to believe He will give it to us.

Read James 1:5-8. If you have doubts, pray for wisdom and then talk them over with your pastor or a trusted Christian friend or counselor. Ask God to give you assurance when you doubt.

for he has not despised or disdained the suffering of the afflicted one; he has not hidden his face from him but has listened to his cry for help. —PSALM 22:24

The Associated Press voted Mildred "Babe" Didrikson Zaharias the outstanding female athlete of the first half of the twentieth century. Not only did the Port Arthur, Texas, native possess amazing athletic ability, she also displayed great courage.

In 1953, Zaharias underwent cancer surgery. The winner of gold medals in the javelin and 80-meter hurdles in the 1932 Olympics faced uncertainty. But the two-time U.S. Women's Open champion returned to golf.

The 1954 Open took place at Salem Country Club in Peabody, Massachusetts. The 72-hole tournament spanned just two days.

Zaharias shot a 72 and 71 in her first two rounds. She moved into first by 7 strokes. On the second day, she carded a 73 on the morning 18 holes.

Visibly spent, Zaharias refused to quit. She managed two pars and three bogeys on the final 5 holes, finishing with a 75. Her 72-hole total 291 bested Betty Hicks by 12 strokes in capturing a third U.S. Open title. Cancer took her life two years later.

Babe was an amazing athlete. Though best known for her track-and-field and golf accomplishments, she also competed in tennis, basketball, baseball, diving, and swimming. As a child, she was nicknamed for Babe Ruth because of her many home runs. She helped found the Ladies Professional Golf Association (LPGA) and once won 17 straight tournaments.

But she suffered, competing in spite of pain and weakness. She wasn't at her best, but she was still better than most people even on their best days.

The psalmist tells us God hears us in our suffering. He loves us and supports us through sickness and disease. He keeps us going when we don't think we can.

If you're interested, read a book about Babe Didrikson Zaharias. She wrote an autobiography titled This Life I've Led. *Thank God for His presence in suffering.*

for the word of God is living and active. Sharper than any double-edged sword, it penetrates even to dividing soul and spirit, joints and marrow; it judges the thoughts and attitudes of the heart. —HEBREWS 4:12

Track fans call the 100-meter record holder the world's fastest man or woman. In 1983, two pacesetters emerged at virtually the same time.

America's best track athletes gathered at the National Sports Festival in Colorado Springs. Many complained about the lack of top performances. But the critics were silenced after the women's 100-meter dash.

Evelyn Ashford ran the straightaway in a blistering 10.79 seconds. The time edged Germany's Marlies Gohr's month-old record by .02 seconds.

When the UCLA sprinter learned of her record-breaking race, she ran a victory lap and collapsed, falling flat on her back and staring at the sky. But the stunned crowd and runner scarcely settled before another mark fell.

Only minutes later, Calvin Smith lined up for the men's 100. He scorched the track with a 9.93. The clocking bested track's oldest record, Jim Hines' mark of 9.95 set in the 1968 Mexico City Olympics.

The double records penetrated the crowd with excitement. They changed the thoughts and attitudes of the sportswriters who felt track performances had declined. In their hearts, U.S. runners were living and active again.

God's Word remains alive and active today. The Bible provides both loving and condemning words. Through it we learn how to live and the way to heaven. Scripture, when taken to heart, powerfully changes thoughts, attitudes, and actions.

Carefully look through your Bible. What are the two major divisions? Which four books contain the recorded words of Jesus? Where do you find the Ten Commandments? Thank God for the Bible. Commit to read at least a few verses every day.

The seventh time around, when the priests sounded the trumpet blast, Joshua commanded the people, "Shout! For the Lord has given you the city!" —JOSHUA 6:16

Americans have celebrated the Fourth of July with fireworks for over 200 years. In 1985, however, the rocket's red glare was delayed.

The Atlanta Braves hosted the New York Mets. Rain postponed the game's start for over two hours.

The contest went into extra innings tied at 8. The Mets went ahead 10–8 on Howard Johnson's 2-run homer in the top of the thirteenth. But Tom Gorman allowed a 2-out, 2-strike, 2-run home run to Brave Terry Harper, sending the marathon matchup to the fourteenth.

The Mets plated a run in the top of the eighteenth and appeared to have victory in hand. But with two outs and no other hitters available, Rick Camp batted. Amazingly, the reliever clubbed a home run, tying the score. Camp never registered another hit in the majors.

New York erupted for 5 runs in the nineteenth. Atlanta put 2 on the scoreboard in its half, but the rally fell short. The contest required 6 hours and 10 minutes to complete.

At 4:01 A.M., the Braves lit the fireworks display for a few hundred remaining diehards. The noise woke Atlanta residents who believed they heard exploding bombs and called police.

In the Bible's Book of Joshua, the residents of Jericho must have been startled too, to wake to loud noises. The trumpets blew. The Israelites shouted. The city walls collapsed, and God gave a victory.

In your Old Testament, read Joshua 6:1-20. Notice especially how victory came because the people were patient and followed the Lord's instructions exactly. Ask God for patience and the ability to follow His leading.

> Then Peter came to Jesus and asked, "Lord, how many times shall I forgive my brother when he sins against me? Up to seven times?" Jesus answered, "I tell you, not seven times, but seventy-seven times." —MATTHEW 18:21-22

The seven elements of the heptathlon challenge the best female athletes. The event tests the ability to run, sprint, hurdle, jump, and throw. In 1986, Jackie Joyner-Kersee tested herself.

The woman named after Jacqueline Kennedy competed in Moscow's Goodwill Games. Jackie set a first-day record with 4,151 points.

The sister of Al Joyner, 1984 Olympic triple jump gold medalist, continued her outstanding performance on day two. Heading into the final event, the 800-meter, the East St. Louis native needed a time of 2 minutes 24.64 seconds to break the world record.

Jackie ran an unbelievable 2:10.02 and received a wild ovation from the Russian fans. Her total of 7,148 points exceeded the previous record by 202 and won the hearts of the Russian people.

Joyner-Kersee competed seven times in an unforgiving athletic contest. Her efforts so impressed the Russian spectators that they forgave her for being a foreigner. They cheered her on and genuinely appreciated her performance.

Peter asked Jesus about forgiveness, too. The disciple wanted to know how many times he should forgive one person. Peter thought he was being generous by offering seven times. Jesus' surprise answer of seventy-seven wasn't meant to be a number to write down and keep up with. Instead, Christ could have answered, "As many times as necessary."

Forgiving isn't easy, but it's necessary not only for the forgiven but also for the forgiver. Harboring a grudge, seeking revenge, and dwelling on the past keeps the wronged person from moving forward. God wants us to forgive and move on.

Count out seventy-seven toothpicks or pennies. If there are wrongs you haven't forgiven, let them go as you pick up the items. Ask God to help you be a forgiving person.

May the God who gives endurance and encouragement give you a spirit of unity among yourselves as you follow Christ Jesus. —ROMANS 15:5

It takes a two-game margin to win a tennis set. Wimbledon Tournament rules prohibit tiebreakers in the final set. Theoretically, a match there could last forever. Spectators at the 1992 Wimbledon doubles finals probably thought that would happen.

John McEnroe and Michael Stich paired against Richey Reneberg and Jim Grabb, the fourth-ranked players. McEnroe and Stich lost the opening set 5–7, but rebounded to take set two 7–6.

Reneberg and Grabb went into the lead with a 6–3 victory in the third. But McEnroe and Stich evened the score with a second 7–6 tiebreaker win in the fourth.

With the match tied, the doubles teams prepared for the final decisive set without tiebreakers. Game after game neither gained an advantage. Darkness settled in with the game's score tied at 13. Officials halted the match.

In the ninth game of the second day, McEnroe and Stich broke their opponents' serve. When the match concluded at 19–17, Stich spontaneously lifted his partner into the air. The celebration delighted the capacity crowd. After 2 days, 5 hours, and 1 minute, the longest Wimbledon final was finally over in 83 games.

The winning twosome had entered the tournament not ranked. Both were known more for singles than doubles. But point after point, game after game, they endured. They encouraged each other. They played as one. McEnroe and Stich became more and more a unit.

Dissension can cause the greatest team to lose. Unity, loyalty, and encouraging each other can make a mediocre team winners.

The same holds true of a choir, Sunday School class, or church. A spirit of unity enables the group to accomplish Christ's goals.

Find a piece of rope and play tug-of-war with some friends or just think about the contest. Does the strongest team usually win? Or is it the one that pulls together? Ask God to help you be a team player.

Those who are wise will shine like the brightness of the heavens, and those who lead many to righteousness, like the stars forever and ever. —DANIEL 12:3

Baseball's All-Star game has been played since 1933. The contest marks the midpoint of the season and allows fans to see the sport's best both in combination and competition.

Chicago Tribune sportswriter Arch Ward arranged the initial American League–National League matchup to coincide with the Century of Progress Exposition. A crowd of 47,595 ventured to Comiskey Park to watch their heroes in action. Legends Connie Mack and John McGraw managed the respective teams.

The American Leaguers struck first. Starting pitcher Lefty Gomez singled in the second, driving in Jimmie Dykes. In the third, aging superstar Babe Ruth hit a 2-run homer. Baseball's first 700-plus home run hitter also made a marvelous running catch of Chick Hafey's line drive in the eighth.

The Nationals narrowed the margin to 3-2 in the sixth with Frank Frisch's home run. But the AL countered with a run in the bottom of the inning and won the first midsummer classic, 4-2.

That day in Chicago, baseball stars shone brightly. The fans were grateful for the wisdom Ward displayed in beginning the tradition. Forever since 1933, the American and National League best have met.

But others besides athletes star in life. God's Word tells us that those who are wise shine brightly. People who lead others to Christ become heaven's stars forever and forever.

If you are a Christian, name the stars who led you to Jesus. Thank God for them, and if you can, tell them how much you appreciate their efforts. Begin to bring others to Christ yourself. If you don't yet follow God, talk to a minister or a Christian friend about accepting Him.

> The nations will see your righteousness, and all kings your glory; you will be called by a new name that the mouth of the Lord will bestow. —ISAIAH 62:2

Boris Becker brought a new face and new life to the 1985 Wimbledon tennis tournament. Although few recognized the German's name at the tournament's beginning, everyone knew him by the end.

The unranked player faced Kevin Curran in the men's final. Many expected Curran to defeat the 17 year old decisively because of previous wins over established players Jimmy Connors and John McEnroe.

But Becker handled the pressure like a veteran. He held service in the first set, winning 6–3.

Neither competitor suffered a service break in set two. Curran took the tiebreaker on a fine backhand passing shot.

Up 4–3 in the third set, Curran lost 3 points on serve. His lapse gave Becker the upper hand. The German forced a tiebreaker and took the lead with 6 straight points.

Curran appeared unnerved. Becker's bullet serves and volleys carried the Leimen native to a 6–4 victory and the singles title. The virtually unknown German became the youngest and only unranked player to capture a championship on Centre Court.

In the 1985 English tournament, old made way for new. Tennis gave rise to a fresh star, Boris Becker, as more established players fell. Sportswriters called a new name.

A similar event occurs when we choose to follow Christ. We become new people. We throw off our sinful selves and work to obey God's commands. We leave behind bad habits, questionable behavior, and poor influences. We get a new name—Christian. We begin to make right choices motivated by Jesus' love.

Practice your tennis backhand shots against a backboard or with a partner. Concentrate on making good choices on ball placement. Ask God to help you make good choices in life.

You will tread our sins underfoot and hurl all our iniquities into the depths of the sea. —MICAH 7:19

Baseball's second All-Star game moved to New York's Polo Grounds. The National League sought revenge against the American League for its previous defeat. The NL slated Giant ace Carl Hubbell as its starter.

The left-hander yielded a leadoff single to Charlie Gehringer and a walk to Heinie Manush. But Hubbell found a groove. Crosstown rivals Babe Ruth and Lou Gehrig and Philadelphia slugger Jimmie Foxx struck out in the first inning.

Chicago White Sox Al Simmons led off the bottom of the second. The outfielder went down on strikes for the first out. Washington shortstop Joe Cronin stepped up. King Carl put Cronin on the bench with strikeout number two.

Yankee catcher Bill Dickey singled to break Hubbell's string, but pitcher Lefty Gomez struck out to end the frame. The Giant pitcher struck out the side in two straight innings. Each victim later received enshrinement in Baseball's Hall of Fame.

What a performance by NL pitcher Carl Hubbell. Just imagine striking out six Hall of Famers in two innings: Babe Ruth, Lou Gehrig, Jimmie Foxx, Al Simmons, Joe Cronin, and Lefty Gomez. One or two would be quite an achievement for most pitchers.

God has the ability to strike out all evil. He can take our sins and throw them as far away as the deepest ocean. But the Lord waits to use that power until we ask.

Read about oceans in an encyclopedia or on the Internet. Note especially the depth of the deepest sea. Thank God for His power to remove our wrongs far from us.

"To whom will you compare me or count me equal? To whom will you liken me that we may be compared?"

—ISAIAH 46:5

Critics accuse women's tennis of lacking excitement. But in 1995, Steffi Graf and Arantxa Sanchez Vicario brought the staid Wimbledon crowd to celebration.

Sanchez Vicario opened the match with precision and focus. She captured the first set 6-4 in 30 minutes, losing only 4 points on serve.

Graf reversed course in set two, winning 6-1. With the match tied 1-1, the German and the Spaniard battled on even terms.

With the deciding third set tied 5-5, Sanchez Vicario served game 11. Neither competitor could gain the advantage. The two went to deuce 13 times in 20 minutes.

The players traded tense shots, with the Spaniard attacking the German's forehand and Graf defusing Sanchez Vicario's lobs with overhand smashes. Steffi faced 6 break points, and Arantxa had 8 game points.

After 44 serves in the humid conditions, Sanchez Vicario fell. Graf pinned her opponent into a corner with a deep forehand, and Arantxa's backhand failed to reach the net. Steffi served out the final game to take the set 7-5 and capture her 6th Wimbledon single's title.

That day, two tennis stars compared favorably to each other. Their games proved similar. Both played effectively. Theirs was a great match.

But none compares to God—not the greatest king or the most unselfish leader. The Lord alone is all-knowing, all-powerful, ever-present, and everlasting.

Compare all the schoolteachers you have had. Which ones were the best? Who taught you the most? Did one make learning fun? Praise God that He has no equal.

> "I am the Lord your God, who teaches you what is best for you, who directs you in the way you should go."

—ISAIAH 48:17

Golfers strive for a Grand Slam victory. The United States Open, the British Open, the Masters, and the Professional Golfers Association (PGA) tournament make up the coveted crowns. In 1970, Lee Trevino vied for the lead in the British Open.

Trevino held a 3-stroke edge over Jack Nicklaus, Doug Sanders, and Tony Jacklin after three rounds. His 207 total put him in excellent shape for the final 18 holes.

But Trevino faltered badly in the final round. The crowning blow occurred on the fifth hole. The fifth green at historic St. Andrews houses two cups for two separate holes.

As the Texas golfer lined up his approach, he looked at the wrong flag. The ball landed 80 feet away from the correct pin. Trevino slapped his head in dismay at his costly mistake.

The errant shot resulted in a bogey on the hole. Trevino never recovered. Nicklaus and Sanders passed him on the leader board and tied after four rounds. The Golden Bear, Jack Nicklaus, took the British Open in a playoff.

Lee Trevino lost sight of what was best for his golf game. He lacked direction in hitting his approach shot on the fifth hole. The golfer's failure to focus cost him a possible championship with its prestige and prize money.

God is not a god of confusion. If we let Him control our lives, we move in the right direction. Our Heavenly Father always leads us into what is best.

Take a walk in your neighborhood or in a nearby park. Use a compass to keep track of the direction you move. When you pray and read the Bible, listen for God's direction. Thank Him for always wanting what is best for you.

If anyone serves, he should do it with the strength God provides, so that in all things God may be praised through Jesus Christ. —**1 PETER 4:11**

Tennis stars Pete Sampras and Boris Becker both make bullet-like serves. When the two met in the 1995 Wimbledon finals, tennis balls flew fast and furious.

Two weeks of hard play and hot sun had baked Centre Court into a brickyard. The final featured quick points and short rallies. Only two lasted longer than five strokes.

Becker held serve in the first set, winning in a tiebreaker, 7–6. But Sampras took the loss hard and served with a vengeance.

The American blitzed the German in three straight sets, 6–2, 6–4, 6–2. Sampras recorded 23 aces in the match. Becker scored only 22 points in 22 games off his opponent's serve, 7 coming on double faults. The 23-year-old Sampras captured his 3rd consecutive Wimbledon title and 6th Grand Slam championship.

Sampras made incredible serves. They overpowered Becker and won the young champion praise.

God commands us to serve Him by serving others. Our Lord asks that we do good deeds with all our strength demonstrating an unselfish attitude. Then the praise goes to Jesus Christ and not to ourselves.

Spend an hour this week helping others. You might mow an elderly person's lawn, baby-sit for a young mother, run errands, visit in a hospital or a nursing home, or plan a special treat for your pastor or another church staff member. If the person offers to pay you or give you a gift, don't accept. Let the person know your good deed is service to God.

So do not throw away your confidence; it will be richly rewarded. —**HEBREWS 10:35**

There is no more imposing pitcher in baseball than Randy Johnson of the Seattle Mariners. The tall left-hander's blazing fastball makes the best hitters weak in the knees. But in 1997, Bobby Witt and the Texas Rangers neutralized the Big Unit with some power pitching and hitting of their own.

Johnson dominated the Texas batters. He struck out 14 before leaving the game in the seventh.

But in the fourth, Texas scratched out 2 runs on a walk and two doubles. Seattle matched the score with solo home runs by Paul Sorrento and Jay Buhner.

Lou Piniella inserted Bobby Ayala for Johnson. The reliever struck out the side in the top of the eighth.

The ninth, however, belonged to Texas. Damon Buford homered to lead off the inning, and Mark McLemore tripled. Ivan Rodriguez plated McLemore on a sacrifice fly.

John Wetteland shut the door on Seattle in the bottom of the ninth. The Mariners went down one, two, three, with Rob Ducey striking out to end the game.

Johnson, Ayala, Witt, Patterson, and Wetteland combined for 31 strikeouts. The total broke the record of 30 set by Seattle and Oakland in 1986.

The pitchers threw with confidence. Knowing they could do it led to a reward, the strikeout record.

Of course, there are some things we know are impossible, but *can't* is a sad word. Lack of confidence leads to not trying. Not trying breeds failure, both in athletics and in life.

God provides the ultimate in confidence. Through Him, we have the promise of forgiveness for the wrongs we do and the good we avoid. Through Him, we have assurance of eternal life in heaven. In Christ, we find the strength to try without fear of failure.

Try something new—a new food, a new sport, a new book, a new computer program, a new activity, or a new friend. Ask God to give you the confidence to try new things for Him.

The eye cannot say to the hand, "I don't need you!"
And the head cannot say to the feet, "I don't need you!"

—1 CORINTHIANS 12:21

What the rest of the world calls "football," Americans call "soccer." The United States has taken years to embrace "football" as a sport. "Football" has always been dominated by South America. However in 1995, the United States national team proved that it takes soccer seriously.

Twelve teams in three divisions played for the America Cup. Officials invited two non-South American countries, the United States and Mexico, simply to fill out the field.

Pretournament favorite Argentina engaged the Americans in the finals of the first round. The United States jumped on the two-time World Cup champion early.

Americans Frank Klopas and Alexi Lalas scored first-half goals. The undefeated Argentines, who had rested many of their starters, substituted furiously.

But the margin never narrowed. Eric Wynalda added a third goal in the second half. The Americans shut out the Pride of the Pampas, 3–0. The United States achieved only its second win in South America since 1930.

Probably more in soccer than in any other sport, a player needs all parts of his body. After seeing the ball, he moves it with his head, knees, feet, or shoulders, just about any body part except his hands. And he does use his hands on inbound plays.

God's church is the same way. He needs every person to worship, to pray, to learn, to minister in His name, and to do work.

Make a list of all jobs you can think of in your church. Could the pastor do them all? Could one or two people do them all? If you're not already involved, think of something you could do. Pray about volunteering. Thank God for giving every Christian a way to serve.

Your arm is endued with power; your hand is strong, your right hand exalted. —PSALM 89:13

Nothing approaches the baseball media circus of New York. Newspaper and television reporters appear everywhere asking countless questions.

Bo Jackson tried to avoid the distractions of the press in 1990. But a combination power hitter and National Football League running back like Jackson seldom goes unnoticed. The Kansas City Royal outfielder batted in the top of the first. New York Yankee pitcher Andy Hawkins threw an inside fastball on a 2–2 count. Jackson powered the ball over the 408-foot mark on the center-field wall.

Bo faced Hawkins again in the third. He looked for an outside pitch. The Yankee hurler threw one into Jackson's power zone. It landed 464 feet in right center field, the longest homer in Yankee Stadium that year.

The Royal outfielder batted again in the fifth. Amazingly, Hawkins still manned the mound. Jackson expected junk. The Yankee right-hander served a slider slightly out of the strike zone. Bo barely reached it, but the ball carried toward the right field wall. It finally cleared the fence for his third home run.

Jackson's 100th home run placed him on the brink of baseball history. Fewer than a dozen players had homered four times in a game, and none had ever clouted five.

Bo's chance never came. In the sixth, Jackson lunged for Deion Sanders' slicing fly. His body twisted in midair and fell awkwardly. The fall dislocated his shoulder, and the 3-homer man left the game.

Even a magnificent athlete like Bo Jackson can be injured. No one except God is invincible.

It's hard to accept mortality. People take unnecessary risks. Sometimes recklessness costs dearly.

A close relationship with God brings balance. We cherish life but realize at some point it will end. We find comfort in knowing when this life is over, we begin a new one with God.

Make a list of people you know who have died recently. Recall something special about each one. Thank God for their memory.

A wise man fears the Lord and shuns evil, but a fool is hotheaded and reckless. —**PROVERBS 14:16**

Hale Irwin remained high on the leader board after the first two rounds of the 1983 British Open. In round three, his ball rested 3 inches from the cup on the 14th hole. The cinch tap-in would result in a par.

The American golfer approached the ball casually. Rather than line up a putt, he swiped at it with the backhand of his two-sided club. Incredibly, the putter hit the ground and skipped over the ball without touching it. The miscue cost Irwin a stroke because his intent had been to hit the ball.

In Sunday's round the sheepish golfer finished before, but one stroke behind, Tom Watson. Irwin hoped Watson would birdie the last hole. He believed a two-stroke victory would make everyone forget Saturday's mistake.

Watson, however, made par and won by a single stroke. The careless putt cost Irwin a playoff spot and an opportunity for a Grand Slam championship.

Carelessness and recklessness almost always cost. Hotheads act or speak before they think. They damage property and friendships. Careless mistakes lead to poor grades, subpar performances, and lost income. Reckless driving leads to accidents.

God dislikes foolish behavior. He commands us to be wise and stay away from evil and recklessness. And if we fear the Lord, we will think before we act or speak.

Think of some things you do every day. Discuss with a friend how carelessness could be costly in doing the routine. Confess any carelessness in your life to God.

"Whoever believes in me, as the Scripture has said, streams of living water will flow from within him." —JOHN 7:38

Records usually fall in the 100-meters by hundredths of a second. In 1988, Florence Griffith-Joyner moved the decimal point.

The wife of Al Joyner, the 1984 triple jump gold medal winner, competed at the United States Olympic trials in Indianapolis. With her fashionably long fingernails and brightly colored outfits, energy flowed from Griffith-Joyner's body.

In a traditionally low-key quarterfinal heat, the sprinter took her mark. At race's end, Flo-Jo clocked a reading of 10.49 seconds.

The time bested Evelyn Ashford's four-year record by .27 second. Officials checked the wind gauge to verify the new mark would be accepted. The instrument read 0.00.

Observers felt the machinery malfunctioned, but Peter Huertzler, the Omega technician, certified the equipment. The International Amateur Athletic Federation ratified the record. Griffith-Joyner became the world's fastest woman.

Flo-Jo broke the world record by so much no one believed the automatic timer. But streams of energy and quickness seemed to flow from within the sprinter. The record held.

Jesus says that streams can flow from within us, too. Those streams come from Christ, Who gives us living water. If we believe in God, He will satisfy our thirst for right and give us the Holy Spirit to live within us and guide us.

Read in an encyclopedia or a Bible dictionary about the Dead Sea. If you live near a fountain, stream, or river, visit the water. Note the freshness and aliveness of the flowing water compared to the Dead Sea. Thank God for the living water He gives.

For a little while they are exalted, and then they are gone. —JOB 24:24

Nothing requires greater concentration than a hitting streak. In 1941, Joe DiMaggio kept his eye on the ball.

On May 15, the New York Yankee singled against the Chicago White Sox. Day by day, the center fielder continued to hit safely. The streak grew longer and longer.

DiMaggio had stroked hits in 56 consecutive games when New York engaged the Cleveland Indians. The string appeared to stretch to 57 as the outfielder smashed a hot grounder down the third base line. But Indian third baseman Ken Keltner backhanded the ball, wheeled, and threw true for the out.

Joltin' Joe walked in the fourth and hit another hot grounder in the seventh. Keltner fielded the ball and recorded another out.

The San Francisco native had a final at-bat in the eighth. But Lou Boudreau gloved his grounder up the middle and turned a double play. The hitting streak ended.

For more than two months, the world listened to the radio and read the newspaper anxiously watching Joe DiMaggio's hitting streak. For weeks after game 57, people talked about the hitter and exalted him. But then the Yankee Clipper entered fewer and fewer conversations. Finally he was gone from baseball.

In life, fame is fleeting. Today's sports hero becomes tomorrow's has-been. Few people live on in history books. But doing your best for God and trusting in Him lasts forever.

Without using Bible heroes, name as many famous people as you can who lived more than 1,000 years ago. Compare your list with a relative's or friend's. Praise God for His enduring exaltation.

"As for God, his way is perfect; the word of the Lord is flawless." —2 SAMUEL 22:31

Gymnastics judges score performances on a 10-point scale. A mark of 10 represents perfection. In the 1976 Montreal Olympics, fans witnessed perfection.

Fourteen-year-old Nadia Comaneci competed on the Romanian team. Analysts considered the 4-foot-11-inch teen a slight favorite.

In the first round, Comaneci stunned the world by receiving a 10 for her performance on the uneven parallel bars. No gymnast had ever achieved a perfect score.

The mark took Olympic officials completely by surprise. The electronic scoreboard, programmed to flash only three digits, read 1.00. But the capacity Forum crowd understood.

Comaneci's perfect form energized the entire field. During the fifteen days of competition, the Romanian registered seven 10s, and Russian gymnast Nellie Kim tallied two. Never had the world witnessed such a level of artistry and skill.

The electrifying gymnastics dazzled millions of television viewers and made Comaneci a folk hero. Nadia captured 5 medals: 3 golds in all-round, balance beam, and uneven bars, a silver in team competition, and a bronze in floor exercise.

The 1976 Olympic gymnastics 10s surprised the world. Perfection had always been an elusive goal, achieved only in theory but never in practice. Many in gymnastics circles felt the scores too high. They didn't believe perfection possible.

But God is always perfect. Period. No debate. The Bible, His Word, is flawless. Period. No argument.

Share with a friend your idea of a perfect vacation. Would you choose the beach or mountains, sports events or historic sites, activity or rest? Ask God to help you live as perfectly as possible.

Then you will lift up your face without shame; you will stand firm and without fear. . . . You will be secure, because there is hope; you will look about you and take rest in your safety. —JOB 11:15, 18

Justin Leonard seldom changes facial expression during a golf match. His work ethic and focus make him one of the world's brightest young golf stars. In the 1997 British Open, Leonard trailed the leader after three rounds by 5 strokes. Few considered him a serious contender for the title.

But the linkster from Dallas started the fourth round strong. He birdied six holes on the front nine. By the 12th, Leonard had narrowed the gap to 2.

The University of Texas alum sank a 15-foot putt on 16, moving into a tie for the lead. On the next hole, Leonard drilled another from 30 feet to pass Jesper Parnevik.

The 25 year old finished with a 6-under-par 65. Leonard's four-day total 272 bested runner-up Parnevik by 3 for the British Open title.

Even though he was behind, Justin's face didn't change expression. He stood firm and played without fear. His patience and preparation paid great rewards. Leonard held on to hope. The young golfer earned the victory and a well-deserved rest.

If we put our faith in the Lord, pray, read the Bible, and worship, we can stand firm in hope through Christ. We rest in the security of the Heavenly Father's love.

Warm up and spend thirty minutes or more exercising or playing a sport with a friend. Then rest. Thank God for security and rest.

The Spirit of God has made me; the breath of the Almighty gives me life. —JOB 33:4

As a youngster, Amy Van Dyken suffered from asthma. High school classmates considered her gangly and awkward. But at the 1996 Atlanta Olympics, the Colorado native swam with speed and grace.

After years of dominating, the American female swimmers slipped to second-class status in the 1988 and 1992 games. Few expected a stellar performance from the 1996 squad.

Van Dyken surprised everyone with a win in the 100-meter butterfly. The unexpected victory inspired the entire United States swimming team.

The 23 year old anchored the 4 x 100 freestyle relay and the 4 x 100 medley relay. The 6-foot swimmer propelled the teams to the gold. The freestyle tandem of Van Dyken, Beth Botsford, Amanda Beard, and Angel Martino set an Olympic record of 3 minutes 39.29 seconds.

The young woman from Colorado saved her best performance for the final night of competition. She zipped to an American record of 24.87 in the 50-meter freestyle, nipping China's Le Jingyi by .03 second for the gold. Van Dyken became the first American female athlete to capture four gold medals in a single Olympics.

The girl who had difficulty breathing, breathed life into American swimming. Amy overcame awkwardness to fly through the water for four golds. She became the swimmer God created her to be.

God made each of us and breathed His life into us. He created us for a purpose, His purpose. Our responsibility is to be all the Lord wants us to be.

If possible, go for a swim. Take a deep breath and swim as far as you can. Praise God for giving you life and a purpose.

He will endure as long as the sun, as long as the moon, through all generations. —PSALM 72:5

Emil Zatopek captured the 10,000-meter gold medal and the 5,000-meter silver in 1948. He repeated the 10K feat and won the 5K gold in 1952. But in the Helsinki games, the 30-year-old Czech also participated in the ultimate race.

Despite lacking experience, Zatopek ran the marathon. The Czechoslovakian Army major sought and shook the hand of world record holder Jim Peters prior to the race. The three-time gold medalist devised a simple strategy—follow Peters.

The rigorous pace exhausted Peters before the halfway point. Zatopek and Gustaf Jansson moved in front.

At the 20-mile mark, the Czech took the lead. He ran apart from the field, chatting with policemen and spectators along the route. Zatopek entered the stadium alone, and the crowd robustly chanted his name.

The runner set an Olympic marathon record of 2 hours, 23 minutes, 3.2 seconds. Zatopek could not walk for a week after his remarkable performance. He described the feeling as "the most pleasant exhaustion ever known."

Emil endured what few others could. He finished the marathon exhausted but a winner. The distance runner couldn't have gone much farther. Zatopek had reached the limit of his endurance.

But God has no such limit. He has existed through all the generations of the earth. He will endure as long as the sun glows and the stars shine.

Ask your oldest living relatives about your ancestors. Get them to tell you stories about their grandparents or as many generations back as they remember. Talk about their memories of church. Thank God for His endurance through all generations.

We writhed in pain, but we gave birth to the wind.

—ISAIAH 26:18

Records and medals often escape the memories of Olympic fans. But some images endure.

The 1996 United States women gymnasts dreamed of the team title, and they had a chance. The last of six competitors on the final apparatus, Kerri Strug felt her left ankle pop after her first vault. She limped down the runway, not even glancing at her mediocre score, a 9.162.

As she looked to her coach for guidance, Bela Karolyi shouted she needed a 9.6 on the second vault. Her teammates screamed, "You can do it!"

Strug approached the apparatus faster. The Houston native catapulted herself into the air, rotated one and a half times, and landed solidly.

With pain searing through her leg, the 4-foot-9-inch dynamo lifted her left foot a few inches to relieve some pressure. She held that pose until certain the judges properly registered her performance, a 9.712.

Medical personnel took Strug off the mat and onto a stretcher. Doctors cast her leg to immobilize the ankle.

Karolyi carried the 18 year old in his arms to the medal stand. Strug stood with her teammates as the United States gymnasts accepted their first team gold.

The pressure was on. The color of the U.S. medal came down to one vault by one gymnast. But Kerri Strug writhed in pain. The serious injury threatened to deny a once-in-a-lifetime chance.

Kerri chose to ignore her agony. She rushed down the runway and lifted like the wind. Though not a perfect 10, the vault was good enough for gold.

Sometimes in life we face pain. The agony may be physical or it might be emotional. Either way, God gives the courage to move through like a wind across the earth—sometimes gently, sometimes in a gust.

Experiment with a fan. Stand where you can feel the breeze. Change fan speeds and rotation. Notice the differences on your skin and hair. Thank God for moving us through pain.

"Woe to you experts in the law, because you have taken away the key to knowledge." —**LUKE 11:52a**

In 1983, New York Yankee manager Billy Martin summoned ace reliever Goose Gossage. New York clung to a 4–3 lead, but the Kansas City Royals had a runner on first and George Brett at bat.

The All Star third baseman drove Gossage's pitch into the right-field stands. But Kansas City's jubilation evaporated.

Martin bolted from the dugout the moment Brett touched home. He remembered an obscure rule stating no more than 18 inches of pine tar, a sticky substance to improve a batter's grip, was allowed. Any excess made the equipment illegal and the hitter out.

The Yankee field general picked up Brett's bat and showed it to umpire Tim McClelland. Martin claimed the batter was out and the game over.

McClelland called in crew chief Joe Brinkman. The head umpire measured against the 17-inch width of home plate. The pine tar definitely exceeded the limit. Brinkman called the third baseman out.

Brett went ballistic. The field eventually cleared, and the Yankees walked away winners.

American League president Lee MacPhail reviewed the controversy. Four days later, he surprisingly reversed Brinkman's decision. MacPhail allowed Brett's homer to stand and declared the game suspended.

New York and Kansas City met again on August 18. Four men, one Royal and three Yankees, batted and made outs. Brett's team finally emerged victorious twenty-four days after his home run.

Christians tend to judge others by very strict standards. Like Billy Martin, they know all the rules and want them enforced. Sometimes, however, the big picture overshadows individual points of law.

Jesus recognized this trait among the Jewish religious leaders. They practiced the rules of faith but lost sight of the meaning.

Review last week's church service. Did you think about the message of the hymns or mindlessly mouth the words? Did you listen to the pastor's sermon or did your mind drift? Ask God to help you find meaning instead of motions.

Then you will find your joy in the Lord, and I will cause you to ride on the heights of the land. —ISAIAH 58:14a

An American in Paris often finds distractions. But in 1989, Greg LeMond focused solely on riding to the heights.

The 1986 winner of the Tour de France bicycle race entered the final day of the 22-day event in second place. He trailed the leader, France's Laurent Fignon, by 50 seconds.

No one believed a margin that large could be overcome. But LeMond refused to accept what everyone else took as fact.

The Reno, Nevada, native declined to have the pace cars call out his time splits. He concentrated completely on the finish line.

LeMond finished the 15-mile course in 26 minutes, 57 seconds. Fignon fell to 27:55.

The American totaled 87 hours, 38 minutes, 35 seconds for the 21-stage, 2,030-mile marathon. LeMond nipped the Frenchman by 8 seconds, the closest margin in 76 years of competition.

Greg LeMond found great joy in his performance. He rode to the heights of victory.

Sports and athletics lead to satisfaction. Participants, coaches, and fans enjoy the competition. Some even reach the heights of fame.

But we can find even greater joy in knowing Christ. Worship takes us to the heights with God.

Discuss with a Christian friend or relative your favorite ways to worship God. Your list might include music, drama, prayer, sermons, or quiet thought. Read Psalm 24 as a worship psalm to the Lord.

Remember this: Whoever turns a sinner from the error of his way will save him from death and cover over a multitude of sins. —**JAMES 5:20**

Errors occur in baseball. Most games, however, never contain more than one or two. But in 1988, New York Yankee pitcher Tommy John managed to commit three on a single play.

New York and the Milwaukee Brewers faced off. John worked through three shutout innings with his usual pinpoint control.

With one out in the fourth, the sinkerball pitcher walked Jim Gantner. Jeffrey Leonard followed and nubbed a dribbler to the left of the mound.

The Yankee ace should have fielded the ball cleanly and gotten an easy out. Instead, he bobbled it for error number one.

With Gantner already at second and Leonard half a step away from first, John fired the ball toward first baseman Don Mattingly. It sailed into right field for the pitcher's second error.

Dave Winfield retrieved the errant throw and rifled the baseball to the plate, attempting to nail Gantner. The six-time Gold Glove winner's aim was true, but John unexplainedly cut the throw.

The New York hurler turned and uncorked a throw toward third base. The ball wound up in the Brewers' dugout for John's third error. Gantner scored, and Leonard trotted home. The scene looked more like Little League than major league.

Too bad a teammate couldn't stop John's errors and save two unearned runs. Even after the first and second miscues, an out could have negated them.

Sometimes in life another person keeps us from making a mistake. It may be a friend, a relative, or someone we don't even know. But when that happens, we are thankful.

Have you ever almost made a big mistake? What kept you from making it? Watch for ways to keep others from making errors. Thank God when others keep you from your own.

I will praise you, O Lord, with all my heart. . . . For You have upheld my right and my cause; you have sat on your throne, judging righteously. —PSALM 9:1, 4

The 1996 United States Olympic softball team earned an opportunity to medal by blanking China, 1–0. Former UCLA pitcher Lisa Fernandez hurled the 3-hit masterpiece, striking out 13.

The Chinese defeated Australia to set up a rematch for gold. Michele Granger took the mound for the Red, White, and Blue.

In the third inning, tied 0–0, shortstop Dot Richardson stepped to the plate with one on. The 34-year-old orthopedic surgeon lofted a towering fly down the right-field line.

China's Wei Qiang chased the ball, watched it sail over the fence, and hook into controversy. She screamed, "Foul!" But umpire Geralyn Lindberg yelled, "Fair!" Richardson trotted around the bases.

Coaches Li Minkuan and Li Xiaoshebg protested for ten minutes. Television replays indicated the umpire had judged the ball's flight correctly.

The quarrel rattled the Chinese. They allowed the Americans an unearned run on a booted grounder and a fly.

China rebounded and put runners on second and third with two out in the sixth. Coach Ralph Raymond summoned Fernandez.

A passed ball gave the Chinese a run. But the All-American struck out Wang Ying.

Fernandez retired the side in order in the seventh. The United States claimed the first Olympic softball gold.

The fair ball made the difference. The umpire judged rightly, but Wei Qiang argued. The ump upheld her call. But the Chinese continued. They lost focus on the important by dwelling on a past that would not change.

Sometimes we do the same. We argue with the Lord and dwell on what might have been instead of what can be. We try to uphold our own cause in place of God's.

The next time you're tempted to argue the umpire's call, ask yourself, "Will it change?" Instead take a deep breath and move on. Forget the past. Look to the future. Praise God for His right judgment.

We all stumble in many ways. If anyone is never at fault in what he says, he is a perfect man, able to keep his whole body in check. —JAMES 3:2

Spectators visiting the Ballpark in Arlington in 1994 arrived with mixed emotions. The sparkling new stadium contrasted with a looming player strike.

Texas Rangers pitcher Kenny Rogers quickly forced the crowd of 46,581 to focus on the game. In the top of the first, he struck out California Angel leadoff hitter Chad Curtis.

Texas quickly staked its pitcher to a 4–0 lead. Rogers needed no additional support. Mixing his pitches to perfection, he threw fastballs to get ahead in the count. Batters then faced an assortment of baffling curves and changeups. One after another California hitter stood at the plate and returned to the dugout without reaching base.

With each inning, those watching sensed history unfolding. Through eight frames, the Ranger left-hander retired 24 consecutive Angel batters.

Rex Hudler led off the top of the ninth. Rogers came within one pitch of walking the second baseman, but Hudler hit a looping line drive toward center fielder Rusty Greer. Greer normally would have allowed the ball to drop for a hit. But he took a chance. Diving full length, the Ranger out-field-er snared the ball in his outstretched glove. The perfect game stayed alive.

Rogers snuffed out the final two batters. Chris Turner grounded out to short, and Gary DiSarcina flied to center. The 14th perfect game went into the record books.

Perfection occurs rarely in any aspect of life. We constantly strive for it but seldom achieve it.

God recognizes our imperfections. Throughout history we have disappointed Him with pride, deception, and cruelty.

Rather than punish us, God chose to save us. He sent His perfect Son to teach us and to die for us.

Through our belief in Christ, we walk toward perfection. When we stray, faith draws us back. Imagine you can plan an entire day. What activities would make it perfect? Praise God for His perfection.

> Whoever loves discipline loves knowledge, but he who hates correction is stupid.—**PROVERBS 12:1**

Seattle Mariner Ken Griffey Jr.'s home run into Yankee Stadium's right field stands on July 20, 1993, was not particularly spectacular. His father, a New York Yankee coach, watched it and signaled congratulations. Griffey Sr. witnessed another home run by his son the next day.

The Mariners then traveled to Cleveland for a four-game series. Griffey Jr. continued his string, tying a Seattle record with homer number five and breaking it with number six.

After a welcome off-day, Junior returned to the Kingdome. He stunned the hometown crowd with a massive grand slam shot. The 4-run blast off Kevin Tapani carried 441 feet to dead center field.

The next day, leading off the seventh inning, Griffey Jr. launched a 400-foot homer into the third deck of the Kingdome. The shot off Minnesota's Willie Banks marked Junior's eighth straight game to belt a round-tripper. The pieces had fallen in place for the young superstar to tie the baseball record for consecutive-game home runs.

Mariner fans anxiously awaited game nine and a chance to see the record breaker. Griffey singled and doubled early in the contest, but Minnesota retired the superstar in his final two plate appearances. The streak ended.

Hitting a home run requires a keen eye, power, strength, and a quick bat. Hitting home runs eight games in a row seems nearly impossible.

In daily living, however, the tools of a home run hitter don't give power and strength. We need knowledge and wisdom. We can obtain knowledge each day.

Wisdom doesn't come as easily. Learning God's teachings and following His Word enable us to make good decisions and become wise.

Thank a coach, teacher, family member, coworker, or friend for the guidance he or she gives. Pray for the discipline to learn God's teachings and the wisdom to apply them.

For this son of mine was dead and is alive again; he was lost and is found. **—LUKE 15:24**

Anthony Young's victory in July 1993 didn't end with a strikeout, a groundout, or a fly ball. In fact, he watched it from the dugout when the New York Mets rallied for 2 runs in the bottom of the ninth against the Florida Marlins. But the win couldn't have been sweeter.

Baseball's longest string of losses dated back to May 6, 1992, and covered over 81 mound appearances. Starting or relieving didn't matter. Young lost 14 as a starter and 13 in relief.

Collecting the win appeared doubtful. Manager Dallas Green called on Young to relieve Bret Saberhagen in the top of the ninth with the score tied 3–3. The consecutive loss record holder allowed the Florida Marlins to score a run but eventually retired the side.

Eddie Murray saved Young further embarrassment. His line drive to right field plated Ryan Thompson with the winning run. The losing streak had ended, and Young earned his lone victory of the 1993 season.

Anthony Young's pitching ability appeared to be lost. His career seemed dead. But with his teammates' help, the pitcher found the joy of victory.

Losing anything makes us sad. God doesn't like it either when we lose Him. We lose Him when we forget to pray, read the Bible, or follow His teachings. But God is always there for us to find. He never loses us. We simply have to look.

Read Luke 15:11-31, the parable of the lost son. Picture yourself as each character. Why do you think the brother was jealous? If you had been the father, what would you have done? What do you believe the son learned? Remember the story is about God's love.

When I said, "My foot is slipping," your love, O Lord, supported me. —PSALM 94:18

The International Olympic Committee approved women's soccer for competition in 1996. The Americans faced the Chinese for the gold medal. A crowd of 76,481, the largest ever to view a women's sporting event, packed the University of Georgia's Sanford Stadium.

The U.S. took a 1–0 lead in the game's 19th minute. Mia Hamm drove the ball past goalie Gao Hong. The sphere careened off the left post, but Shannon Miller kicked the rebound into the net.

Still in the first half, American goaltender Briana Scurry moved out too fast and got caught in no-man's land. Forward Sun Wen skipped past her to knot the score 1–1.

In the contest's 68th minute, Hamm and fullback Joy Fawcett teamed on a give-and-go. Fawcett carried the ball to midfield and dished to Hamm. The University of North Carolina grad returned the pass. Fawcett kicked the ball through the box to a waiting Tiffeny Milbrett for the game-winning shot.

Hamm, suffering from a sprained ankle, left the game. Moments after the 2–1 triumph, Dr. Mark Adams and trainer Patty Marchak carried her to the center circle to join her celebrating teammates. Spectators leaped to their feat and shouted the familiar "U-S-A! U-S-A!"

Mia Hamm's foot slipped but not before she had assisted in the medal-winning goal. And when she slipped, her teammates picked up the slack. Two special supporters carried her back to join the excitement.

When we slip in life, God's love is there. Not only do we feel His presence through the quietness of prayer and meditation but also through reading the Bible. He sends Christian friends to support us, and we find security in the arms of our Savior.

If you've never played soccer or seen a match, attend one or watch on television. Learn the significance of the center circle. Thank God for circling us with His love.

Do you not know that in a race all the runners run, but only one gets the prize? Run in such a way as to get the prize. —1 CORINTHIANS 9:24

Track-and-field fans expected great things from Michael Johnson in the 1996 Olympics. The previous summer he stunned the running world by winning both the 200- and 400-meter races in the World Track and Field Championships. No man had accomplished this feat in the twentieth century.

Johnson wanted to prove something to himself. The gold medal favorite at the 1992 games had fallen victim to food poisoning and failed to make the finals. He won the gold as a member of the 4 x 400 relay, but Barcelona remained a bittersweet memory.

The 400 meters was scheduled first in Atlanta. Critics complained Johnson loafed through the preliminaries. But the world class runner silenced their voices with an Olympic record 43.49 seconds in the finals.

The 200 meters took place three days later. Michael followed the same strategy and ran only fast enough to qualify.

But with the gold medal on the line, the sprinter shot from the blocks. He rushed past the field on the curve and bolted toward the finish line. The timer flashed a clocking of 19.32. Johnson broke his own world record of 19.66 set in June at the trials.

Michael Johnson ran an unbelievable race. He deserved the prize and the glory.

Our lives lack the excitement and glamour of an Olympic race, but we are no less important to God.

In a race, the runner cannot win if he doesn't run hard and concentrate on the finish line. Christians must do the same. The center and focus is God.

Sometime this week visit a local track with a friend or relative. Walk around once together discussing the day's events. Then time a lap. Remember to look straight ahead and keep your eyes on the finish. Ask God to help keep your life on track for Him.

I will praise God's name in song and glorify him with thanksgiving. —PSALM 69:30

Lindsay Davenport heard "The Star Spangled Banner" over and over during the 1996 Atlanta Olympics. After listening to the music pay tribute to others, the Californian determined the national anthem would play for her as well.

The Newport Beach native barely made the United States Olympic tennis team. Officials ranked her fourth on the American squad.

But Davenport concentrated on fitness. A strict training regime melted 20 pounds. Former star and coach Billie Jean King encouraged the daughter of a 1968 Olympic volleyball team member to go for the gold.

A favorable draw improved the 20 year old's chances. Monica Seles, Arantxa Sanchez Vicario, and Jana Novotna, the three favorites competed against other players.

Davenport won 5 matches, advancing to the gold-medal round against Sanchez Vicario. The contest appeared to be a mismatch. The American had never beaten the Spaniard in five tries.

Both competitors held serve in the first set and entered the tiebreaker. Lindsay gained a 6–4 lead but squandered 2 set points to tie. She responded with a strong serve and deep volley to go up 7–6. Fortune smiled on the American. Her two-handed backhand ticked the net and trickled over to win set one.

Davenport broke Sanchez Vicario's serve in her first two service games of the second set. The Spaniard never recovered and lost, 2–6. The most unlikely American candidate captured tennis gold.

Tears welled in the champion's eyes as Olympic officials praised her name and glorified her country by playing "The Star Spangled Banner." As they raised the American flag, Lindsay was thankful for the training and the draw that helped her win.

The psalmist says we should also sing praises to God and glorify Him with thanksgiving.

Sing a praise song to God. He doesn't care whether it's off-key or beautifully in tune. Then glorify the Lord by thanking Him for all He is and does.

Therefore, as we have opportunity, let us do good to all people, especially to those who belong to the family of believers. —GALATIANS 6:10

The American League installed the designated hitter (DH) in 1973 to add offense. American League pitchers have rarely batted since. But in 1991, Texas Ranger hurler Mike Jeffcoat stepped to the plate and made the most of his opportunity.

In the top of the ninth inning, the Rangers led the Milwaukee Brewers, 12–1. Manager Bobby Valentine pulled many of his regulars. He switched the game's DH, Geno Petralli, to third base. The move forced the Texas pitcher into the batting order.

Mike Jeffcoat replaced starter Brian Bohanan in the eighth. In the next inning, the southpaw strode to the plate for the first time since 1985.

Edwin Nunez went ahead in the count, 0–2. Nunez tried for the strike-out with a fastball, but Jeffcoat ripped it into the alley for a double. No American League pitcher had hit safely since October 2, 1974.

Mike Jeffcoat had not swung a bat in a game for six years. But down to his last strike, he delivered in the clutch.

Christians have an obligation to deliver too. Although faith saves us, good works prove our beliefs. Those who call themselves Christians but never show it make poor witnesses. And good deeds never go unrecognized, even if they're only seen by God.

Recall a time when someone did a special favor for you. How did it make you feel? Plan an unexpected good deed for a another person. Ask God to help you demonstrate your faith through good works.

Oh, the depth of the riches of the wisdom and knowledge of God! —ROMANS 11:33

The 1996 Olympic men's basketball team rolled through its opposition. The Dream Team of Charles Barkley, Anfernee Hardaway, Grant Hill, Karl Malone, Reggie Miller, Hakeem Olajuwon, Shaquille O'Neal, Scottie Pippen, Mitch Richmond, John Stockton, David Robinson, and Gary Payton hardly broke a sweat en route to the gold medal.

The Americans met Yugoslavia in the finals. Charlotte Hornet center Vlade Divac anchored the Slavic team. Like most teams, Yugoslavia played close in the first half. The U.S. team didn't take the lead until 3 minutes, 14 seconds before halftime.

But the Dream Team's deep bench took over. Its second-half lead grew and grew. The Red, White, and Blue coasted to its seventh win and took the gold, 95–69. The Yugoslavs settled for silver.

The Americans knew the game well. They instinctively threw the ball to the right place at the right time. They played heads-up defense, anticipating the opponents' every move.

In his wisdom, coach Lenny Wilkens made key substitutions. The men stayed fresh, ready to claim the richest Olympic prize. Knowledge and wisdom paid off.

The same holds true for us. The better we know God, the wiser we become about Him. The closer we draw to our Heavenly Father, the greater our riches.

Search the internet or the business section of a newspaper to find the relative value of silver and gold. Compare the two. Which would you rather have? Work hard to have a golden relationship with God. Ask for His help.

For riches do not endure forever, and a crown is not secure for all generations. —**PROVERBS 27:24**

From 1934 to 1976, the College All-Star Game raised millions for charity as the colleges' best faced the football world champions. But the recent graduates stood little chance.

In 1963, experts favored the Green Bay Packers by at least 2 touchdowns. Vince Lombardi's crew lit up the scoreboard early. The collegians fumbled. Green Bay recovered. Jim Taylor plunged over from the 2 to give the pros a 7–0 lead.

The All-Stars kicked a 20-yard field goal. Tommy Janik intercepted a Packer pass, and Larry Ferguson converted the turnover into a touchdown.

Jerry Kramer kicked a 21-yard field goal for the pros, tying the contest at halftime. After a scoreless third quarter, Bob Jencks booted a 33-yarder, giving the collegians a 13–10 lead.

With three minutes to play, quarterback Ron Vanderkelen connected with Wisconsin teammate Pat Richter. Richter turned the short pass into a 74-yard touchdown. The collegians held on for a 20–17 victory, their last before the game was discontinued.

The collegiate bunch played together only once. The Green Bay Packers worked together all season. The Green and Gold had been crowned world champions.

But that crown was not secure. Lombardi's team had to earn it each time it took the field. On that August day, the crown fell.

Winning a title once doesn't guarantee we'll win again. Having money doesn't indicate we'll always keep it. Following a successful parent or grandparent doesn't mean we'll also achieve.

God's plan is for the individual. Our parents' faith does not guarantee our own. The past does not predict the present.

In a sports encyclopedia, review the list of pro football world champions. How many teams have won more than two crowns in a row? Has any one team totally dominated? Ask God to help you build on the salvation of previous generations with your own faith.

> They serve at a sanctuary that is a copy and shadow of what is in heaven. —HEBREWS 8:5a

Seven-year-old Mary Lou Retton watched Nadia Comaneci nail a perfect 10 at the 1976 Montreal Olympics. Eight years later the young woman from West Virginia had a chance to copy her idol.

Retton and Romania's Ecaterina Szabo squared off in UCLA's Pauley Pavilion for the all-around gymnastics title. Luck of the draw placed Szabo in her strongest events first. The American faced the opposite.

The Romanian began the evening with a perfect 10 on the beam. She then scored a 9.95 in the floor exercise. Suddenly, Retton trailed by .15 points.

But Szabo fell to a 9.9 on the vault. Mary Lou took advantage of her slipup, garnering a 10 in the floor exercises. The gap narrowed to .05 points.

The Eastern European pulled another 9.9 on the uneven bars. A minor imperfection gave the American a chance.

Retton toed the mark for the vault, her strongest event. She raced down the runway, hit the springboard, twisted, somersaulted in the air, and stuck the landing.

The 4-foot-9-inch pixie smiled. The crowd roared, and the judges recorded their marks. Retton received a perfect score and the gold medal. The 16 year old won the first Olympic medal ever by an American gymnast.

Mary Lou Retton copied the accomplishment of the star she had watched. The American moved from the shadow of Olympic gymnastics competition and into the spotlight. Two perfect scores resulted in gold.

On earth we can only try to copy Jesus' perfect life. Unfortunately, we'll never measure up. But by trusting Christ for our salvation, we move out of the shadows of evil and into God's perfect light.

Make a copy of a picture, letter, cassette, or CD. Note the difference in quality between the original and the duplicate. While the copy may be quite useable, it's never perfect. Thank God for Christ's perfection. Pray for help in copying Him.

Who among you fears the Lord and obeys the word of his servant? Let him who walks in the dark, who has no light, trust in the name of the Lord and rely on his God. —ISAIAH 50:10

Bob Mathias' high school coach in Tulare, California, suggested he take up the decathlon. The coach obviously had a keen eye for talent. Three months later, the 17 year old competed on the 1952 United States Olympic team.

At the London games, Mathias' inexperience cost valuable points in the field events. But his dogged determination and athletic ability kept him from shutouts. After the first day, the California schoolboy trailed only Argentina's Enrique Kistenmacher and France's Ignace Heinrich.

Heavy rains delayed the second day of competition. Darkness fell. Since England's Wembley Stadium had no infield lights, officials lined cars along the javelin runway to illuminate the track.

Mathias staggered across the shadowy 1,500-meter finish line at 10:35 P.M., over twelve hours after the day's beginning competition. He fell far behind the pack but earned enough points to claim first place. The future United States Congressman became the Olympics' youngest gold medalist.

Bob Mathias practically finished the decathlon in the dark. But the track star obeyed his coach, trusted his instincts, and relied on the headlights of parked cars. He saw enough.

Sometimes in life we feel as if we're stumbling in the dark. We don't know which way to turn. Through those times, we must trust in the Lord and rely on Him. After all, God created light and gave Jesus Christ to be the light of the world. He will let us see far enough.

Take a drive after dark or simply turn on the headlights of a car at night. How far does the light shine? Far enough to keep going. Thank God for always giving enough light.

And God said, "Let there be light," and there was light.

—GENESIS 1:3

Cubs' owner Phil Wrigley purchased lights and scheduled their installation at Wrigley Field for early 1942. But when World War II began, he donated them to the war effort.

For years, Chicago remained the only professional baseball team performing solely in the sunshine. Many loved the distinctive feature. But outsiders pressured Cubs ownership, and the light standards appeared.

Officials chose 8-8-88 as the day. Hall of Famers Ernie Banks and Billy Williams threw out the first pitch. Lifelong fan Harry Grossman, age 91, pulled the switch. Fifteen brass musicians from the Chicago Symphony Orchestra played Richard Strauss' *Also Sprach Zarathustra* as Mr. Edison's invention illuminated the city's north side.

For seventy-four minutes, the plan played perfectly. But in the top of the fourth with the Cubs leading 3–1, lightning, thunder, wind, and torrential rain descended.

After a 2 hour, 10 minute, delay, umpires postponed the contest. Wrigley Field's first official night game waited one more day.

It took forty-six years and two sets of lights to let the Cubs play at night. What an ordeal! But the results were good.

It took God only a day to make light and to separate that light into day and night. And the Lord saw that it was good.

God can do in an instant what people struggle to do in a lifetime. Isn't it amazing that the Heavenly Father works in and through us when He could do things so much better Himself? But He chose each of us to be His hands and His feet on earth. What an awesome responsibility that the Lord should see what we do is good.

Read about Thomas Alva Edison and his inventions. Compare the time it took him to make light to the time it took God to create light. But think of what the world would be like if Edison had never lived. Praise God for allowing people to be part of His plan.

A cheerful look brings joy to the heart, and good news gives health to the bones. —**PROVERBS 15:30**

Canada's Silken Laumann captured the 1991 world championship in single scull rowing by a 3-second margin. The impressive victory made her an overwhelming favorite for the gold medal at the 1992 Barcelona Olympics. But a devastating tragedy intervened.

On May 16, the German team of Peter Holtzenbein and Colin von Ettingshausen accidentally rammed Laumann's shell. A piece of wood pierced her lower right leg, fracturing the bone, cutting the muscle, and causing extensive nerve damage.

Doctors estimated six months for recovery. After five operations, the Mississuaga, Ontario, native traveled to Barcelona. But she walked with a cane and could not stand unassisted for more than fifteen minutes.

However, to the astonishment and excitement of spectators, the 27-year-old oarsman strapped her injured leg to hold it steady. She placed second in the first qualifying heat. The world champion won her semifinal. Laumann advanced to the final field of eight.

Rowing mightily, Laumann captured the bronze medal, covering the 2,000-meter course in 7 minutes, 28.85 seconds.

Fans joyfully watched Silken compete and medal. The good news that she could row brought enough health to her fractured bone to let her go on. A bronze in Laumann's condition was as good as gold.

The writer of the Book of Proverbs knew that a smile and encouraging look brighten every day, especially the tough ones. He knew, too, that when we're feeling down, good news always makes us feel better.

For one day, try smiling and saying an encouraging word to everyone. Make a promise to yourself that each person you contact will be glad she saw you. Ask God to help you always be the bearer of a cheerful look and good news.

> Much dreaming and many words are meaningless.
> Therefore stand in awe of God. —ECCLESIASTES 5:7

American professional basketball players had never participated in the Olympic games. Pressure from FIBA (Federation Internationale de Basketball) forced the rule change for Barcelona's XXV Olympiad. But when the National Basketball Association all-stars took the court, the players spent as much time posing for photographs as they did shooting baskets.

Sportwriters immediately dubbed the group the Dream Team. Indeed they were. The United States team averaged over 120 points per game and held their opponents to 70.

Coach Chuck Daly's team of Michael Jordan, Charles Barkley, Karl Malone, Chris Mullen, Clyde Drexler, Patrick Ewing, Scottie Pippen, David Robinson, Larry Bird, Magic Johnson, Christian Laettner, and John Stockton faced Croatia in the finals.

The contest was a mismatch just like the others. The Dream Team captured the 1992 Olympic gold with a 117–85 victory.

But few cared about the final score. Watching the world's best provided entertainment enough. Playing against the greatest gave motivation enough. Seeing or touching living legends wove dreams.

Every person needs to dream. Dreams enable us to use our gifts and talents in the way God intended. But dreams must be mixed with reality. Most of us will never play NBA basketball or win an Olympic medal. Most will never meet a member of the Dream Team.

Too often we stand in awe of superstars. We want to be like them, to enjoy widespread fame, and to make million-dollar salaries. We dream of being like them instead of working to be like the most awesome hero of all time, Jesus.

Who is your earthly hero? Why? Write or tell the person how much you admire him or her and the reason. Thank God for your heavenly and earthly heroes.

> *Rid yourselves of all the offenses you have committed, and get a new heart and a new spirit.* —EZEKIEL 18:31

No one knew how long Wilson Alvarez's stint in the major leagues would last. In his debut on July 24, 1989, he pitched miserably, giving up 3 runs on 3 hits without getting an out. But in the Venezuela native's second start in 1991, he made baseball history.

Fresh from the Chicago White Sox Birmingham farm club, the 21-year-old hurler challenged the Baltimore Orioles. Frank Thomas spotted him a 2-run cushion with a homer in the top of the first.

Alvarez survived his jitters and got through the first without allowing a hit. Inning after inning, the Orioles could not connect with their bats.

In the seventh inning, Cal Ripken Jr. tapped a slow roller. Catcher Ron Karkovice fielded it, but his throw pulled Frank Thomas off the bag. The official scorer ruled an error on Karkovice and kept the no-hitter alive.

In the eighth, Chris Hoiles lined a shot to center. Lance Johnson raced toward the infield, spearing the ball with a head-first dive. The no-hit game remained intact.

Alvarez retired the rest of the Orioles without difficulty. The Baltimore crowd cheered every out registered by the rookie.

At game's end Alvarez entered baseball's record book. The second youngest no-hitter pitcher walked 5 and struck out 7 en route to his first major league victory.

Before he could be successful, Wilson Alvarez had to put aside the past. He had to forget his first game in the majors. He entered the Baltimore contest nervous but with a new spirit.

Once we learn from them, God forgives our failures and lets us forget them. Then we can move forward with a new heart, ready for the future.

Think of a problem or failure that has been bothering you. Write it on a piece of paper. Ask God to forgive you and help you forget. Then wad the paper up and throw it in a trash can.

There they will exclaim, "Pharaoh king of Egypt is only a loud noise; he has missed his opportunity." —JEREMIAH 46:17

The 1994 baseball strike hurt everyone. Fans, players, and owners missed the national pastime. The World Series was canceled for the first time in ninety years.

The pain may have been greatest for Frank Thomas. The Chicago White Sox first baseman had tallied remarkable numbers when the work stoppage occurred.

At the time of the strike, the Big Hurt carried a .353 batting average. He had belted 39 homers and driven in 101 runs. Thomas had scored 106 times and coaxed over 100 walks. The Auburn alum had accumulated the numbers with almost a third of the season remaining.

The statistics put the White Sox first baseman in highly select company. In 1995, he joined Lou Gehrig and Ted Williams as the only ballplayers to hit over 20 home runs, bat over .300, walk over 100 times, score over 100 runs, and drive in over 100 runs in their first four seasons. In 1996, the two-time Most Valuable Player stood alone as the only player to achieve the levels in his first five campaigns.

On strike day, Chicago led the AL Central division. The team hoped to advance beyond the previous year's first-round exit. But the shutdown eliminated all opportunity.

Life is full of missed chances. Sometimes they're our fault. We wait too long or make a poor choice. At other times, as with Thomas and the White Sox, the fault lies with someone else.

God wants us to use our opportunities wisely. He desires we make good choices, learn all we can when we have a chance, and treat others with Christian love.

Remember a time you had a chance to do something but didn't and were sorry. Share the story with a friend or write it down. Ask God to help you take advantage of the opportunities He gives.

There are three things that are stately in their stride, four that move with stately bearing: a lion, mighty among beasts, who retreats before nothing; a strutting rooster, a he-goat, and a king with his army around him. —PROVERBS 30:29-31

Carl Lewis has been compared to the legendary Jesse Owens. In the 1984 Los Angeles Olympics, the brash University of Houston runner captured gold medals in the 100 meters, 200 meters, and long jump. But King Carl set no records.

One race remained for the flamboyant athlete, the 4 x 100 relay. The Olympic coaches selected Lewis to anchor.

Sam Graddy, the 100-meter silver medalist, lined up in the blocks. His time of 10.29 seconds started a record-setting pace.

Future Los Angeles Ram wide receiver Ron Brown turned in a blistering 9.19. Calvin Smith, the 100-meter world record holder, posted a 9.91. He handed the baton to Lewis with a commanding lead.

King Carl ran against the clock, igniting the track with an 8.94. The Americans not only captured gold, they established a new world mark of 37.86 seconds, the only track-and-field world record in the games. Lewis exactly matched Jesse Owens' 1936 Olympic gold medal performance—four first places in the same four events.

The foursome never backed down. Graddy, Brown, Smith, and Lewis matched strides with the greatest and outdid them. Their stately victory lap showed them as kings of the track.

Sometimes it's easy to feel intimidated. But God gives us the strength not to retreat. Great people may awe us. But the Heavenly Father provides confidence. Armed with God's love, mercy, and grace, we can hold our heads high, as stately as a king.

Think of a time you or your team were intimidated during an athletic event. How did you overcome the intimidation? Or if you didn't, how could you have overcome it? Share your story with a friend or teammate. Praise God for the confidence He gives.

In his heart a man plans his course, but the Lord determines his steps. —**PROVERBS 16:9**

Joan Benoit never allowed any obstacle to stop her from running the marathon. She expected pain in every race, but determination carried her.

The International Olympic Committee scheduled the first women's marathon in the 1984 Los Angeles games. The Maine native craved competition. Benoit ran in the United States Olympic Trials just 17 days after undergoing orthoscopic knee surgery, but she made the team.

The weather cooperated to ease the runner's burden. The race began with a temperature of 67 degrees and rose only to the mid-70s.

The field started slowly. Benoit grew weary of the pace and took the lead at the 3-mile mark. No one moved up to challenge her, not even the undefeated Norwegian, Greta Waitz.

The 5-foot-2-inch ball of energy focused solely on the race. She smiled once when she glimpsed a spectator holding a banner of her alma mater, Bowdoin College.

Benoit ran with confidence and assurance. She slowed slightly, conserving energy for a possible last-minute surge. But the American never needed it.

The former skier entered the Los Angeles Coliseum to the ovation of 77,000 fans. Benoit captured the first women's marathon gold medal with a time of 2 minutes, 24.52 seconds—the third fastest ever.

In her heart, Joan had set her Olympic course. She planned to run with the pack, at least early on. But the other competitors and the race determined her actual steps.

In our hearts, we plan our lives. We may dream of playing pro sports, winning an Olympic medal, becoming famous, or making lots of money.

But whatever our plans, God determines our steps. He leads us on the path of love, joy, peace, patience, kindness, goodness, faithfulness, gentleness, and self control.

Write each of the qualities listed above on a sheet of paper. Evaluate on a scale of 1 to 10, 10 being best, how far along God's path you are in each area. Ask God's direction in reaching perfections.

It was not by their sword that they won the land, nor did their arm bring them victory; it was your right hand, your arm, and the light of your face, for you loved them.

—PSALM 44:3

No one expected Dave Dravecky to return to baseball in 1989. An eleven-hour operation to remove a cancerous tumor and the surrounding muscle left his career in doubt. But Dravecky never quit.

The San Francisco Giants pitcher began rehab two weeks after his surgery. By spring, he engaged in full-scale workouts. Dravecky progressed so rapidly he pitched three minor league games to test his recovery. The lefty won all three.

Manager Roger Craig scheduled Dravecky's comeback for August 10 in Candlestick Park. The pitcher faced the division-leading Cincinnati Reds.

Dravecky allowed only one hit through seven innings, and the Giants staked him to a lead. A year and a half away from baseball, Dravecky had achieved a comeback win.

Five days later, he started in Montreal. Through four innings, the game went well. But in the fifth, Dravecky's arm began to tingle.

Tim Raines stepped to the plate. Dravecky threw with all his might. A loud crack resounded through the stadium.

The pitcher fell to the ground in pain. His arm had broken. The comeback was over.

In spite of seeming failure, Dave Dravecky had won, not by strength and not even in baseball. God's right hand extended determination. The Lord's arm gave strength.

The light of God's face directed Dave in dark days. And he felt the Father's love around him. Dravecky didn't continue playing baseball, but he continued playing the game of life.

Disease and disaster put life in perspective. What isn't important when we're healthy becomes important when we're not. Some things we used to take for granted become things to thank God for every day.

For an hour, don't use your right hand if you're right-handed or your left if you're left-handed. Ask God to keep you from taking all His gifts for granted.

Greater love has no one than this, that he lay down his life for his friends. —JOHN 15:13

Luz Long surprised Jesse Owens, the world record holder in the long jump, at the 1936 Berlin Olympic games. The American knew nothing of the tall, blond German taking practice jumps remarkably close to his world mark.

Startled, Owens took a practice run wearing his sweat suit. Surprisingly, officials counted the jump in the qualifying round.

Shaken, the Ohio State alum fouled on his next attempt. Long, sensing Owens' nervousness, approached the American and introduced himself.

The German jumper suggested Owens mark a spot several inches before the takeoff point, ensuring a qualifying jump. The world record holder listened to Long's advice and advanced to the finals by a single centimeter.

Spurred by the competition, Owens opened the finals with a leap of 25 feet, 5 1/2 inches, an Olympic record. Each jump went farther. The American's final attempt carried 26 feet, 5 3/4 inches, giving Owens his fourth gold medal. Long won silver.

Luz Long knew of Jesse Owens' greatness. The German surely guessed the American could beat him. But Luz helped Jesse anyway. The unselfish act sealed Owens' gold medal and friendship.

Long and Owens maintained their long-distance relationship. Although the German lost his life in 1943 at the battle of St. Pietro, the American continued to correspond with his family. We sometimes read about parents giving their lives to save their children. But God said the most unselfish love is that of a friend putting his life on the line for a friend.

That's what Jesus did. He gave His life to save ours. That's why children sing "My Best Friend Is Jesus."

Do you have good friends? Would they give their lives for you? Would you give your life for them? Praise Jesus for dying for you.

> The crowds that went ahead of him and those that followed shouted, "Hosanna to the Son of David!" "Blessed is he who comes in the name of the Lord!" "Hosanna in the highest!"
>
> **—MATTHEW 21:9**

Major league baseball entered new territory in 1996. The New York Mets and San Diego Padres experienced south of the border hospitality.

The two National League clubs met for a three-game series in Monterrey, Mexico. Fernando Valenzuela, a native of the Mexican state of Sonora, manned the mound for the Padres.

The 23,699 fans packing Estadio Monterrey cheered Valenzuela's every pitch. San Diego backed its hurler with a 15–1 lead before he left in the seventh. Fernando exited the field to a standing ovation and shouts of *"Toro! Toro! Toro!"*

But not a single *beisbol* fan left early. The Monterrey partisans stayed until the end and watched the Mets explode for 7 ninth-inning runs. San Diego hung on for a 15–10 victory in the first major league baseball game played outside of the United States or Canada.

The crowds shouted their approval of the home country star. The Mexican people loved their own hero.

In a Bible scene centuries before, the crowds shouted their approval for their countryman. The Jewish people sang praises to Jesus.

But unlike the baseball fans, Jesus' crowd turned on Him. Those who shouted "Hosanna" on Sunday shouted "Crucify Him" on Friday.

Judas, Caiaphas, the Sanhedrin, Pilate, and Herod all played a role in Jesus' death. But so did the crowd. Three times the crowd could have let Christ go. Three times the people called for His death.

Jesus gave His life for the crowd, a crowd that included us.

Have you ever been caught up in the crowd and done something you never would have done otherwise? Read Luke 23:13-25. Note the power of the crowd. Thank God for the sacrifice of His Son. Ask the Lord to keep you from simply following the crowd.

For our struggle is not against flesh and blood, but against the rulers, against the authorities, against the powers of this dark world and against the spiritual forces of evil in the heavenly realms.

—**EPHESIANS 6:12**

Sports fans seldom see Greco-Roman wrestling outside the Olympic games. In the sport, competitors can't hold or grip their opponent's legs. A wrestler can't trip, hook, or lift with the lower limbs.

In high school, Jeff Blatnick dreamed of joining the United States wrestling team. He majored in physical education at Springfield College and competed on varsity. Blatnick's training paid off with selection to the 1980 Olympic squad. His dreams crashed, however, when President Jimmy Carter declared a boycott against the Moscow games.

The New York wrestler immediately set his sights on 1984. But in 1982, doctors discovered Blatnick suffered from Hodgkin's disease, a treatable but serious form of cancer. His spleen and appendix were removed, and Blatnick underwent radiation. The surgery and therapy weakened him. But the determined young man refused to quit.

The United States Olympic Committee selected Blatnick for the 1984 Greco-Roman wrestling team. The games would take place in Los Angeles.

Competing in the super heavyweight class, the 6-foot-2-inch, 238-pound wrestler faced heavier opponents. One by one, Blatnick defeated them.

He lost one match when a Greek wrestler bit him. But the Greek lost his next match. Blatnick advanced to the finals where he defeated Sweden's Thomas Johansson for the gold medal, the first ever for the United States in the event.

Jeff Blatnick overcame much to win his Olympic wrestling gold. The Apostle Paul recognized Christians wrestle with opposing powers every day.

God gives us many tools, however, to fight wrong. Bible study, prayer, and Christian fellowship are some of the best. If we practice, we are ready for combat.

Challenge a friend to an arm-wrestling match. Praise God for the extra power He supplies.

The least of you will become a thousand, the smallest a mighty nation. —ISAIAH 60:22

Observant fans noticed a strange name on their baseball scorecards, "Gaedel 1/8." Most assumed it to be a printing error.

The crowd quickly forgot the unusual listing as the last place 1951 St. Louis Browns lost the doubleheader opener to the Detroit Tigers. The stadium erupted, however, as St. Louis prepared to bat in the nightcap's bottom of the first.

Instead of scheduled center fielder Frank Saucier, the PA announcer boomed forth, "Batting for Saucier, number 1/8, Eddie Gaedel."

Chaos reigned for several minutes. The umpires forced manager Zach Taylor to produce official papers listing Gaedel on the roster. They finally allowed the 3-foot-7-inch man into the batter's box with his toy bat.

Tiger pitcher Bob Cain threw four straight balls, each high over Eddie's head. The tiny batter trotted briskly to first base as photographers furiously shot the action. Outfielder Jim Delsing replaced baseball's smallest player, and the crowd cheered loudly while Gaedel left the field.

Eddie Gaedel lacked the strength to swing a regular bat. But he displayed great courage by stepping to the plate when the announcer called his name.

The shepherd boy David faced the same situation with Goliath. Logically, the giant should have defeated him. Yet David's faith in God told him he could win.

Rejecting King Saul's heavy armor, Israel's future ruler went into battle armed with only a sling and five smooth stones. Hours of practice and inner strength from God guided the missile to its mark. The young man killed the Philistine warrior, and the Israelite nation celebrated.

Ask a parent, grandparent, or friend to share an event from her childhood that took courage. Then share one with her about your life. Pray for strength to face each day and its challenges.

> *"But my righteousness will last forever, my salvation through all generations."* —ISAIAH 51:8b

Numerous brothers have played major league baseball. Scores of fathers and sons have also participated. But only one three-generation family has set foot on a big league diamond. In 1992, Bret Boone joined his father, Bob, and his grandfather, Ray, to complete the trio.

Shortstop and third baseman Ray Boone debuted on September 3, 1948. He played for Cleveland, Detroit, Chicago, Kansas City, Milwaukee, and Boston before retiring in 1960.

Bob Boone caught for the Phillies, Angels, and Royals. He began his big league tenure behind the plate in 1972 and called it quits in 1990.

Both father and son participated in the All-Star game. Ray appeared twice, and Bob made the squad four times.

The Seattle Mariners called up grandson Bret Boone from minor league Calgary. Manager Bill Plummer inserted the rookie second baseman in the seventh spot in the batting order.

Bret faced hard-throwing southpaw Arthur Rhodes of the Baltimore Orioles. In his first at bat, Bret singled. Just as his father and grandfather before him, the youngest Boone had embarked on a major league career.

For the Boone family, Bret's debut was a red-letter day. For any father, a child following in his footsteps feels very special. But for both a son and grandson to take the same path yields even greater pride.

The talent, the hard work, and the desire all came together for three men. Each helped and encouraged the next. But each made the big leagues on his own.

God, too, is faithful to all generations. While parents and grandparents cannot become Christians for the next generation, they can pray. They can set an example. They can encourage.

Ask relatives to help you draw a family tree. Record as many full names as you can, as many generations back as you can. Thank God for those who have gone before you. Pray that God will help you set an example for those who come after you.

He sends his command to the earth; his word runs swiftly. —**PSALM 147:15**

A fast field makes for a fast race. In 1991, a swift set of runners forced Carl Lewis into a record-setting performance.

The nine-time Olympic gold medal winner competed in the 100-meter race at the Tokyo World Championships. World record holder Leroy Burrell paced the eight-man contingent.

The 75,000 spectators expected an exciting contest. Lewis posted 9.93 seconds, the third fastest time ever in the semifinals.

In the finals, the gun sounded, and the runners started in a flash. Lewis pulled ahead of Burrell in the final 10 meters. His time of 9.86 broke Burrell's world record by .02.

Burrell placed second with a 9.88. Six of the eight competitors finished under 10 seconds. The briefest of races run with unbelievable speed sent the crowd into wild celebration.

The 100 meter is the swiftest of all races. Once the start command is sent, the contest runs in the blink of any eye.

When God sends His commands to the earth, His Word works swiftly, faster than a 100-meter race. His blessings flow. He sustains the hurting. He punishes the wicked. The weather obeys. He makes grass grow and winds blow. He creates upheaval and grants peace. He melts snow and the hardest heart.

Make a list of things you can do in under ten seconds. Praise the Lord for the swiftness of His Word.

From heaven the Lord looks down and sees all mankind;
from his dwelling place he watches all who live on earth.

—PSALM 33:13-14

During the 1930s, scientists discovered a process enabling images to be transferred into electronic signals and transmitted over long distances. Such knowledge led to the development of television. The marriage of television and professional sports soon followed.

In 1939, Brooklyn Dodger radio broadcaster Red Barber convinced general manager Larry MacPhail to experiment with television. Two cameras, one at ground level by home plate, and one in the upper deck near third base, covered the baseball action. Barber sat near the third-base camera describing the plays without knowing exactly what image the camera projected.

Following the Cincinnati Reds' 5–2 victory, Barber rushed to the field to interview managers Bill McKechnie and Leo Durocher. An estimated 400 viewers on station W2XBS watched television's first professional sports coverage.

Today we can't imagine not being able to turn on the television to watch sports. We can even choose a favorite team and rarely miss a game. We may stay up late to see live Olympic action from the other side of the world. We tune in to sports events we'd never view in person.

We watch the screen in airports, hotel lobbies, cars, homes, and even in the stadium. The sports camera looks down everywhere and seems to see it all.

But one television camera can't capture every player in every game at every moment. The sport's camera seems to see all, but God does see us all. The Lord watches us and watches over us every second of every day.

Look at the day's television listing in the newspaper or a weekly media magazine. Circle all the sporting events set for broadcast. Decide which ones you will watch. Thank the Heavenly Father for watchful care every moment of your life.

But many who heard the message believed, and the number of men grew to about five thousand. —ACTS 4:4

Nolan Ryan's strikeout legend grew with time. The Express overtook Walter Johnson in 1983 and added to his record with every appearance. In 1989, Ryan edged closer and closer to a baseball mark once believed unobtainable.

The Texas Rangers hosted the Oakland Athletics. Ryan's stats totaled 4,994 opponents called out on strikes.

Fans packed Arlington Stadium to witness the historic 5,000th strikeout. Supporters posted "K" signs along the rails whenever an Oakland batter struck out.

The excitement reached a fever pitch in the third. Ron Hassey took a 2–2 pitch for a called third strike. Strikeout number 4,999 entered the record books.

Rickey Henderson led off the top of the fifth. The speedster worked the count full, and Ryan threw his best fastball. Henderson swung and missed the 96 mph pitch and returned to the bench as victim 5,000.

Catcher Chad Kreuter walked to the mound to shake Ryan's hand. Every teammate on the field followed suit. The fans rose for a minute and a half standing ovation.

Five thousand strikeouts took Ryan over twenty years. Five thousand of anything is more than most people can imagine.

In the Bible, Peter and John preached the Good News of Jesus to crowds in Jerusalem. Many who heard believed, and the number of Christians grew to about 5,000.

Read the story in Acts 3:1-10 and 4:1-12. Pay special attention to verse 12. Praise God for His gift of salvation through Christ Jesus.

A man who strays from the path of understanding comes to rest in the company of the dead. —PROVERBS 21:16

Getting picked off embarrasses a baserunner. In baseball's major leagues, pickoffs seldom occur, but they give the defensive team a big boost. In 1983, the Baltimore Orioles astounded the Toronto Blue Jays.

In the top of the tenth, Toronto led 4–3. The Orioles had substituted all their regular catchers and were forced to insert infielder Lenn Sakata behind the plate.

With no outs, Bobby Bonnell took a large lead off first. But the outfielder strayed too far, and relief pitcher Tippy Martinez whipped the ball to the bag, nailing Bonnell.

Dave Collins batted next and walked. The speedster anticipated an easy steal off Sakata. But the outfielder took too large a lead. Martinez picked Collins off, too.

First baseman Willie Upshaw came to the plate. He beat out an infield hit and prepared to steal second. Incredibly, the relief pitcher picked off his third runner of the inning.

The Orioles took their turn at bat. They quickly tied the score, and Sakata added the final nail in Toronto's coffin. He blasted a 3-run homer to give Baltimore a 7–4 victory.

Bonnell, Collins, and Upshaw wished there had been a place to hide walking back from first base. But they could not escape the eyes of the crowd.

Each strayed too far from the base and paid the price, an out and a potential run erased. When we stray from what God wants, we pay the price too. Our punishment may be embarrassment or hurt, or it might be something more serious.

Recall a time you did something wrong. What price did you have to pay? Ask God to help you stay on His path.

The Lord takes his place in court; he rises to judge the people. —ISAIAH 3:13

The women's 100-meter race requires under 11 seconds to run. Victory sometimes narrows to centimeters.

In the 1993 World Track and Field Championship at Stuttgart, Germany, Gail Devers headed an all-star field. The American struggled for two years with Graves' disease before coming back to capture the 100-meter gold medal at the 1992 Barcelona Olympics.

The UCLA grad and Jamaica's Merlene Ottey crossed the finish line neck and neck. Officials studied the photographs to determine placement.

An image taken from the outside of the track indicated Devers' head crossed first, but Ottey's torso broke the plane before Devers'. In track, a tie goes to the torso.

But after viewing another photo shot from the inside, judges unanimously awarded the American first place. The decision-making took over an hour of study, discussion, and debate. Officials assigned Devers a time of 10.81 seconds and Ottey 10.82.

The judges wanted to be right. They desired to be fair, so they took their time. They examined the finish from every angle. They made the best decision possible.

God also takes His place as a judge. He makes just decisions. But if we ask, He also pardons us through the death of His Son, Jesus Christ. That's not fair. That's mercy.

Interview a legal judge or a sports official. Talk about justice or fairness and mercy. Invite him or her to share stories about some difficult judgments. Thank the person for willingness to make right decisions. Thank God for His judgment and His mercy.

Watch out that you do not lose what you have worked for, but that you may be rewarded fully. —2 JOHN 8

No hit thrills baseball fans like an inside-the-park home run. Watching a batter circle the bases with the ball in play brings everybody to his feet. But sometimes strange circumstances prevent a fielder from reaching the ball.

In 1929, the Cincinnati Reds traveled to Wrigley Field to face the Chicago Cubs. Third baseman Norm McMillan stepped to the plate in the bottom of the eighth with the bases loaded and the score tied 5–5.

McMillan bounced a base hit down the left-field line. The ball rolled into foul territory and appeared to be a sure double.

The baseball came to rest near the Cubs bullpen bench. The relief pitchers scattered to let Reds left fielder Evar Swanson field the ball. The rookie searched frantically but with no luck. He looked under, over, and around the bench.

Of course during Swanson's search, the Cubs' runners dashed around the bases. Finally McMillan crossed the plate with an inside-the-park homer, giving Chicago a 9–5 lead and ultimately the win.

The Reds outfielder picked up relief pitcher Ken Penner's warm-up jacket in disgust and threw it to the ground. The ball rolled out. It had been hidden up Penner's sleeve all the time.

Sometimes, like Swanson searching for the ball, we lose what we've worked for. It may have been there. We just couldn't find it.

Had the outfielder been more careful and moved the jacket, he might have held McMillan to a double or at most a triple. Being careful is often worth the trouble.

God asks that we guard against deceit. People pretend to be His followers but are not. Friends may tempt us to do wrong. Our Heavenly Father expects us to be alert.

Play a game of "keep-away-take-away" using a small ball that can easily be hidden. Pray, asking God to help you recognize people who try to lead you astray.

He pursues them and moves on unscathed, by a path his feet have not traveled before. —ISAIAH 41:3

The United States Amateur golf tournament uses match play rather than medal play. In the match play scoring system, winners are determined on a hole-by-hole basis rather than by total strokes.

In 1996, the two-time champion Tiger Woods pursued Steve Scott, trailing the 19 year old by two holes with three remaining. Hopes sank for a third straight title.

But the University of Florida golfer put his second shot on 16 into the bunker and salvaged a par. Woods birdied the hole, narrowing the gap to 1.

Woods' 6-iron approach shot to the 17th left him 30 feet from the pin. The Stanford alum guided the ball to the cup for another birdie and tied the match.

The linksters both parred the final hole and entered a playoff. Both missed birdie putts and collected pars on the first extra hole to remain tied.

On the next hole, the 38th of the day, Woods tapped in a 2-foot putt for a par. Scott 2-putted the par 3 for a bogey. After 8 hours and 20 minutes of play, Tiger became the first golfer to capture three consecutive U.S. Amateur titles.

Tiger Woods had been down that path before but not in quite the same way. He had never come from behind late on the course, and he hadn't won the other two in playoffs. But Tiger traveled the path well and emerged unscathed.

Isaiah described another Who pursued a path He hadn't traveled before and emerged unscathed. Isaiah described God.

Walk or hike down a new path. Be alert to obstacles so that you can return home unscathed. Praise God for His guidance down untraveled paths.

If you return to the Almighty, you will be restored.

—JOB 22:23

Resuming normal activity following a trauma requires determination. In 1995, Monica Seles returned to the tennis court with courage and resolve.

Seles entered the Canadian Open following a twenty-eight-month layoff. Fans wondered how the 21 year old would fare after a knife attack by a mentally unstable spectator in Hamburg, Germany. Seles breezed through the early rounds without losing a set.

The returning superstar faced Amanda Coetzer in the finals. The South African had also played outstanding tennis, defeating three higher-ranking players—Steffi Graf, Mary Pierce, and Jana Novotna—on her path to the final.

Seles displayed her solid form in the championship match. She dispatched Coetzer in 51 minutes, winning straight sets 6-0, 6-1.

Seles returned to tennis. She rehabilitated, practiced, concentrated, and was restored to her previous championship form.

God assures us, too, that if we do wrong we can return to Him. If we repent, ask His forgiveness, and concentrate on following His Word, we will be restored to Him.

Find something in your home that needs restoring. It might be an old photograph, a book, an appliance, a piece of furniture, or a flower bed. Do your best to return it to its original state or find someone who can do the restoration for you. Thank God for forgiveness and restoration.

My disgrace is before me all day long, and my face is covered with shame. —**PSALM 44:15**

Track meets run with precision. If a competitor misses the start time, there's no second chance.

In the 1972 Munich Olympics, Americans Ray Robinson, Ed Hart, and Robert Taylor advanced to the second round of the 100-meter race. Following their morning heats, coach Stan Wright informed them the semi-finals would begin at 7 P.M. Unfortunately, Wright's eighteen-month-old schedule had been changed.

Robinson, Hart, Taylor, and Wright left the Olympic village in late afternoon. While waiting for the bus to the stadium, they wandered into the ABC television headquarters.

Watching the monitors, the Americans viewed a shot of the 100-meter race. The quartet asked if the broadcast was a tape of the earlier heats. ABC officials informed them it was live.

The coach and his runners panicked. Bill Norris, an ABC employee, shoved the group into a car and sped to the arena. Only Taylor arrived in time.

Without a warm-up, Robert Taylor placed second and qualified for the finals. The Texan repeated his second-place finish the following day and captured the silver medal. Robinson and Hart lost their chances.

Ray Robinson, Ed Hart, and especially coach Stan Wright felt the shame of the honest mistake. For days, they pictured empty lanes and the completed race. The disgrace and what-might-have-beens would haunt them for a long time and every Olympic season.

In such times, we second-guess ourselves and feel far from God. We ask why He lets bad things happen. We want to know why He allows honest mistakes. But the Heavenly Father never promised life would be perfect. He promised mercy and grace. The difficulty is not His forgiveness. The problem is forgiving ourselves.

Does something you have said or done continue to bother you even though you've asked for God's forgiveness and the forgiveness of other people involved? If so, ask God to help you forgive yourself.

> *"He makes his angels winds, his servants flames of fire."*
>
> **—HEBREWS 1:7**

Bob Beamon's long jump record held for 23 years. In the 1980s, Carl Lewis won gold, but never the world mark. But Tokyo's 1991 World Track and Field Championships provided an excellent opportunity.

King Carl faced only one major challenger. Mike Powell had finished runner-up to Lewis in more than a dozen competitions. But Powell possessed the talent to set a world record if he could only master technique.

Excitement and emotion affected the UC–Irvine grad's first attempt. He leaped only 25 feet, 9 inches. Lewis went over 28.

Powell calmed. His jumps increased to 28 feet plus inches but so did his competition. Lewis cleared 29 feet, 2 3/4 inches, 1/4 inch above the world mark. Due to excessive wind, however, the leap could not count.

The Californian knew what was needed. On his fifth attempt, he studied the approach. Powell took four slow steps then burst into a full gallop. To avoid fouling, he leaped 2 inches short of the bar.

The challenger drove off his left leg and propelled himself into the air. In midflight, Powell performed a hitch kick. As he neared the landing, the man who finished second so many times threw his legs in front.

Powell bolted from the pit. Officials measured. The tape showed 29 feet, 4 1/2 inches. The wind gauge read under the allowable. The man so often in Lewis' shadow established a new world record.

With his heart on fire with desire, Powell leaped like the wind. He moved from a forever second to the man in first.

When we become Christians, God promises us His power. With the flame of His Spirit inside us, we can measure up to what our Heavenly Father desires for us.

Using a tape measure or yardstick, measure 29 feet, 4 1/2 inches. See how far you can long jump. How close did you come to Powell's record? Ask God to help you measure up to His standards.

"All things have been committed to me by my Father. No one knows the Son except the Father, and no one knows the Father except the Son and those to whom the Son chooses to reveal him." —MATTHEW 11:27

Ken Griffey Jr. debuted in the major leagues in 1989 as an 18-year-old outfielder. He quickly earned a reputation as a top hitter and defensive center fielder.

While Junior embarked on his professional career with the Seattle Mariners, his father, Ken Griffey Sr., continued as a contributor to the Cincinnati Reds. However, playing in rival leagues prevented the father from watching his son in action.

In late August 1991, a dream situation unfolded. Griffey Sr. accepted a late season trade from the Reds to Seattle. The situation created a media event. The first father-son tandem in major league history took the field.

The Griffeys trotted to the outfield before the national anthem sounded. Junior played his familiar center, and Senior manned left.

The father-son combo batted second and third. Dad held the second slot. Son hit third.

With one out, Griffey Sr. punched a single past second. Junior kept the scoring threat alive with a hit to center. Both father and son eventually scored, and Seattle breezed to a 5–2 victory.

It's never easy for a son to follow in his father's footsteps. Comparisons always happen, and many can't handle the stress.

Christ could have chosen not to follow His Father's plans. No one would have blamed Him for avoiding the pain and suffering He endured.

But Christ did come to live as a man. He experienced emotions. He knew joy and sadness, pleasure and pain, acceptance and rejection.

Most importantly He gave His life to save us. No father ever received, or son ever gave, a greater gift.

Ask your father, mother, grandfather, grandmother, son, or daughter to describe his or her work in detail. Pray for God's guidance as you follow the Heavenly Father.

The commander of the Lord's army replied, "Take off your sandals, for the place where you are standing is holy." And Joshua did so. —JOSHUA 5:15

Marathons often produce strange results. In the 1960 Rome Olympics, spectators witnessed one of the strangest ever.

Officials made significant changes for the event. The race ran entirely at night. It started and ended outside the stadium.

Just before the halfway mark, two front-runners emerged. Rhadi Ben Abdesselem of Morocco and Abebe Bikila of Ethiopia paced side by side, never glancing at one another.

Bikila, a member of the Ethiopian Imperial Bodyguard, caught everyone's eye. He competed barefoot.

The Ethiopian and his coach, Onni Niskanen, had surveyed the route several days earlier. They determined Bikila would make his final move at the Obelisk of Axum, about a mile from the finish.

As the pacesetters passed the landmark that had been plundered by Italian soldiers during World War II, Bikila pulled away from Abdesselem. He increased his lead to almost 200 yards before breaking the tape. The barefoot runner sliced .8 seconds off Sergei Popov's world record in capturing the gold.

Abebe removed his shoes for the marathon. He competed barefoot for fear shoes would rub blisters on the soles of his feet.

Centuries before, another leader also removed his shoes. But his shoes were sandals, and he wasn't running a race. Joshua stood on holy ground.

Today we demonstrate respect by removing hats, opening doors, or standing when the person is introduced or enters the room. In other countries and cultures, bowing or covering the head shows homage.

We honor the Lord through kind words, appropriate speech, right choices, and good deeds. We show respect for God through prayer, praise, worship, and obedience.

Think of the three most important people in the world. How would you act and what would you say if you met them? Pray to God with honor and respect.

Strengthen the feeble hands, steady the knees that give way. —ISAIAH 35:3

In the 1950s, polio left thousands of children barely able to walk. Wilma Rudolph, the twentieth of twenty-two children, weighed only 4 1/2 pounds at birth. She suffered from polio, double pneumonia, and scarlet fever as a child. Disease damaged her left leg, leaving it useless.

Doctors placed a brace on the injured limb when she turned 6. Eventually, an orthopedic shoe replaced the brace.

Rudolph's mother and brothers massaged the leg every day. At 11, Wilma threw away the corrective shoes and began playing basketball with her siblings.

Her body developed quickly. In 1956, she won a bronze medal in the Melbourne Olympics as a member of the 4 x 100 meter relay.

After high school graduation, Rudolph entered Tennessee State University. The TSU Tigerbelle competed in the 1960 Rome Olympics.

The once sickly child dominated the 100-meter race. She won by three strides and broke the world's record with an 11.0. The new mark could not hold, however, because the wind exceeded the allowable 2 meters per second. Rudolph also won gold medals in the 200 meters and 4 x 100 relay.

Premature birth, polio, double pneumonia, scarlet fever—any one of these can result in death or permanent disability. But Wilma Rudolph overcame all four. She not only overcame, she conquered.

How did the young woman do it? Her family stood behind her, beside her, and around her. They massaged, encouraged, played, and supported her every stride of the way. Without their help, Wilma wouldn't have won gold or run for her college education.

God created families for love, nurturing, guidance, and support. Parents, grandparents, brothers, sisters, aunts, uncles, and cousins steady us when we're weak and pick us up when we fall. Like the Heavenly Father, they love us no matter what.

Remember when someone in your family helped you through a difficult time. Remind the relative of the experience and thank him or her again for the support. Praise God for His gift of families.

For men will hear of your great name and your mighty hand and your outstretched arm. —1 KINGS 8:42

Jim Abbott wanted to stay ahead of the batters. He set a goal of being competitive and avoiding self-destruction. But on a Saturday in 1993, the New York Yankee left-hander went beyond his objective and pitched the baseball game of his life.

New York hosted the Cleveland Indians. Abbott had faced the Tribe six days earlier and lasted fewer than four innings. The frustrated University of Michigan alum gave up 10 hits and 7 runs.

The hurler noticed little difference in how his pitches felt. But his fastball exploded, and his breaking ball moved sharply.

Abbott walked five batters, but none advanced past first base. Not a single Indian tallied a base hit.

The 27,225 Bronx fans jumped to their feet and screamed in the bottom of the ninth. Kenny Lofton enraged them by attempting to bunt before grounding out.

Felix Fermin flied out to deep center. The final batter, Carlos Baerga, hit a soft ground ball to short. Randy Velarde charged, fielded cleanly, and threw to first baseman Don Mattingly for the final out. Jim Abbott became the eighth New York Yankee to pitch a no-hitter in the team's ninety-year history.

Throwing a no-hitter is in itself an amazing feat. But Jim Abbott became a collegiate All-American, played on the 1988 Olympic team, and made the pros—all without a right hand. He was born with just a stub.

To take the mound, the creative pitcher placed the glove on this right arm. After Abbott threw with his left hand, he immediately slipped the glove to his left hand so he could field.

God gives us each talents and abilities. Sometimes He asks us to overcome obstacles to use them.

Volunteer at a Challenger Division baseball game or for the Special Olympics. If that's not possible, read about President Franklin Roosevelt. Note the physical challenge he faced. Ask God to help you overcome obstacles in your life.

When the righteous triumph, there is great elation.

—PROVERBS 28:12a

The Northwestern University Wildcats opened the 1995 collegiate football season with a trip to South Bend, Indiana. The Notre Dame Fighting Irish envisioned the celebration of Lou Holtz's 200th victory.

The Wildcats opened the scoring with a 7-yard first-quarter touchdown pass to Dave Beazley. Notre Dame narrowed the gap with a second-period field goal, but Northwestern quickly matched it.

One of the game's key plays came just before halftime. Robert Farmer scored the Irish's first touchdown on a 5-yard run. But the extra point attempt went awry, and the Wildcats maintained a 1-point lead.

In the second half, Steve Schnur passed to D'Wayne Bates for a 26-yard score, upping Northwestern's lead to 17–9. The Irish rallied with Randy Kinder taking the ball in from 2 yards out in the fourth quarter. But Ron Powlus' 2-point conversion pass fell harmlessly incomplete. The Wildcats held on for a 17–15 upset win, their first victory over Notre Dame in 33 years.

Holtz's team suffered shock instead of wild celebration. The comeback had fallen short. Northwestern had triumphed. The Wildcats felt the elation.

Sometimes, like the Fighting Irish, we get behind and can't catch up. Our efforts seem to fall just short.

But God stands ready to give us a clear mind and an energetic spirit. Through biblical examples and Christian leaders, we can learn to be more organized, to get tasks completed, and to catch up.

Make a list of things you need to do this week. Next to each item, note a day you can do it and about how long it will take to complete the task. Be flexible, but stick with your basic plan. Ask God to help you accomplish your goal.

I know that everything God does will endure forever; nothing can be added to it and nothing taken from it. God does it so that men will revere Him. —ECCLESIASTES 3:14

Phil Regan, the Baltimore Orioles manager, penciled Ripken's name on the lineup card. This September baseball game with the California Angels, however, had special meaning. It marked the 2,131st consecutive time Cal Ripken Jr. had appeared on the diamond.

The moment the Baltimore shortstop took the field, he broke Hall of Famer Lou Gehrig's record. Baseball faithfuls had considered the Yankee's streak almost sacred.

Ripken's streak began May 30, 1982, when his father, Cal Sr., plugged him in at third base. Cal, Jr., moved to shortstop soon afterward, and for the next thirteen years he remained a fixture on the Orioles infield.

At one point, a shoulder injury suffered in a scuffle almost ended Ripken's string of consecutive games. Fortunately, the Orioles did not play the following day, and the shoulder healed enough for the iron man to continue.

With all eyes on him, Baltimore's favorite player belted a home run in the bottom of the fourth. When the game became official in the fifth, the stands exploded with a 22-minute standing ovation. Ripken celebrated the moment with a stroll around the field, tipping his cap to the adoring crowd.

Someday Ripken's long series of consecutive games will end. Another name will be penciled in his spot.

God, however, never changes. He was present at the beginning of time and will remain until its end. God is the constant in a universe of change.

What God creates lasts forever, so we honor Him. The glory belongs to Him now and forever more.

Make a list of things that last a long time. Compare them with the lasting nature of God. Thank God for always being there.

Then Jesus said to Simon, "Don't be afraid; from now on you will catch men." —**LUKE 5:10b**

The Los Angeles Raiders waived James Lofton at age 33. But at age 36, the wide receiver continued to snare passes for the Buffalo Bills. In the 1992 season opener, the seven-time Pro Bowler needed just 55 yards to break Steve Largent's NFL receiving record of 13,089.

The Bills hosted the Los Angeles Rams. The former number one draft choice bought nearly sixty tickets for family and friends to watch what he hoped would be his record-breaking performance.

Buffalo coasted to an early lead on Thurman Thomas' 3 touchdown runs. Late in the fourth quarter, with the Bills in front 40-7, Lofton snagged his fourth reception of the game. The 6-yard curl brought enough yardage for Lofton to best Largent's record by 2 yards.

Officials stopped the game momentarily as teammates mobbed the wide receiver. The sellout crowd of 80,290 cheered madly as Lofton received the commemorative ball and left the field.

Lofton made his living catching passes. The Packers drafted him for just that purpose. His fearless grabs enabled him to gain more yards than anyone, even when some thought he was a has-been.

Jesus called Simon Peter. He asked him to be fearless and to catch men instead of his usual fish. Catching men meant bringing them to Christ. It meant telling them of Jesus' love.

God reminds us not to be afraid. He calls us to catch men, women, boys, and girls for Him. Our Heavenly Father asks us to tell them of Jesus' love.

Play catch with a friend or relative. As you throw, talk about how Jesus called Simon Peter to catch men. Think of someone you can tell about Jesus. Ask God to keep you from being afraid.

The Lord your God has blessed you in all the work of your hands. He has watched over your journey through this vast desert. —DEUTERONOMY 2:7a

Mark Whiten fits the mold of a classic journeyman baseball outfielder. Moving from team to team, he struggles every spring to make the roster. But in the second game of a 1993 doubleheader, Whiten rewrote several entries in baseball's record book.

In the top of the first inning, the St. Louis Cardinal outfielder faced Larry Luebbers of the Cincinnati Reds. With the bases loaded, Whiten clubbed a home run.

After fouling out in the fourth, the Cardinal came up with two men on, in both the sixth and seventh. Both times Whiten connected for 3-run homers on Mike Anderson pitches.

The St. Louis slugger got a final at bat in the ninth. With one man aboard and Rob Dibble pitching, Whiten belted his fourth round-tripper.

The final long ball put the much-traveled outfielder in elite company. Only 12 men in baseball history have blasted 4 homers in a single contest. The 12 RBIs in a game tied Hall of Famer Jim Bottomley's record. One RBI in the first game, plus the 12 in the second equaled Nate Colbert's double-header mark.

Every baseball player dreams of a game like Mark Whiten's. Most go through an entire career and never come close.

Each of us dreams of doing great things too. Sometimes our dreams come true, but often our lives seem dull and ordinary.

In God's eyes, however, our lives are special. He watches as we travel through this world. No activity is too insignificant for His concern. No place is too remote.

Plan a short trip. Make a list of places to visit and things to do. Praise God for being with you on life's journey.

The world and its desires pass away, but the man who does the will of God lives forever. —1 JOHN 2:17

Ty Detmer entered his senior year as the NCAA's number two quarterback in passing yardage. In Brigham Young University's second football game of the 1991 season, he jumped to the number one spot.

The UCLA Bruins entertained the BYU Cougars. Both teams ranked in the top 25 and hoped to use the game as a spring to the top 10.

Detmer, the 1990 Heisman Trophy winner, displayed his great passing arm. He connected on 29 of 46 attempts for 377 yards and threw 2 touchdown passes. In the second quarter, the quarterback's passing yardage pushed him past San Diego State's Todd Santos for the number one spot.

UCLA refused to be impressed with the BYU signal caller. The Bruins went ahead 27–23 in the fourth quarter. On its next possession, UCLA gambled on fourth-and-two at the BYU 14. But the Cougar defense held.

Detmer attempted a legendary BYU comeback. Mixing his plays with perfection, the Cougars entered Bruin territory. The All-American play caller drove his troops inside the 20 and faced fourth-and-seven with 1:27 to play.

Ignoring the needed first down, Detmer went for all the marbles. He lofted a pass into the end zone for wide receiver Bryce Doman. But Carl Greenwood, a redshirt freshman playing his first collegiate game, batted the ball harmlessly to the ground. Detmer had the record, but UCLA had the win.

As they look in the record book, few remember Detmer's team lost the day he broke the passing record. Some day another quarterback will surpass his feat.

Athletic accomplishments fade. New players replace the old who are soon forgotten. Unless they are alive at Christ's return, each person on earth will one day pass away. But if we trust in God, we will live forever with Him.

Practice passing a football to a friend or relative. Thank God for His gift of eternal life.

> Even a child is known by his actions, by whether his conduct is pure and right. —**PROVERBS 20:11**

Talent determines a champion on the tennis court. In 1979, two young and talented players challenged each other for the United States Open title.

In the finals, 24-year-old Chris Evert met 16-year-old Tracy Austin. Oddsmakers favored Evert, the winner of four straight Opens.

But Austin, an emerging star from California, carried strong credentials. She advanced to the championship by upsetting second-ranked Martina Navratilova in straight sets.

Both competitors checked their emotions and played with calm control. Both worked hard. The match lacked drama.

Austin won the mental battle. She routinely hit hard two-handed backhand cross-court shots, forcing Evert into errors. Her toughness and determination surprised the capacity crowd and the millions watching via television.

The 11th-grade Austin defeated former champion Evert in straight sets, 6-4, 6-3. Tracy Austin became the youngest female champion in U.S. Open history.

Actions gave the teen the crown. Her conduct playing pure tennis on the court brought victory.

Whether an adult or a child, we are known by our actions. People usually are aware if our conduct is right or wrong, good or bad. But even if they don't, God does.

Look up the word pure *in the dictionary. See how many items labeled "pure" you can find in your home. What does a manufacturer mean when it advertises that its products are pure? Ask God to help you be known for pure and good conduct.*

"Do this in remembrance of me." —LUKE 22:19b

September Friday nights provide a familiar landmark in Texas towns. The towers of the local high school football fields light the way across the Lone Star state.

The illumination not only signals the start of a school year and football season, but also brings fresh hopes and new beginnings. In 1997, when the small town of Jarrell saw the Friday night lights, remembrance mixed with anticipation.

The previous May, a deadly tornado had ripped through central Texas. Twenty-seven Jarrell residents lost their lives. Six played on the football team. Media flocked in for the season opener. Satellite trucks ringed the field, their antennas reaching high above the light standards. Newspapers and magazines from across the nation sent reporters. But the residents largely ignored them.

Prior to the kickoff, the Jarrell Cougars and Bruceville-Eddy Eagles knelt in prayer. The Cougars wore a black stripe on the blue jerseys to commemorate their friends. The team needed no other outward signs of mourning. Memories were enough.

The contest reflected the drama of high school football. Bruceville-Eddy jumped to a quick 18–0 first-half lead. But Jarrell battled back and scored a touchdown four seconds before halftime.

The Cougars took control after intermission. They gained the lead in the fourth quarter and held on for a 27–24 victory. Coach Tracy Burke praised his team for playing with honor.

The Jarrell team didn't talk about it. Yet every snap of the ball, every pass, every tackle brought back thoughts of players who should have been there but weren't. They remembered.

Jesus asked His followers to remember Him, too. As they shared the Passover supper, Christ reflected on His body and blood. Today as we take part in the Lord's Supper or Communion, we remember Christ's death for our sins.

Observe or participate in the Lord's Supper. Pay attention to the meaning of the bread and wine and read Luke 24:14-20. Spend a few minutes remembering Jesus' sacrifice.

"I am the first and I am the last; apart from me there is no God." —ISAIAH 44:6

Pete Sampras wanted to be ranked the number one tennis player in the world. What better place to showcase his skills than the 1993 United States Open?

The defending champion faced France's Cedric Pioline in the finals. Sampras dominated the challenger from the start.

A forceful forehand, precision volleys, and an overpowering serve befuddled the Frenchman. A dozen aces unmercifully blew past Pioline as Sampras completed the match in barely over two hours. The higher-ranked player swept his competitor 6–4, 6–4, and 6–3.

Sampras had won his first Wimbledon crown the previous July. The victories brought him the rare distinction of Grand Slam triumphs on both grass and hardcourts. The consecutive U.S. Open titles coupled with the English crown moved Sampras to first place in the world rankings over Jim Courier.

In athletics, many earn first-place finishes and blue ribbons. We debate about who is the number one quarterback, the best pitcher, the most out-standing rebounder, the greatest goalie, or the top-ranked tennis player. Each year, sports stars shine, fade, and are forgotten.

But God is the first, the last, and the only God. He is Creator, Father, Lord, and Savior. He loves us, hears us, guides us, and protects us. Our Heavenly Father will never fade. He is forever.

Make a mental list of sports stars you remember from past years. Compare notes with some other people. Are they still stars or have they faded? Do you know what they're doing now? Praise God for being an everlasting God.

"Will a man rob God? Yet you rob me." —MALACHI 3:8

In seven Olympiads, the United States had never lost a single basketball game. At the 1972 Munich games, the Americans advanced to the finals against the Russians.

The game began 15 minutes before midnight to accommodate television. Coach Hank Iba's team had better speed, but the Oklahoma State coach preferred a controlled style.

The Eastern Europeans inched ahead. With 6 minutes to play, they led by 8.

The Americans switched to a full-court press and cut the margin. But with 6 seconds to play, the U.S. trailed by 1; the Russians had the ball.

Sasha Belov accidentally threw the ball to Doug Collins. Sako Sakandelidze intentionally fouled Collins, and the Illinois State collegian sank both free throws.

The Russians inbounded, but a referee halted play with 1 second remaining. After a second inbound pass, the final buzzer sounded.

But R. William Jones, Secretary-General of the Federation International de Basketball (FIBA) ordered a replay without cause and put 3 seconds on the clock. Ivan Edeshko threw a long pass to Belov. The Russian caught the ball, knocked aside two defenders, and scored the winning basket. No foul whistle blew.

The United States appealed, but a five-member committee upheld the score by a 3–2 vote. The Americans refused their silver medals in protest.

Officials rarely favor one team. But when they do, it feels like robbery. The U.S. team felt robbed of the gold medal.

On earth, robbers both take things that aren't theirs and keep things that should go to others. As Christians, we might never steal in the legal sense. But we steal a good name through gossip. We take praise for another's ideas or work. We fail to give our tithes and offerings. We spend God's time on ourselves. In short, we rob God.

If you've been robbed, remember the experience. If not, interview a victim. Inquire about his feelings. Ask God to keep you from stealing legally, morally, or spiritually.

Surely he will never be shaken; a righteous man will be remembered forever. —PSALM 112:6

Jimmy Connors dominated tennis in the 1970s and early 1980s. Age and injuries eventually wore down the Illinois native. But in 1991 Jimbo showed the world that true champions never quit.

The former number one, ranked 174th, faced Peter McEnroe in the opening match of the United States Open. The younger brother of John McEnroe captured the first two sets. Peter was down three games to none in set three, and many thought the aging veteran would make a hasty exit.

McEnroe went to 40–0 in game four. Nine points away from elimination, Jimbo rallied. The five-time U.S. Open champion took three straight sets in a grueling 4 1/2-hour match. The vocal New York crowd cheered.

Connors discovered a fountain of youth and played like the champion of old. The 39 year old blitzed by Michael Schapers and Karl Novacek.

Next came 24-year-old Aaron Krickstein. The youngster pushed the former superstar. With the match tied 2–2, Krickstein led the fifth set, 5–2. But the miracle comeback continued, and Connors won the set and match in a tiebreaker.

Paul Haarhuis met the sentimental favorite in the quarterfinals. Connors endured another five-set match and advanced to the semifinals against Jim Courier.

The Cinderella tale ended. Courier won the match easily in straight sets. But none forgot Connors' exhibition. He exited with the grace and style of a legend.

The aging star was never shaken. Tennis fans still remember the 1991 tournament and Jimmy Connors' courage.

The psalmist reminds us that when we put our faith in God, we cannot be shaken. And if we are righteous, the Lord will remember us forever with the gift of eternal life through Christ Jesus.

Make yourself a milkshake or frosted soda by blending ice cream with either milk or soda pop. Watch the ingredients shake together. Thank God for His unshakeable love.

I give you this charge: Preach the Word; be prepared in season and out of season. —2 TIMOTHY 4:1-2

Marshall Faulk didn't expect much action. As a freshman tailback, he played behind T. C. Wright. But when Wright's injury forced Faulk into the lineup, he carried his name into the NCAA football record book.

The San Diego State Aztecs hosted the University of the Pacific Tigers. Faulk entered the contest with 3:55 left in the first quarter. By the end of the third, the tailback had rushed for 323 yards.

Faulk finished the game with 386 yards on 37 carries. His totals surpassed the NCAA record of 377 yards in 52 tries held by Indiana's Anthony Thompson.

The freshman running back from New Orleans scored 7 touchdowns and 44 total points to set NCAA freshman records. His scoring runs of 9, 5, 61, 7, 47, 2, and 25 yards lifted the Aztecs to a 55–34 victory over the Tigers.

When coach Ted Tollner looked down the bench and motioned to the young running back, Faulk grabbed his helmet, listened to the coach's instructions, and trotted onto the field. He was ready.

Faulk had practiced hard, learned the plays, and kept his head in the game. Playing was a surprise, but he was prepared.

God asks that we prepare for the expected and the unexpected. By eating right, staying in shape, and keeping our bodies healthy, we're ready for the unexpected physically. Prayer, worship, and Bible study keep us spiritually prepared.

Plan a fun surprise for a friend or family member. Watch how she reacts. Was she ready? Ask God to keep you prepared to face whatever happens in life.

He lifted me out of the slimy pit, out of the mud and mire; he set my feet on a rock and gave me a firm place to stand. —**PSALM 40:2**

Field conditions sometimes make playing football difficult. In 1940, the Detroit Lions and Chicago Cardinals discovered how miserable nature's elements can be.

The two teams tangled at a neutral site, Buffalo's War Memorial Stadium. About 18,000 fans hoped to watch high-caliber National Football League action.

Shortly after kickoff, a blinding, chilling thunderstorm turned the turf into a sea of mud. To save money, the NFL used only one football per game. The pigskin soon became waterlogged.

Mud covered every player. No one could tell who played for which team. The players on the field resembled pigs wallowing in a sty.

Neither team could muster any offense. Detroit almost scored in the third quarter when Lloyd Cardwell snared Dwight Sloan's wobbly pass for a 26-yard gain to the Chicago 1-yard line. But the Cardinals sacked Sloan twice and intercepted his third-down desperation pass.

After that, neither team attempted any offense. During the fourth quarter, the teams exchanged punts eight straight times without running a play from scrimmage. The game mercifully ended in a scoreless tie, before the days of overtime.

Playing in the mud may be fun for a while, but not for long. The weight of wet dirt makes moving difficult. Slipping makes traction impossible.

In life we may feel as if we're bogged down or slipping. We can't move forward because we dwell on the bad or the past.

God can help us out of life's mud and put us firmly on His rock, Jesus. By focusing on Him, we find solid footing.

Wearing old clothes, make a small amount of mud. Run the slime through your fingers. Then pick up a rock. Consider the difference. Thank God for being your rock.

Show me the way I should go, for to you I lift up my soul. —**PSALM 143:8b**

Stefka Kostadinova overwhelmed the competition in the high jump. From 1985 to 1987, the Bulgarian won 73 of 77 meets and set three world records. Her mark of 6 feet, 10 1/4 inches, topped the record books. But in the 1988 Olympics, a Texan matched the Eastern European inch for inch.

Louise Ritter grew up in Red Oak, Texas, a small town on the southern outskirts of Dallas. Her high-jumping career had shown bright promise but produced limited success. But the 30 year old had bested Kostadinova twice in 1987.

Ritter and Kostadinova eliminated all challengers by clearing seven heights without a miss. At 6 feet, 8 inches, both competitors missed three times forcing a jump-off.

The Bulgarian jumped first and missed. Ritter knew she had to give her best or the opportunity would be lost.

Fighting off aching legs, the American moved her approach point back a foot. Running at full speed, she leaped with every ounce of her strength.

Ritter cleared the bar. On the way down her right thigh grazed it. But the standard held, and the Texan captured the victory and the gold.

Stefka and Louise both got great lift. They jumped heights taller than themselves. They found their way to records and medals.

When we lift our hearts and souls to God, we feel Him very near. If we ask and listen, the Lord will show us the way to live. The Heavenly Father will guide us in making good choices and choosing lasting Christian friends.

Visit a local track and observe the high jumpers or watch the event on television. Notice the lift of the competitors. Lift your thoughts to God through prayer and praise.

You were taught . . . to be made new in the attitude of your minds; and to put on the new self, created to be like God in true righteousness and holiness. —EPHESIANS 4:22-24

The Cleveland Browns anticipated the opening game of the 1950 season. After four years of competing in the All-American Football Conference, coach Paul Brown's team would finally showcase its talent in the National Football League.

The Browns traveled to Philadelphia to engage the defending champion Eagles. Brown had sent his two assistant coaches, Fritz Heisler and Blanton Collier, to scout the 1949 title game. He designed a game plan using a man-in-motion to neutralize the Eagles' 5–4 defense.

Cleveland threw 3 straight passes on its first possession. All fell incomplete, but the Browns found the key to victory. The Philadelphia linebackers had covered the man-in-motion, leaving the wide receivers in single coverage.

The Eagles opened with a field goal. But Otto Graham and the Cleveland offense kicked into high gear.

Graham tossed scoring strikes to Dub Jones, Dante Lavelli, and Mac Speedie. With a 21–3 lead, the Browns turned to ball control, using Marion Motley and Rex Bumgardner. Cleveland prevailed 35–10. The upstart Browns proved to the National Football League they belonged.

Cleveland put on new uniforms in a new conference for a new season. Coach Brown knew he had to think with a new attitude. He taught the players. And the team showed its worth. The new kids won.

When we become Christians, God gives us a new heart and a new beginning. But He also gives us freedom. He will help us, but He lets us choose how we act and how we live.

Like the Browns, we can work hard and show our worth. We can be God's people. Or we can forget His teachings. The decision is ours.

Look on the sports page of a newspaper at the National Football League standings. Note the records of the newer expansion teams. Thank God for the new beginning He gives.

And they asked each other, "Who will roll the stone away from the entrance of the tomb?" —MARK 16:3

Last-second victories sometimes require desperate measures. In 1978, the Oakland Raiders faced fourth down with the ball on the San Diego Charger 14-yard line. They trailed 20–14 with only ten seconds remaining.

Quarterback Ken Stabler stepped back to pass. But a strong Charger rush flushed the Raider signal caller from the pocket.

An incompletion or a sack would end the game. The quick-thinking Stabler intentionally fumbled the ball forward. Running back Pete Banaszak reached the pigskin around the 8-yard line and slapped it toward the goal line.

Tight end Dave Casper watched the ball roll into the end zone and fell on it for a Raider touchdown. Oakland kicked the extra point and captured an incredible 21-20 win.

The chance for a victory roll will never happen again. In 1979, the National Football League rules committee disallowed an offensive team from advancing the ball on a fumble in the final two minutes of either half.

Oakland had one chance, a forward fumble. Stabler and his teammates looked like young children rolling the ball. But the plan worked. The concerned Raiders won.

Centuries before, some women were also concerned. They wanted to properly anoint Jesus' body for burial. But a stone sealed the tomb's entrance. How could they roll it away?

They didn't need to worry. The stone was moved. Jesus conquered death. He arose. Hallelujah!

Read Mark 16:1-6. Praise God for the risen Savior.

Create in me a pure heart, O God, and renew a steadfast spirit within me. —PSALM 51:10

Dan O'Brien missed an opportunity to compete for the decathlon gold medal when he failed to clear the pole vault in the 1992 U.S. Olympic Trials. But the 1991 world champion had a chance to recover a measure of success at the Talence Invitational after the Olympics.

On the first day of competition, the American set new highs in the long jump and shot put. The following day, he broke his individual discus mark and bested his javelin record with each successive throw. His point total positioned the decathlete perfectly to break the world record in the final event, the 1,500 meters.

O'Brien required a time of 4 minutes 49 seconds to beat Daley Thompson's record-setting mark of 8,847 points. The American ran the race in 4:42.10. The crowd of 5,000 track-and-field enthusiasts roared with every lap and cheered wildly when officials posted the final time. O'Brien became the first American to hold the world record since Bruce Jenner in 1976.

O'Brien could have given up and quit after missing the Olympic team. Instead he searched his heart and spirit and returned to his training determined to win.

He renewed his efforts. He focused on each event and what he could do to improve. He put aside the distractions of failure and the Olympics.

His hard work paid off. The crowd's cheers broke the silence of Dan's solitary training. He won.

Just as O'Brien had to train by himself, we must spend time alone with God. In quietness, God renews our spirits.

Turn off the television, computer, radio, and CD player. Set a timer and spend five minutes in silence. Think about God and read Psalm 93 in your Bible. Pray for a clean heart and a new spirit.

Remember the former things, those of long ago; I am God, and there is no other; I am God, and there is none like me. I make known the end from the beginning, from ancient times, what is still to come. —ISAIAH 46:9-10

Most people remember Terry Bradshaw as the Pittsburgh Steelers quarterback who won four Super Bowl championships. Younger fans know him as a television commentator. But few recall Bradshaw's first National Football League game.

The Steelers drafted the Louisiana Tech quarterback as the NFL's number one player in 1970. The Pittsburgh faithful put high hopes in his ability to lead the team from professional football's cellar.

Bradshaw had great physical talent, but small college competition had not prepared him for the rigors of the pros. Coach Chuck Noll started the rookie in the Steelers' season opener against the Houston Oilers despite his inexperience.

The performance was ugly. The quarterback's passes wobbled or bounced off receivers like rockets. Ron Shanklin worked free for a sure touchdown, but the pass arced so high defenders tackled him 20 yards from the goal line.

The Steeler play caller misfired on 9 straight passes and gave up a safety when he backed out of the end zone. Coach Noll mercifully ended the embarrassment by substituting Terry Hanratty in the third quarter. Bradshaw completed only 4 of 16 passes for 70 yards.

Terry Bradshaw made a poor first impression. In time, however, he improved.

It's the same when we become new Christians. We are filled with energy and vigor. But sometimes we stumble and fall as we attempt to share our faith.

Telling the Good News is exciting. A little practice and study make a difference. Enthusiasm for spreading His Word plus public speaking experience form an unbeatable combination.

Share your personal testimony with a Christian you respect. Review the strong and weak points. Polish it until the words flow and the message rings true. Ask God to help you as you share your faith.

Then Jesus answered, "Woman, you have great faith! Your request is granted." —**MATTHEW 15:28**

Female athletes have made great strides in recent years. In 1992, a woman won the right to play with the male professional elite.

The Tampa Bay Lightning of the National Hockey League signed Manon Rheaume in August 1992. Rheaume had competed in junior hockey from the day she could skate. She tended goal for the Women's Canadian National Team at that year's Women's World Championships, winning a gold medal.

After a few weeks of training camp, Tampa Bay started its new goalie in an exhibition game against the St. Louis Blues. The young woman per-formed like a rookie. Rheaume displayed occasional flashes of promise and committed no major mistakes. In one period of play, the Canadian blocked 7 shots and allowed 2 goals.

Tampa Bay released the female goalie after her single performance. But she holds the distinction of being the only woman to ever play in a major professional men's league.

Manon Rheaume had great faith in her skating ability. She felt confi-dent she could compete in the men's contests. So did the coach and general manager. They gave her a chance to play with the best. Even if for a brief time, her request was granted.

Jesus encountered another woman with great faith. Her daughter was suffering, but the mother knew Christ could heal her.

She asked for His gift of healing. Because of her faith, the request was granted.

Read Matthew 15:21-28. How great is your faith? Ask God to strengthen your faith in your own talents and abilities and your faith in Him.

Do not follow the crowd in doing wrong. **—EXODUS 23:2a**

Colorado embraced major league baseball enthusiastically in 1993. The Rockies, a National League expansion team, drew a record 4,483,350 fans to Coors Field during their first season. The Toronto Blue Jays had been the only team to draw more than four million until Colorado shattered the attendance mark.

The Rockies weren't particularly good. They won just 67 contests and lost 95. The team finished 37 games in back of the division-winning Atlanta Braves. Only the lowly San Diego Padres kept Colorado out of the cellar.

But the Rockies could swing the bat, and baseball fans loved the offense. Denver's thin air made the stadium a hitter's paradise. Andres Galarraga won the league batting crown with a .370 average. Dante Bichette and Charlie Hays each hit over .300.

The offensive fireworks made Colorado very competitive at home. On their own turf, the Rockies won 39 of 81. An average of 55,350 fans turned out for every Rockies home game to cheer one of the National League's newest entries.

Coloradans followed the crowd to the baseball diamond. They enjoyed exciting baseball and family entertainment. They had fun.

But sometimes following the crowd is a problem. When everyone does wrong, it's hard not to join in. But God requires more of His followers. He wants us to do right even if we're the only one.

Try to attend an athletic contest in person. If that's not possible, watch on television. Observe the crowd. Do you see people yelling inappropriately, throwing trash, or doing other things they shouldn't? Ask God to help you do right even when the crowd does wrong.

Save me from all my transgressions; do not make me the scorn of fools. —**PSALM 39:8**

The New York Giants and Chicago Cubs played baseball on an autumn afternoon in 1908 for the National League lead. About 18,000 fans jammed the Polo Grounds to see Giant Christy Mathewson battle Cub Jack Pfiester.

The game lived up to its expectations. New York entered the bottom of the ninth tied 1–1.

With two out and Moose McCormick on first, Fred Merkle singled sharply to right, advancing the runner to third. Al Bridwell, the next batter, lined the first pitch to center field.

McCormick trotted home thinking the Giants were victorious. Merkle watched the action at the plate and headed to the Giants' clubhouse without touching second base.

A quick-thinking Johnny Evers, the Cubs second baseman, screamed for the ball. He realized a run could not count if a force play ended the inning.

Getting a ball and stepping on second, Evers appealed to umpire Hank O'Day. O'Day ruled Merkle out and disallowed McCormick's run. Darkness forced the game to end in a 1–1 tie.

The Giants and Cubs tied for the National League title and scheduled a playoff on October 8. The Cubs won 4–2, whisking the championship away from New York. Since Merkle's mental error cost the Giants the pennant, newspapers tagged him Bonehead.

Each day Christians make boneheaded mistakes like Fred Merkle. Unkind words, harsh looks, and evil thoughts enter quickly in the heat of the moment. We regret these actions. But the damage is done and can't easily be repaired.

Through our relationship with Him, God prevents errors before we commit them. The closer we move to Him, the more we live in Christ. If we think before we act, God guides us to do right.

Recall something dumb you've done. Compare it with a time you made fun of someone else's mistake. Pray for wisdom to choose your words and actions carefully.

"I will lead the blind by ways they have not known, along unfamiliar paths I will guide them; I will turn the darkness into light before them and make the rough places smooth."

—ISAIAH 42:16

Paul Ereng switched from the 400-meter race to the 800 early in 1988. Representing the University of Virginia, the Kenyan captured first place in the NCAA meet. He received an invitation to the Kenya Olympic trials because a fan sent a clipping.

In the trials, the inexperienced Ereng used too much energy too soon. He faded and barely qualified.

A highly talented field took the track for the 1988 Seoul Olympics. Analysts considered Ereng a noncompetitor. But he and teammate Nixon Kiprotich devised a strategy.

Kiprotich suggested he set the early pace and let Ereng surprise the field. Brazilians Joaquim Carvalho Cruz and Jose Luis Barbosa followed a similar scheme. Barbosa went out fast and hoped to box out favorite Said Aouita while Cruz surged ahead.

The race unfolded as planned. Barbosa led after lap one with Kiprotich second and Cruz third. Ereng trailed in seventh.

A scramble began on the back straightaway. Kiprotich took the lead, then Cruz. Elliot and Aouita battled. Kiprotich faded. Meanwhile, Ereng slipped ahead of Elliot and Aouita on the inside. The dark horse passed the shocked Cruz and claimed victory.

Paul's teammate led him through the unfamiliar race. Kiprotich and Barbosa made the rough path smooth. Their plans worked, and Ereng found the light of victory.

In life, we face unfamiliar challenges. Relocating to a new city, changing schools or jobs, the birth of a baby, the death of a loved one, illness, or natural disaster all bring upheaval.

But God promises His guidance. He gives us Christian family and friends and the Bible. The Heavenly Father turns dark into light and makes the rough places smooth.

With a friend or family member, plan a strategy for an unfamiliar race or game. Thank the Lord for His leading through the new and different.

If I rise on the wings of the dawn, if I settle on the far side of the sea, even there your hand will guide me, your right hand will hold me fast. —**PSALM 139:9-10**

In football, quarterbacks and running backs receive most of the headlines. Offensive linemen rarely rate a second glance unless they commit a penalty.

In 1962, the Dallas Cowboys hosted the Pittsburgh Steelers. Pittsburgh led 21–14 and pinned the Cowboys on their own 1-yard line.

Eddie LeBaron dropped back behind the goal line. He spied a wide open Frank Clarke. Clarke snared LeBaron's pass and bolted 99 yards for an apparent tying touchdown.

But officials called a hold on offensive lineman Andy Cvercko. The penalty happened in the end zone. The refs invoked a rarely used rule. Holding in the end zone results in a 2-point safety for the defense.

Instead of tying the game with a touchdown, Dallas gave the Steelers 2 points, upping their lead to 23–14. The safety proved the difference in Pittsburgh's 30-28 victory.

Cvercko's hand held fast, and the officials saw it. The lineman couldn't hide. The referee made the right call and assessed a safety.

Likewise, we can't hide from God. Whether in the east on the wings of dawn or on the other side of the sea in the west, He guides us. The Lord holds us safe in His hand.

Name as many ways of scoring in football as you can. Thank God for the safety He gives wherever you are.

Examine yourselves to see whether you are in the faith; test yourselves. Do you not realize that Christ Jesus is in you—unless, of course, you fail the test? —2 CORINTHIANS 13:5

Canada's Ben Johnson lingered in the shadow of America's Carl Lewis. The sprinter sought public respect and admiration. In the 1987 Rome World Championship, Johnson lowered the 100-meter world record to 9.83 seconds. Endorsements and adulation followed.

The next year at the Seoul Olympics, the sprinter appeared in top form. Johnson ran in lane six and Lewis in lane three.

The world record holder shot from the blocks like a bullet. Halfway through the race, he moved to a meter and a half lead, but Lewis believed he could close the gap.

At the 80-meter mark, Johnson maintained the margin. As he crossed the finish line, the Canadian turned back and thrust his index finger in the air. His 9.79 second time astonished everyone.

Following the race, officials performed a mandatory drug test. Results indicated the presence of stanozolol, a banned anabolic steroid.

Three days later, the International Olympic Committee stripped Johnson of his gold medal and awarded it to Carl Lewis. Three months later, the International Amateur Athletic Federation retroactively rescinded the Rome world record.

At the moment of his greatest triumph, Ben Johnson failed the test. Officials examined the results and found drugs. The sprinter lost everything—a world record, gold medals, and a chance for money and fame.

The Apostle Paul suggests that we examine ourselves. If Christ lives in us, we pass the test. If not, we fail for eternity. But as long as we live, God allows a retest.

Have you ever failed a test—academic, physical, or maybe for a driver's license or professional certification? How did you feel? Give yourself a one-question test: Does God live in me?

Who shall separate us from the love of Christ? Shall trouble or hardship or persecution or famine or nakedness or danger or sword? —ROMANS 8:35

The United States Military Academy opened the 1958 football season with a strange offensive formation. Number 87, junior end Bill Carpenter, stayed 15 yards away from the huddle. Sportswriters quickly dubbed Carpenter the "Lonely End."

Army rolled through every opponent. Only a tie to the University of Pittsburgh marred its perfect season. But a question nagged every foe and fan. How did the Lonely End know the plays?

Carpenter never blew an assignment. He ran routes and blocked to perfection.

At the conclusion of the '58 campaign, coach Red Blaik retired. In January 1959, at a dinner of the Touchdown Club of New York, he revealed the confidential information.

Quarterback Joe Caldwell signaled the play with his feet. Two feet together indicated a run. A left foot out front also meant a run, and a front right foot out meant a pass. Carpenter acknowledged the play by rubbing his nose or tugging his helmet.

Despite the lack of secrecy, Carpenter enjoyed a fine senior season. He made every major All-American team and commanded his cadet battalion. Six years later, he won the Silver Star and the congressional Medal of Honor for service in Vietnam.

Carpenter was seemingly separated from his team while being a big part of its success. The end looked, observed, concentrated, responded, and succeeded. Though opponents tried to set him apart, they could not.

The officer's concentration served him well on the football field and in the battlefield. Nothing could separate him from his task.

Satan tries to cut us off from God with hard times. But no matter what happens, nothing can separate us from Christ's love. And Christ's concentration on us is forever if we trust Him. Though God may seem far away, we can use prayer as our signals to keep in close communication.

With a friend or relative, try Caldwell's and Carpenter's signals. How did you do? Did it get easier as you concentrated? Thank God that you can never be separated from Him.

The Lord will save me, and we will sing with stringed instruments all the days of our lives in the temple of the Lord. —ISAIAH 38:20

Any string can be broken. But in 1988, Orel Hershiser established a baseball string that may last all the days of his life. On August 30, the Los Angeles Dodger right-hander held the Montreal Expos scoreless for the game's final four innings. In the following weeks, Hershiser shut out Cincinnati, Houston, and San Francisco once, and Atlanta twice.

Los Angeles had clinched the division crown when the seventeenth-round draft choice made his final 1988 start. The Ohio native faced Andy Hawkins of the San Diego Padres.

Hershiser and Hawkins battled in a classic pitchers' duel. The scoreboard posted zero after zero. After nine innings, neither team had scored.

Dodger manager Tommy Lasorda allowed his ace to pitch the tenth. Marvell Wynne struck out, but the third strike skipped away from catcher Mike Scioscia. Wynne reached first on the wild pitch.

Benito Santiago bunted the runner to second. Randy Ready grounded out with Wynne advancing to third. The Dodgers intentionally walked Gary Templeton, and Keith Moreland pinch hit for the pitcher.

Hershiser threw two quick strikes. Moreland fouled off a pitch, then lofted a lazy fly to left. Jose Gonzalez gloved the ball for the inning's final out.

The Most Valuable Player of the 1988 National League Championship Series and the World Series pitched 59 consecutive innings without a run. The string broke Dodger Hall of Famer Don Drysdale's mark of 58.

Orel Hershiser pitched quite a record. Some of his fellow players saved the string with outstanding defense. And the achievement will last a long, long time. But longer than that, we will sing praises to God for He has made us and saved us.

Compete with a friend to see who can name the most stringed instruments. Which ones does your church use in worship? Praise God by playing if you can. If not, sing or speak a song of praise.

I am the Alpha and the Omega, the First and the Last, the Beginning and the End. —**REVELATION 22:13**

Players never forget their debuts in professional sports. For some, the first also becomes the last.

The Houston Colt .45s brought minor league baseball prospect John Paciorek from Modesto, California, to Texas for back treatment. In the 1963 season finale, manager Harry Craft started an all-rookie lineup. He asked the outfielder if his back felt well enough to play. Paciorek leaped at the opportunity to start in the big leagues.

Batting seventh and manning right field, the Detroit native singled three times and walked twice to complete a perfect three-for-three day. He also scored 3 runs and batted-in 2 as the Colt .45s battered the Mets 13–4.

Paciorek underwent back surgery later that year. Although he played five more seasons in the minors, the brother of former major league out-fielder Tom Paciorek never appeared in the majors again. Of the more than sixty former major leaguers with perfect 1.000 batting averages, Paciorek heads the lists in number of hits with three.

For John Paciorek, the first was the last. Nine innings and three hits were sandwiched in between. The rookie's career came and went in less than a day. The beginning became the end.

But God is the beginning and the end of all time. In Greek, He is the Alpha and Omega. In English, that would be the A and the Z, the first to the last and everything in between.

Make yourself a sandwich. Put a piece of bread down first. Add meat, cheese, vegetables, and other good foods. Place another slice of bread on last. Remember God knew you in your beginning and will be with you to the end. Ask the Lord to help you fill the in-between with good.

And over all these virtues put on love, which binds them all together in perfect unity. —COLOSSIANS 3:14

Edson Arantes do Nascimento "Pele" brought Brazil three World Cup soccer titles. He scored 1,281 goals as a professional.

In 1974, following his retirement from Santos of Brazil, the world's most popular player signed with the New York Cosmos of the North American Soccer League. For the next three years, Pele traveled throughout the United States spreading the game's popularity. Millions who barely recognized the sport turned out to see the superstar.

The Cosmos arranged a special final game against Santos to honor the great Pele. The Brazilian played the first half with New York and the second half for Brazil.

A crowd of 75,646 packed Giants Stadium to watch Pele's swan song. At halftime, he stripped off the familiar number 10 of the Cosmos and donned the 10 of the Santos. At game's end, Pele handed his jersey to his Brazilian coach. Teammates carried the shirtless soccer star off the field as he waved tiny American and Brazilian flags.

The two countries were bound together that day in their love of soccer and their love for Pele. The virtue unified the teams and the fans even in competition.

Although we may be fierce rivals on the soccer field, baseball diamond, or basketball court, God asks us to put on love with our uniforms. Love of the game and love for the Lord should bind us together. That's true sportsmanship.

Choose someone on a rival team to get to know, either personally or through the media. Focus on the player's positives and enjoyment of the sport. Ask God to help you put on love as you play or cheer your teams.

In your hands are strength and power to exalt and give strength to all. —1 CHRONICLES 29:12b

Baseball fans revere power hitters. In 1961, the power surged.

New York Yankee outfielders Mickey Mantle and Roger Maris assaulted Babe Ruth's season record of 60 home runs. Mantle missed several September games due to injury, but Maris continued his feverish pace.

The much-traveled outfielder belted number 59 in the season's 154th game. Eight games remained to break or tie the mark. He tied the mark on September 26.

Maris felt enormous pressure. He lost sleep and hair from the constant scrutiny of the press.

The Yankee right fielder entered the season finale with 60 round-trippers. In his first at bat, the Minnesota native flied out. His next time up, Maris slugged a 2–0 pitch off Boston pitcher Tracy Stallard fifteen rows into the right-field stands. The 23,154 fans screamed in delight. They demanded Maris take several bows on the dugout steps.

A 19-year-old fan from Brooklyn, Sal Durante, retrieved the ball and received a $5,000 prize. Three Yankee pitchers combined to shut out the Red Sox, and New York took the season's final game 1–0.

Yankee Roger Maris demonstrated his strength 61 times in 1961. His power surged the ball out of the park and into the stands.

When we become Christians, God surges His power into us. He gives us courage to stand for right. He provides boldness to tell others about His love and grace. He helps us endure difficulties and live energetic lives for Him.

Survey computers and other expensive electrical equipment in your home to make sure they're equipped with surge protectors to prevent damage from power surges. Thank God for His power surges.

She is clothed in fine linen and purple. —**PROVERBS 31:22b**

Coach Bob Kersee discovered Florence Griffith Joyner working as a bank teller. He helped her get financial aid so she could run track at UCLA. Once Flojo tasted a little success, she thirsted for greatness.

Griffith Joyner won a silver medal in the 200-meter race at the 1984 Los Angeles Olympics. But the hometown press paid more attention to her 6-inch nails than her running.

The seventh of eleven children began serious training in 1987. Married to 1984 triple jump gold medalist Al Joyner, the sprinter concentrated on her start technique. She added weight lifting and endurance running to her regime.

At the 1988 Olympic trials, Flojo set a world record in the 100 meters. Her unbelievable times and spectacular running outfits endeared her to the media.

Griffith Joyner didn't disappoint her fans. She set an Olympic record in the opening round of the 100 meters and improved with each race. The Californian captured gold with 10.54 seconds, nearly .3 seconds faster than second place.

The sprinter set another world record, 21.34 seconds, in winning the 200 meters. The flamboyant runner closed her Olympic career with a gold in the 4 x 100 relay and a silver in the 4 x 400.

Florence Griffith Joyner not only wore silver and gold, she clothed herself in attractive racing outfits. She kept her hair and nails beautifully groomed. She looked as great as she ran.

God wants us to make ourselves pleasing. Our hair, nails, clothes, and shoes should reflect positively who we are in Christ. Staying neat and clean helps draw people to us and gives us opportunities to make friends and share our faith. The Lord always wants us to act as good as we look.

This week, pay extra attention to how you look. Make sure your nails are clean and filed and your hair attractively groomed. Check your clothes for spots and tears. Polish or clean your shoes. Ask God to help you look good both inside and outside.

No one could distinguish the sound of the shouts of joy from the sound of weeping, because the people made so much noise. And the sound was heard far away. —EZRA 3:13

On August 12, 1951, the New York Giants trailed the Brooklyn Dodgers by 13 1/2 games. The Giants won 16 consecutive baseball games and narrowed the gap. They closed with 37 victories and 7 losses, deadlocking with identical 96–58 records.

Brooklyn and New York met in a three-game playoff. The Giants took game one, 3–1. The Dodgers bounced back with a 10–0 shutout by Clem Labine. The championship came down to a single game.

The contest matched two 20-game winners, Don Newcombe and Sal Maglie. Brooklyn scored 1 in the first and 3 in the eighth to take a 4–1 lead into the ninth.

Dodger Newcombe told manager Charlie Dressen his strength was fading. But Dressen and Jackie Robinson convinced their ace to continue.

Shortstop Alvin Dark opened with a single for the Giants. Right fielder Don Mueller followed. Monte Irvin fouled out, but Whitey Lockman doubled to left, scoring Dark.

Dressen summoned Ralph Branca from the bullpen. Third baseman Bobby Thomson stepped up to bat with two Giants on base. Thomson hammered the ball for a 3-run homer.

The Polo Grounds crowd of 34,320 erupted. Radio announcer Russ Hodges screamed over and over, "The Giants win the pennant!" Sportswriters called Thomson's home run "the shout heard 'round the world." Fans shouted and cried. Some wept for joy, others in sorrow.

Emotions often overflow into each other. We cry when we're happy or laugh when embarrassed. We shout in both anger and excitement.

When God's temple was rebuilt in Ezra's day, people showed their emotions. Some wept. Others shouted. Even their enemies heard. It was the most important event in hundreds of years and generations of the Children of Israel.

Think about how you handle your feelings. Do others readily know where you stand? Do you display anger too quickly? Do you show genuine excitement? Ask God for the freedom to display your emotions and the discipline to control them.

"The terror you inspire and the pride of your heart have deceived you, you who live in the clefts of the rocks, who occupy the heights of the hill. Though you build your nest as high as the eagle's, from there I will bring you down," declares the Lord. —JEREMIAH 49:16

Experts predicted Ralph Boston and Igor Ter-Ovanesyan would battle for the 1968 Olympic long jump gold medal. Many expected a record due to Mexico City's altitude.

Unheralded Bob Beamon took his first jump, hoping for respectability. Suddenly, the leaper was airborne. His arms and legs pumped. He seemed to fly.

The athlete landed toward the end of the sand pit. Officials measured. Astonished, they took second and third looks. Beamon leaped an incredible 29 feet, 2 1/2 inches. He surpassed the world record by 21 3/4 inches.

Scientists calculated the thin atmosphere might have contributed 8 inches. But Beamon by his own effort added over a foot. The gold medal winner never jumped more than 27 feet again. His record stood for 23 years.

In the altitude of Mexico City, Bob Beamon leaped to the heights and covered the distance quickly. He shocked fans and sports writers. The unheralded long jumper surprised favorites Boston and Ter-Ovanesyan. In a sense, his accomplishments also brought them down.

Sometimes we need bringing down too. We're proud of who we are, how much we own, and what we've done. We tell over and over about that out-of-the-park home run, the last-second basket, the scoring pass, or the hole in one.

But God says that pride deceives. The first dictionary definition of pride is conceit—an undue sense of superiority. When we build ourselves, our possessions, and our accomplishments up too high, the Lord promises to bring us down to earth.

Stack dominoes, books, or cans one on top of the other. How high is the stack when it topples and falls? Ask God to give you a healthy and realistic opinion of yourself rather than deceitful pride.

"I'm going out to fish," Simon Peter told them, and they said, "We'll go with you." So they went out and got into the boat, but that night they caught nothing. —JOHN 21:3

An odd baseball rule requires the catcher to catch a two-out third strike. If he fails, the batter can run to first base. The catcher must throw to first to register the final out.

In the fourth game of the 1941 World Series, Brooklyn led the New York Yankees 4–3 in the top of the ninth. Three more outs and the Dodgers would even the world championship chase.

Johnny Sturm and Red Rolfe grounded out. Tommy "Old Reliable" Henrich approached the plate.

Pitcher Hugh Casey worked the count full. The Dodger hurler toed the rubber, took his windup, and fired. Henrich swung.

Umpire Larry Goetz raised his right hand, calling strike three. But catcher Mickey Owen missed. Henrich reached first base.

The final out eluded Casey. Joe DiMaggio singled, Charlie Keller doubled, Bill Dickey walked, and Joe Gordon doubled. New York turned a 4–3 loss into a 7–4 win when the game should have ended.

At that last moment, Mickey Owen caught nothing. The Dodgers lost the following day 3–1, and the Yankees won their ninth world championship. Brooklyn had experienced baseball's most costly drop.

One night as Jesus' disciples fished, they caught nothing. But Jesus came. He suggested they move their net to the other side. Fish seemed to jump into their nets. But Jesus also made the apostles fishers of men as they brought others to salvation.

Early Christians used the fish as a symbol. It's appropriate for us to use it today because God has made every Christian a fisher of people. The Lord asks us to tell His story and catch others for Him.

Note symbols on sports equipment, clothes, restaurants, etc. Some of those symbols are recognized around the world. What Christian symbols do you wear or use? Do you use the fish? Thank God for making you a fisher of men.

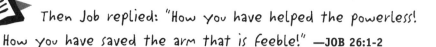

Then Job replied: "How you have helped the powerless! How you have saved the arm that is feeble!" —JOB 26:1-2

The 1968 Mexico City Olympics brought heartache to Maxine "Micki" King. The springboard diver led the competition through eight of the ten required dives.

On her ninth attempt, a reverse one-and-a-half layout, King's body struck the board, breaking her left forearm. With a fractured limb the fierce competitor completed her final dive, even though she had lost her power. Micki slipped to fourth in the standings. What could have been gold faded to nothing.

The native of Pontiac, Michigan, returned to Olympic competition in the 1972 Munich games. The United States Air Force captain took over the lead from Sweden's Ulrika Knape on her eighth attempt. Her final drive, the same reverse one-and-a-half somersault that broke her arm in 1968, clinched the gold.

Micki King's diving had become powerful again. Her feeble arm was restored. She stood on the 1972 Olympic victory stand to accept her medal and hear "The Star Spangled Banner" play in her honor.

God heals brokenness. He saves the feeble and helps the powerless. Job knew what he was talking about. He had been there just like Maxine King.

Sometimes God chooses to use us to help the powerless. Read to a needy child sometime this week. If that's not possible, give a children's book to an underprivileged boy or girl or the school or public library. Praise God for the help He gives. Ask the Lord to also help others through you.

But thanks be to God! He gives us the victory through our Lord Jesus Christ. —1 CORINTHIANS 15:57

Coach John Heisman of Georgia Tech didn't want to add Cumberland to his 1916 schedule. Sportswriters insisted, however, on comparing scores, and Heisman needed a weakling to demonstrate his team's power.

The Georgia Tech Yellow Jackets won the coin toss and chose to kick off. Cumberland ran off tackle for 3 yards on its first offensive play. It was its largest gain of the entire game.

The mismatch soon became apparent. The Yellow Jackets scored 63 points in the first quarter and matched it in the second.

Cumberland kicked off after each score to move Georgia Tech as far away from their goal as possible. This strategy backfired as the Yellow Jackets returned 5 kickoffs for 220 yards. Georgia Tech scored 32 rushing touchdowns before the rout finally ended, defeating Cumberland 222–0. Displaying true sportsmanship, Tech never attempted a single forward pass.

Heisman's team achieved a great gridiron win that day, but every Christian has experienced a much greater triumph. We rejoice in the victory of salvation through Jesus Christ.

He sacrificed His life for us to obtain eternal life. His death represents the final defeat of Satan and death.

Jesus provided us the means to overcome all enemies, including fear, hatred, jealousy, and envy. Our faith helps us combat life's problems.

Mathematically calculate the number of touchdowns and extra points Georgia Tech scored in its win. Pray for those who do not know salvation through Jesus. Give thanks for those who have won victory in Christ.

"In the same way, let your light shine before men, that they may see your good deeds and praise your Father in heaven." —MATTHEW 5:16

Eddie Robinson began coaching at Grambling University in 1941. In 1985, he became college football's winningest all-time coach. In 1995, the coach of the small Louisiana university reached a milestone none will pass any time soon.

The Grambling Tigers hosted the Delta Devils of Mississippi Valley State. After a scoreless first quarter, Robinson's team erupted for 3 touchdowns. Jason Bratton ran 17 yards for a score, Jay Johnson bolted for a 10-yard touchdown three minutes later, and Jeff Nichols ended the half with a 3-yard jaunt.

The Tigers dominated the second half. Grambling added 3 touchdowns to Mississippi Valley's 1. Robinson and his charges prevailed 42–6.

The victory registered as number 400 for Eddie Robinson. The Tiger band formed the number 400 on the field. Mobs of fans and players stayed in the stands cheering the coaching legend.

Robinson remained in the same job for 55 football seasons. He began with World War II and continued through the end of the Cold War.

The world changed, but Robinson stayed. And he won. The Tigers averaged more than 7 victories a year. His actions made Grambling shine in the football world.

Robinson will live on in the players he coached. Fans will long remember his teams and the Saturday fun they provided. Coaches will strive for his milestone.

God values goodness and righteousness. He promises our good deeds will shine and lead others to Him. Our actions are remembered by people long after we have moved on.

Interview someone who remembers World War II. Ask him or her to talk about changes in the world and in football between 1941 and today. What are some good things that stand out in that person's mind?

God's voice thunders in marvelous ways; he does great things beyond our understanding. He says to the snow, "Fall on the earth," and to the rain shower, "Be a mighty downpour."

—JOB 37:5-6

Throwing the discus requires strength, agility, and concentration. Romanian Lia Manoliu competed in her fifth Olympic games in 1968. She captured bronze medals in 1960 at Rome and in 1964 at Tokyo, but feared an ailing elbow would limit her success in Mexico City.

Analysts favored world record holder Liesel Westermann to win in 1968. She stood alone as the only woman to hurl the discus over 200 feet.

Manoliu threw hard on her first attempt. The disk carried 191 feet, 2 inches, and put her in the lead. She later fouled three times and made one weak throw.

A massive rainstorm arrived in the second round, and the throwing circle became wet. No one could match Manoliu's first toss.

At age 36, the Romanian became the oldest female to capture a gold medal. In the 1972 Munich games, she competed for a sixth time, the only female track-and-field athlete ever to achieve this distinction.

Nature helped determine the 1968 Olympic discus champion. The rain shower, with its thunder and lightning, outplayed the competition.

Those natural elements are God's. He commands the snow to fall and the rain to drop. The Lord causes thunder to roll and lightning to flash. He controls the earth and everything in, around, over, and beyond it.

Remember the biggest storm you've ever seen. How did it make you feel? Happy? Scared? Excited? Praise God for His power over nature.

"I am sending you out like sheep among wolves. Therefore be as shrewd as snakes and as innocent as doves."

—MATTHEW 10:16

Baseball historians consider the 1926 World Series a classic. The New York Yankees and St. Louis Cardinals split the first six games. With the supremacy of baseball on the line, two future Hall of Famers played major roles.

Cardinal knuckleballer Jess Haines nursed a 3–2 lead into the seventh inning. With two out and the bases loaded, St. Louis manager Rogers Hornsby called for relief. He summoned Grover Cleveland Alexander. The aging right-hander had pitched a complete game the previous day.

Rookie shortstop Tony Lazzeri stood in the box for New York. With the count at 1 and 1, the Yankee infielder lined a shot to left that hooked foul at the last moment.

Alexander threw a curve to run the count even at 2. Lazzeri saw another curve and took a mighty cut. But he missed and struck out.

The St. Louis stopper retired the Yankees in order in the eighth. He recorded 2 outs in the ninth before walking slugging outfielder Babe Ruth. Cleanup hitter Bob Meusel stepped in with Lou Gehrig on deck.

Suddenly, Ruth broke for second. Catcher Bob O'Farrell hesitated for a moment, then easily nailed the Sultan of Swat attempting to steal. The Cardinals won their first World Championship.

With the Yankee batting lineup, Hornsby seemed to send the troubled Alexander to the wolves. The aging pitcher still suffered problems from a World War I injury and battled epilepsy. But he innocently walked to the mound and shrewdly faced the heavy hitters.

Christians, too, feel like sheep among wolves when we work and witness in the world. When things become difficult, we must listen to Jesus' advice. Be as shrewd as snakes. Be as pure and innocent as doves.

Rent the video or watch The Winning Team *on a classic movie channel. The story chronicles the life of Grover Cleveland Alexander and stars former President Ronald Reagan. Ask God for the right combination of shrewdness and innocence to tell others about Christ.*

Make level paths for your feet and take only ways that are firm. —**PROVERBS 4:26**

Few fans knew runner Billy Mills prior to the 1964 Tokyo Olympics. The United States had never medaled in the 10,000 meters, and Mills seemed an unlikely candidate.

But Mills had joined the United States Marine Corps. The military regime had improved his training and diet.

Mills adopted a strategy of following the favorites, Australian Ron Clarke and Tunisian Mohamed Gammoudi. The Native American believed he could sprint past them in the final 200 meters.

Clarke set a rapid pace. On the twenty-fifth and final lap, the trio ran neck and neck. Stragglers caused problems. In the backstretch, the Australian bumped the American while passing another runner. The Tunisian, seeing the brief opening, shot to a 10-meter lead.

But the bump pushed Mills into the path of good fortune. The outside of the track provided better traction.

As the runners entered the homestretch, Clarke and Gammoudi battled for the lead. But Mills suddenly bolted down the outside lane to win the gold and set an Olympic record of 28 minutes 24.4 seconds.

Billy Mills didn't choose his own path. Someone else did. But the American runner found a level trail and firm footing that served him well.

Sometimes in life we do things the hard way. We don't listen to the experts. We don't seek help. We don't let experienced Christians guide us. We don't read our Bibles or pray. In short, we try to walk uphill in the mud.

But that's not what God wants for us. He wants us to move in His direction. He will make our paths straight and put our lives on firm ground. But we have to let Him.

Make a list of some things you do or don't do that make life more difficult. Share the list with a special Christian leader, friend, or relative. Consider how you can let go of the problems. Ask God to help you take the path He has prepared for you.

If you, O Lord, kept a record of sins, O Lord, who could stand? But with you there is forgiveness. —PSALM 130:3-4

The National Football League has produced many great receivers. In 1992, Art Monk rose to the NFL's summit in number of career receptions.

The Washington Redskins hosted the Denver Broncos on Monday Night Football. Washington jumped to a 21–3 first-quarter lead, and the national television audience quickly lost interest. Monk, however, remained attentive.

The wide receiver needed 7 catches to pass Steve Largent for the all-time record. He chipped away at the record with single receptions in the first, second, and third quarters.

The Redskin wideout caught pass number 4 in the opening stages of the fourth quarter. With 4:14 remaining, and victory sealed, quarterback Mark Rypien focused on getting Monk the record.

The Washington signal caller threw three consecutive passes to his All-Pro receiver. Monk caught a 6-yard hook and an 18-yarder in the flats. By hauling in a 10-yard sideline out, the Syracuse wideout owned the all-time receiving mark.

Athletes strive to write their names in record books. Being the all-time best earns fame and a place in history. People remember the most out-standing performances. Everyone wants to be remembered. But we want to be remembered for good, not bad. We all sin. We may sin by doing wrong. We might sin by not doing something we should.

If we ask Him, God forgives us for our sins. Once He forgives us, He forgets and takes away the record of the wrong.

List some things that might be sins. Don't forget selfishness and disobedience. Tell God about your sins. Ask Him to forgive you.

Each one should test his own actions. Then he can take pride in himself, without comparing himself to somebody else, for each one should carry his own load. —GALATIANS 6:4-5

Monday Night Football brings out the best and worst in NFL teams. On a cold, snowy night in 1984, the Green Bay Packers wished they had stayed home.

An early blizzard covered Denver with a blanket of white. A howling wind roared through Mile High Stadium.

The Denver Broncos won the coin toss but elected to kick. Their wisdom was quickly revealed.

On the game's first play from scrimmage, Packer halfback Gerry Ellis plunged into the line. Linebacker Tom Jackson popped the ball free, and Denver safety Steve Foley scooped it up. He slipped and slid into the end zone for a 22-yard touchdown.

The Broncos kicked off again. Green Bay quarterback Lynn Dickey handed off to Jessie Clark. Unbelievably, he fumbled.

Denver cornerback Louis Wright danced down the field for a 27-yard score. Only 37 seconds had elapsed, and the Packers faced a 14–0 deficit.

The foul weather played havoc with Denver's offense. They scored a single field goal. But the 3 points put the Broncos in the win column. Green Bay could counter only the two defensive touchdowns, and the national TV audience watched Denver prevail 17–14.

The Packers could have turned their misfortunes into a rout. Instead they regrouped and played a competitive game.

It's frustrating to make mistakes. Sometimes we give up. But quitting accomplishes little. Rather than compare ourselves to others, we must give our best effort every day.

Christ serves as our example. He had many opportunities to avoid hurt and pain, but He always chose to face the challenge.

The Lord aids us in carrying our loads. Daily prayer and Scripture reading make everyday problems easier to handle. The more we study and pray, the more help we receive.

Visit your library. Ask the librarian to recommend a book about someone who refused to quit. Read it and note the turning point in the person's life. Pray for perseverance.

For everyone who exalts himself will be humbled, and he who humbles himself will be exalted. —**LUKE 14:11**

The Pittsburgh Pirates stood on the brink of making the World Series in 1992. After falling behind three games to one in the National League Championship Series, they fought back to tie the Atlanta Braves.

Pirate pitcher Doug Drabek totally dominated Atlanta in game seven. He took a 2–0 lead into the bottom of the ninth.

But Drabek tired. Brave Terry Pendleton doubled. David Justice hit a weak ground ball, but it ticked off Chico Lind's glove for an error.

The exhausted pitcher walked Sid Bream to load the bases. Manager Jim Leyland called in reliever Stan Belinda.

Belinda yielded a sacrifice fly to Ron Gant and walked Damon Berryhill to reload the bases. But Brian Hunter popped up, and Pittsburgh needed only one more out to play for the world championship.

Leyland's substitutions had been countered at every turn by Braves' manager Bobby Cox. He needed a pinch hitter for pitcher Jeff Reardon, but his bench was depleted except for backup catcher Francisco Cabrera.

Cabrera made the postseason roster on August 31 due to Greg Olson's injury. He collected only three hits in September and faced a pressure-packed at bat.

The pinch hitter punched a 2–1 pitch through the infield, scoring Justice. Pirate left fielder Barry Bonds charged the ball and fired a strike to catcher Mike LaValliere. The throw came in slightly up the line, and Bream slid into home just ahead of the tag. The Braves celebrated as the National League champions.

Francisco Cabrera was an unlikely hero. But the humble backup received the exaltation that comes with victory.

Christ described His followers much the same way. Some Christians brag and boast about their relationships with God.

Others, however, quietly serve God and seek no recognition. But God knows what they've done. They will receive the greatest glory in Christ's kingdom.

Name some individuals who perform service for others, but few seem to notice. Thank God for them.

He called you to this through our gospel, that you might share in the glory of our Lord Jesus Christ.

—2 THESSALONIANS 2:14

Kirk Gibson's pulled hamstring and strained knee benched him for the first game of the 1988 World Series. He watched the baseball game on television while treating his injuries.

The Los Angeles Dodger outfielder stewed as his teammates struggled against the Oakland Athletics. When L.A. entered the bottom of the ninth trailing 4–3, he couldn't stomach his inactivity. Gibson secretly huddled in the dugout.

The American League's top reliever, Dennis Eckersley, rapidly retired Mike Scioscia and Jeff Hamilton. With just one out remaining, manager Tommy Lasorda held Gibson back and sent Mike Davis to pinch hit. He then kept his power hitter hidden and put Dave Anderson on deck.

Davis disrupted the A's stopper by stepping in and out of the batter's box. He finally coaxed a walk, and the Dodgers stayed alive.

When Gibson emerged, the noise reached epic levels. Eckersley swiftly went ahead with two foul ball strikes. Gibson fouled another before evening the count at 2 and 2.

The Dodgers' last hope remembered the right-hander usually threw a slider in this situation. Gibson anticipated the pitch and pulled it down the right-field line for a game-winning 2-run homer. The fans cheered as their hero limped around the bases pumping his fist into the air.

It's tempting for Christians to remain on the bench. We enjoy the comfort and safety there.

But we should follow Kirk Gibson's example. Rather than sit and watch, we need to take an active role in spreading Christ's Word.

God doesn't expect us to stand on a street corner shouting. But He does require a loving spirit and a lifestyle consistent with His message. These qualities serve as a Christian's most effective tools to share the Gospel.

Ask some Christians you admire how they witness to others about their faith. List the ways you can witness too. Pray for God to help you.

Be careful that you do not forget the Lord.

—DEUTERONOMY 6:12

Ken Stabler caught the nation's eye quarterbacking the Oakland Raiders. The Snake led Oakland to a world championship in Super Bowl XI.

Stabler played collegiate football for the University of Alabama Crimson Tide. In 1965, senior signal caller Steve Sloan struggled against the University of Tennessee Volunteers. Late in the fourth quarter, with the score tied 7–7, Coach Bear Bryant inserted Stabler.

With less than a minute remaining, Alabama launched its final drive. Stabler drove to a first-and-goal just inside the Vols 10-yard line, but no time-outs remained.

A plunge gained 2. A pitchout lost 10. A third down quarterback scramble netted 14 and moved the ball to the 4-yard line.

But Stabler failed to get out-of-bounds. The clock read ten seconds and counting. Time would expire before Alabama could attempt a field goal.

The Alabama quarterback lined up for a desperation pass. Stabler took the snap and quickly threw. But instead of aiming for the end zone, he rifled it out-of-bounds. The clock stopped on six seconds, and Tennessee took over on downs.

Kenny Stabler lost track of the down in an important game. His forgetfulness let possible victory slip away.

It's natural to forget. No one is immune from it. But God is too important to slip our minds.

We often let it happen. We become entangled with dozens of activities. God simply gets shoved aside.

We drift from His plan. We don't stop to pray. But if we work on our relationship, God shapes our lives. He communicates with us. We feel the Lord's presence when we need Him.

Recall an occasion when you forgot something important. What kind of problems did it cause? Ask God to forgive you when you forget to pray or read His word.

We have come to share in Christ if we hold firmly till the end the confidence we had at first. —**HEBREWS 3:14**

Football fans love high-scoring contests and great comebacks. That's what Big Eight partisans witnessed in 1992 when the twenty-fifth-ranked Kansas Jayhawks squared off against the Iowa State Cyclones.

Kansas jumped to a 21–7 first-quarter lead on the strength of quarterback Chip Hilleary's two touchdown passes. But the Cyclones roared back. Iowa State scored 20 unanswered points in quarters two and three to take a 47–21 margin into the fourth.

However, as coaches say, the fat lady had not sung. The Jayhawk signal caller attacked. He scored on an 18-yard run and called his own number for the 2-point conversion.

Hilleary's touchdown passes of 30 and 12 yards closed the gap to 47–42 with 6:28 left. Iowa State fumbled just 21 seconds later. Larry Thiel grabbed the loose pigskin and rumbled 37 yards for the go-ahead touchdown. Kansas went for 2 and converted successfully. The Jayhawks held on to win, 50–47.

Kansas knew it could beat the Cyclones in Iowa even though it had been eleven years. The Jayhawks were confident. When they fell behind by more than 3 touchdowns, they still believed in themselves. And they won.

When we first become Christians, we feel God's power. We know He will help us live and grow.

But life isn't always easy. When good things happen, we may neglect God. When bad things happen, we sometimes blame Him.

Having confidence in Christ means that from beginning to end and every day in between, we trust in Him. We know God will guide us. And we let Him.

Choose a sports skill. It can be throwing, catching, kicking, shooting, or anything you want. Practice until you gain confidence. Ask God to help you always have confidence in Him.

And God said, "Let there be lights in the expanse of the sky to separate the day from the night, and let them serve as signs to mark seasons and days and years." —GENESIS 1:14

Reggie Jackson attracted attention wherever he played baseball. In the 1977 World Series, the New York Yankees faced the Los Angeles Dodgers. Jackson batted poorly in the first three games, collecting only 2 hits in 9 at bats. But the 1973 American League Most Valuable Player broke his slump with a double and a home run in game four. Jackson continued his hot streak in game five with a home run in his final plate appearance.

The Dodgers led 3–2 when Reggie batted in the fourth inning of game six. The Yankee slugger sent Burt Hooton's first pitch into the right field stands and put New York in front 4–3.

One inning later, Jackson faced Elias Sosa with two out and a runner on base. Sosa threw his first pitch. The Yankee outfielder powered it into the right field stands, upping New York's margin to 7–3.

In the eighth, the Yankee Stadium crowd shouted Reggie's name in unison as he stepped into the batter's box. He hammered Charlie Hough's first pitch 450 feet into center field. The three home runs on three straight pitches earned Jackson the nickname Mr. October.

The fall brings thoughts of football games, bonfires with roasting marshmallows, beautiful autumn-colored leaves, crisp air, and the World Series. Reggie Jackson always found October and the playoffs his best season.

God created the seasons for us to enjoy. Fall, winter, spring, and summer—each offers a different perspective of the earth. Each marks the passing of time.

Think about your favorite autumn events. Either plan to roast marshmallows or make s'mores (a warm roasted marshmallow and chocolate smashed between two graham crackers) or participate in a fun fall family activity. Thank God for the beauty and freshness of changing seasons.

In the beginning was the Word, and the Word was with God, and the Word was God. —JOHN 1:1

The Fighting Irish of Notre Dame met the United States Military Academy at the Polo Grounds before 55,000 fans. Grantland Rice, the nation's best-known sportswriter, covered the event for the *New York Herald-Tribune*.

On the 1924 autumn afternoon, Harry Stuhldreher, Don Miller, Jimmy Crowley, and Elmer Layden entered a scoreless tie early in the second quarter. The backfield rampaged through the defense. Running left, running right, and running up the middle, Notre Dame opened a 2-touchdown lead. Army scored late in the contest, but the Irish held on for a 13–7 victory.

Rice focused the spotlight on the Notre Dame running backs. Drawing an allusion from the Four Horsemen of the Apocalypse, the reporter penned his lead, "Outlined against a blue-gray October sky, the Four Horsemen rode again. In dramatic lore they are known as Famine, Pestilence, Destruction, and Death. These are only aliases. Their real names are Stuhldreher, Miller, Crowley, and Layden."

The colorful imagery caught the nation's imagination. An enterprising photographer convinced the players to mount steeds and snapped their picture. The photo ran throughout the world.

Grantland Rice knew the power of words. He chose them carefully to convey a clear view.

The writer of the Gospel of John also knew words could change people's lives. He chose to describe Jesus Christ simply as "the Word."

He picked an apt description. No writing contains such power. No book has affected so many.

Christ indeed is "the Word." We speak His name in praise. We call His name in prayer. We say His name with reverence and shout it with joy.

Take a pen and paper and write down what Jesus means in your life. Share it with your pastor, Bible study teacher, or a friend. Ask the person for some pointers to polish the writing. Make the finished copy a gift to God.

More strength is needed but skill will bring success.

—ECCLESIASTES 10:10b

Some Sundays, National Football League quarterbacks do little wrong. The Miami Dolphins' Dan Marino has been one of the most successful.

A 1992 game at Miami's Orange Bowl featured the Dolphins and New England Patriots. The winless Patriots gained a quick 10–0 lead, but Marino and his scoring machine went to work.

The University of Pittsburgh alum tossed second-quarter scoring strikes to Mark Duper and Keith Jackson. Miami led at the half 17–10.

Less than five minutes into the third period, Marino hit Mark Clayton with a 43-yard touchdown pass. On Miami's next possession, the signal caller rolled out and scared the Orange Bowl crowd by stumbling over the New England bench. But the record-breaking quarterback bounced to his feet and moments later threw his fourth touchdown pass to Keith Jackson.

Touchdown throw number four tied Marino with Hall of Famer Johnny Unitas. The two rifle-armed play callers tossed four or more touchdown passes in a single game 17 times.

Marino showed strength and skill when he threw a fourth touchdown pass after suffering an injury. Strength without skill wouldn't have broken the record. Neither would skill without strength.

God expects us to combine the two. He wants us to be strong and skilled—physically, spiritually, intellectually, and socially. We perfect skills through practice. We gain strength through food and exercise.

Make a list of good things you can put into your mind and body. Think of some things best left out. Ask God to help you choose only the best.

He who has ears, let him hear. —**MATTHEW 11:15**

New Orleans Saints punter Tommy Barnhardt knew his punts carried a bit long. On a Sunday afternoon in 1993, the kicker found out a football can actually be booted too far.

Ideally, his kick would pin the St. Louis Rams inside the 5-yard line. The ball, however, rolled into the end zone and stopped. No Saints player touched the pigskin to down it. Nor did the football roll out-of-bounds. It just sat motionless. No whistle sounded.

Both teams drifted toward the sidelines. Rams defensive back Robert Bailey suddenly realized he had not heard a whistle. The ball stayed alive.

The punt returner scooped the pigskin off the Superdome carpet, 3 yards deep in the end zone. As he sprinted toward the Rams goal, the referee followed.

Bailey crossed the goal line, and the official signaled touchdown. The scoring jaunt put the Rams cornerback in the National Football League record book with the longest punt return in history, 103 yards.

Of the twenty-two players on the field, only one listened. Bailey's keen hearing paid dividends both for his team and himself. His ears put him in the record book.

Listening gives us an edge. It can keep us safe and put us in touch with other people. Our ears help us learn and enjoy nature.

But more important, our ears let us hear about Jesus. We learn how He came to earth and gave His life to save us from our sins. All we have to do is listen to His love and trust.

Go outside in the early morning or late evening. Listen. Take note of all the sounds you hear. Thank God for the gift of hearing.

We must pay more careful attention, therefore, to what we have heard, so that we do not drift away. —**HEBREWS 2:1**

Centers rarely attract football fans' attention. The middle of the offensive line usually looks like a jumble of bodies.

Snappers prefer to avoid the limelight. A center drawing the eyes of the crowd has usually made a mistake.

The Seattle Seahawks prepared to kick a field goal against the Denver Broncos on a fall afternoon in 1989. Grant Feasel crouched over the ball anticipating the count from holder Jeff Kemp.

Kemp checked the defense and spotted a blitz formation. He yelled to the blockers, "Watch it, left."

Feasel misunderstood, thinking his holder called out, "Red Set," the signal for a quick snap. He rifled the ball between his legs.

Unfortunately, Kemp had turned his head to speak to kicker Norm Johnson. The ball glanced off his helmet and rolled loose on the ground. The backup quarterback recovered the pigskin, but since it was fourth down, the Broncos took possession.

The missed opportunity cost the Seahawks 3 possible points. Seattle ultimately lost the game, 24–21.

Grant Feasel's inattention led to a mistake. He embarrassed himself and let down his teammates.

We let down God if we ignore His Word. Often, we think we know all the answers.

There's a fine line between self-confidence and arrogant cockiness. A kind heart and loving spirit make the difference.

Practice some deep snaps. Pay close attention to the count and cadence. Be alert for God as well.

The Spirit searches all things, even the deep things of God. —1 CORINTHIANS 2:10b

The Toronto Blue Jays led the Philadelphia Phillies three games to two in the 1993 baseball World Series. But in the ninth inning of game six, the situation appeared bleak for Canada's team.

The Phillies led 6–5, and Mitch "Wild Thing" Williams took the mound to shut Toronto down. Two days earlier, Curt Schilling had blanked the Blue Jays 2–0 on five hits. Another win would even the score and set up a final game seven.

In the ninth inning, Williams broke a closer's cardinal rule. He walked Rickey Henderson on four straight pitches.

The "Wild Thing" seemed to calm down. Devon White flied out. But 37-year-old Paul Molitor singled, and the tying and winning runs were aboard.

Joe Carter stepped into the box. He worked the count to 2 and 2, then drilled a low, inside fastball over the left-field fence for a 3-run homer.

Carter leaped as he rounded the bases, celebrating the 8–6 victory and Canada's second straight World Series triumph. Amazingly, the slugger's deep shot marked the first time a team had won a World Series on a come-from-behind ninth inning home run.

Going deep enabled Joe Carter and the Toronto Blue Jays to prevail in the World Series. As Christians, we must seek the depths of God.

But we don't have to wander aimlessly while we search. God provides the Holy Spirit as a guide.

It's difficult to understand the nature of the Holy Spirit. Religious scholars have debated its role for centuries.

One element is certain, however. The Holy Spirit is always there. The closer we grow toward God, the stronger the presence becomes.

Think of some questions about the Christian faith. Discuss them with your Bible study teacher, pastor, or other mature Christian.

Be wise in the way you act toward outsiders; make the most of every opportunity. —**COLOSSIANS 4:5**

A pitcher achieves great honor starting the first game of the World Series. Many dream of opening the fall classic in New York Yankee pinstripes.

Andy Pettitte took the mound for 1996's contest against the Atlanta Braves. After retiring the side one, two, three, in the top of the first, the left-hander ran into serious trouble.

Andruw Jones stepped to the plate with a runner on. The 19-year-old outfielder belted Pettitte's pitch out of the park, becoming the youngest player to homer in World Series history.

Manager Joe Torre pulled his ace in the third. The 20-game winner had allowed 7 earned runs.

After dropping games one and two, the Yankees tied the Series. Pettitte drew the assignment for game five.

Yankee catcher Jim Leyritz rooted his mitt on the outside corner. Pitch after Pettitte pitch caught the plate. Brave after Brave went down.

Pettitte threw 8 1/3 shutout innings, allowing only 5 hits. He also contributed two defensive gems on the field.

The Yankees scored the only run when Cecil Fielder's fourth-inning double plated Charlie Hayes. New York's 1–0 win propelled the team to its 23rd world championship.

Andy Pettitte redeemed himself. He performed well both pitching and fielding. He displayed wisdom in his actions and made the most of his opportunity.

Wisdom means showing common sense combined with knowledge and learning. Opportunity is a favorable occasion or a convenient time.

The Bible says we should learn and gain knowledge so that we can use good judgment when the right time comes. That isn't always easy, as Andy Pettitte found in game one. But it does brings rewards, as he discovered in game five.

Play baseball or softball with friends, using at least a pitcher, catcher, and batter. Take turns at different positions. Picture yourself in the World Series. Ask God to help you be wise and make the most of every opportunity He gives.

for the grace of God that brings salvation has appeared to all men. . . . While we wait for the blessed hope—the glorious appearing of our great God and Savior, Jesus Christ.

—TITUS 2:11, 13

The Boston Red Sox waited anxiously for the final out in game six of the 1986 World Series. Another New York Met erased, and the Red Sox could fly the championship flag for the first time since 1918.

Roger Clemens pitched seven strong innings before giving way to Calvin Schiraldi. The stopper held the Mets scoreless.

Dave Henderson's tenth-inning homer put the Red Sox ahead 5–3. Hope surged.

Schiraldi quickly retired Wally Backman and Keith Hernandez. Gary Carter kept the Mets' faint hopes alive with a single. Kevin Mitchell lined a hit. The New York fans began to chant.

Ray Knight poked a third straight single into center field. Carter scored and cut the lead to one.

Boston manager John McNamara signaled for Bob Stanley to pitch. Mookie Wilson stepped to the plate. Stanley worked the count to 2–2 and bore down to throw a final strike.

The Met outfielder fouled off four straight pitches. Tension grew. The right-hander uncorked another pitch, but it skipped past catcher Rich Gedman. Mitchell scored to tie, and Boston's hopes dimmed.

With the Red Sox bench silent, Wilson dribbled a ball. It bounced between Bill Buckner's legs as Ray Knight crossed the plate. The Mets' unbelievable comeback crushed the heart of every Boston fan.

It's hard to wait for the things we really want. Sometimes we have no choice. Red Sox followers have waited 75-plus years for another championship, but they never lose hope.

Christians have awaited Christ's return for almost 2,000 years, but only God knows the time of His Son's return.

Calculate the number of days until Christmas. Compare that time to the years since Christ's birth. Ponder how glorious His return will be. Praise God.

"'Call to me and I will answer you and tell you great and unsearchable things you do not know.'" —JEREMIAH 33:3

The Kansas City Royals stood on the edge of elimination from the 1985 World Series. They trailed the St. Louis Cardinals three games to two, and faced a 1–0 deficit in the bottom of the ninth of game six.

The odds favored St. Louis. The Cardinals owned an 84–0 season mark when they led in the ninth inning. Ace reliever Todd Worrell took the mound to shut the door on the Royals.

Pinch hitter Jorge Orta led off. He bounced a ground ball to first baseman Jack Clark. Clark fielded the ball cleanly and tossed it to Worrell covering the bag.

Orta appeared out by a step, but umpire Don Denkinger waved his arms safe. The Cardinals protested vigorously.

The play unraveled St. Louis. Steve Balboni's popup fell harmlessly in the dugout. With new life, he stroked a single to left.

Jim Sundberg attempted to bunt, but the Cards forced out the runner at third. However, catcher Darrell Porter allowed a ball to skip away, and the runners advanced.

Manager Whitey Herzog ordered Hal McRae walked to load the bases. Pinch hitter Dane Iorg stepped to the plate.

Iorg, a former Cardinal, looped a shallow single. One run scored, and Sundberg followed close behind. His spectacular headfirst slide around Porter's tag gave the Royals a comeback 2–1 victory.

An umpire's call turned the Kansas City Royals from also-rans into champions. When Christians call on God, He turns us into champions too.

But getting in touch with God requires effort. We can't dial long distance or shout to Him from the backyard.

Communicating with the Creator is a long-term process. As we grow in our faith through prayer and fellowship, we learn about God. The more we learn, the closer we grow. Eventually, calling on God becomes natural.

Make a long-distance telephone call to someone special. Make an effort to call on God more often. Begin today.

For in the gospel a righteousness from God is revealed, a righteousness that is by faith from first to last, just as it written: "The righteous will live by faith." —ROMANS 1:17

The 1991 World Series matched two improbable teams. Both the Minnesota Twins and Atlanta Braves had finished last in their divisions the prior year.

The Twins had made World Series history four years earlier. The Minnesota team had claimed the crown with four victories on its home field.

The 1991 classic began the same way. Minnesota won games one and two in the Metrodome. Atlanta rebounded and emerged victorious in contests three, four, and five, at Fulton County Stadium.

Game six was a classic. The Twins took an early 2–0 lead, but Atlanta tied. Minnesota went ahead by a run in the fifth, but the Braves knotted it again in the seventh. Kirby Puckett's eleventh-inning homer brought home the victory to the Metrodome crowd and set the stage for game seven.

Jack Morris and John Smoltz squared off in the decisive game. Inning after inning, the hurlers shut down the offense. The scoreless contest went into extra innings.

Dan Gladden led off the bottom of the tenth with a double. Chuck Knoblauch sacrificed him to third. Braves' manager Bobby Cox ordered Kirby Puckett and Kent Hrbek walked intentionally.

Minnesota manager Tom Kelly inserted Gene Larkin as a pinch hitter. With the outfield drawn in, Larkin lifted a shallow fly ball over the right fielder's head. Gladden trotted home with the winning run, and the Twins celebrated as world champions.

What a thrill for a team to go from last place to World Champions. But what a bigger thrill to know God's righteousness.

Christians must supply one element to achieve His gift, faith. Without faith, we cannot know God. With faith, we have unlimited potential.

Have someone blindfold you. Navigate through your house without sight but with the other person at your side. Remember we cannot see God, but He guides us, too. Thank Him.

"Have I not commanded you? Be strong and courageous. Do not be terrified; do not be discouraged, for the Lord your God will be with you wherever you go." —JOSHUA 1:9

Back injuries and Hodgkin's disease forced Mario Lemieux to leave the ice rink for a while. But the Pittsburgh Penguin center recovered in 1995 and left his mark in the National Hockey League record book.

Pittsburgh visited the New York Islanders. Lemieux's first-period goal put the Penguins up 2–0. But New York tallied 4 times in period number two to lead 4–3 going into the final period.

Super Mario tied the score only 19 seconds into the third frame. He fed Tomas Sandstrom for the go-ahead goal 10 minutes later. The Penguins beat the Islanders 7–5.

Pittsburgh's all-time scorer earned his 32nd hat trick—hockey slang for scoring three goals in a game—with a shot past Tommy Soderstrom with 2:48 remaining. The final score was Lemieux's 500th career goal.

The center reached the mark after 605 contests. Only Wayne Gretzky achieved the feat faster.

Lemieux could have quit hockey when his back hurt. He might have retired with the Hodgkin's disease diagnosis. But he didn't. He came back. He showed strength. He had courage.

Sometimes we hurt. Sometimes we get sick. We become afraid and discouraged. But God promises to be with us no matter what, no matter where.

Call or visit someone you know who is hurt, sick, or discouraged. You might choose a friend, relative, or someone in a nursing home. Tell him Mario Lemieux's story and relate God's promise. Ask God to give him strength and courage.

Be joyful in hope, patient in affliction, faithful in prayer. —ROMANS 12:12

Colleges quickly learned the recognition a winning football team brings. In 1916, Centre College, a small school in Danville, Kentucky, began big-time gridiron action.

Trustees hired Charles "Uncle Charlie" Moran as head coach. Moran, an experienced collegiate headmaster and former baseball umpire, brought a wealth of experience.

During halftime against the University of Kentucky, Uncle Charlie delivered a rousing pep talk. Suddenly, he said, "Boys, I believe in God, and I'm sure He looks after folks who are doing their best." Moran concluded, "Won't one of you say a word of prayer?"

Lineman Bob Mathias began a prayer. Before he finished, every Centre player joined in. The press reported the incident and nicknamed the team the "Praying Colonels."

The Colonels' football prowess earned an engagement with the Harvard Crimson in 1920. The Crimson prevailed 31–14 but scheduled a rematch for the following year.

Going into the second game, Harvard rode a 28-game winning streak. The Crimson dominated play in the first half, but failed to score.

Early in the third quarter, Centre lined up at Harvard's 32-yard line. Tailback Bo McMillin took the snap and ran right.

Just before going out-of-bounds, he reversed direction. Only two Harvard players adjusted.

At the 10-yard line, he stopped completely. One defender overran the play, and the other missed the tackle. McMillin bounded into the end zone. The Praying Colonels upset mighty Harvard, 6–0.

The Centre College football team made great contributions to the sport. The players knew that God wanted them to do their best. The Colonels enjoyed the game. They played patiently and prayed faithfully.

God expects the same from us—joy, patience, and faithfulness.

Watch a college football game on television. Imagine the difference between 1916 and today. If you're interested, read about the history of American football. Ask God to give you those same qualities that the Centre team had.

And the words of the Lord are flawless, like silver refined in a furnace of clay, purified seven times. —PSALM 12:6

Some sprinters run almost flawlessly. For a dozen years, Irena Kirszenstein Szewinska reigned as queen of the track.

In the 1964 Tokyo games, her first Olympics, Irena captured two silvers and a gold. She placed second in the 200-meter race and the long jump and ran the second leg on the winning 4 x 100-meter relay.

Four years later, Szewinska reached a higher level. In Mexico City, the Polish runner set two world records. Irena established a new mark of 11.1 seconds in the early rounds of the 100 meters but settled for bronze in the finals. In the 200, however, Szewinska captured gold in a record-setting performance of 22.58.

By 1972, Irena no longer dominated the shorter sprints. She finished a disappointing third in the Munich 200 meters.

Szewinska converted to the 400 meters. At the 1976 Montreal games, Irena won her final gold medal with a world record time of 49.29.

Her quest for a medal in the 1980 Moscow games fell short when she pulled a hamstring muscle in the semifinals. The star garnered seven medals: three gold, two silver, and two bronze, in five separate Olympic competitions.

For many years, Irena Szewinska ran flawlessly. She refined her style with practice and purified her determination with competition.

Few things in the world are flawless. Diamonds typically contain imperfections. Only careful cutting diminishes them. Metals include impurity. Refining silver or gold in white-hot fire eliminates them.

But God's word is absolutely, unquestionably flawless. No errors appear. No falsehoods can be found. Our Lord is perfect.

Read about jewelry in an encyclopedia or visit a jewelry store. Ask the jeweler to explain how the purity of gold or silver is calculated and to show you a diamond through a magnifying glass. Praise God for His flawless Word.

Live as free men, but do not use your freedom as a cover-up for evil; live as servants of God. —1 PETER 2:16

As doctors stitched a seven-inch gash under his nose, Montreal Canadien goalie Jacques Plante gave coach Toe Blake an ultimatum: no mask, no play. No other National Hockey League goaltender had ever covered his face in a game. Since teams carried no backup goalies in 1959, Blake had to comply.

Two broken cheekbones, four smashed noses, and a fractured skull convinced the four-time Vezina Trophy winner to seek protection. A Montreal businessman developed a plastic mask molded to fit his face.

Fortunately, the Canadiens' goaltender played well with his face covered in a 3–1 victory over the New York Rangers. The coach told Plante to wear the mask until his wounds healed.

Then Blake allowed his goalie to wear the face guard only in practice. He feared the mask would limit Plante's vision.

Montreal, however, lost to the Detroit Red Wings when the goalie bared his face. Blake changed his mind. He informed Plante if the mask worked, he could wear it. The Canadien never removed the face protector again in a game. He won three additional Vezina Trophies as the league's most outstanding goaltender.

Sometimes, as in a hockey goalie's case, masks serve a useful purpose. They protect. At other times, masks become disguises. They hide the criminal's identity or provide playful fun.

God desires that we never cover up evil or hide from doing good. After all, He has the power to see through any mask or disguise.

Some Christians don't trick-or-treat because of the origins of the Halloween holiday. Instead, consider going to a party at your church or collecting donations for a charity while trick-or-treating.

Although the Lord gives you the bread of adversity and the water of affliction, your teachers will be hidden no more; with your own eyes you will see them. Whether you turn to the right or to the left, your ears will hear a voice behind you, saying, "This is the way; walk in it." —ISAIAH 30:20-21

Michael Larrabee failed twice to make the United States Olympic track team. His mathematics students at a Los Angeles high school laughed when he told of his intentions to qualify in the 400-meter race.

But Larrabee accidentally used a new training program. A high school student delivered a judo chop to his stomach. The bruised abdominal muscles forced the sprinter to reduce his training. Surprisingly, Larrabee found the lighter workouts increased his closing kick.

At the U.S. Olympic trials, the 30 year old not only won, he also tied the world record of 44.9 seconds. The following month at the 1964 Tokyo games, Larrabee ran in sixth place at the halfway point. He had moved up only one slot coming out of the final curve.

But the high school teacher shifted into high gear. He churned past runner after runner. Ten meters from the finish line, Larrabee passed frontrunner Wendell Mottley of Yale. The twice-rejected runner won the gold by less than a meter.

Michael Larrabee first became a teacher and then became an Olympic medalist. As a teacher, he made a mark on the hearts and minds of teenagers. As a runner, he wrote his name in the book of Olympic winners.

Which would you rather do? Which would God find more important?

Write a thank-you note to a favorite teacher or nominate him or her for a teaching award. Praise God for being the best teacher and providing the best textbook, the Bible.

"But I, when I am lifted up from the earth, will draw all men to myself." —JOHN 12:32

Bill Toomey suffered through hepatitis, mononucleosis, and a shattered kneecap in training for the 1968 Mexico City Olympics. But leading the Olympic decathlon after seven events, the California English teacher missed on his first two attempts at the pole vault's opening height. One more miss would result in 0 points and eliminate any possibility of a medal.

Toomey tried to analyze his inability to lift himself but failed. Pressure blocked out the years of training and practice.

The 29 year old decided to make his final leap with nothing but pure determination. Toomey cleared the bar and remarked, "I'm not sure I even needed the pole."

The American worked his way up to 13 feet, 9 1/2 inches, his best effort ever in competition. He held off the field in the remaining two events and captured the gold medal with 8,193 points.

Bill's lift lifted him over the bar. It drew the eyes of the world to him on the winner's stand.

On earth, Jesus also drew crowds to Himself. In death, He was lifted up on the cross. Through the Resurrection, God made it possible for every man, woman, boy, and girl to be lifted up with Him to everlasting life.

Read John 6:1-13 about a crowd drawn to Jesus. Note particularly the little boy whose gift the Lord lifted up and multiplied. Thank God for lifting you to Him and multiplying your efforts.

So we fix our eyes not on what is seen, but on what is unseen. —2 CORINTHIANS 4:18

Spectators often picture themselves in a football game. They dream of scoring the winning touchdown or making a game-saving tackle. In 1961, a fan managed to become the twelfth man.

The Dallas Texans visited the Boston Patriots. The Texans trailed 28–20 but completed a 70-yard flea-flicker play to Chris Burford in the final seconds. The ball rested on the 3-yard line.

Hundreds of Bostonians spilled from the stands, thinking the contest over. The officials, however, ruled time permitted one more play.

The crowd finally left the field but ringed the gridiron. Dallas quarterback Cotton Davidson called for a slant pass over the middle to Burford.

Davidson set the offense and barked the signals. Suddenly, a man wearing a trenchcoat appeared in the middle of the Patriot defense. Without thinking, the Dallas quarterback continued the play.

Burford broke open, and the play caller rifled the ball. At the last second, the man in the trenchcoat leaped and batted the ball away.

Davidson protested furiously, but no one, not even coach Hank Stram believed the tale. But the game films revealed the truth. The Patriots' unseen defender had made the game-saving play.

The unseen in the Patriot–Texan game became more important than the seen. The unseen determined the game's outcome.

The unseen in life also becomes more important than the seen. We can't see God, but we can feel Him. We can't take a picture of Him, but we can follow Him. We can't live with Him, but we can live in Him and trust Him. Faith in the unseen Lord determines whether we spend eternity in heaven.

Compete with a friend to see who can name more things that are unseen but important. Examples might include electricity or the wind. If you haven't put your faith in God Who is unseen, consider doing so. If you have trusted the Lord, thank Him for His impact on your life.

In reading this, then, you will be able to understand my insight into the mystery of Christ, which was not made known to men in other generations as it has now been revealed by the Spirit to God's holy apostles and prophets. —EPHESIANS 3:4-5

No American woman had ever medaled in the long jump.

Experts considered the 1956 Olympic squad weak and anticipated a continuation of the shutout string.

Willye White, a 17 year old from Money, Mississippi, scarcely rated a second glance. But she intrigued writers and spectators by reading the New Testament between jumps.

Poland's Elzbieta Krzesinska dominated the field. Her leap of 20 feet, 10 inches, exceeded all challengers by nearly a foot.

But White wanted to perform at her best. On her final attempt, the teenager went all out. The Mississippi native hit the sand with a jump of 19 feet, 11 3/4 inches. She edged Russia's Nadezhda Dvalischvili for the silver medal by a fraction of an inch.

White competed in the next four Olympic games. She garnered another silver as a member of the 1964 4 x 100-meter relay.

Since retiring from competition, Willye has headed a summer camp and has created and directed the Robert Taylor Homes Girls Athletic Program. The program, in the largest U.S. public housing system, builds self-esteem through physical education for girls, ages 5–12.

Reading the Bible wasn't a talisman or good luck charm. Instead, it gave Willye strength, hope, and peace.

Faith in God isn't a magic potion to bring victory and medals. But God's Word provides the foundation for success. That success may not necessarily be success defined by the world. It is victory over sin, evil, and death.

Do you have a good luck charm? Does it really help you?

Read at least one Bible verse or Scripture passage today and every day. Ask God to make His Word the foundation of your life.

When one rules over men in righteousness, when he rules in fear of God, he is like the light of morning at sunrise on a cloudless morning, like the brightness after rain that brings the grass from the earth. —2 SAMUEL 23:3-4

In 1967, the American Basketball Association challenged the established National Basketball Association. To draw fans away from the older league, officials tinkered with the rules.

The new organization instituted a colorful red-white-and-blue ball, automatic time-outs following a basket in the final 2 minutes, and a 3-point shot. The latter two innovations created one of basketball's most amazing plays.

The Dallas Chaparrals hosted the Indiana Pacers. John Beasley's short jumper put Dallas in front 118–116 with 1 second to play. But the revised rules immediately stopped the clock.

Indiana inbounded to reserve forward Jerry Harkness just inside the baseline. The former New York Knick grabbed the ball and heaved it 90 feet downcourt like a shot put.

The buzzer sounded with the ball in the air. The sphere clanged off the back of the rim and bounced straight up. The ball fell through the hoop for 3 points and gave Indiana a 119–118 victory.

Some felt the ABA rules were made to add excitement. Others believed they were created to be more fair and right. Either way, they often changed the outcome of games. A trailing team could catch up quickly. And the brightness of hope remained until the final buzzer.

God gives us earthly rulers and governments. When we choose godly rulers, they make fair and just laws. We live each day in national peace, hope, and harmony.

When we choose wicked officials, they create rules that favor their personal interests. We face unhappiness and dark days.

Choose a local, state, national, or international government official whom you admire. Write, call, or send an email message of thanks and encouragement. Ask God to guide the decisions of the leader you chose.

At the end of ten days they looked healthier and better nourished than any of the young men who ate the royal food. So the guard took away their choice food and the wine they were to drink and gave them vegetables instead. —DANIEL 1:15-16

In weightlifting, the competitor hoisting the greatest weight wins. But on some occasions, less can be more.

In the 1956 Melbourne Olympics, oddsmakers favored Georgian Paul Anderson. But Anderson developed strep throat and faced the 1952 bronze medalist, Humberto Selvetti of Argentina.

Selvetti took the lead with a press of 175 kilograms. In the final phase, the jerk, the South American successfully lifted 180 kilograms before missing at 185.

Anderson decided to open at 187.5. The American failed on his first two attempts. On his final try, Anderson strained and jerked the weight over his head. He tied Selvetti exactly with a total of 500 kilograms.

Although both contestants weighed over 300 pounds, Selvetti exceeded Anderson 316 1/2 to 303 1/4. Under Weightlifting Federation rules, Anderson captured the gold due to his lesser body weight.

Americans seem obsessed with weight. Doctors record a newborn's weight. Grandparents comment to a child, "My you're getting big!"

Girls begin dieting in elementary school. Many continue through teen years and adulthood. A few develop eating disorders.

Athletes lift weights and load up on carbohydrates. Coaches have become nutrition conscious. Some teams hire professional dietitians.

Nutrition and health are important. The Bible mentions the subject. Chapter 3 of Judges describes Moab's King Eglon as fat and explains how weight contributed to his death. On the other hand, the Bible attributes some of Daniel and his friends' success to their nutrition.

Extremes aren't for us: Obsession with losing weight is just as bad as obsession with food. God wants us to eat healthful foods, not to conform to the world's ideal, but to His.

For one day, read the nutrition labels on what you eat. Note especially fat and salt content. Strive to eat healthful foods without becoming obsessed by weight. Ask God for His help.

"Go, walk through the length and breadth of the land, for I am giving it to you." —**GENESIS 13:17**

Born without a right hand and only half a right foot, Tom Dempsey hardly looked athletic. But the California native starred in the National Football League.

The San Diego Chargers signed Dempsey after scouting him in the Atlantic Coast Football League. The team had experts design a special shoe to fit his deformed foot.

After the Chargers released him, Dempsey signed with the New Orleans Saints. He earned the Saints' kicking job.

In 1970, New Orleans hosted the Detroit Lions. The Lions took the lead, 17–16, with eighteen seconds remaining.

The Saints received the kickoff. New Orleans quarterback Billy Kilmer connected with Al Dodd at the Saints' 45-yard line. The receiver stepped out-of-bounds, stopping the clock with two seconds to play.

Coach J. D. Roberts opted for a field goal attempt. Holder Joe Scarpati set up a yard deeper than normal to give Dempsey a little more approach time. The goal posts stood 63 yards away.

Some of the Lions laughed at the lengthy attempt. But the Saints kicker hit the ball hard and true. The pigskin sailed through the uprights to give New Orleans a 19–17 win. The kick set an NFL record for length.

That Sunday, the man who faced a challenge to learn to walk owned the length and breadth of the football field. Tom Dempsey turned his disability into an ability. It was almost as if someone had said, "I'm giving you the field."

In the Bible, God did give His people fields. He rewarded Abraham for his obedience and faithfulness.

Read Genesis 13:14-18. Praise God for His faithfulness. Ask God to help you be obedient to Him and to those over you on earth.

Do not hide your face from me when I am in distress.
Turn your ear to me; when I call, answer me quickly.

—PSALM 102:2

Monday morning quarterbacking is a popular sport. Most fans think they could have done better than the coach. In 1965, circumstances forced the president of Susquehanna University, Dr. Gustave Weber, to coach for real.

The small Pennsylvania school's coach, Jim Garrett, resigned seven games into the season. He felt he could no longer run a program that had lost every game.

Dr. Weber accepted the resignation and made a monumental decision. He would take over the football program for the remaining two games.

The president had lettered in three sports as a collegian. But his coaching experience extended only to the high school junior varsity level.

Weber called a team meeting. He told the squad the first item on his agenda was to make football fun. Secondly, the Crusaders would pass more.

The next Saturday, Susquehanna played Geneva. On the first play, Dr. Weber surprised everyone by faking an off-tackle run and throwing a long pass. The winless squad went up 6–0.

Several times during the game, Susquehanna successfully gambled on fourth down. The score seesawed.

With two and a half minutes to play, Susquehanna scored a touchdown and trailed 29–28. Dr. Weber in his go-for-broke style opted for a 2-point conversion. It failed, but the team regained its confidence. The 28 points represented more than the squad had totaled in its seven previous defeats.

Like Dr. Weber's situation, God sometimes calls us to stretch ourselves. He asks us to do something we've never done. It might be in sports. It could be at church. When the call comes, God will work for our good if we love Him.

Talk to your pastor or another church leader about volunteer jobs. They may be one-time or ongoing opportunities. Listen for God's call to stretch yourself for Him.

All men are like grass, and all their glory is like the flowers of the field; the grass withers and the flowers fall, but the word of the Lord stands forever. —1 PETER 1:24-25

The New York Knickerbockers began the 1969 season on a hot streak. The team challenged the National Basketball Association record for consecutive victories.

New York faced the Cincinnati Royals coached by former point guard Bob Cousy. Although he had not played for seven years, the 41 year old activated himself. Cincinnati took a 30–23 lead. But Cazzie Russell sparked the Knicks to a 55–52 halftime margin.

The game stayed close. The Royals gained the lead 101–98 with 1:49 to play. But future Hall of Famer Oscar Robertson fouled out.

Surprisingly, Cousy entered the game. The contest resembled 1959 rather than 1969. The former Celtic fired a crosscourt hook pass. At the foul line, the aging playmaker calmly hit 2. Cincinnati upped its lead to 105–100 with only 26 seconds left.

But great teams make great plays. Willis Reed sank 2 free throws. Dave DeBusschere stole the inbounds pass and streaked for a layup. The Knicks cut the margin to 105–104 with just 2 ticks on the clock.

A clean inbound pass would assure a Royal victory. But Willis Reed deflected the throw-in to Walt Frazier. Frazier went to the hoop, but was fouled.

The point guard sank both shots. The Knicks won 106–105 and set a new record of 18 consecutive victories.

Records are made to be broken, and the New York Knicks knew they could do it. No record stands forever, just as no person stands forever. We all die. Our glory fades, maybe not as quickly as grass or flowers, but in God's time.

The Word of God lasts forever. Hallelujah. Amen.

Pick some flowers or buy a fall bouquet. Change the water frequently, but note how long the flowers look fresh. Praise the Lord for His everlasting Word.

You shall not steal. —EXODUS 20:15

No football play kills a touchdown drive like an interception. A defensive turnover is one of the gridiron's most exciting plays. But Bernie Kosar's sharp skills approached the National Football League record for most pass attempts without a pickoff.

The error-free string began in late 1990. Kosar continued the streak into 1991. After nine games, the Miami signal caller stood one short of Bart Starr's all-time record of 294.

The Dolphins met the Philadelphia Eagles in game ten. Kosar quickly broke the mark by avoiding interceptions in his first two attempts. Although they resulted in only a short gain and an incompletion, the quarterback kept the ball out of the opposition's hands. He continued the error-free streak until the middle of the second quarter.

Under a heavy Philadelphia rush, Kosar lobbed a weak pass over the middle. Cornerback Ben Smith nabbed the errant throw, ending the play caller's string at 308.

For almost two years, Bernie Kosar kept the other team from intercepting his passes. But the purpose of defense in football or basketball is not only to keep the opponent from scoring, but to steal the ball.

In games, stealing may be okay. In life, God commands us not to steal. Theft includes taking things that don't belong to us. It also includes copying work someone else does and saying it is ours.

Think about the following situations.

• *Situation one: You find a wallet that contains $100, credit cards, and a driver's license in a public restroom. The wallet belongs to a stranger. What would you do?*

• *Situation two: You find the same wallet, but it belongs to someone you know. Would you do anything differently from situation one?*

• *Situation three: You lose your wallet that contains all the money you have. What would you want the person who finds it to do?*

Ask God to keep you free from the temptation to steal.

Endure hardship with us like a good soldier of Christ Jesus. —2 TIMOTHY 2:3

Veterans Day holds special meaning for Kansas City Chiefs linebacker Derrick Thomas. In 1990, the holiday proved quite emotional for the football player.

The Chiefs' defensive stalwart lost his father, Captain Robert Thomas, at age 5. The Air Force pilot went down flying a mission over Vietnam in 1972. The Department of Defense declared him legally dead in 1980. The Alabama alum always paid special homage to his dad on the day honoring those who served their country.

Prior to the Seattle Seahawks contest, four Air Force jets flew over Arrowhead Stadium in tribute to the United States military. The sight of the airplanes charged Thomas emotionally and physically.

The linebacker played ferociously. Play after play, he blew past offensive tackle Andy Heck, wreaking havoc in the Seattle backfield. The Chief sacked Seahawk signal caller Dave Krieg 7 times, setting a new National Football League record.

Captain Robert Thomas and his family endured the hardship of a good soldier. Derrick grew up with only the memory of a father. The Air Force pilot missed special moments with his son. Captain Thomas made the ultimate sacrifice for the United States of America—his life.

Paul understood the hardships and responsibilities of those who served in the military in his day. He used them as an example to young Timothy.

God knows the sacrifices today's veterans have made. And He stands with them and their families.

Participate in the Veterans Day activities in your community. If you own one, fly a flag outside your home. Honor the veterans and service women and men you know in some special way. Thank God for the gift they have given to keep America free.

Consequently, you are no longer foreigners and aliens, but fellow citizens with God's people and members of God's household. —EPHESIANS 2:19

Garo Yepremian never saw a football game until 1966. But one month after watching his first game, the Cyprus native kicked for the Detroit Lions.

Yepremian worked as a salesman in London and played soccer. His powerful leg could kick a ball straight and long.

The foreigner traveled to the United States to visit a brother. His sibling suggested Yepremian practice kicking a football and contacted the National Football League. The Atlanta Falcons and Detroit Lions gave try-outs. Yepremian signed with the Lions.

At first, it appeared Detroit had made a huge mistake. But in pregame warm-ups before the Minnesota Viking contest, Yepremian looked good. Coach Harry Gilmer decided to let his new acquisition kick.

The Vikings jumped to an early 10–0 lead. But the foreign-born kicker booted 4 field goals through the uprights. The Lions led at halftime, 12–10.

Although Minnesota put up 2 third-quarter touchdowns, Yepremian kicked 2 more field goals. Number six broke the record for most field goals in a single game.

Detroit edged the Vikings, 32–31. The diminutive Lion wearing number 1 established himself.

As Garo Yepremian discovered, sports skills developed on one side of the world can translate into sports skills on the other. Athletic ability doesn't depend on country. On the playing field, all are equal. Talent makes the difference. And Yepremian had the talent to become a Detroit Lion.

The same holds true in God's kingdom. In His house, there are no foreigners. We are equal citizens and members of His family. Accepting Christ makes the difference.

Do you know someone from another country or whose parents or grandparents were? If so, make certain that you treat them as equals. If they've recently arrived in the U.S., help them feel at home. You might watch football with them and help them understand the game. Ask God to make you sensitive to all people.

Then Moses said, "Now show me your glory." And the Lord said, "I will cause all my goodness to pass in front of you, and I will proclaim my name, the Lord, in your presence."

—EXODUS 33:18-19

When football teams fall behind 20–0, quarterbacks throw. In 1994, Drew Bledsoe and the New England Patriots found themselves in this predicament.

The Minnesota Vikings visited Foxboro Stadium. By mid-second quarter, the Vikings forged ahead 20–0. The plodding New England offense managed only a field goal before intermission.

Coach Bill Parcells switched to a no-huddle scheme. But Minnesota maintained a 20–10 lead with less than three minutes to play.

The New England offense suddenly shifted into high gear. Bledsoe hit Leroy Thompson on a 5-yard scoring pass with 2:21 remaining.

Minnesota punted. The Patriots' play caller moved the team from New England's 39-yard line to Minnesota's 16. Matt Bahr kicked a 23-yard field goal with fourteen seconds left. The game moved to overtime.

The Vikings won the toss but didn't score. Bledsoe took over. The signal caller completed 6 of 6. His final completion, a 14-yard scoring strike to fullback Kevin Turner, brought New England a 26–20 victory.

After connecting for only 8 of 17 in the first half, Bledsoe filled the second half with records. The strong-armed passer hit 37 of 53 after halftime and finished the day 45 for 70. The New England quarterback broke both George Blanda's record for attempts and Richard Todd's for completions.

Quarterback Bledsoe and the Patriots showed the Vikings their glory. They kept their opponents off-balance with no huddle and passed the ball in front of Minnesota for completion after completion. The overtime win felt good.

God, too, shows us His glory. He proclaims it in all of His creation.

Think of a Christian who shows the glory of God. Thank God for the person. Let him know you admire the way he lives by calling, writing a note, or telling him personally.

Your gates will always stand open, they will never be shut, day or night, so that men may bring you the wealth of the nations. —ISAIAH 60:11

The "swinging gate" is one of football's strangest plays. But it often succeeds through the element of surprise.

In 1994, the Chicago Bears met the Miami Dolphins. After Miami took an early 3–0 lead, the Bears lined up for a 40-yard field goal.

Instead of a standard formation, Chicago split all the blockers to one side and left snapper Marv Cook alone. Kicker Kevin Butler and holder Chris Gardocki stood behind Cook.

But the snap went diagonally to wideout Chris Conway. Conway heaved the ball to guard Jerry Fontenot, an eligible receiver in the strange alignment.

The pass deflected off Fontenot's hand into the arms of tight end Keith Jennings. The weird "swinging gate" formation resulted in a 23-yard touchdown pass and put Chicago in the lead.

The Bears needed the points as Miami tied the contest 14–14 with 5:46 to play. But quarterback Steve Walsh directed a 47-yard drive, and Butler booted a 40-yard field goal with 59 seconds remaining to put Chicago in front.

Dan Marino moved the offense in position for a last-second tie, but James Williams blocked Pete Stoyanovich's 45-yard field goal attempt. The Bears clung to a narrow road win.

The "swinging gate" opened the way for the Bear touchdown and a victory. Likewise we must be open to God at all times, day and night. If the gates of our hearts and minds stay locked to our Heavenly Father, God cannot help us or give us His blessings. Opening our gates means thinking about Him, listening to Him, praying to Him, serving Him, and loving Him with our whole selves.

Diagram the "swinging gate." If necessary, enlist a coach to explain. Run the play with some friends if possible. Ask God to help you always keep the gate to your heart open to Him.

Be still, and know that I am God; I will be exalted among the nations, I will be exalted in the earth. —PSALM 46:10

Sprinter Bobby Morrow remained perfectly motionless in the starting blocks. He considered a "rolling start" that anticipated the starter's gun unsportsmanlike. But the speed of the cotton and carrot farmer from San Benito, Texas, more than compensated.

In the 1956 Melbourne games, Morrow tied the 100-meter Olympic record in the second-round preliminaries. The Abilene Christian University graduate competed against a strong field in the finals.

Five-time Australian champion Hector Hogan surged to the early lead. Morrow passed him at the halfway point and won the gold medal in a time of 10.5 seconds.

The American also captured golds in the 200 meters and the 4 x 100 relay. He attributed his success to eleven hours of sleep each night and total relaxation.

Bobby Morrow knew what being still could do for him. Being still at night brought rest and readiness for competition. Stillness in relaxation kept him calm before a race. Staying still in the starting blocks showcased him as a good sport.

Being still helps Christians, too. Quietness and calmness provide a chance to listen and talk to God. Enough sleep gives us energy to serve God through helping others. Being relaxed and friendly draws non-Christians our way so we can tell them about Jesus.

Choose a room or outside area free from distractions. Use a stopwatch or kitchen-type timer to see how long you can be quiet and still. During the quiet time, concentrate on God and His blessings, including family, friends, and sports activities. How long did the stillness last? Do you need to work on getting more sleep, relaxing, and not moving? Ask God to help you be still and think about His greatness.

"Do not be afraid or discouraged because of this vast army. For the battle is not yours, but God's."

—2 CHRONICLES 20:15

Number one and number two teams seldom tangle in a late season game. But in 1991, the top-ranked Florida State University Seminoles and the runner-up University of Miami Hurricanes fought for college football supremacy.

The Hurricanes took the opening kickoff and drove 74 yards for the contest's first touchdown. But the Seminoles rolled off 16 straight points. Miami moved within striking distance with a 45-yard field goal by Carlos Huerta. Hurricane signal caller Gino Torretta used the strong legs of fullback Stephen McGuire on a final drive. Larry Jones' 1-yard touchdown dive put Miami in front 17–16.

Over three minutes remained. Florida State moved from its own 20 to the Miami 18 but burned its time-outs.

Fifty-three seconds remained. Amp Lee rushed for a yard. Quarterback Casey Weldon lost a shoe and wasted twenty-eight seconds.

The clock showed twenty-three ticks. Coach Bobby Bowden decided to attempt a field goal on third down rather than risk time expiring. Gerry Thomas' 34-yard boot sailed inches wide. Miami had toppled the nation's number one team.

Number two won. Miami could have been discouraged by its second ranking and failed to try. The Hurricanes could have been so afraid that they choked.

Instead, they relied on hard work and a quarterback's lost shoe. They battled until they won.

We all have times when we're discouraged or afraid. Instead of quitting, we must know that God is with us. Our lives belong to Him. He even controls the little things.

With some friends or relatives have a shoe scramble. Place everyone's shoes in a big pile. Mix them up. Race to see who gets her shoes back on and returns to the starting point first. Think about how losing a shoe might have made the difference in the game. Thank God that He cares about the little things in our lives.

I will hasten and not delay to obey your commands.

—PSALM 119:60

Millions watch professional football on Sunday afternoon. A close contest keeps fans glued to their televisions. But in 1968, a network executive pulled the plug early.

The New York Jets visited the Oakland Raiders. Both teams led their divisions. The game featured two of pro football's most potent offenses.

The Jets' Jim Turner kicked a 26-yard field goal with sixty-five seconds remaining, putting New York in front, 32–29. Oakland moved to the Jet 43-yard line with fifty seconds to play before calling time-out.

When NBC returned from commercial break, football had disappeared. The children's special *Heidi* lit up the silver screen.

Fans by the thousands called the NBC switchboard, blowing fuses. The New York City Police Department had its telephone system jammed.

Game watchers missed a fantastic finish. On the first play after the time-out, Daryle Lamonica threw a 43-yard touchdown pass to Charlie Smith, giving Oakland the lead.

The Jets return man, Earl Christy, fumbled the kickoff into the end zone. Preston Ridlehuber recovered the ball for a Raider touchdown. Oakland won in the final seconds, 43–32.

Network executives learned a valuable lesson from the *Heidi* fiasco. Since then, all regularly scheduled programming is delayed until the completion of a football game.

The people commanded that the network show the end of the game. But the NBC executive didn't listen. Today, the switchover to regular programming waits. The media obey the wishes of their viewers.

Many decisions must be made in a split second. There's no going back. There's no undoing. What's done is done.

God insists that in the split second when we have a choice to obey Him or disobey, we obey. And we obey quickly.

Watch a football game sometime during the week. Notice particularly the number of delay-of-game penalties given and the times when a delay in throwing results in a quarterback sack. How costly were they? Pray for quickness in being obedient to God.

You turned my wailing into dancing; you removed my sackcloth and clothed me with joy, that my heart may sing to you and not be silent. O Lord my God, I will give you thanks forever. —PSALM 30:11-12

Olga Fikotova Connolly grew up on a Czechoslovakian street filled with boys. Her parents encouraged her to practice the violin, but the Prague native preferred soccer.

Fikotova later switched from team sports to the discus throw. After finishing last in a meet, the young woman returned to the stadium's throwing ring in the evening to meditate.

There she encountered Nina Ponomaryeva, the 1952 Olympic champion. The Russian spent two hours the following day tutoring Fikotova and parted with the words, "So long, until Melbourne."

The Czech athlete combined Ponomaryeva's tips with her coach's suggestion that she treat the discus throw as a dance step. Fikotova often practiced to the sounds of "The Blue Danube."

At the 1956 Melbourne Olympics, the 23 year old set an Olympic record and captured the gold with a toss of 176 feet, 1 inch. Fikotova later married American hammer thrower Harold Connolly and competed for the United States in four subsequent Olympiads. The American squad honored her in 1972 as the flag bearer in the opening ceremony.

A chance meeting with an Olympic star turned Olga's disappointment into potential. Her coach moved the potential into dancing. And Fikotova changed dancing into the joy of a gold medal. Discus success enabled the Czech to meet and marry a fellow Olympian. How could anyone be silent over such wonderful events?

And how could anyone be silent over God's blessings? He carefully choreographs our lives with joy. He turns sorrow into gladness and despair into hope.

Listen to all or part of "The Blue Danube" waltz by Johann Strauss. If you don't own a copy, it's available on cassette or CD at most libraries. Close your eyes and picture throwing the discus to the music. Praise God for the music He gives.

Many of them will stumble. —ISAIAH 8:15a

Some of pro football's strangest events have occurred on Monday Night Football. No one knows what causes them, but they have provided many years of great entertainment.

In 1978, the New York Giants led the Philadelphia Eagles 17–12 with twenty-eight seconds to play. New York had the ball and faced third-and-two at its own 29-yard line. Philadelphia couldn't stop the clock.

Offensive coordinator Bob Gibson sent in a play, "Pro 65 Up," requiring quarterback Joe Pisarcik to hand off to fullback Larry Csonka.

The Giants yelled at Pisarcik to forget Gibson's call. They wanted their signal caller to fall on the ball. Time would expire before Philadelphia could regain possession.

But Pisarcik had been reprimanded in the past for not following orders, so he carried out Gibson's instructions. The result spelled disaster.

As the Giant play caller took the snap, he stumbled. The ball bounced off Csonka's hip onto the turf.

Eagle defensive back Herman Edwards fielded the ball on the bounce. He ran untouched into the end zone for a Philadelphia touchdown. The Giants had snatched defeat from victory and lost 19–17.

A win could have come easily for the Giants. But Pisarcik stumbled, and the team stumbled with him into defeat.

The quarterback faced a dilemma, a choice between two equally un-desirable alternatives. He could disobey, risk the wrath of the coach, and take a knee for a sure victory. Or he could obey the coach, risk the wrath of his teammates, and face a possible loss.

Life is filled with dilemmas. Sometimes we face two awful choices and must decide which is least bad. At other times, we find ourselves caught choosing between two wonderful options. When those times come, seek God's help. Talk the dilemma over with a trusted Christian friend.

Had you been Joe Pisarcik, what would you have done? Discuss the situation with another sports fan. When you face a dilemma in life, pray to the Heavenly Father for guidance.

Therefore I do not run like a man running aimlessly; I do not fight like a man beating the air. —1 CORINTHIANS 9:26

The Stanford University Cardinals believed victory was a lock. Kicker Mark Harmon booted a field goal with four seconds remaining to give the Cardinals a 20–19 lead over arch rival University of California. A kickoff put in play would conclude the finale of the 1982 season.

Harmon deliberately squibbed the pigskin on the ground, forcing Cal to field it. It bounced into the arms of Kevin Moen on his own 43-yard line.

After zigging and zagging upfield, Moen lateraled the ball to Richard Rodgers. Rodgers took a few steps and tossed it backward to Dwight Garner.

Stanford zeroed in on the new ball carrier, but before Garner went down, he flipped the football back to Rodgers. Spectators and the marching band filled the field, thinking the game over.

The Cardinal kickoff team hemmed in Rodgers, but amazingly he found teammate Mariet Ford trailing behind. Ford sprinted down the sideline to the Stanford 20. Before going out-of-bounds, he blindly tossed the ball over his shoulder. Moen caught it on the dead run.

Dodging and weaving through the band, Moen bowled into the end zone. After five laterals, Cal had returned a kickoff for a touchdown with no time on the clock. Stanford took the kickoff lightly and lost, 25–20.

It's rare when a football team can improvise and win a game as Cal did against Stanford. Winning usually requires planning, practice, and execution.

Christians also suffer if they take their faith lightly. Those who fail to practice or refuse to study often wind up doubting and confused.

No skill can be developed without hard work. Living the Christian life is no different.

Observe football practice at a local high school or college. Watch how the drills are repeated. Focus on the coaches and take note how much time they spend teaching. Praise God for those who give direction.

Again and again he bursts upon me; he rushes at me like a warrior. —JOB 16:14

In 1977, Walter Payton battled the flu. His chances of playing football against the Minnesota Vikings remained doubtful.

The Chicago Bear running back filled his body with fluids and swallowed aspirin to reduce the fever. When the opening whistle sounded, Payton took his regular slot in the Chicago backfield.

Quarterback Bob Avellini handed off time and time again to his star running back. The Jackson State grad scored on a 1-yard plunge in the second quarter, giving the Bears the lead.

By halftime, number 34 had rushed for 144 yards on 26 carries. A fourth-quarter 58-yard dash pulled Payton within 5 yards of the National Football League single-game rushing record.

Two consecutive runs, one for 3 and another for 4, broke O. J. Simpson's mark. Payton finished the game with 275 yards on 40 carries as the Bears defeated the Vikings, 10–7.

The Viking defense surely felt that Walter Payton would never stop gaining yards. He just kept rushing and rushing and rushing like a warrior refusing to give up.

That's the way Job felt, too, when he faced Satan. Satan kept coming with problem after problem after problem. But unlike the Minnesota players, Job turned the tide. His faith kept coming and coming and coming.

God restored Job's prosperity. Seven sons and three daughters were born to him. And he lived 140 more years.

By yourself or with a friend, name as many things as you can that keep coming. Praise God for His steadfast love. Ask Him to give you faith that keeps on coming.

"I tell you that in the same way there will be more rejoicing in heaven over one sinner who repents than over ninety-nine righteous persons who do not need to repent."

—LUKE 15:7

Coach Jordan Olivar installed a special play for the 1952 Harvard–Yale football game. He involved Yale's senior manager, 5-foot-6-inch, 140-pound, Charlie Yeager.

Olivar issued his manager a jersey with the number 99. The extra-point team practiced a fake with the quarterback throwing to Yeager. The coach promised to use the play if the score was out of reach.

Yeager performed his usual managerial duties. But he packed the number 99 shirt.

That day, the game belonged to Yale. During intermission, Yeager excitedly changed. He stood on the sidelines close to Olivar.

Leading 39–14 in the second half, the Yale coach sent the manager-turned-player in for the extra point. Yeager lined up at end. Ed Molloy barked the signals.

A Harvard defensive tackle knocked the tiny end to the ground. But Yeager bounced up. Molloy launched the ball. The pigskin hit number 99 square in the chest for a 2-point conversion.

The radio announcer had no 99 on his roster. He dispatched the Yale spotter to the bench. The answer surprised everyone. Charlie Yeager, the equipment manager, became a football hero.

Yale fans everywhere rejoiced over both the 41–14 victory and the play of number 99. The one, football manager Charlie Yeager, had worked hard for four years out of the spotlight. But his turn came.

God, too, is concerned about the one who strays out of the spotlight. He wants every person to receive the gift of salvation, no matter how big or small. All the angels in heaven sing with joy when one becomes a Christian.

Talk to a current or past equipment manager of a football or other sports team. Find out how many hours he puts in and what his responsibilities are. Odds are he probably gives more time than the players do. Thank God for the importance of one person to Him.

But those who hope in the Lord will renew their strength. They will soar on wings like eagles; they will run and not grow weary, they will walk and not be faint. —ISAIAH 40:31

The day after Thanksgiving in 1984, the Boston College Eagles visited the University of Miami Hurricanes. Two of the nation's premier quarterbacks, Doug Flutie and Bernie Kosar, lit up the scoreboard.

Boston College jumped to an early 14–0 lead as Flutie completed his first 11 passes. But Kosar rallied with 2 first-half touchdown passes. Miami trailed 28–21 at the break.

The Hurricanes pulled even, 31–31. The final quarter showcased one of collegiate football's most fantastic finishes.

Miami appeared to clinch the victory, 45–41, with Melvin Bratton's 1-yard touchdown plunge with twenty-eight seconds left to play. But Flutie and the Eagles wouldn't surrender.

Boston College took over on its own 20-yard line. Two short passes moved the ball to the Miami 48. A scant six seconds remained.

Miami knew what was coming. Boston College had no choice but to go for the end zone.

Flutie took the snap and rolled left. A fierce rush pushed him back to his own 36. Time expired.

The Eagle signal caller flung the pigskin with every ounce of strength. Gerard Phelan leaped and battled defenders. He clutched the pass to his chest and fell into the end zone. Boston College triumphed, 47–45.

Flutie and his teammates never lost hope. The Eagles gained strength as they saw a chance. The weariness of a hard-fought game faded.

The quarterback's final pass soared. The ball seemed to hang in the air. The receiver jumped higher than ever before. He made a miraculous catch.

If we hope in the Lord, He promises us strength, endurance, and perseverance. He will help us soar above the everyday problems and disappointments of life.

Copy Isaiah 40:31 onto a notecard. Put it in a place where you can read it often. Ask God to help you soar.

"I am the Lord; that is my name!" —ISAIAH 42:8a

Clever nicknames sometimes find their way into the world of sports. In 1981, the New York Jets' defensive line earned the title the "New York Sack Exchange."

Joe Klecko, Mark Gastineau, Marty Lyons, and Abdul Salaam sacked Kenny Stabler seven times in the football season's fourth game. In contest number six, the defensive linemen downed Steve Grogan on eight occasions. An enterprising fan hung a cloth banner from the heights of Shea Stadium, praising the "NY Sack Exchange."

Jets publicity director Frank Ramos began releasing weekly sack reports. The catchy slogan soon caught the nation's fancy.

On November 24, the New York Stock Exchange hosted the front four. As they walked across the floor, cries of "Jets! Jets! Jets!" rang out.

After lunching with brokers, Klecko, Gastineau, Lyons, and Salaam stood on a balcony overlooking the exchange floor. This time, cheers of "Defense! Defense! Defense!" filled the air.

Unfortunately, the sack rate fell, and the Jets' defensive line split up. The term "Sack Exchange" became a part of the past.

Our name is an important part of who we are. That's how we're known. Parents agonize over selecting names for their newborns. Some names are more popular than others.

Some are easily made fun of or turned into nicknames—Mike or Mikey for Michael, Tom or Tommy for Thomas, Marshy for Marshall. Nicknames may come from a physical, personal, or family trait, such as, Red, Junior, Trooper, Trey, Rabbit, or Freckles. Others comes from events or jobs—Coach, Teach, Catch, Brick, or Speedy.

Do you have a nickname or does a friend have one? How did you get it? Do you like it? In a library or bookstore, find a book of names. Look up the meaning of your name. Ask God to help you live up to your name and the name of Christ you carry as a Christian.

So whether you eat or drink or whatever you do, do it all for the glory of God. —1 CORINTHIANS 10:31

Grant Teaff's Baylor Bears had experienced a lackluster 1978 football season. Injuries and last-second defeats left their record at 2 wins, 8 losses. But Coach Teaff dug up the perfect motivation for their season finale.

The University of Texas Longhorns needed a victory to earn a repeat trip to the Cotton Bowl. The Bears had lost their first- and second-string quarterbacks and tabbed walk-on Mickey Elam to start.

The Bruin coach told his team a joke just before taking the field. He related how two Eskimos went fishing. One caught everything. The other caught nothing.

When the unsuccessful fisherman asked for the secret, the successful one only mumbled. He repeated the question. This time, the fisherman opened a mouthful of crawling bait and replied, "You've got to keep the worms warm."

Teaff informed his team, "I'll do my part. I'll keep the worms warm." The coach plunked a four-inch night crawler into his mouth.

Filled with emotion, the players rushed from the locker room. The Baylor offense marched swiftly down the field, and the defense stifled the Longhorn attack. At game's end, the scoreboard read Baylor 38, Texas 14. The Bears finished their season on a high, and Texas lost its Cotton Bowl berth.

When told the story, many fans wondered if Teaff actually swallowed the worm or managed to spit it out later. Either way, his story worked.

At Thanksgiving time, we especially enjoy sitting down to a feast with family and friends. As we eat and visit around the table, we should remember that the Lord wants whatever we eat and drink and whatever we do and say to be to His honor and glory.

Dedicate your Thanksgiving celebration to God. Plan a time before or during the meal to remember and thank the Heavenly Father for the blessings of the year.

"Blessed is she who has believed that what the Lord has said to her will be accomplished." —**LUKE 1:45**

Elizabeth Cuthbert improved her sprinting dramatically, setting a 200-meter world record in June 1956. The 18 year old became Australia's folk hero, winning gold medals in the 100-meter, 200-meter, and the 4 x 100 relay in the Melbourne Olympics. The press nicknamed her the "Golden Girl."

But the adulation and attention confused the shy and self-conscious young woman. Her athletic skills diminished, leading to further frustration and disappointment. In the 1960 Rome Olympics, she withdrew after one race due to a hamstring injury.

Two years later, her original coach, June Ferguson, suggested Cuthbert switch to the 400-meter race. The move inspired her.

In the 1964 Tokyo Olympics, the Golden Girl coasted through the preliminaries. In the finals, Cuthbert ran "the only perfect race I have ever run" and captured her fourth gold medal. Her time of 52.0 set an Olympic record.

Elizabeth Cuthbert's worth seemed to be bound to her victories. The press and fans idolized the gold, not the girl. But when she went back to believing in herself and trusting in her original coach, the sprinter regained her form. Elizabeth ran the perfect race. The gold medal was important but not as important as the runner herself.

Another Elizabeth, the mother of John the Baptist in the Bible, found her worth tied to having a child. But she was childless. Yet, Zechariah's wife remained faithful to God. She observed His commands and she believed. The Heavenly Father gave her a son, the one who prepared the way for Christ. And Elizabeth gave thanks.

Read the story of Elizabeth and her husband in Luke 1:5-45. Ask God to strengthen your beliefs.

There is surely a future hope for you, and your hope will not be cut off. —**PROVERBS 23:18**

Rose Bowl football hopes often hinge on the outcome of the Ohio State Buckeyes vs. Michigan Wolverines game. In 1950, the Wolverines' hopes were few.

Michigan not only needed to defeat Ohio State, but Northwestern also had to upset Illinois.

An icy blizzard struck the day before the big game. Many expected it to be cancelled. But radios across the Midwest announced the contest would continue.

About 50,000 fans ventured into the 10-degree temperature. Blinding snow fell. A sheet of white covered the field.

From the outset, both teams knew traditional football strategy would not work. One lucky play could mean victory.

Both the Buckeyes and the Wolverines often punted on first down. Ohio State caught the first break by blocking a Michigan kick. Vic Janowicz punched through a 38-yard field goal, giving the Buckeyes a 3–0 first-quarter lead.

But the Wolverines answered Ohio State's block with one of their own. The Buckeyes' punt attempt rolled through the back of the end zone for a Michigan safety.

Late in the first half, Ohio State faced third-and-six on its own 14-yard line. Forty-seven seconds remained.

The Buckeyes opted to punt. Michigan overshifted for the block. It succeeded. The ball bounced into the end zone. Tony Momsen recovered it for a touchdown and the 9–3 lead.

Michigan fans waited anxiously by radios for the Illinois vs. Northwestern score. The final outcome was Northwestern 14, Illinois 7. Despite the faint hope, roses bloomed in the snow.

As long as the two games had not ended, hope remained for Michigan.

As long as we live and breathe, hope remains for a joyful future on earth. And thanks to God, hope remains even in death.

Examine a rose or other flower. What makes it beautiful? Until its final petal falls, the blossom adds color and life to its surroundings. Praise God for coloring our world with hope.

How often are they like straw before the wind, like chaff swept away by a gale? —JOB 21:18

The Reverend Bob Richards traveled to the 1956 Melbourne Olympics to defend his gold medal in the pole vault. Gusty winds, a patchy runway, and the warm Australian sun bothered the 30-year-old vaulter during warm-ups.

Officials opened the competition at 13 feet, 1 1/2 inches. Richards watched competitor after competitor clear the low height.

The time arrived for the pastor of the Church of the Brethren in La Verne, California, to leap. He charged down the runway and hoisted himself skyward. But his foot hit the crossbar, knocking it down.

The embarrassed Richards had to endure another round of qualifying vaults. Finally, his time came.

The two-time Olympic medalist approached the bar with practiced skill. He cleared the top by a wide margin, but as he lay in the sawdust pit, the bar fell from its perch. A gust of wind had blown it off.

Richards stood on the brink of elimination. But he nailed his last try perfectly.

In the finals, the Californian inched farther and farther upward. He missed his first attempt for victory at 14 feet, 11 1/2 inches.

But on his second try, Richards grazed the bar. He lay on his back watching it quiver. But the wind held it steadfast. Richards won his second consecutive gold.

The wind almost broke Richards' chances to medal. In the end, the wind helped him win.

Job compares wicked men to straw. God sweeps them away as the wind sweeps away worthless husks of grain. But the breeze of the Lord's love can gently bring people back to Him.

Take a handful of oatmeal or cereal outside. If it's a windy day, hold your hand open and watch how quickly the grain disappears. If it's still, gently blow across your hand. Thank the Heavenly Father for the refreshing breath of His love.

I do not trust in my bow, my sword does not bring me victory; but you give us victory over our enemies, you put our adversaries to shame. —**PSALM 44:6-7**

From their beginning, the New Orleans Saints experienced little success. Fans felt disappointed and disillusioned.

Team owner Tom Benson decided to end his team's frustration. He hired quiet but forceful Jim Mora as head coach.

Mora emphasized defense and a no-frills offense. On November 1987's final Sunday, New Orleans traveled to Three Rivers Stadium to engage the Pittsburgh Steelers. At 7–3, the Saints' record led the NFC West.

But Pittsburgh dominated and jumped to a 14–3 lead. New Orleans rallied, however, and reeled off 17 straight points to move ahead 20–14.

The Steelers refused to quit. They marched downfield and faced first-and-goal from the Saints 4-yard line.

The New Orleans defense took charge. On fourth down, linebacker Sam Mills slipped through a gap and stopped Frank Pollard inches short.

The Saints ran three plays. On fourth down, punter Brian Hansen stepped out of the end zone. The safety gave Pittsburgh 2 points but allowed New Orleans a free kick. Only sixty-five seconds remained.

The Steelers threatened once more with twenty ticks left. Pittsburgh camped on the New Orleans 3-yard line with a first-and-goal.

Mora's fine-tuned defense responded. Linebacker Pat Swilling sacked quarterback Mark Malone on first down. David Waymer intercepted Malone's pass to clinch the win. New Orleans' loser reputation ended.

Losing is contagious. When we hear the term, we accept it as truth.

It's easy to label someone a loser, especially those who don't excel in the classroom, on the job, or on the athletic field. But God makes everyone winners.

Think of someone who struggles with schoolwork, his job, or athletics. Offer encouragement. Be positive. Focus on assisting him without drawing attention to yourself. Ask God to help him feel like a winner.

You will call and I will answer you; you will long for the creature your hands have made. Surely then you will count my steps but not keep track of my sin. —JOB 14:15-16

Shirley Strickland de la Hunty studied mathematics and physics at the University of Western Australia. She became a professor at Perth Technical College. But in the midst of her studies, the Australian lined up with the world's best athletes.

Strickland competed in her first Olympics in London in 1948. She won bronze medals in the 80-meter hurdles and 100-meter sprint and a silver in the 4 x 100 relay. Although officials ranked her fourth, a discovered photo later showed the sprinter had actually placed third in the 200 meters.

In the 1952 Helsinki games, the math and science whiz captured the gold and set world records on back-to-back days in the 80-meter hurdles. She added another bronze in the 100 meters.

Australian officials failed to select de la Hunty for the 1954 Commonwealth Games. Running in her final Olympics, Strickland magnified the slight by winning gold medals in the 80-meter hurdles and 4 x 100 relay. Competing and achieving gold in her native land at the 1956 Melbourne games proved especially gratifying for the 31 year old.

Strickland longed to compete in the Commonwealth Games. But Shirley didn't receive the call. Instead, officials chose her for the Olympics only after others failed.

Shirley carefully counted her steps as she prepared to run the hurdles and hand off the baton in the relays. She practiced until she could perform on the track without thinking.

Unlike the track selection committee, God always calls us. He longs for us to answer. The Heavenly Father watches every step we take. And if we ask, He forgets all our mistakes. Aren't we glad?

Count the Olympic medals Shirley Strickland de la Hunty won. Include the mistake the timers made. Praise God for counting your steps but forgetting your stumbles.

The great street of the city was of pure gold, like transparent glass. —REVELATION 21:21b

ABC television could not have created a better matchup. Two undefeateds—the University of Texas Longhorns and the University of Arkansas Razorbacks—met to determine the country's number one college football team.

By mutual agreement, the schools moved the date from mid-October to early December. The entire nation focused on the Fayetteville contest. President Richard Nixon made a special visit on Air Force One to present a plaque to the winner.

Arkansas dominated three quarters. Running back Bill Burnett scored on a 1-yard first-quarter plunge, and split end Chuck Dicus caught a 29-yard third-quarter touchdown pass.

Down 14–0 early in the fourth quarter, the Longhorns rallied. Quarterback James Street broke free for a 42-yard touchdown dash on the period's first play. Texas opted to go for 2, and Street ran into the end zone.

With under five minutes remaining, Texas faced fourth-and-three on its own 43-yard line. Following a time-out, Street executed a memorable play.

The Texas quarterback shocked everyone by throwing deep to tight end Randy Peschel. Arkansas tackled the receiver on its own 13-yard line. Two plays later, Jim Bertelsen scored on a 2-yard run to give Texas a 15–14 lead. The Longhorns won the legendary 1969 national championship. The media termed the contest the "Game of the Century."

James Street managed to surprise Arkansas and complete the key pass. That day, Street's memorable play was pure gold. The trophy and the championship belonged to the University of Texas.

In Revelation, Saint John describes a street of pure gold. He describes heaven, where salvation provides life with God forever.

Read the description of heaven in Revelation 21:18-21. Note all the precious stones mentioned. Picture the setting in your mind. Praise God for the richness of eternal life with Him.

But for you who revere my name, the sun of righteousness will rise with healing in its wings. And you will go out and leap like calves released from the stall. —MALACHI 4:2

No fiercer rivalry exists in college football than Alabama and Auburn. The citizens of Dixie's heartland divide their loyalties equally whenever the two powerhouses tangle.

In 1972, the Alabama Crimson Tide ranked number two and sported a perfect record heading into the final game against the Auburn War Eagles. But rankings and records mean little when traditional rivals meet.

Alabama led 16–3 with slightly over five minutes to play. The Crimson Tide fans felt confident of victory.

Facing fourth down at midfield, Alabama lined up to punt. Punter Greg Gantt took the snap, but Auburn linebacker Bill Newton leaped and blocked the kick with his hands.

The ball bounced. David Langer gathered the pigskin at the 25 and scampered untouched for a War Eagle touchdown.

With the lead cut to 16–10, the Crimson Tide played ball control. Almost four minutes elapsed before Auburn forced another punt.

A minute and a half remained. The crowd at Jordan Hare Stadium stood. The War Eagle partisans yelled at the top of their lungs, "Block that kick! Block that kick!"

Gantt awaited the snap. The Tide blockers expected a massive rush, but they could not contain Bill Newton. With an outstretched hand, he deflected Gantt's kick.

Once again, David Langer positioned himself in the right place at the right time. He scooped up the loose football on the 20 and bolted into the end zone. Auburn kicked the extra point to take the lead, 17–16. Alabama failed to score and saw its dreams of a perfect season vanish.

Bill Newton's leaps brought his team an upset victory. Our spirits should soar when we think of God. His presence brings peace. His Word provides wisdom. His power works miracles.

Measure your vertical leap. How does it compare with your friends' or teammates'? Practice your spiritual leaps in some quiet time with God.

Now there is in store for me the crown of righteousness, which the Lord, the righteous Judge, will award to me on that day. —2 TIMOTHY 4:8

The presentation of the Heisman Trophy has turned into a media event. The selection committee brings the potential winners to New York for a nationally televised announcement. But in 1988, one finalist, Oklahoma State's Barry Sanders, couldn't attend due to a late season game in Tokyo, Japan. The announcement made late Saturday afternoon preceded Sanders' final collegiate game by several hours. The Oklahoma State Cowboys and Texas Tech Red Raiders faced off across the Pacific. Promoters wanted to bring the Japanese a taste of American collegiate football.

Both squads lit the scoreboard with offensive fireworks. The Cowboys edged the Red Raiders in the high-scoring contest, 45–42. Sanders scored 4 rushing touchdowns and gained a career-high 328 yards.

The senior running back broke Marcus Allen's single season rushing yardage mark with a 15-yard sprint late in the first quarter. Sanders finished his senior season with 2,624 yards and 39 touchdowns, both NCAA records.

Barry Sanders won the Heisman by a large margin over Southern Cal's Rodney Peete. But Sanders received his trophy only after he returned home from Japan.

The Oklahoma State running back missed the ceremony and the media attention of the moment. Imagine the excitement on the plane trip home. The Cowboys had won. The star knew college football's highest award awaited him. The media would meet the jet. He looked forward to that touchdown.

God promises His followers an award. If we trust, love, and serve Him, we will receive a crown of righteousness at the end of our lives. We can look forward to that day.

Name as many Heisman Trophy winners as you can. Who do you think should win it this year? Thank God for the eternal trophy He promises.

"As the heavens are higher than the earth, so are my ways higher than your ways and my thoughts than your thoughts." —ISAIAH 55:9

Romania's Iolanda Balas set her first high jump world record in July 1956. The 6 foot-3/4 inch jumper used a modified scissors style after most athletes had switched to the straddle technique. Her long legs greatly aided her leaping ability.

Balas had high hopes for a gold medal in the 1956 Melbourne games but finished a disappointing fifth. After the setback, Balas' win totals went higher and higher. The Romanian won 140 straight competitions between 1957 and 1967.

Balas captured gold medals in both the 1960 Rome and 1964 Tokyo games. She exceeded her world record sixteen times, increasing the mark from 5 feet, 8 3/4 inches to 6 feet, 3 1/4 inches.

Unlike Iolanda, most of us spend our lives staying as close to earth as possible. If we jump, we leap a curb or short hedge. We don't even think about going higher.

But just as a high jumper concentrates on taller bars, God concentrates on higher thoughts and higher actions that aren't possible for people.

Yet we can try. And with God's help in the trying, we will think deeper thoughts and perform more beautiful deeds than otherwise possible.

Use an encyclopedia, atlas, or the internet to discover the world's highest mountain, the tallest peak in the United States, and the greatest elevation in your state. Praise God for His lofty thoughts and actions. Ask the Lord to help you achieve higher thoughts and actions.

"It is not by strength that one prevails; those who oppose the Lord will be shattered." —1 SAMUEL 2:9b-10

Darryl Dawkins bypassed the college game and went straight from high school to the National Basketball Association. He soon thrilled crowds with his jumps and monstrous dunks.

His antics above the rim earned Dawkins several colorful nicknames including "Master of Disaster," "Sir Slam," and the "Demon of Destiny." But on a December evening in 1979, the Philadelphia 76ers center created a real disaster.

The dunk specialist had gone to the hoop against Kansas City Kings center Bill Robinzine twenty-two days earlier. Dawkins' two-handed jam shattered the board and sent glass flying in all directions. The game stopped for over an hour while workers swept up debris.

Dawkins continued his awesome power displays. Fans speculated on when and where the next exploding backboard would occur.

It happened soon. Playing at home, the 76ers faced the San Antonio Spurs. The center worked free under the basket and jammed the ball through. The force ripped the hoop right off the board. Officials required an hour and fourteen minutes to replace it.

NBA commissioner Larry O'Brien decided the spectacular display should cease. He mandated breakaway rims at all arenas and backup goals in case of emergency.

Dawkins' displays were no doubt spectacular. But consider a thunderstorm or a sunset. Are these any less awesome?

God's power can easily be seen but it is difficult to understand. We must rely on faith.

But faith has to grow and develop. We can't see God or touch Him. The only ways to hear Him are through prayer, Bible study, and the insights He gives through others and nature.

Borrow or purchase a CD or video of natural sounds. Listen or watch closely and sense God through His handiwork.

"This is to my father's glory, that you bear much fruit, showing yourselves to be my disciples." —JOHN 15:8

No National Football League receiver has been more productive than Jerry Rice. The offense run by the San Francisco 49ers suits the wideout perfectly. In 1992, Rice had a chance to top the touchdown receptions list.

The 49ers met the Miami Dolphins at Candlestick Park. After a scoreless first quarter, Tom Rathman's 2 touchdowns put San Francisco in front 13–0 at the half. Amp Lee upped the margin to 20–3 with a third-quarter 1-yard scoring plunge.

The 49er defense limited Miami to 40 yards rushing and contained Dan Marino's potent passing attack. With victory almost certain, quarterback Steve Young looked to his favorite receiver for the record-breaking catch.

From the Dolphin 12-yard line, Young called Rice's hallmark play, the slant over the middle. Number 80 broke free from J. B. Brown and hauled in the touchdown pass. Touchdown reception number 101 broke Steve Largent's previous record of 100.

The media waited eagerly to interview Rice. Adoring fans lined up to catch a glimpse of number 80 leaving Candlestick Park. The glory came because he made receptions. His play bore the fruit of touchdowns.

God asks Christians to bear fruit. He wants others to know we are His because of what we say and how we act. We bear fruit when we show Jesus' love in us.

Eat an apple or other piece of fruit. Think about the tree it came from. Note that the name of the tree is the same as that of the fruit, and the owner will cut down the tree if it doesn't have fruit. Ask God to help you bear His fruit.

"But understand this: If the owner of the house had known at what hour the thief was coming, he would not have let his house be broken into." —LUKE 12:39

College football fans could not have asked for more in the 1992 inaugural Southeast Conference Championship game. The undefeated University of Alabama Crimson Tide took on the University of Florida Gators.

The Gators grabbed a 7–0 lead on Errict Rhett's 5-yard touchdown reception. The Crimson Tide defense tightened, however, and the Alabama offense scored a touchdown in each of the first three quarters.

Down 21–7, Florida quarterback Shane Matthews cranked up his team. A late third quarter touchdown reception by Willie Jackson narrowed the gap to 21–14. Rhett's fourth-quarter 1-yard plunge tied the contest at 21.

But the Tide defenders refused to roll over. The Gators faced first-and-ten at their own 21 with slightly over three minutes remaining. Matthews readied his team for a comeback victory.

The Florida signal caller threw a normally safe sideline pass. For 41 straight passes, Matthews read the defense correctly. Number 42 spelled disaster.

Cornerback Antonio Langham decoyed the Gator play caller. The Alabama junior saw the quarterback's release and broke in front of receiver Monty Duncan. Langham intercepted the pass and bolted down the sideline. His 27-yard romp put the Tide in front 28–21 and clinched Alabama's victory. The nation's number two-ranked, undefeated Crimson Tide earned the right to face the number one University of Miami in the Sugar Bowl.

Matthews wished he had seen Langham coming. If he had known the thief was near, he wouldn't have thrown the pass.

Just as in the game, we don't know what life will bring. Attending worship services, studying the Bible, praying, and helping others prepares us for whatever comes, good or bad.

Make a safety survey of your home. Work with your family to correct any problems that you find. Ask God to help you be prepared for the unexpected.

"Be perfect, therefore, as your heavenly Father is perfect." —**MATTHEW 5:48**

A little over a month into the 1992–93 National Basketball Association season, the Atlanta Hawks hosted the two-time champion Chicago Bulls. The home court advantage gave Atlanta a slight edge, but playing the Bulls is never easy.

The Hawks kept the contest close and led by 5, 33–28, at the conclusion of the first quarter. Atlanta maintained the momentum and upped its margin to 13, 67–54, at the half. The Bulls regained some ground, but Atlanta held off Chicago and won 123–114.

The Bulls played like a very ordinary NBA team that night in the Omni. They shot only .490 from the floor and .632 at the free-throw line.

The Hawks, on the other hand, played a near perfect game in one regard. From the field, they shot only slightly higher than Chicago, but at the foul line, Atlanta excelled.

Led by forward Dominique Wilkins, the home team connected on 39 of 40 free throws. Rookie Adam Keefe misfired in the opening minute of the second quarter for the team's sole miss.

Wilkins set an NBA record with a 23 for 23 performance. He eclipsed the previous mark of 19 for 19 shared by Bob Pettitt, Bill Cartwright, and Adrian Dantley.

Perfect. That night from the foul line Dominique Wilkins was perfect. His team nearly made the goal, too. Athletes rarely play perfect ball. But when a pitcher throws a perfect game, a basketball player makes all his shots, or a receiver catches every pass thrown his way, the world takes note.

Only God is perfect. Yet He asks us to work toward that goal. Sometimes we fail completely. At other times with His help, we come close. The world may not take note. But we know. And God knows.

Look for a chance this week to do something especially kind for someone you don't know. Keep it a secret from everyone except God. Praise Him for being perfect.

He will not let your foot slip—he who watches over you will not slumber. —**PSALM 121:3**

The New York Giants and Chicago Bears tangled for the National Football League championship in 1934. The two teams had met the previous year with Chicago prevailing 23–21.

A frigid winter storm turned the Polo Grounds into a skating rink. The metal cleats slipped and skidded on the icy surface.

Assistant coach Ray Flaherty remembered his collegiate team wearing gym sneakers in similar conditions. He and head coach Steve Owen dispatched clubhouse attendant Abe Cohen to Manhattan College. The coaches ordered him to gather as many pairs of basketball shoes as he could find.

The game began. The Bears jumped to a 10–3 halftime lead. A third-quarter field goal upped the score to 13–3. Cohen returned from the mission with 10 minutes left to play.

The Giants quickly swapped shoes. The increased traction helped. Quarterback Ed Dankowski hit Ike Frankian for a 28-yard scoring pass, closing the gap to 13–10. When New York regained the ball, Ken Strong's 42-yard touchdown run put the Giants in the lead.

The hometown defense stiffened. Bears fullback Bronko Nagurski attempted a fourth-down run at midfield, but the Giants held. A short drive ended with another Strong touchdown.

The New York defenders intercepted a desperation Bears pass to set up a final score by Dankowski. The Giants rallied for 27 points with their new shoes and became NFL champions, 30–13, in what has been called the "Sneaker Bowl."

A quick-thinking football coach used basketball shoes to prevent his team from sliding on the ice. God watches over Christians to keep us from slipping into bad habits.

The psalmist wrote, God never sleeps. His vigil is constant. Recall the first time you skated. How many times did you fall? Praise God for steadiness on life's journey.

In this way the word of the Lord spread widely and grew in power. —ACTS 19:20

Sometimes games get out of hand. One team takes a lead, and suddenly the margin becomes insurmountable. In 1991, the Cleveland Cavaliers and Miami Heat played such a contest.

Mark Price paced the Cavs in the first half with 14 points. Three of his teammates hit for double figures, and Cleveland enjoyed a 20-point half-time cushion, 73–53.

The Heat turned ice cold in the third quarter. The Cavaliers scored 17 of the stanza's first 19 points. Coach Kevin Loughery benched his starters and let the subs have a field day.

Cleveland outscored Miami 75–27 in the second half and 42–13 in the final quarter. At game's end, the scoreboard read Cavs 148, Heat 80. The 68-point winning margin set an NBA record.

The Cavs' dominance of the game continued from beginning to end. Their power grew as the game went on. Coach Loughery spread the scoring among everyone and let them all have a part in the record.

The good news about Jesus began with a small group of believers. They had no power. The Roman emperors tried to stop them. But they couldn't.

From one person to another, the word spread. The message of Jesus Christ grew in power. It reached around the world.

No matter how old or how young, we're all on the Lord's team to spread the word. Without our telling others about Jesus' death and resurrection, they may not hear.

Look for chances to tell someone who doesn't know about Christ. Invite the person to a church activity or worship service. Be prepared to express your faith clearly and simply. Ask God for help.

"But he who sent me is reliable, and what I have heard from him I tell the world." —JOHN 8:26b

Jan Stenerud started kicking in the National Football League in 1967. In 1983 at age 41, the NFL's oldest player could still consistently boom the football.

The soccer-style kicker began the 1983 season 19 field goals shy of George Blanda's all-time record. By early December, the Norwegian native needed only 1 to tie.

Stenerud got the opportunity as the Green Bay Packers met the Tampa Bay Buccaneers on Monday Night Football. The 16-year veteran tied Blanda on Green Bay's first possession. An interception set up a short drive, and Stenerud booted a 33-yarder for career number 335.

Late in the third quarter with the score tied 3–3, the Packers moved to the Buccaneers' 14-yard line. When the offense stalled, coach Bart Starr called on his reliable kicking machine for the record breaker. With millions watching, Stenerud hit a 32-yarder for the record.

The 6–3 Green Bay lead disappeared. Tampa Bay scored a touchdown but missed the extra point.

Quarterback Lynn Dickey drove to the Bucs 5-yard line with twenty-eight seconds remaining. The sure-footed Stenerud trotted out. His 23-yarder tied the score and sent the game to overtime.

The Packers won the coin toss and marched methodically toward the goal. Eleven plays later, Stenerud hit another 23-yarder to give Green Bay a 12–9 victory. Not only did the kicker break the all-time record, he added two to spare.

Jan Stenerud kicked professionally for nearly twenty years. His career lasted because coaches could rely on his leg for points. Before retiring in 1985, the sidewinder made 66.8 percent of his attempts and kicked 373 field goals.

Christians can rely on God 100 percent of the time. He never fails or deserts us. His promises are eternal and everlasting.

Review the promises and commitments you made during the past week. How many did you fulfill completely? Focus on improving your reliability. Praise God for being reliable.

There is no one like the God of Jeshurun, who rides on the heavens to help you and on the clouds in his majesty.

—DEUTERONOMY 33:26

Monday Night Football provides a stage for weird and strange events. A cold, snowy night in Foxboro, Massachusetts, saw one of the strangest.

A roaring blizzard and frigid winds kept the Miami Dolphins and New England Patriots from crossing the goal line. Both teams attempted and missed field goals due to the foul weather.

With 4:45 remaining in the scoreless game, New England drove to the Miami 16-yard line. The drive stalled. Coach Ron Meyer called time-out to allow kicker John Smith to clear away the snow.

Suddenly Meyer had a better idea. The Patriots employed a snow plow to clear the yard lines during time-outs. He signaled for the driver to remove the snow near the 23-yard line for Smith's kick.

Mark Henderson, the snow plow operator, revved his John Deere and chugged onto the Superturf. He followed his original path along the 20, then swerved to the left. The plow left a perfect spot, and Smith booted the game-winning field goal.

Help comes in unusual forms and from unexpected sources. For John Smith and the New England Patriots, assistance drove a snowplow.

God hears requests for help and answers. Often, however, we miss the aid because we see our situation in only one way. We must open our eyes and be receptive if we want to be in tune with God.

Many wrongly quote the Bible, "God helps those who help themselves." The adage isn't biblical and isn't correct. God helps everyone, but unfortunately not everyone can see the help when it arrives.

Ask an older person if she can recall an incident when help seemed to arrive out of nowhere. Thank God for those who serve as His helpers.

Whatever your hand finds to do, do it with all your might. —ECCLESIASTES 9:10

The Minnesota Vikings and Detroit Lions battled for National Football League supremacy in game fifteen of the 1994 season.

The Lions had salvaged a dismal season. At one point, they faced play-off elimination with a 5–6 record. But veteran quarterback Dave Krieg and running back Barry Sanders sparked Detroit to a three-game winning streak.

The Vikings experienced the opposite. They once led the Central Division with a 7–2 mark but faltered in the stretch.

On paper, Minnesota appeared to be the better team. Its defense ranked fifth in the League, and quarterback Warren Moon had been one of the NFL's best for many years.

But the Lions totally dominated. Barry Sanders rushed for 110 yards and 2 touchdowns. Mel Gray reached the end zone on a 98-yard kickoff return. The final score read Detroit 41, Minnesota 19.

The Vikings could find one bright spot in the entire contest. Cris Carter's hands snagged 8 receptions to break Sterling Sharpe's year-old record. Carter had trailed by 1, 111 to 112, prior to the game. He snared 3 more the following week to set a single-season record of 122.

Carter's sure hands brought home the record as he ran each route with all his might. In life, God expects us, like the Vikings' receiver, to do whatever our hands find to do with all our might.

It may be easier to let things slide, put them off, or give half an effort. But coaches, parents, teachers, and bosses often say, "If it's worth doing, it's worth doing right." That's good advice. That's God's command.

For just one day, give full effort in everything you do. If it's running pass routes, concentrate and run your hardest. If it's helping around the house, do the best job you can. If it's talking with other people, be the nicest person possible. Notice the difference, and try to do everything with all your might. Ask God to help you.

for what I received I passed on to you as of first importance: that Christ died for our sins according to the Scriptures.

—1 CORINTHIANS 15:3

The Miami Dolphins engaged the Dallas Cowboys in 1984's final game. Miami used the contest as a springboard to the playoffs and a showcase for the passing talents of Dan Marino.

In the first quarter, the Miami signal caller hit Nat Moore for a 22-yard touchdown pass. The completion broke Dan Fout's single-season passing record of 4,802 yards.

Five plays later, a touchdown pass to Mark Clayton established a new mark for touchdown passes in a season. Marino added 2 more to set a new NFL mark of 70.

The Miami quarterback finished the day with 23 completions out of 40 attempts. His 340 yards passing gave him the single-season record of 5,084 yards. Marino stands alone as the only NFL play caller to exceed 5,000.

In addition to the records, the game ended perfectly for the Dolphin faithful. Dallas tied the contest at 21 with a minute and forty seconds remaining. Marino expertly moved the offense and connected with Clayton for a 63-yard scoring strike with fifty-one seconds to play. Miami held on for a 28-21 triumph.

Just as Dan Marino passed the Dolphins to victory, parents and teachers pass on valuable information. Without their instruction, we would be ill-equipped to handle life's obstacles.

The passing on of religious training is important also. An uninformed and uneducated Christian can be easily influenced.

Bible study, Sunday School, mission training, Christian schools, and church services all provide opportunities for learning about God and His teachings. The more time we spend in study, the stronger our minds become. A well-developed Christian intellect serves God well.

Make a list of past school and church teachers. Which ones taught you the most? Say a prayer of thanks and gratitude for them.

"Therefore the Lord himself will give you a sign: The virgin will be with child and will give birth to a son, and will call him Immanuel." —ISAIAH 7:14

The National Football League awarded New Orleans an expansion franchise in 1966. The team selected Saints as its nickname. Ownership based the decision on New Orleans' musical heritage. Trumpeter Al Hirt, an original limited partner, played the Dixieland classic, "When the Saints Go Marchin' In," as his trademark song.

Choosing a team logo proved to be more difficult. Management settled on the fleur-de-lis, a tribute to New Orleans' French influence.

According to legend, King Clovis I of France used the fleur-de-lis as his personal symbol in the early sixth century, after an angel gave him an iris for accepting Christianity. The coat of arms of Louis VI first depicted the symbol.

Carefully chosen symbols mark the New Orleans Saints. Team members proudly wear the gold fleur-de-lis on their helmets.

As Christians, we proudly display Christ's symbols at Christmas. Poinsettias, stars, angels, candles, wreaths, and special ornaments grace our homes. Some choose to decorate a special chrismon tree. The word *chrismon* is a contraction of *Christ* and *monogram*.

All chrismon ornaments specifically symbolize Christ. One is the fleur-de-lis cross, which symbolizes purity. Other chrismons include the sand dollar, double triangle, seven flames, lamb, three fish united to form a circle, anchor cross with fish, Christmas rose, chalice, brazen serpent on tau cross, and the cross of Christ and the twelve apostles. Each carries a special meaning.

Consider decorating a small tree exclusively with chrismons. Christian bookstores and craft shops have patterns or sets. See if you can find out the history and meanings of some of these symbols from a Christian bookstore, the local library, or your pastor. Each time you see a symbol of Christ during this season, pause to thank God for His Son.

Then Herod called the Magi secretly and found out from them the exact time the star had appeared. He sent them to Bethlehem and said, "Go and make a careful search for the child."

—MATTHEW 2:7-8

Bob Simmons worked hard to succeed. The former Bowling Green linebacker coached football two years at his alma mater before accepting a position at the University of Toledo.

In 1980, Simmons joined the University of West Virginia staff. Eight years later, he began tutoring linebackers for Bill McCartney at the University of Colorado. In 1993, Colorado promoted Simmons to assistant head coach.

McCartney announced his retirement after the 1994 season and recommended Simmons as his replacement. But the University regents selected Rick Neuheisel instead.

Though disappointed, Simmons refused to be discouraged. He began his search and applied for the vacant Oklahoma State University head-coaching position.

In a rare move, OSU made a careful but secret search and hired the Colorado assistant. Simmons fulfilled his dream and became Oklahoma State's twentieth head coach.

Sometimes life involves making careful searches. We look for just the right gift, the perfect outfit, the greatest school or job, or the best friend.

Twenty centuries ago, the Magi made a careful search. They traveled thousands of miles through foreign lands to find what they sought—the Christ Child.

Share with a friend what you're searching for during the holiday season. Is it that one dreamed-about present? Is it tasty food and parties? Is it being with relatives and friends? Is it feeling the Christmas spirit deep inside? Whatever your wish, ask God to keep the true meaning of the holiday first in your heart.

The angel went to her and said, "Greetings, you who are highly favored! The Lord is with you. . . . You will be with child and give birth to a son, and you are to give him the name Jesus." —LUKE 1:28, 31

Sheryl Swoopes has achieved virtually every goal imaginable. The young woman captained an NCAA champion basketball team, won the NCAA tournament Most Valuable Player award, and captured an Olympic gold medal. She signed a lucrative shoe contract and played one-on-one against Michael Jordan.

In 1997, Swoopes awaited the fulfillment of a lifelong dream, playing professional basketball in the United States. Two new women's leagues, the American Basketball League and the Women's National Basketball Association prepared for their inaugural seasons.

But Sheryl's plans had to be put on hold. The former Olympian and her husband, Eric Jackson, discovered she was pregnant.

Swoopes gave birth to a boy on June 25, 1997. Eric and Sheryl named him Jordan.

The former NCAA tournament MVP joined the Houston Comets of the WNBA in late July. Although she played a limited role, the Comets captured the first WNBA title over the New York Liberty in the championship game, 65–51.

Jordan Jackson wasn't born at a convenient time for his mother. But his birth brought great joy and the opportunity to name him for a special superstar. Magazines and television carried the news.

Mary's pregnancy wasn't convenient either. But Jesus' birth brought rejoicing in heaven and on earth as the angels and a star spread the news.

Spread the news. Listen to or sing the carol "Go, Tell It on the Mountain." Communicate the true meaning of Christmas to someone who has never heard. Ask God to lead you to that person.

In a loud voice, she exclaimed: "Blessed are you among women, and blessed is the child you will bear!" —LUKE 1:42

Jackie Joyner-Kersee left her home in East St. Louis to play basketball and run track at UCLA. Her mother called the college freshman every night.

One late November evening, Jackie's mother asked if she would be coming home for Christmas. Although the young woman wanted to visit her family more than anything, Joyner-Kersee knew the airfare would strain finances.

Two weeks before Christmas, Mary Joyner telephoned her daughter following a game with California State at Long Beach. Jackie excitedly related her exploits, but her mother sounded ill. She promised to see a doctor.

In early January, Jackie received a call from her mother's younger sister. Her mom had been stricken with meningitis and was on life support.

The basketball and track star returned to East St. Louis. Her mother died shortly after her arrival.

Left with two younger sisters and a brother in college, Jackie considered leaving UCLA. But the family discovered a small life insurance policy purchased only months before, possibly with money saved by working at a movie theater. The proceeds enabled all the Joyner children to remain in school.

Mary Joyner felt blessed to be the mother of four. Two of her children won Olympic medals after her death. But the children were even more blessed by a mother who loved them, sacrificed for them, and helped them accomplish their dreams, even in her death.

God blessed the biblical Mary when He chose her to be the mother of Jesus. And He blessed Jesus with a mother who loved Him and sacrificed for Him, even until His death.

Mothers around the world will sacrifice this year so that their children will have a wonderful Christmas. Participate in a toy drive during the holidays or adopt a prisoner's son or daughter and provide appropriate Christmas gifts. Thank God for Mary and other mothers whose children are blessed by them.

An angel of the Lord appeared to him in a dream and said, "Joseph son of David, do not be afraid to take Mary home as your wife, because what is conceived in her is from the Holy Spirit." —**MATTHEW 1:20**

The Soviet sports system paired ice skaters Sergei Grinkov and Ekaterina Gordeeva at ages 14 and 10. They performed together for over a dozen years.

The Russians captured the 1988 and 1994 Olympic gold medals in pairs figure skating. But Sergei and Ekaterina became more than just a precision team. They fell in love. In April 1991, the couple wed. In September 1992, a daughter, Daria, was born.

Daria looked like her father. She had his shocking blue eyes and the white hair Sergei had as a little boy.

But tragedy struck the loving family. On November 24, 1995, while skating, Grinkov died from a heart attack. Thousands mourned.

Three months later, the cast of Stars on Ice, along with Viktor Petrenko and Oksana Baiul, performed a tribute to their fallen colleague. Gordeeva hosted the event.

For the finale, the entire cast came out in pairs and recreated a position from previous Grinkov and Gordeeva performances. Ekaterina wove through them as they skated. Gordeeva took the microphone at the conclusion and spoke these words, "I did not skate alone, I skated with Sergei."

Sergei and Ekaterina were not afraid to love each other with their whole hearts. That evening on the ice, Ekaterina felt Sergei's spirit with her.

In the Bible, Matthew explains how Joseph, the carpenter, was afraid to marry Mary. But the angel assured Him of Mary's love and faithfulness. The baby had come from the Holy Spirit. And Mary and Joseph loved each other with their whole hearts.

Think about Joseph's feelings about Mary's pregnancy and then his excitement about Jesus' coming birth. Imagine how he planned and used his woodworking skills to prepare for the baby. If you can, make or buy a wooden Christmas ornament. Thank God for Joseph and loving earthly fathers.

> When the angels had left them and gone into heaven, the shepherds said to one another, "Let's go to Bethlehem and see this thing that has happened, which the Lord has told us about."
>
> **—LUKE 2:15**

Less than a month after winning the 1945 National Football League championship, owner Dan Reeves whisked the Rams from Cleveland and replanted them in Los Angeles. Football became the first professional sport to locate on the West Coast.

The City of Angels immediately embraced the Rams. Former UCLA quarterback Bob Wakefield's flashy passing and ball handling brought thousands of fans to the Los Angeles Coliseum. His marriage to movie actress Jane Russell kept the press clamoring for every scrap of news.

Halfback Fred Gehrke enhanced the Rams' stylish Hollywood image. He added a creative touch by painting a pair of curly ram horns on his leather helmet. Teammates quickly imitated him. Other franchises followed, and team logos became the rage.

Another group of people worked with rams. But their clothes weren't stylish. They didn't make lots of money. In fact, nobody really wanted to be around them. They smelled bad and wandered around the countryside. They were shepherds.

But an angel appeared to them. A heavenly host praised God in their presence. The shepherds felt fear and honor and awe and joy. They left their fields and followed the words of the angel to Bethlehem. There they found Mary, Joseph, and the Baby lying in an animals' feeding trough.

These lowly shepherds spent the rest of their lives glorifying God and spreading the word about the Christ Child.

Spread the word. Plan to gather a group of family and friends to sing Christmas carols in your neighborhood. Enjoy telling about Jesus' birth through song. Glorify God.

On coming to the house, they saw the child with his mother Mary, and they bowed down and worshiped him. Then they opened their treasures and presented him with gifts of gold and of incense and of myrrh. **—MATTHEW 2:11**

U.S. Basketball offered Tara VanDerveer the opportunity to coach the 1996 women's Olympic team. The team would train and play exhibitions for ten months instead of the customary six weeks. She took a leave of absence from coaching Stanford University.

The women chosen to represent the United States trained relentlessly in Colorado Springs during October 1995. On November 1, they embarked on a six-week nationwide tour, playing collegians and making public appearances.

The hectic schedule strained the team. VanDerveer coped with eleven personalities and egos, ranging in age from 22 to 31. She enforced strict rules but fought hard to ease her players' burdens. VanDerveer convinced U.S. Basketball to pay for private hotel rooms and provide a full-time athletic trainer.

Just before their eleven-day Christmas break, the team exchanged gifts. The women pushed so hard by VanDerveer presented her with a framed set of their trading cards.

The coach realized the team had jelled. The 1996 United States women Olympians won 60 games without a loss en route to the gold medal.

The team chose the perfect gift. It contained a part of themselves. But the trading cards also evoked priceless memories and would serve as a permanent reminder of a special time.

The Magi brought Jesus worthy gifts. The journey they took honored Him, and the presents they brought reflected their feelings. The precious metal, sweet incense, and myrrh would serve as permanent reminders of a perfect King.

Choose to give Christmas gifts that are worthy of the person. The present needn't be expensive, but should reflect your feelings. Remember, Jesus wants just one gift—yourself. Ask God to make you a worthy present for Him.

But his mother treasured all these things in her heart.

—LUKE 2:51b

On Christmas Eve 1961, the Houston Oilers played the San Diego Chargers in the American Football League championship. Just prior to halftime, Charger defensive back Charley McNeil hit Oiler wide receiver Charley Hennigan in the back and knocked him virtually unconscious.

Hennigan revived slightly in the locker room but left early to clear his head. When the receiver sat down on the bench, officials angrily pushed him away. Hennigan had wandered to the San Diego sideline.

During the second half, the wideout couldn't remember the plays quarterback George Blanda repeated. Running back Billy Cannon caught a 35-yard fourth-quarter touchdown pass, giving Houston a 10–0 lead. The Oilers held on for their second AFL title, 10–3.

The return trip to Houston in a turboprop plane took six hours. The Oilers didn't arrive until early Christmas morning. The blow jarred Hennigan so hard, he had no memories of the plane ride or his family's Christmas celebration.

Charley Hennigan's mind totally lost Christmas 1961. The holiday will forever be a blur remembered only in family album pictures. But his memory lapse occurred by accident.

Often we lose Christmas by our own actions. We miss the holidays by running from one activity to another, too busy to enjoy or remember the season. Sometimes, we focus on what we can't get or do, and ignore the blessing of the special time. We may lose the days in a blur of eating, drinking, and late-night parties.

Surely God wants us, like Mary, to treasure the sights, sounds, feelings, and memories of Christmas. But unlike Charley Hennigan, it is our choice.

Share special memories of holidays past with your family or a group of friends. Plan ways to make this a memorable celebration without losing its joy in perfection. Ask God to help you treasure this Christmas season in your heart.

Do not forget to entertain strangers, for by so doing some people have entertained angels without knowing it.

—HEBREWS 13:2

In December 1971, Montreal Expos baseball players Ron Brand, Steve Renko, and Boots Day agreed to visit a local hospital. The trio felt apprehension because the children had birth defects.

A cheerful nurse led the ballplayers to a brightly decorated room. About thirty children anxiously waited.

Brand commented on the beautiful drawings and ornaments. The nurse replied, "The children made them."

For the next few minutes, the young patients entertained their guests with Christmas carols sung in both French and English. Brand particularly noticed a 6 year old with an abnormally large head. She suffered from hydrocephalus, commonly known as water on the brain.

When the singing concluded, the three Expos went from bed to bed, signing autographs and passing out mementos.

Brand approached the girl with the enlarged head.

The catcher autographed a photo. He handed it to her and said, "Thank you for the beautiful music, sweetheart."

The girl broke into a huge smile and looked straight at Brand with the bluest, most beautiful eyes he had ever seen. She shyly asked, "Could you kiss me good-bye?"

The Expo bent down and softly kissed her on the cheek. Brand felt as if he kissed an angel.

Each Christmas, Ron Brand thinks about the year he was entertained by the children. But most of all, he remembers the little angel's special request.

The Lord asks that we, like Brand, Day, and Renko, give a part of ourselves to people we don't yet know. At Christmastime, we may offer our loving presence to those in nursing homes or hospitals, or on military bases or college campuses who can't return home for the holidays. But God's command to entertain strangers lasts all year. He doesn't limit angels to this season.

Plan to visit a nursing home or hospital or invite someone who can't go home for Christmas to enjoy the day with your family. Thank God for new friends He brings into your life.

While they were there, the time came for the baby to be born, and she gave birth to her firstborn, a son. She wrapped him in cloths and placed him in a manger, because there was no room for them in the inn. —LUKE 2:6-7

Luke and Diane Prestridge eagerly anticipated their daughter Kristin's first Christmas. But the 1982 National Football League players' strike delayed the season's conclusion until after New Year's. Luke, the Denver Broncos' punter, had to leave for Los Angeles on Christmas Day.

Diane planned to fly to Albuquerque to be with her parents. But a major blizzard hit Denver, canceling all commercial flights.

With no plans, the freezer held only ground meat and french fries. Diane fixed burgers and fries for their meager holiday meal.

Deep snowdrifts prevented Luke from driving to the airport. Shortly after lunch, he hiked to a major highway. A teammate picked up the punter and shuttled him to the Broncos' charter flight. There was no room for families, so Diane and Kristin stayed home alone.

Mary and Joseph must have felt alone without plans in Bethlehem the night before their first child's birth. The young husband looked everywhere for a comfortable room. No one would take them in. At last an innkeeper bedded the young family in a stable. A manger became the baby Jesus' crib.

Children in Mexico traditionally commemorate the search with *Las Posadas. Las Posadas* means "the inns." Families make a candlelight journey from house to house singing special songs, asking for lodging.

The processional is led by a young man who guides a donkey carrying a girl. The group is refused shelter at each stop until at last they are welcomed with carols of joy. The families then feast on Mexican hot chocolate, *buñuelos* (fried bread), *capirotada* (bread pudding), flan, and other special treats. They may break a star-shaped piñata as they celebrate the birth of the Christ Child.

Read about traditional Christmas celebrations and foods in several cultures. Choose one to add to your own holiday. Ask God to help you always to find room in your heart for Jesus.

But the angel said to them, "Do not be afraid. I bring you good news of great joy that will be for all the people. Today in the town of David a Savior has been born to you; he is Christ the Lord." —LUKE 2:10-11

Walter Abercrombie felt confused. The cold, gray skies and the calendar told the Pittsburgh Steeler rookie running back he should be spending Christmas with family and friends in Texas. But Abercrombie had to play football.

The Steelers hosted the New England Patriots. A player strike had extended the season and shortened it to nine games. After two years of missing the playoffs, Pittsburgh needed a victory to assure a postseason slot.

Terry Bradshaw directed the Steelers to a 20–0 lead before New England registered a first down. Abercrombie logged some playing time and scored the final touchdown in Pittsburgh's 37–14 win. Football season would continue.

The 50,515 fans at Three Rivers Stadium cheered. But Walter felt lonely as he drove away. He returned to an empty apartment far from his family in Texas. He picked up the phone to call them.

Abercrombie's family congratulated him for the win and wished him Merry Christmas. Walter received their words with mixed feelings. Championships and victories were his ultimate goals, but nothing could replace his family.

Walter Abercrombie had to work away from home that Christmas. Each year, many spend holidays serving in jobs the rest of us couldn't do without. Police, firefighters, medical personnel, nursing home staffs, hotel and restaurant employees, and radio/television teams among others perform necessary, 365-days-a-year tasks. They sacrifice their celebrations for ours.

God's news belongs to them, too. A Savior has been born. Hallelujah!

As you see people working on this day, be especially courteous and say a special "thank-you" to each one. Ask God to bless their Christmas celebrations and yours.

After Jesus was born in Bethlehem in Judea, during the time of King Herod, Magi from the east came to Jerusalem and asked, "Where is the one who has been born king of the Jews? We saw his star in the east and have come to worship him."

—MATTHEW 2:1-2

Some professional sports franchises bounce around the country and never find the success they seek. The Sacramento Kings are a prime example.

The club began in 1948 as the Rochester Royals. Rochester won the National Basketball Association championship in 1951, the only title in franchise history.

The Royals moved to Cincinnati in 1957. Hall of Famer Oscar Robertson joined the team in 1960, but his talents failed to lead Cincinnati to an NBA crown.

In 1972, another relocation placed the Royals in Kansas City. The team changed its mascot to the Kings to avoid confusion with the baseball Kansas City Royals.

The final franchise shift occurred in 1985. The former Rochester Royals, Cincinnati Royals, and Kansas City Kings became the Sacramento Kings.

Kings also appear throughout the Bible. We find the pharaohs, King Saul, King David, King Xerxes, King Ahab, and scores of others on the pages of the Old Testament. Some ruled well. Others loved evil and wickedness.

The New Testament begins with the story of kings and their gifts: King Herod, the kings from the East or Magi, and the King of the Jews. Herod decreed death. The Magi offered gold, incense, myrrh, and adoration. And Jesus Christ, King of the Jews, brought hope.

King Herod's decrees covered a short while. The Magi's gifts survived a lifetime. But Jesus' present lasts forever.

Reflect on the gifts you received and gave yesterday. How long will each last? Praise God for the gifts He gives.

A man's steps are directed by the Lord. How then can anyone understand his own way? —**PROVERBS 20:24**

The Dallas Cowboys once ruled the National Football League. But age and poor drafts pushed them to the bottom of the heap. In 1992, however, Emmitt Smith's running brought Dallas back.

The Cowboys entertained the Chicago Bears in the season finale. The game's outcome meant little except pride. Dallas had clinched the division title and home field advantage.

For Smith, the contest provided the chance to earn a second straight NFL rushing title. Because of the late starting time, the Cowboy tailback knew exactly how many yards he needed to pass Pittsburgh's Barry Foster.

Smith gained 94 yards in the first half, leaving him 15 short. Offensive mistakes limited the Cowboys to a single field goal before intermission.

Almost four minutes into the second half, the running back broke into the secondary for a 31-yard touchdown run. The gallop pushed Smith past Foster and gave Dallas a 10–0 lead.

The Cowboys iced the game two plays later. Darren Lewis bobbled a pitchout into the arms of defensive tackle Russell Maryland. The Outland Trophy winner lumbered 26 yards for the touchdown and belly flopped into the end zone. Dallas coasted to an easy victory, 27–14.

Smith retired for the day with 131 yards and 1,713 for the season. He edged Foster for the rushing title by 23 yards and set a Cowboy single season mark. Smith broke Tony Dorsett's eleven-year record of 1,646 by 67 yards.

The coaches, quarterback, Smith, and his blockers—especially fullback Daryl Johnston—and the playbook directed Emmitt's steps. Once he saw daylight, he powered his way through.

God directs our steps. The Bible gives guidelines. Many times, as for a running back, God uses other people.

Pastors, church leaders, parents, other relatives, and wise friends offer advice. We must follow.

Practice diagramming some football running plays. Show the steps the ball carrier should take. Be sensitive to God's direction in your life.

They all joined together constantly in prayer, along with the women and Mary the mother of Jesus, and with his brothers. —ACTS 1:14

The Dallas Cowboys visited the Minnesota Vikings in the first round of the 1975 National Football League playoffs. Brent McClanahan put Minnesota in front with a fourth-quarter touchdown plunge.

Cowboy quarterback Roger Staubach faced the improbable task of moving the team 85 yards. On every play, Staubach lined up 7 yards behind the center. The shotgun formation provided an extra second of protection.

The Cowboys converted a fourth-and-sixteen with a 25-yard completion. But the ball rested on the 50-yard line with thirty-two seconds to play. Dallas had used its time-outs.

The Dallas signal caller sent Drew Pearson deep down the right sideline. Defensive end Jim Marshall charged, and Staubach hurried.

The ball lacked zip. Pearson adjusted. Cornerback Nate Wright bumped the receiver and fell.

Pearson caught the ball against his hip, then cradled it in his arms. He trotted into the end zone to bring Dallas a come-from-behind 17–14 victory. After the game, Staubach called his desperation pass a "Hail Mary," after a traditional Catholic prayer.

Staubach and the Cowboys saw only a faint glimmer of hope, so the quarterback lifted his pass on a prayer. Pearson gently became the answer as the entire Dallas team joined together to beat the Vikings.

Another group united in prayer twenty centuries ago. Jesus had died, risen, ascended into heaven, and left His followers with a promise. Christ pledged to send His power to live in each of them. But the time hadn't come. The disciples, Mary, some of the other women, and Jesus' brothers waited. And while they waited, they prayed. The Holy Spirit became the answer, not gently, but with the rush of wind.

And the power of prayer and the power of the Holy Spirit remain available to us today, especially when we join together.

Unite in prayer with your family, a group of friends, or just one other person. Read Acts 1:1-14 and 2:1-4 as you begin.

Who led them through the depths? Like a horse in open country, they did not stumble. —ISAIAH 63:13

For many years, American sports fans preferred professional baseball to pro football. But in 1958, the public discovered the excitement and drama of the newer sport.

The New York Giants hosted the Baltimore Colts in the National Football League championship game. The Giants had won the NFL title in 1956, and their reputation grew nationwide.

Baltimore surprised the favored Giants, leading 14–3 at the half. But New York struck for 2 second-half touchdowns and led 17–14 with less than three minutes to play.

Colts quarterback Johnny Unitas took over on his own 14- yard line. Unitas completed key passes to Lenny Moore and Raymond Berry and moved the ball to the Giants' 13. Only thirty seconds remained.

Steve Myhra booted a 20-yard field goal. Time expired with the game tied 17–17.

A never-used rule went into effect. The teams would play "sudden death" overtime until one scored.

The Giants won the coin toss and took the ball. The Colts defense held, and New York punter Don Chandler pinned Baltimore back on its 20-yard line.

Unitas directed the Colt attack with precision. L. G. Dupre and Alan "The Horse" Ameche carried for large gains. Berry caught clutch receptions.

The Colts drove to the New York 1-yard line. Baltimore handed off. Ameche plunged into the end zone to bring the Colts the NFL title, 23–17.

Johnny Unitas led the Colts nearly the length of the field. The Horse Ameche ran through the open country. He did not stumble.

God leads us the same way through life. If we stumble, it's because we chose a difficult path, not because the Lord did.

Read about horses or arrange to ride horseback if possible. Observe the animals in movies and on television. Notice how steady they are, only stumbling in a hole or when something is in their path. Ask God to help you choose His path.

But no man can tame the tongue. It is a restless evil, full of deadly poison. —JAMES 3:8

The 1962 American Football League title game ended in regulation time with the score tied 17–17. The Dallas Texans and Houston Oilers met at midfield for the overtime coin flip.

Texan coach Hank Stram made an unconventional decision. He chose to take the wind rather than the ball. Stram reasoned his defense could contain the Oiler offense, and a kick would battle the breeze.

As visiting captain, Abner Haynes called heads. The coin fell heads. The Dallas back informed referee Harold Bourne, "We'll kick to the clock."

But the Texan captain made a crucial mistake. His choices were kick, receive, or which goal to defend. Haynes could not choose two. His first words, "We'll kick," determined Dallas' option.

The gleeful Oilers took the wind. With the ball and the breeze, victory seemed certain. Oiler quarterback George Blanda came out passing, but Johnny Robinson intercepted an errant throw and returned the ball to the Houston 37-yard line.

Dallas failed to score and punted. Houston regained possession on its own 12. Blanda worked the ball downfield once more. But the Oiler signal caller threw another interception.

The Texans ran one play, and the first overtime period ended. With the wind at their back, quarterback Len Dawson moved the Texans to the Houston 19. Two running plays positioned the ball in the middle of the field. Kicker Tommy Brooker booted a 25-yard field goal, and Dallas gained its first title.

Abner Haynes' slip of the tongue almost cost the Dallas Texans an AFL championship. Our tongues can cause great trouble too. Harsh words inflict pain. And wounds to the heart heal slowly.

We can hurt God with our speech too. He always hears our words. Thinking before speaking is a good rule.

Tape-record a conversation and play it back. Listen to how you sound. Ask God to help you think about the words you speak.

From whose womb comes the ice? Who gives birth to the frost from the heavens when the waters become hard as stone, when the surface of the deep is frozen? —JOB 38:29-30

The Green Bay Packers hosted the Dallas Cowboys in the 1967 National Football League championship. An Arctic front dropped the temperature to minus 13 degrees and froze Lambeau Field into a solid, slippery mass.

The Packers jumped to a 14–0 lead with a pair of touchdown passes. But Dallas rallied before halftime with a 7-yard fumble return by George Andrie and a 21-yard Danny Villanueva field goal.

Neither team crossed the goal line in the third quarter. As the teams switched ends, Cowboy halfback Dan Reeves suggested a fire pitch to quarterback Don Meredith. Reeves would fake a sweep then throw deep to flanker Lance Rentzel.

The play worked. Rentzel slipped behind the Packer secondary and scampered into the end zone.

Time ticked down. Green Bay took possession with four-and-a-half minutes remaining.

Bart Starr threw short passes. Dallas defenders slipped on the ice. The Packers reached the Dallas 3-yard line with under a minute to play.

Three Donny Anderson plunges gained 2 yards. Green Bay used every time-out. Only sixteen seconds remained.

Starr and Coach Vince Lombardi opted to go for victory. Starr wedged forward and scored. The Packers captured their third straight NFL championship, 21–17 in the Ice Bowl.

When the cold wind blows and God frosts the world in snowy white, the Heavenly Father warms our hearts with His love. We find time to stay inside, read His Word, and pray. The quietness of the frozen world lets us reflect on the One Who created all things.

As another year slides away and slips into memory, make yourself a cup of cocoa or spiced tea. Sit in a cozy chair, possibly in front of a roaring fire. Enjoy the quiet moment. Reflect individually or as a family on the year past. Dream and plan for the year ahead. Ask God's guidance and blessing for the future.

Big Eight Conference: A collegiate athletic conference established in 1928, made up of eight Great Plains schools. In 1996, the conference merged with four Texas universities to form the Big Twelve Conference.

MVP: Most Valuable Player, the highest award given in many sports.

NCAA: The National Collegiate Athletic Association, the governing body for collegiate sports.

. . B A S E B A L L . .

American League: A professional baseball major league founded in 1901, counterpart to the National League.

Batter's box: The 6-foot by 4-foot rectangle on each side of home plate in which batters must stand when they are hitting.

Bullpen: The area where pitchers warm up before and during games, usually located behind the outfield wall.

Bunt: A soft hit resulting from the batter holding the bat out and letting the ball hit it instead of swinging the bat.

Curveball: A pitch that curves as it reaches the plate. It is thrown by snapping the wrist sharply away from the body as the pitch is released, so the ball spins rapidly and veers to the left (if thrown right-handed) or right (if thrown left-handed).

Error: A misplay by a fielder that allows a runner to reach base safely or score.

Fastball: A pitch that is thrown with great speed and power.

Knuckleball: A slow pitch thrown by gripping the ball with the knuckles or fingertips. The ball barely spins after it is released, so breezes and air current cause it to flutter and jump in unpredictable ways.

National League: A professional baseball major league founded in 1876, counterpart to the American League.

No-hitter: When a pitcher or pitchers on the same team do not allow a base hit during a game.

Passed ball: When a catcher fails to stop a pitch he could have caught, allowing a base runner to advance. If a passed ball comes on a third strike, the batter can run to first.

Perfect game: When a pitcher does not let a runner reach first base for an entire game.

Rookie: A player in his or her first season.

Sacrifice: A bunt or fly ball that allows a runner to score or advance to another base at the expense of the batter, who is out.

Shutout: When a team loses a game without scoring a run.

Spitball: An illegal pitch thrown with saliva, sweat, or any slippery substance on the ball that makes it break more sharply.

Strikeout: An out made by a combination of three swings and misses at pitches or having the pitches called strikes by the umpire.

Strike zone: The area over the plate from the batter's knees up to his armpits. If a pitch passes through this area and the batter doesn't swing, the umpire calls a strike.

. . B A S K E T B A L L . .

Assist: A pass that results in a basket.

Charity stripe: A slang term for the basketball free-throw line.

Dunk: To slam the ball into the basket from above the rim.

Foul: Illegal contact by an opposing player.

Free throw: A free shot from the foul line by a player who has been fouled. It is also called a foul shot.

Hook shot: A high-arcing shot, using a sweeping motion.

Jump shot: A shot taken from medium to long range at the top of a jump. The jump allows the shooter to free himself from the defender and gives the shot more power.

Layup: A shot from close range, often banked off the backboard.

Post: The area where the center usually sets up on offense, with his back to the basket.

Tip-in: A field goal made by tipping a rebound into the basket.

. . F I G U R E   S K A T I N G . .

Axel: The only jump made as the skater moves forward. In a single axel, a skater jumps off one foot, turns one-and-a-half times in the air, and lands on the back outside edge of the opposite foot, skating backward. (In a triple axel, the skater spins three-and-a-half times.) The jump is named for Axel Paulsen, who introduced it in the early 1900s.

Salchow: A basic jump, in which the skater, moving backward, jumps off one foot, makes a full turn in the air, and lands on the other foot. It is named after skater Ulrich Salchow, the 1908 Olympic gold medalist.

. . F O O T B A L L . .

AFC: The American Football Conference.

An NFL conference comprised primarily of teams from the former American Football League.

Audible: A change of the play shouted in code by the quarterback at the line of scrimmage.

Backfield: The area behind the line of scrimmage where the running backs line up and the quarterback passes.

Backup: A substitute player who is not in the starting lineup.

Ball control: A strategy that enables the offensive team to maintain possession of the football for the longest period of time.

Blitz: A rush at the quarterback involving linebackers and/or defensive backs.

Blocking: The legal effort by an offensive player to obstruct a defensive opponent from stopping the passing or running plays of the offensive team.

Bootleg: A deceptive move by the quarterback on which he fakes a handoff, then hides the ball against his hip and runs around one of the ends.

Completion: A forward pass caught by an eligible receiver.

End zone: The area, 10 yards deep,

bounded by the goal line, end line, and both sidelines.

Field goal: A scoring placekick worth 3 points that may be attempted from anywhere on the field. The ball must go between the goal post's uprights and over the crossbar.

Fumble: A loss of possession of the football by the ball carrier, punter, or kick holder.

Goal line: The line that marks the start of the end zone.

Goal post: A Y-shaped, 40-foot, bright gold post positioned at each end line.

Halftime: The intermission between the first and second halves of a game.

Handoff: Giving the ball, hand to hand, to another player.

Interception: A change of possession that occurs when a defensive player catches a pass intended for an offensive player.

Man-in-Motion: A running back who moves parallel to or away from the line of scrimmage prior to the snap.

NFC: The National Football Conference. One of two conferences comprising the National Football League. Counterpart to the American Football Conference.

NFL: The National Football League. The professional football league comprised of the National and American Football Conferences.

Onside kick: A short kickoff that the kicking team attempts to recover. The kick must travel at least 10 yards or be touched by the receiving team to be a "live" ball.

Option: A play in the which the quarterback or halfback has the option to run or pass.

Overtime: The extra 15-minute period added to games to break ties. Also called "sudden death" overtime, because the first team to score in any manner wins the game.

Pitchout: A long, underhanded toss, usually from a quarterback to a running back.

Punt: A type of kick used primarily on fourth down that ordinarily results in change of possession.

Sack: A tackle made on a ball carrier behind the line of scrimmage, usually a quarterback attempting to pass.

Safety: A 2-point scoring play often caused by tackling a ball carrier in his own end zone.

Scrimmage (Line of): The imaginary line running from sideline to sideline at the point where the ball is snapped.

Signal caller: A slang term for a football quarterback.

Tackle: To stop a ball carrier and force him to the ground.

Touchdown: A 6-point scoring play that occurs when one team crosses the other team's goal line with the ball in possession.

Yard line: The numerical designation of the line across the playing field that denotes the distance from the end zones.

. . G O L F . .

Birdie: A score of 1-under-par for a hole.

Bogey: A score of 1-over-par for a hole.

Drive: A golfer's first shot off the tee.

Eagle: A score of 2-under-par for a hole.

Green: The smooth grass area around each hole.

Hole in one: A golfer's drive that goes into the hole.

Par: The accepted number of strokes a good player should need when hitting the ball from the tee into the hole.

Putt: A short stroke used on the green to roll the ball into the hole.

Tee: A small peg that balances the ball just above the ground.

. .GYMNASTICS. .

Balance beam: A board 15 feet long, 4 feet high, and 4 inches wide on which female gymnasts perform.

Floor exercise: A gymnastic routine performed on a 40-foot by 40-foot mat.

Vault: A padded piece of equipment 5 feet long, 4 feet high and 14 inches wide over which gymnasts leap.

Uneven bars: Two wooden bars connected by cables or wooden poles. One bar is 7 feet, 9 inches tall, the other is 5 feet, 2 inches.

. .HOCKEY. .

Assist: Passing to a player who scores a goal.

Bodychecking: Using the body to bump an opponent off-balance, away from the puck, or out of the play.

Crease: A marked 8-foot by 4-foot area immediately in front of each goal.

Hat trick: Scoring three goals in a single game.

Penalty shot: A free shot awarded to a player who has been dragged down from behind before he could take a clear shot at the net.

Power play: An offensive play used when a team outnumbers its opponents because of a penalty.

Save: A stop of a shot by a goalie by blocking or catching the puck.

Slap shot: A hard shot that is taken by drawing the stick back and swinging forcefully at the puck.

Wrist shot: A shot made without the stick blade leaving the ice.

. .ROWING. .

Sculling: The type of racing in which each rower uses two oars.

. .TENNIS. .

Backhand: One of two groundstrokes. A right-handed player uses a backhand to hit a ball that lands to the left.

Deuce: A score in which each player or side has 40 points or five or more games each. Either player or side must win two successive points or games to win the game or set.

Forehand: The other common groundstroke. A right-handed player uses a forehand to hit a ball that lands to the right.

Groundstrokes: Shots hit from baseline to baseline in a rally.

Lob: A high-arcing shot designed to go

over the head of an opponent at the net.

Match: A contest decided on the basis of victory in a specified number of sets. Women's matches are normally two out of three. Men usually play a three of five format.

Set: A group of six games forming one unit of a match.

Straight sets: A tennis contest in which one contestant wins every set in the match.

Tiebreaker: A sudden-death finish that is played when a set reaches 6–6. A tiebreaker is won by the player who scores 7 points first, though the player must win by 2.

Volley: A ball hit before it bounces on the surface of the court.

. .TRACK AND FIELD. .

Closing Kick: A runner's last sprint toward the finish line at the conclusion of a race.

Discus: A wooden disk with a metal rim weighing 2 kilograms and thrown from a 2.5-meter circle.

High jump: A vertical jump made from a running start and then over a horizontal bar supported between two upright standards.

Hurdles: Artificial barriers spaced equally on the track.

Javelin: A pointed, spear-shaped stick not less than 8.53 feet in length and 1.765 pounds in weight.

Long jump: A horizontal jump for distance, usually made with a fast short sprint and a take-off from a wooden slab 8 inches wide and 4 inches long set firmly in the ground.

Pole vault: A vertical jump made from a running start using a 12- to 16-foot pole to assist the jumper in clearing the bar.

Relay: A four-person race in which each team member runs a part of the total distance.

Shot put: A 16-pound metal sphere thrown from a circle 7 feet in diameter.

Dec 28
Stenerud, Jan, Jan 15, Dec 11
Stich, Michael, Jul 6
Stockton, John, Feb 1, Feb 21, Apr 17, Apr
  25, May 25, May 29, Aug 4, Aug 10
Stoudamire, Damon, Mar 18
Street, James, Dec 1
Street, Picabo, Mar 10
Strock, Don, Jan 2
Strug, Kerri, Jul 23
Stuhldreher, Harry, Oct 19
Sugden, Joe, May 18
Swann, Lynn, Jan 19
Swoopes, Sheryl, Mar 26, Dec 17
Szabo, Ecaterina, Aug 6
Szewinska, Irena Kirszenstein, Oct 30

Taylor, Robert, Aug 29
Teaff, Grant, Nov 25
Ter-Ovanesyan, Igor, Oct 4
Thomas, Debi, Mar 21
Thomas, Derrick, Nov 11
Thomas, Frank, Aug 12
Thomas, Isaiah, Feb 21
Thomas, Thurman, Jan 27, Sep 5
Thompson, David, Apr 10
Thomson, Bobby, Oct 3
Thorpe, Jim, Jan 18
Toomey, Bill, Nov 2
Torretta, Gino, Nov 16
Torvill, Jayne, Feb 15
Trevino, Lee, Jul 11

Uelses, John, Feb 2
Unitas, Johnny, Jan 17, Oct 20, Dec 29
Upshaw, Willie, Aug 24

Valdano, Jorge, Jun 25
Valenzuela, Fernando, Aug 17
Valvano, Jim, Apr 2, Apr 3
Van Dyken, Amy, Jul 21
Vanbiesbrouck, John, Apr 23, Jun 12
VanderKelen, Ron, Aug 5
VanDerveer, Tara, Dec 21
Verchota, Phil, Feb 24
Vicario, Arantxa Sanchez, Jul 10, Aug 2

Waitz, Greta, Aug 14

Wakefield, Bob, , Dec 20
Walker, Erick, Mar 13
Walker, Herschel, Mar 6
Walker, Larry, Apr 24
Walsh, Steve, Nov 14
Walton, Bill, Mar 25
Warmerdam, Dutch, Apr 12
Watson, Tom, Jul 16
Webber, Chris, Apr 5
Weber, Dr. Gustave, Nov 8
White, Willye, Nov 4
Whiten, Mark, Sep 7
Wilkens, Lenny, Jan 6, Aug 4
Wilkins, Dominique, Dec 8
Wilkins, Mac, May 2
Williams, Billy, Aug 8
Williams, Doug, Jan 31
Williams, Michael, Apr 25
Winslow, Kellen, Jan 2, Jan 9
Witt, Bobby, Jun 29, Jul 13
Witt, Katarina, Mar 14, Mar 21
Woods, Tiger, Apr 13, Aug 27
Wynalda, Eric, Jul 14

Yamaguchi, Kristy, Feb 18
Yeager, Charlie, Nov 22
Yepremian, Garo, Jan 14, Nov 12
Young, Anthony, Jul 30
Young, Steve, Mar 6, Dec 6

Zaharias, Babe Didrikson, Jul 2
Zatopek, Emil, Jul 22
Zayak, Elaine, Mar 14

If you want to learn more about combining sports and Christianity, check out these organizations.

Athletes in Action
P.O. Box 588
Lebanon, OH 45036
513-933-2421
Fax: 513-933-2422
Website: www.aiasports.org/aia

Fellowship of Christian Athletes
8701 Leeds Road
Kansas City, MO 64129-1680
816-921-0909
Fax: 816-921-8755
Website: www.fac.org

Athletes in Action (AIA), a ministry of Campus Crusade for Christ International, has a mission, "to reach the world for Jesus Christ through the influence of sports."

AIA uses testimonies, videos, and athletic competition to achieve its goal. The organization has produced videotapes such as *Joe Gibbs—Fourth and One,* and *Give Me the Rock!* highlighting NBA players, and an NFL Films video titled *Spirit of the Game.*

AIA men's and women's basketball teams travel the world engaging collegiate and national teams. The players present personal Christian testimonies to fans during halftime.

Each summer Athletes in Action offers summer camps for ages eight through high school on a 120-acre campsite outside of Cincinnati, Ohio.

The Fellowship of Christian Athletes (FCA), founded in 1954, has a mission, "to present athletes and coaches and all whom they influence, the challenge and adventure of receiving Jesus Christ as Savior and Lord, serving Him in their relationships and in the fellowship of Christ."

FCA offers summer camps around the country for seventh graders through high school. Each camper receives a one-year subscription to its magazine, *Sharing the Victory*. The magazine is also available through individual subscription.

The Fellowship of Christian Athletes sponsors "huddle groups" on campuses from junior high school through college. These groups grew from a desire to continue the FCA camping experience during the school year. Huddle groups commit to grow spiritually and reach out to others in word and deed.

John Hillman is a CPA who devotes his energies to consulting and writing. As a noted authority on sports history, John has written articles that have appeared in *Sports Collectors Digest, Junior League Baseball, Boys Quest*, as well as the *Waco Tribune-Herald* and the *Dallas Morning News*, where he is on special assignment to cover sporting events in central Texas. He is a sports fan in the truest sense.

Kathy Hillman, also an avid sports fan, serves as Associate Professor and Acquisitions and Collection Development Librarian for Baylor University. She has written over fifty articles for Woman's Missionary Union, which she has served in varying capacities since 1981.

She and John are raising three children and live in Waco, Texas. They are actively involved in the Columbus Avenue Baptist Church.

John and Kathy believe that God should be the "main thing" in life. It's not a decision between sports and God. But if God is at the center, everything else will be balanced and in proper perspective.

> *Therefore, since we are surrounded by such a great cloud of witnesses, let us throw off everything that hinders and the sin that so easily entangles, and let us run with perseverance the race marked out for us. Let us fix our eyes on Jesus, the author and perfecter of our faith.*
>
> **—Hebrews 12:1-2**

If you would like to email the Hillmans with your comments about this book, they can be reached at either guardeen@aol.com or kathy_hillman@baylor.edu.